WRITIN

ON IRISH HIS
1993 & 1994

INCORPORATING ADDENDA FROM
PREVIOUS YEARS

COMPILED BY
MÁIRÍN CASSIDY • CIARAN NICHOLSON

EDITED BY
SARAH WARD-PERKINS

IRISH COMMITTEE OF HISTORICAL SCIENCES
AND
IRISH HISTORICAL STUDIES

DUBLIN 1999

ISBN: 0 9502097 8 3

Printed in Ireland by Paceprint Ltd, Dublin

CONTENTS

ANNUAL LISTS of 'Writings on Irish History' for the period 1936 to 1978 were published in *Irish Historical Studies* from 1938 to 1979. 'Writings on Irish History' 1979 to 1983 appeared in microfiche published by the Irish Committee of Historical Sciences. Since 1984 'Writings on Irish History' has appeared as a separate publication. It was decided to publish two years of 'Writings on Irish History' in one issue starting with 1989 & 1990 in an effort to catch up.

The preparation and publication of these lists is the responsibililty of the bibliographical subcommittee of the Irish Committee of Historical Sciences consisting of the compilers (Máirín Cassidy and Ciaran Nicholson), Seán Duffy, Jacqueline Hill and Sarah Ward-Perkins (convenor). The present list is published jointly by the Irish Commitee of Historical Sciences and *Irish Historical Studies*.

The editors and compilers gratefully acknowledge assistance and help received from the staff of the National Library of Ireland, the Royal Irish Academy, Trinity College Dublin library, University College Dublin library, Peggy Morgan, and John Breslin of Paceprint.

The lists continues the chronological classification introduced in the previous microfiche lists. Items that refer to more than two chronological periods are assigned to the general section. Essays on family history and records of the memorials of the dead are usually in the general section, as are other entries which for one reason or another defy analysis. It follows that a reader interested in any specific period should consult the general section also. Excluded from the list are current works of reference, parliamentary publications, and items appearing in newspapers.

Readers who notice errors in or omissions from the list are invited to write the bibliographical subcommitte, care of Sarah Ward-Perkins, Department of Modern History, Trinity College, Dublin 2, or send by email (to wvaughan@tcd.ie).

Sarah Ward-Perkins

Corrigenda
Writings on Irish History 1991 & 1992

(0837) For Maureen Walsh read Maureen Wilson.

(1417) For John Ravell read Joseph Ravell.

Administration: Institute of Public Administration, xxvi, xxxv, xxxviii (1978, 1988, 1990).

Ainm: bulletin of the Ulster Place-name Society, vi (1994/95).

An Aisling, iii (1991).

Albion, xix-xxii, xxv (1987-90, 1993).

Alumnus: Trinity College Dublin, Graduate Students Union, 1993, 1994.

Amer. Jn. Sociology, c (1994/95).

Amer. Philos. Soc. Proc., cxxxiii (1989).

Annales de Bretagne, xcii (1985).

Antiq. Jn., lxxiii (1993).

Antiquity, lxvii, lxviii (1993, 1994).

Archaeol. Jn., cxlvii (1990).

Arch. Ire., ii-iv, vii, viii (1988-1990, 1993, 1994).

Archives of Natural History, xx (1993).

Archiv. Hib.: Irish Historical Records, xlvii, xlviii (1993, 1994).

Archiv. Hist. Pont., Archivium Historiae Pontificiae, xxxi (1993).

Ardmore Jn.: Irishleabhar Aird Mhor, x (1993).

Area: Institute of British Geographers, xxv (1993).

Arklow Hist Soc. Jn., Arklow Historical Society Journal, 1992/93.

Baile, University College Dublin Geography Society Annual Journal, 1989, 1992, 1993.

The Bann Disc: journal of the Coleraine Historical Society, i (1994).

Bandon Hist. Jn.: Bandon Local History Society, ix, x (1993, 1994).

Bantry Hist. Soc. Jn.: Bantry Historical and Archaeological Society Journal, i (1991).

The Bell: journal of Stewartstown and District Local History Society, v (1994).

Benbradagh, xii, xxiii, xxiv (1982, 1993, 1994).

Bibliog. Soc. American Papers: Papers of the Bibliographical Society of America,lxxxvii,
    lxxxviii (1993, 1994).

Blackrock Society Proc. i, ii (1992/93, 1993/94).

Board Celt. Stud. Bull.: the Bulletin of the Board of Celtic Studies, Univesity of Wales xxxvi,
    xxxvii (1989, 1990).

Breifne: Cumann Seanchais Breifne, vi (24), viii (1986, 1992/93, 1994).

Brit. Acad. Proc. Proceedings of the British Academy, lxxx, lxxxii (1993).

Brit. Jn. of the History of Sport, iii (1986).

Brit. Jn. Polit. Sci., British Journal of Political Science, v, ix, x (1975, 1979, 1980).

Brit. Jn. Sociol., xxxii, xxxiv, xxxvi, xxxviii (1981, 1983, 1985, 1987).

Bullán: an Irish Studies Journal., i, nos 1-2 (1994).

Butler Soc. Jn, iii (no 4) (1994).

Cahiers de Civilisation Médiévale, xxxvi, xxxvii (1993, 1994).

Camb: Med. Celt. Stud., Cambridge Medieval Celtic Studies, ix-xii, xxv-xxviii (1985-1986, (1993, 1994). Cambrian Medieval Celtic Studies from no. xxvi (1993).

Canad. Hist. Assoc. Historical Papers, 1989.

Canad. Hist. Rev., lxxii (1991).

Canad. Jn. Ir. Stud., xix, xx (1993, 1994).

Carloviana: journal of the Old Carlow Society, xxxiii, xl-xli (1985/86, 1992/93, 1993/94).

Cathair na Mart:: journal of the Westport Historical Society, xiii, xiv (1993, 1994).

Cath. Hist. Rev., lxx (1984).

Celtica, Dublin Institute for Advanced Studies, xi (1976).

Clogher Rec.: journal of the Clogher Society, xiv (iii), xv (i) (1993, 1994).

Cloughjordan Heritage, i (1985).

Collect. Hib.: Collectanea Hibernica, sources for Irish history, xxxiv/xxxv (1992/93).

Connemara: Journal of the Clifden & Connemara Heritage Group, i (i) (1993).

Cork Hist. Soc. Jn: Journal of the Cork Historical and Archaeological Society, xcviii, xcix, (1993, 1994).

An Cosantóir, li-liii (1991-1993).

Curr. Archaeol., Current Archaeology, xii (1993/95).

Cymmrodorian Soc. Trans., Transactions of the Cymmrodorian Society, 1983, 1990.

Decies: journal of the Old Waterford Society, lxvii-l (1993, 1994).

Donegal Annual: Journal of the County Donegal Historical Society, xlv, xlvi (1993, 1994)

Dublin Heritage Group Ann.. Report, v, vi (1993, 1994) .

Dublin Hist. Rec.: journal of the Old Dublin Society, xlvi, xlvii (1993, 1994).

Dúiche Néill: journal of the O'Neill Country Historical Society, viii, ix (1993, 1994).

Dun Laoghaire Geneal. Soc. Jn., ii, iii (1993,1994).

Dun Laoghaire Jn.: Dun Laoghaire Borough Historical Society, i, ii, iii (1990-1993).

Early Med. Eur., iii (1994).

Ec. Soc. Rev., Economic and Social Review, xxi, xxv (1990, 1994).

Econ. Hist. Rev., xlvi (1993).

Eighteenth-century Ireland: Iris an dá Chultúr: Eighteenth-Century Ireland Society, viii, ix (1993, 1994).

Éigse, a journal of Irish Studies, xxvii-xxviii (1993, 1994).

Eire-Ireland, a journal of Irish Studies, xxviii, xxix (1993, 1994).

Emania: Bulletin of the Navan Research Group, iii-vii, xi, xii (1987-1990, 1993, 1994).

Eng. Hist. Rev., cviii, cix (1993, 1994).

Ériu, xliv, xlv (1993, 1994).

Ethnic and Racial Stud., v, viii, ix (1982, 1985, 1986).

Etudes Irlandaises, xviii, xix (1993, 1994).

European Jn. Polit. Res., European Journal of Political Research, xv, xx, xxiv, xxvi (1987, 1991, 1993, 1994).

Explor. Econ. Hist, xxx, xxxi (1993, 1994).

Familia: Ulster Historical Foundation, ii (nos 9, 10) (1993, 1994).

Folk Life: a journal of ethnological Studies, xxxi (1992-93).

The Furrow, xxviii, xxxi-xxxviii, xlv (1977, 1980-87, 1994).

Galway Arch. Soc. Jn.: Galway Archaeological and Historical Society Journal, xxxviii, lxv, lxvi (1981/82, 1993, 1994).

Galway Roots: journal of the Galway Family History Society, [i], ii (1993, 1994).

Gateway to the Past (vol i, no i entitled *Irish Family History*) i, nos i-iii (1993, 1994).
(See also *Irish Family History* below.)

Geog. Jn., cliii (1987).

Geographical Viewpoint: journal of the Association of Geography Teachers of Ireland, xvii, xxii (1988/89, 1994).

The Glynns: journal of the Glens of Antrim Historical Society, viii, xxi, xxii (1980, 1993, 1994).

Hermathena: a Dublin University review, cliv (1993).

The Historian, lxxii (1993).

History, lx (1975).

Hist. Europ. Ideas, xvi (1993).

Hist. Jn., xix, xxxvi, xxxvii (1976, 1993, 1994).

Hist. Res.: bulletin of the Institute of Historical Research, lxvii (1994).

Hist. Jahrb.: Historisches Jahrbuch, cx (1990).

Hist. Ire., i, ii (1993, 1994).

History Today, xxxv, xxxviii, xliii (1985, 1988, 1993).

Hist. Work., History Workshop: a journal of socialist and feminist historians, xxxv (1993).

In the Shadow of the Steeple, iv (1994).

Inst. Brit. Geog. Trans, xix (1994).

Int Migration Rev., xx (1986).

Int. Jn. Oral Hist., vii (1986).

Int. Jn. of the Hist. of Sport, x (1993).

Int. Jn. Sociol and Soc. Pol., xiii, (1993).

Int .Jn. Urban and Regional Res., xviii, (1994).

Int. Rev. Soc. Hist.., xxiii, xxxiii (1978, 1988).

Ir. Archeaological Wetland Unit Trans., i, ii (1993).

Ir. Archives: journal of the Irish Society for Archives, (Autumn 1994).

Ir. Arts Rev. Yearbk., 1994.

Ir. Baptist Hist. Soc. Jn. xxv (1992/93), n.s. i, ii (1993/94, 1994/95).

Ir. Communications Rev., i -iii (1991-1993).

Ir. Econ. & Soc. Hist.: Economic and Social History Society of Ireland, xx, xxi (1993, 1994).

Ir. Educational Stud.: Educational Studies Association of Ireland, xii, xiii (1993, 1994).

Ir. Family Hist.: journal of the Irish Family History Society ix, x (1993, 1994). (See also *Gateway to the Past* above).

Ir. Forestry, xxxviii, xlii, xliii (1981, 1985, 1986).

Ir. Garden, i-iii (1992-1994).

Ir. Geneal.: Journal of Irish Genealogical Research Society, ix (1994).

Ir. Geography, xxvi, xxvii (1993, 1994).

Ir. Georgian Soc. Bull.: bulletin of the Irish Georgian Society, xxiv, xxxvi (1981, 1994).

I.H.S., Irish Historical Studies, xxviii, xxix (1993, 1994).

Ir. Home Economics Jn., i (2) ii (2) (1992).

Ir. Jn. Sociol.: Sociological Association of Ireland, ii - iv (1992-1994).

Ir. Jurist, Irish Jurist, xxviii/xxx (1993/95).

Ir. Political Stud.: Political Studies Association of Ireland, viii, ix (1993, 1994).

Ir. Railway Rec. Soc. Jn..: Journal of the Irish Railway Record Society, xviii, 120-122 (1993) xviii, 123, 125 (1994).

Ir. Reporter , xi, xvi (1993, 1994).

The Ir. Rev, xiv, xv, xvi (1993, 1994).

Ir. Roots, 1992 (1-4), 1993 (1-4), 1994 (1-4).

Ir. Stud. in International Affairs, v (1994).

Ir. Studies Rev., i-ix (1992-1994).

Ir. Sword : Military History Society of Ireland, xix (75-76) (1993, 1994).

Ir. Theological Quarterly , lix, lx (1993, 1994).

Ir. University Rev., xxiv (1994).

Irishways, i-iii (1991, 1992).

Irisleabhar Mha Nuad, 1993, 1994.

John Rylands Library Bulletin, lxxvi (1994).

Jn. British Studies, xxii (1993).

Jn. Contemporary History, xxviii (1993).

Jn. Eccles. Hist. , xliv (1993).

Jn. Econ. Hist ., liii (1993).

Jn. European Economic Hist ., v (1976), x-xiii (1981-1984) xxiii (1994).

Jn. Family Hist., xviii (1993).

Jn. Hist. Geog., xiii, xix (1987, 1993).

Jn. Hist. Ideas, xxxi, xxxiv, xxxvi, xxxviii, xlii, xlvi (1970, 1973, 1975, 1977, 1981, 1985).

Jn. Interdisciplinary History, xxiv, xxv (1993/94, 1994/95).

Jn. Ir. Archaeol., i-v (1983,1984, 1985/86, 1987/88, 1989/90).

Jn. Ir. Lit., xxii (1993).

Jn. Medieval History, xii, xiii (1986, 1987).

Jn. Religious History, xii (1983).

Jn. Soc. Hist., xxviii (1994/95).

Jn. of the Statistical and Social Inquiry Soc. Ire., xxvi, no 4 (1991/92).

Jn. Transport History , x, no 2 (1989).

Jn. Urban Hist., xx (1993/94).

Labour History News, Irish Labour History Society, ix (1993).

Labour History Rev.: Society for the Study of Labour History, lviii, lix (1993, 1994).

Lecale Miscellany: Lecale Historical Society, xi, xii (1993, 1994).

Linen Hall Rev., x, xi (1993, 1994).

Local History Rev.: Federation of Local History Societies, vi (1993).

Long Room: bulletin of the Friends of the Library Trinity College Dublin, xxxviii, xxxix
    (1993, 1994).

Louth Arch. Soc. Jn.: journal of the County Louth Archaeological and Historical Society,
    xxiii (1), xxiii (2) (1993, 1994).

Mallow Field Club Jn., xi , xii (1993, 1994).

Medieval Archaeology, xxxviii, xxxix (1993, 1994).

Midland History, ix (1984).

Milltown Studies, ii, viii, ix, xii, xiv, xvi, xxi, xxv, xxxii (1978, 1981, 1982, 1983, 1984,
    1985, 1988, 1990, 1993).

Mizen Jn. , i, ii (1993, 1994).

Mod. Law Rev., xlix, li, lii, lvii (1986, 1988, 1989, 1994).

North Munster Antiq. Jn., xxxv (1993/94).

New Left Review, 207 (1994).

North Mayo Hist. Jn.: journal of the North Mayo Historical and Archeaological Society, iii,
    nos 1-2 (1992/93, 1993/94).

N. Irel. Legal Q.: Northern Ireland Legal Quarterly, xxxiv, xxxvii, xxxix, xliv (1983, 1986, 1988, 1993).

Notes and Queries, xl (1994).

Ó Domhnaill Abú, xx (1993).

Oghma, 1 - 6 (1989-1994).

Old Blarney, journal of the Blarney and District Historical Society, iii (1993).

Old Drogheda Soc. Jn., ix (1994).

Old Kilkenny Rev.: journal of the Kilkenny Archaeological Society, iv (5), xlvi, (1993,1994).

Old Limerick Jn., xxx, xxxi (1993,1994).

O Mahony Jn., xii, xvi (1982, 1993)

Old Wexford Soc. Jn., vi (1976/77) (See also *Wexford Hist. Soc. Jn.* below).

Oola Past & Present, i-iii (1992-1994).

The Other Clare: Shannon Archeaological and Historical Society, i, ii, xvii, xviii (1977, 1978, 1993, 1994).

Oughterany: jounal of the Donadea Local History Group, i (1) (1993).

Parliamentary Hist., xi - xiii (1992-1994).

The Past: : journal of the Uí Cinsealaigh Historical Society, xviii (1992).

Peritia, viii (1994).

An Pobal Éirithe: An Pobal Éirithe - The Risen People, v (1991).

Political Studies, xlii (1992).

Population Studies, xlviii (1994).

Proc. Prehistoric Soc. lx (1994).

Race & Class, xxxiv (1993).

Recusant History: Catholic Record Society Great Britain, xxii (1994/95).

Renaissance and Modern Studies, xxxvi (1993).

Renaissance Quarterly, xlvi (1993).

Review: journal of the Craigavon Historical Society, v (3) (1986/87).

Review - UCG, Review - UCG Womens Studies Centre, i (1992).

R.I.A. Proc., xciii, xciv (1994).

Ríocht na Midhe: Meath Archaeological and Historical Society, ix (1) (1994/95).

Roscommon Hist. Soc. Jn.: Roscommon Historical and Archaeological Society journal (from vol iv - Co Roscommon), iii, iv, v (1990, 1992, 1994).

Roy. Australia Hist. Soc. Jn., lxxix (1993).

R.S.A.I. Jn.: Journal of the Royal Society of Antiquaries of Ireland, cxxiii, cxxiv (1993, 1994).

Royal Hist. Soc. Trans.: Transactions of the Royal Historical Society, 6th series, iii, iv (1993, 1994).

Saothar: Irish Labour History Society, xviii, xix (1993, 1994).

Scottish Hist. Rev., liv, lxxii, lxxiii (1975, 1993, 1994).

Seanchas Ardmhacha: journal of the Armagh Diocesan Historical Society. xv (2), xvi (1) (1993, 1994).

Seanchas Duthalla: journal of the Duhallow Historical Society, ix (1993).

Sliabh Aughty: East Clare Heritage Group, iv, v (1993, 1994).

Soc. Pol. & Admin., xxvi, xxvii (1992, 1993).

Social Studies, v, viii (1976/1977, 1984/1985).

Studia Hibernica, xxvii, xxviii (1993, 1994).

Sudia Monastica, xix, xxix (1977, 1987).

Studies, lxxxii, lxxxiii (1993, 1994).

Swords Voices, i, i (2) (1992/93, 1994).

Teathba: journal of Longford Historical Society, i (1), ii (1), (1969, 1980).

Theatre Ireland, xxxi (1993).

Times Change, i - iii (1994).

Timoleague Hist. Soc. Newssheet, ii (1986).

Tipp. Hist. Jn: Co Tipperary Historical Journal, 1993, 1994.

Traditio , xlix (1994).

Treoir, xxv, xxvi (1993, 1994).

U.C.D. Hist. Rev., iii, v - viii (1989, 1991-1994).

Ulster Folklife, xxxix, xl (1993, 1994).

U.J.A.: Ulster Journal of Archaeology, lvi (1993).

Ulster Local Studies: journal of the Federation for Ulster Local Studies, iii (2), iv, xv, xvi
(1977, 1978, 1993, 1994).

An t-Ultach, lxx, lxxi (1993, 1994).

Victorian Studies, xix, xxi, xxvi, xxviii, xxxi, (1975/76, 1977/78, 1982/83, 1984/85, 1987).

West European Politics, xvi (1993).

Wexford Hist. Soc. Jn.: Old Wexford Society, xv (1994/95). (See also *Old Wexford Soc. Jn.*
above).

Wicklow Hist. Soc. Jn., i (nos 6, 7) (1993, 1994).

A Window on the Past: journal of Rathfeigh Historical Society, [i], iii (1987, 1993).

Women's Studies International Forum, xvi (1993).

World Arch., xv, xxvi (1983, 1994).

Z.C.P.: Zeitschrift fur Celtische Philogie, xlvi (1994).

ABRAMS (Lesley), ed. See *St. Patrick, A.D. 493-1993* (1993)

0001 The age of migrating ideas: early medieval art in northern Britain and Ireland: proceedings of the second international conference on insular art held in the National Museums of Scotland in Edinburgh, 3-6 January 1991. *Ed.* Michael Spearman and John Higgitt. Pp x, 267. Edinburgh: National Museums of Scotland; Stroud: Alan Sutton, 1993.

ALDERMAN (Geoffrey), ed. See *Governments, ethnic groups and political representation* (1993).

ANDERSON (R.G.W.), ed. See *Making instruments count* (1993).

ANDREWS (J.H.), ed. See *Irish country towns* (1994).

0002 Art and the national dream: the search for vernacular expression in turn-of-the century design. *Ed.* Nicola Gordon Bowe. Pp 213. Blackrock, Co. Dublin: Irish Academic Press, 1993.

0003 Art is my life: a tribute to James White. *Ed.* Brian P. Kennedy. Pp xvi, 216. Dublin: National Gallery, 1991.

ASCH (Ronald G.) ed. See *Three nations: a common history?* (1993).

0004 Aspects of Irish genealogy: proceedings of the 1st Irish genealogical congress. [*Ed.* M.D. Evans and Eileen O Duill]. Pp 212. [S.l.]: Genealogical Congress Committee, [1993].

BARRON (Thomas J.), ed. See *Constitutions and national identity* (1993).

BARTON (Brian), ed. See *The Northern Ireland question* (1994).

BEBBINGTON (David W.), ed, See *Evangelicalism* (1994).

BELCHEM (John), ed. See *The Irish in British labour history* (1993).

BENNETT (J.A.). See *Making instruments count* (1993).

0005 The big house in Ireland: reality and representation. *Ed.* Jacqueline Genet. Pp xii, 311. Dingle: Brandon, 1991.

BIRKE (Adolf M.), ed. See *Foderalismus im deutsch-britischen meinungsstreit* (1993).

BIRKS (Peter), ed. See *The life of the law* (1993).

BONNER (Gerald), ed. See *St. Cuthbert* (1989).

0006 The Book of Cloyne = leabhar Chuain Uamha. *Ed.* Padraig O Loingsigh. 2nd ed. Pp [6], 387 [2]. [s.l.]: [the author], [1994?].
　　　Previous ed.: 1977.

0007 The Book of Kells: proceedings of a conference at Trinity College Dublin, 6-9 September 1992. *Ed.* Felicity O'Mahony. Pp xiv, 603. Aldershot: Scolar Press for Trinity College Library Dublin, 1994.

0008   Boundaries & thresholds: papers from a colloquium of the Katharine Briggs club. *Ed.* Hilda Ellis Davidson. Pp 104. Stroud, Gloucs: Thimble Press for the Katharine Briggs Club, 1993.

BOWE (Nicola Gordon), ed. See *Art and the national dream* (1993).

BOYCE (D. George), ed.   See *Political thought in Ireland since the seventeenth century* (1993).

BRADSHAW (Brendan), ed. See *Representing Ireland* (1993).

BRADY (Ciaran), ed. See *Interpreting Irish history* (1994).

0009   British and Irish women dramatists since 1958: a critical handbook. *Ed.* Trevor R. Griffiths, Margaret Llewellyn Jones. Pp viii, 193. Buckingham: Open University Press, 1993. (Gender in writing).

BUCKLAND (Patrick), ed. See *The Irish in British labour history* (1993).

BURNSIDE (Sam) ed. See *The glow upon the fringe* (1994).

BUTTIMER (Cornelius G.), ed. See *Cork* (1993).

0010   Cabinet ministers and parliamentary government. *Ed.* Michael Laver, Kenneth A. Shepsie. Pp ix, 318. Cambridge: Cambridge University Press, 1994. (Political economy of institutions and decisions).
     Includes chapters on Ireland.

CANNY (Nicholas), ed. See *Europeans on the move* (1994).

CARROLL (Peter S.), ed. See *A man raised up* (1994).

CATHCART (Kevin J.), ed. See *The Edward Hincks bicentenary lectures* (1994).

0011   Churches built in ancient times: recent studies in early Christian archaeology. *Ed.* Kenneth Painter. Pp xxvii, 362. London: Society of Antiquaries of London, Accordia Research Centre University of London, 1994. (Specialist studies of the Mediterranean, vol. 1) (Occasional papers (Society of Antiquaries of London): new series, vol. 16).

COLLINS (Neil), ed. See *Political issues in Ireland today* (1994).

COLLINS (Peter), ed. See *Nationalism and unionism* (1994).

COLLINS (Timothy), ed. See *Decoding the landscape* (1994).

0012   Coming into the light: the work, politics and religion of women in Ulster, 1840-1940. *Ed.* Janice Holmes and Diane Urquhart. Pp x, 213. Belfast: The Institute of Irish Studies, Queen's University of Belfast, 1994.

0013   Comparative aspects of Irish and Japanese economic and social history. *Ed.* Taro Matsuo. Pp 350. Tokyo: Institute of Comparative Economic Studies, Hosei University, 1993.

0014   Constitutions and national identity: proceedings of the conference ... University of Edinburgh 3-6 July 1987. *Ed.* Thomas J. Barron, Owen Dudley Edwards and Patricia Storey. Pp xvi, 316. Edinburgh: Quadriga, 1993.

    COOK (Chris), comp. See *The Longman guide to sources in contemporary British history* (1994).

0015   Cork: history and society: interdisciplinary essays on the history of an Irish county. *Ed.* Patrick O'Flanagan, Cornelius G. Buttimer; editorial advisor Gerard O'Brien. Pp xxiv, 1000. Dublin: Geography Publications, 1993.

0016   The course of Irish history. *Ed.* T.W. Moody and F.X. Martin. Revised and enlarged edition edited by F.X. Martin. Pp 504. Cork: Mercier Press in association with Radio Telefís Éireann, 1994.
    Previous ed.: 1984

0017   The creation of the Dáil: a volume of essays from the Thomas Davis lectures. (General editor Michael Littleton). *Ed.* Brian Farrell. Pp v, 177. Dublin: Blackwater Press in association with Radio Telefís Éireann, 1994.

0018   The creative migrant. *Ed.* Patrick O'Sullivan. Pp ix, 246. Leicester: Leicester University Press, 1994. (The Irish world wide: history, heritage, identity, vol 3).

0019   Culture in Ireland - regions: identity and power: proceedings of the Cultures of Ireland Group Conference, 27-29 November, 1992. *Ed.* Proinsias Ó Drisceoil. Pp viii, 242. Belfast: Institute of Irish Studies, Queen's University of Belfast, 1993.

0020   Dáithí Ó hUaithne: cuimhní cairde. *Ed.* Proinsias Mac Aonghusa agus Tomás de Bhaldraithe. Pp 144. Baile Átha Cliath: Clóchomhar, 1994.
    David Greene (1915-1981) Irish language scholar.

    DALSIMER (Adele M.), ed. See *Visualizing Ireland* (1993).

    DAVIDSON (Hilda Ellis), ed. See *Boundaries & thresholds* (1993).

    De BHALDRAITHE (Tomás), ed. See *Dáithí Ó hUaithne* (1994).

0021   Decoding the landscape: papers read at the inaugural conference of the Centre for Landscape Studies ... at University College Galway, November 2nd 1990 and subsequent meetings. *Ed.* Timothy Collins. Pp x, 170. Galway: University College Galway, Social Sciences Research Centre, Centre for Landscape Studies, 1994.

    DENNISON (Gabriel), ed. See *Traditional architecture in Ireland* (1994).

    DICKSON (David), ed. See *The United Irishmen* (1993).

    DOAN (James E.), ed. See *The Scotch-Irish and Hiberno-English language and culture* (1993).

    DUMVILLE (D.N.), ed. See *France and the British Isles in the middle ages and Renaissance* (1991).

DUMVILLE (David N.), ed. See *St. Patrick, A.D. 493-1993* (1993).

ECCLESHALL (Robert), ed. See *Political thought in Ireland since the seventeenth century* (1993).

0022   The Edward Hincks bicentenary lectures. *Ed.* Kevin J. Cathcart. Pp x, 227. Dublin: University College Dublin, Department of Near Eastern Languages, 1994.
Edward Hincks (1792-1866), egyptologist and Church of Ireland pastor.

EDWARDS (Owen Dudley), ed. See *Constitutions and national identity* (1993).

EDWARDS (R. Dudley), ed. See *The great famine* (1994).

ELVERT (Jurgen), ed. See *Nordirland in Geschichte und Gegenwart* (1994).

0023   Ethnic and religious conflicts: Europe and Asia. *Ed.* Peter Janke. Pp xiii, 306. Aldershot: Dartmouth, 1994.

0024   Europeans on the move: studies on European migration, 1500-1800. *Ed.* Nicholas Canny. Pp xii, 329. Oxford: Clarendon Press, 1994.

0025   Evangelicalism: comparative studies of popular protestantism in North America, the British Isles, and beyond, 1700-1990. *Ed.* Mark A. Noll, David W. Bebbington, George A. Rawlyk. Pp xv, 430. Oxford: Oxford University Press, 1994. (Religion in America series).

EVANS (M.D.), ed. See *Aspects of Irish genealogy* [1993].

FARRELL (Brian), ed. See *The creation of the Dáil* (1994).

0026   Féile Zozimus. Vol. 3: two Dubliners, Seán O'Casey, Donn S. Piatt. *Ed.* Vivian Uíbh Eachach, Dónal Ó Faoláin. Pp 93. Baile Átha Cliath: Gael-Linn, 1994.

0027   Foderalismus im deutsch-britischen meinungsstreit. Historische dimension und politische aktualitat = The federalism debate in Britain and Germany: a historical and political controversy. *Ed.* Adolf M. Birke, Hermann Wentker. Pp 177. Munchen: Saur, 1993. (Prinz-Albert Studien, 10).

0028   France and the British Isles in the middle ages and Renaissance: essays by members of Girton College, Cambridge in memory of Ruth Morgan. *Ed.* Gillian Jondorf and D.N. Dumville. Pp 288. Woodbridge: Boydell, 1991.

FRASER (T.G.), ed. See *Men, women and war* (1993).

GENET (Jacqueline), ed. See *The big house in Ireland* (1991).

GEOGHEGAN (Vincent), ed. See *Political thought in Ireland since the seventeenth century* (1993).

GERARD (Alan), ed. See *La Vendée dans l'histoire* (1994).

GILLEN (Gerard), ed. See *Music and the church* (1993).

GILLESPIE (Raymond), ed. See *Ireland: art into history* (1994)

0029   The glow upon the fringe: literary journeys around Derry and the north west. *Ed.* Sam Burnside. Pp ix, 112. Londonderry: Verbal Arts Centre, 1994.

0030   Governments, ethnic groups and political representation. *Ed.* Geoffrey Alderman, John Leslie and Klaus Erich Pollmann. Pp xx, 300. Aldershot: Dartmouth, 1993. (Comparative studies on governments and non-dominant ethnic groups in Europe, 1850-1940, vol 4).

GRAHAM (B.J.), ed. See *An historical geography of Ireland* (1993).

0031   The great famine: studies in Irish history, 1845-52. *Ed.* R. Dudley Edwards, T. Desmond Williams. [New ed. with a new introduction and bibliography by Cormac Ó Gráda]. Pp xxvii, 523. Dublin: Lilliput Press, 1994.
      Previous ed.: 1956.

GREENGRASS (Mark). See *Samuel Hartlib and universal reformation* (1994).

GRIFFITHS (Trevor R.), ed. See *British and Irish women dramatists since 1958* (1993).

HADFIELD (Andrew), ed. See *Representing Ireland* (1993).

HALLINAN (Michael), ed. See *Tipperary county* (1993).

HANNIGAN (Ken), ed. See *Wicklow* (1994).

HATTON (Timothy J.), ed. See *Migration and the international labor market* (1994).

HALTZEL (Michael H.), ed. See *Northern Ireland and the politics of reconciliation* (1993).

HECKMANN (Thierry), ed. See *La vendée dans l'histoire* (1994).

HENDERSON (John), ed. See *Poor women and children in the European past* (1994).

HIGGITT (John), ed. See *The age of migrating ideas* (1993).

HILL (Ronald J.), ed. See *Modern Irish democracy* (1993).

0032   An historical geography of Ireland. *Ed.* B.J. Graham and L.J. Proudfoot. Pp xviii, 454. New York, London: Academic Press, 1993.

0033   The history and legends of Ballyhoura mountains. *Ed.* Ted O'Riordan. Pp 64. [S.l.]: Ted O'Riordan, 1993.
      Co. Limerick.

HOLMES (Janice), ed. See *Coming into the light* (1994).

HOWELL (David), ed. See *Roots of rural ethnic mobilisation* (1993).

0034   An imperial state at war: Britain from 1689 to 1815. *Ed.* Lawrence Stone. Pp ix, 372. London: Routledge, 1993.

0035   Images, identities and ideologies: papers from the 22nd International Ballad Conference, Belfast, 29 June - 3 July 1992. *Ed.* John M. Kirk and Colin Neilands. Pp 286. Enfield Lock, Middlesex: Hisarlik, 1994. (Lore and language, vol 12).

0036   Interpreting Irish history: the debate on historical revisionism, 1938-1994. *Ed.* Ciaran Brady. Pp xii, 348. Blackrock, Co. Dublin: Irish Academic Press, 1994.

0037   Ireland: art into history. *Ed.* Raymond Gillespie and Brian P. Kennedy. Pp 240. Dublin: Town House; Niwot, Colorado: R. Rinehart, 1994.

0038   The Irish Augustinians in Rome, 1656-1994 and Irish Augustinian missions throughout the world. *Ed.* F.X. Martin and Clare O'Reilly. Pp 224. Dublin: Augustinian House of Studies; Rome: St Patrick's College, 1994.

0039   Irish convict lives. *Ed.* Bob Reece. Pp xii, 266. Sydney: Crossing Press, 1993.

0040   Irish country towns. *Ed.* Anngret Simms and J.H. Andrews. Pp 191. Cork: Mercier Press in association with Radio Telefís Éireann, 1994. (The Thomas Davis lecture series).

0041   The Irish in British labour history. *Ed.* Patrick Buckland and John Belchem. Pp vi, 114. Liverpool: Institute of Irish Studies, University of Liverpool with Society for the Study of Labour History, 1993. (Conference proceedings in Irish studies, no. 1).

0042   Irish women's studies reader. *Ed.* Ailbhe Smyth. Pp vii, 279. Dublin: Attic Press, 1993.

JANKE (Peter), ed. See *Ethnic and religious conflicts* (1994).

JEFFERY (Keith), ed. See *Men, women and war* (1993).

JONDORF (Gillian), ed. See *France and the British Isles in the middle ages and renaissance* (1991).

KENNEDY (Brian P.), ed. See *Art is my life* (1991).

KENNEDY (Brian P.), ed. See *Ireland: art into history* (1994).

KEOGH (Dáire), ed. See *The United Irishmen* (1993).

KEOGH (Dermot), ed. See *Northern Ireland and the politics of reconciliation* (1993).

KIRK (John M.), ed. See *Images, identities and ideologies* (1994).

KLAUS (H. Gustav), ed. See *Strong words, brave deeds* (1994).

LAVER (Michael), ed. See *Cabinet ministers and parliamentary government* (1994).

LESLIE (John), ed. See *Governments, ethnic groups and political representation* (1993).

LESLIE (Michael), ed. See *Samuel Hartlib and universal reformation* (1994).

0043   The life of the law: proceedings of the tenth British Legal History Conference, Oxford 1991. *Ed.* Peter Birks. Pp viii, 267. London: Hambledon Press, 1993.

LITTLETON (Michael), general ed. See *The creation of the Dáil* (1994).

LLEWELLYN-JONES (Margaret), ed. See *British and Irish women dramatists since 1958* (1993).

LOGAN (John), ed. See *With warmest love* (1994).

0044   The Longman guide to sources in contemporary British history, 1: organisations and societies. Compiled for the British Library of Political and Economic Science by Chris Cook and David Waller. Pp xii, 372. London: Longman, 1994.

0045   Lúise Gabhánach Ní Dhufaigh agus scoil Bhríde. *Ed.* Mairéad Ní Ghacháin. Pp [3], iii, 43. Baile Átha Cliath: Coscéim, 1993.
       Louise Gavan Duffy (1884-1969) teacher and revolutionary founder of Irish language secondary school for girls in Dublin in 1917.

Mac AONGHUSA (Proinsias), ed. See *Dáithí Ó hUaithne* (1994).

McCONE (Kim), ed. See *Stair na Gaeilge* (1994).

Mac CUARTA (Brian), ed. See *Ulster 1641* (1993).

MacLOCHLAINN (Alf), ed. See *Writers, raconteurs and notable feminists* (1993).

0046   Making instruments count: essays on historical scientific instruments presented to Gerard L'Estrange Turner. *Ed.* R.G.W. Anderson, J.A. Bennett, W.F. Ryan. Pp ix, 492. Aldershot: Variorum, 1993.

MALEY (Willy), ed. See *Representing Ireland* (1993).

0047   A man raised up: recollections and reflections on Venerable Edmund Rice, presented in 1994 on the occasion of the 150th anniversary of his death. *Ed.* Peter S. Carroll. Pp 192. Dublin: Elo Publications in association with the Congregation of Christian Brothers, 1994.
       Edmund Rice 1762-1844.

MARSH (Michael), ed. See *Modern Irish democracy* (1993).

MARTIN (F.X.), ed. See *The course of Irish history* (1994).

MARTIN (F.X.), ed. See *The Irish Augustinians in Rome* (1994).

MATSUO (Taro), ed. See *Comparative aspects of Irish and Japanese economic and social history* (1993).

0048   Medieval codicology, icongraphy, literature, and translation: studies for Keith Val Sinclair. *Ed.* Peter Rolfe Monkes and D.D.R. Owen. Pp xxvii, 395. Leiden: Brill, 1994. (Litterae textuales: a series on manuscripts and their texts).

0049   Men, women and war. *Ed.* T.G. Fraser and Keith Jeffery. Pp x, 242. Dublin: Lilliput Press, 1993. (Historical studies, 18).

0050   Migration and the international labor market 1850-1939. *Ed.* Timothy J. Hatton and Jeffrey G. Williamson. Pp xii, 295. London: Routledge, 1994.

0051   Modern Irish democracy: essays in honour of Basil Chubb. *Ed.* Ronald J. Hill and Michael Marsh. Pp 199. Blackrock, Co. Dublin: Irish Academic Press, 1993

MONKS (Peter Rolfe), ed. See *Medieval codicology, iconography, literature and translation* (1994).

MOODY (T.W.), ed. See *The course of Irish history* (1994).

0052   Music and the church. *Ed.* Gerard Gillen and Harry White. Pp 354. Blackrock, Co. Dublin: Irish Academic Press, 1993. (Irish musical studies, 2.).

0053   Náisiún na hÉireann: mar a bhí agus mar atá. *Ed.* Diarmuid Ó Laoghaire. Pp [5], 100. Baile Átha Cliath: Foilseacháin Ábhair Spioradálta, 1993.
    Irish language and culture.

0054   The national question in Europe in historical context. *Ed.* Mikulás Teich and Roy Porter. Pp xx, 343. Cambridge: Cambridge University Press, 1993.

0055   Nationalism and Unionism: conflict in Ireland, 1885-1921. *Ed.* Peter Collins. Pp x, 207. Belfast: Institute of Irish Studies, Queen's University of Belfast, 1994.

NEILANDS (Colin), ed. See *Images, identities and ideologies* (1994).

NEVIN (Donal), ed. See *Trade union century* (1994).

Ní FHLOINN (Bairbre), ed. See *Traditional architecture in Ireland* (1994).

Ní GHACHÁIN (Mairéad). See *Lúise Gabhánach Ní Dhufaigh agus scoil Bhríde* (1993).

NOLAN (William), ed. See *Wicklow* (1994).

NOLL (Mark A.), ed. See *Evangelicanism* (1994).

0056   Nordirland in Geschichte und Gegenwart = Northern Ireland past and present. *Ed.* Jurgen Elvert. Pp 573. Stuttgart: Steiner, 1994. (Historische mitteilungen Beiheft 9).
    Most contributions are in English.

0057   Northern Ireland and the politics of reconciliation. *Ed.* Dermot Keogh and Michael H Haltzel. Pp x, 267. Washington (D.C.): Woodrow Wilson Center Press; Cambridge: Cambridge University Press, 1993. (Woodrow Wilson Center series).

0058   The Northern Ireland question: perspectives and policies. *Ed.* Brian Barton, Patrick J. Roche. Pp vii, 216. Aldershot Avebury, 1994.

O'BRIEN (Gerard), ed. See *Cork* (1993).

Ó CEALLAIGH (Daltún), ed. See *Reconsiderations of Irish history and culture* (1994).

O'CONNELL (Maurice R.), ed. See *People power* (1993).

Ó DRISCEOIL (Proinsias), ed. See *Culture in Ireland - regions* (1993).

Ó DÚILL (Eileen), ed. See *Aspects of Irish genealogy* [1993].

Ó FAOLÁIN (Donal), ed. See *Féile Zozimus vol 3: Two Dubliners* (1994).

O'FLANAGAN (Patrick), ed. See *Cork* (1993).

0059   Ó ghlúin go glúin: scéal Chonradh na Gaeilge in Aonach Urmhumhan, 1901-1993. *Ed.* Eibhlín Uí Mhorónaigh, Liam Prút. Pp x, 70. [Baile Átha Cliath]: Coiscéim, 1993.
      The Gaelic League in Nenagh.

Ó GRÁDA (Cormac). See *The great famine* (1994).

Ó GRÁDA (Liam). See *Souvenir of re-dedication of Church of the Immaculate Conception, Drangan* (1993)

Ó LAOGHAIRE (Diarmuid), ed. See *Náisiún na hÉireann* (1993).

Ó LOINSIGH (Pádraig), ed. See *The book of Cloyne* [1994?]

O'MAHONY (Felicity), ed. See *The book of Kells* (1994).

O'REILLY (Clare), ed. See *The Irish Augustinians in Rome* (1994).

O'RIORDAN (Ted), ed. See *The history and legends of Ballyhoura mountains* (1993).

O'SULLIVAN (Patrick), ed. See *The creative migrant* (1994).

OWEN (D.D.R.), ed. See *Medieval codicology, iconography, literature, and translation* (1994).

PAINTER (Kenneth), ed. See *Churches built in ancient times* (1994).

0060   People power: proceedings of the third annual Daniel O'Connell Workshop. *Ed.* Maurice R. O'Connell. Pp x, 147. Dublin: Institute of Public Administration on behalf of DOCAL - Daniel O'Connell Association, 1993.

PISTOHLKORS (Gort Von), ed. See *Roots of rural ethnic mobilisation* (1993).

0061   Political issues in Ireland today. *Ed*. Neil Collins. Pp x, 223. Manchester: Manchester University Press, 1994. (Politics today).

0062   Political thought in Ireland since the seventeenth century. *Ed*. D. George Boyce, Robert Eccleshall, and Vincent Geoghegan. Pp viii, 227. London: Routledge, 1993.

POLLMANN (Klaus Erich), ed. See *Governments, ethnic groups and political representation* (1993).

0063   Poor women and children in the European past. *Ed*. John Henderson and Richard Wall. Pp xiii, 347 London: Routledge, 1994.

PORTER (Roy), ed. *The national question in Europe in historical context* (1993).

PROUDFOOT (L.J.), ed. See *An historical geography of Ireland* (1993).

PRÚT (Liam), ed. See *Ó ghlúin go glúin* (1993).

RAWLYK (George A.), ed. See *Evangelicanism* (1994).

RAYLOR (Timothy), ed. See *Samuel Hartlib and universal reformation* (1994).

0064   Reading Swift: papers from the second Munster symposium on Jonathan Swift. *Ed*. Richard H. Rodino, Hermann J. Real with the assistance of Helgard Stover-Leidig. Pp 271. Munchen: Fink Verlag, 1993.

REAL (Hermann J.), ed. See *Reading Swift* (1993).

0065   Reconsiderations of Irish history and culture: selected papers from the Desmond Greaves summer school, 1989-'93. *Ed*. Daltún Ó Ceallaigh. Pp 188. Dublin: Léirmheas, 1994.

REECE (Bob), ed. See *Irish convict lives* (1993).

0066   Representing Ireland: literature and the origins of conflict, 1534-1660. *Ed*. Brendan Bradshaw, Andrew Hadfield, Willy Maley. Pp xxiv, 235. Cambridge: Cambridge University Press, 1993.

ROCHE (Patrick J.), ed. See *The Northern Ireland question* (1994).

RODINO (Richard H.), ed. See *Reading Swift* (1993).

0067   The role of the amateur architect: papers given at the Georgian group symposium 1993. *Ed*. Giles Worsley. Pp 56. London: Georgian Group, 1994.

ROLLASON (David), ed. See *St. Cuthbert* (1993).

0068   Roots of rural ethnic mobilisation. *Ed.* David Howell, Gert von Pistohlkors, Ellen Wiegandt. Pp xxii, 327. Aldershot: Dartmouth; (N.Y.): New York University Press, 1993. (Comparative Studies on governments and non-dominant ethnic groups in Europe, 1850-1940, vol. 7).

RYAN (W.F.), ed. See *Making instruments count* (1993).

0069   Samuel Hartlib and universal reformation: studies in intellectual communication. *Ed.* Mark Greengrass, Michael Leslie and Timothy Raylor. Pp xix, 372. Cambridge: Cambridge University Press, 1994.
Samuel Hartlib c.1600-1662.

0070   The Scotch-Irish and Hiberno-English language and culture. [*Ed.* James E. Doan]. Pp [1], 36. Fort Lauderdale (Fla): Nova University, Dept. of Liberal Arts, 1993. (Working papers in Irish Studies, no. 93-3).

0071   Scotland and Ulster. *Ed.* Ian S. Wood. Pp xi, 212. Edinburgh: Mercat Press, 1994.

SHEEHY SKEFFINGTON (Andrée). See *Writers, recanteurs and notable feminists* (1993).

SHEPSIE (Kenneth A.), ed. See *Cabinet ministers and parliamentary government* (1994).

SIMMS (Anngret), ed. See *Irish country towns* (1994).

0072   Souvenir of re-dedication of Church of the Immaculate Conception, Drangan, 5th December, 1993. [Liam Ó Gráda ... et al]. Pp 24. Drangan, Co. Tipperary: Church of the Immaculate Conception, 1993.

SMYTH (Ailbhe), ed. See *Irish women's studies reader* (1993).

SPEARMAN (R. Michael), ed. See *The age of migrating ideas* (1993).

0073   St Cuthbert, his cult and his community to AD 1200. *Ed.* Gerald Bonner, David Rollason, Clare Stancliffe. Pp xxiii, 484. Woodbridge, Suffolk: Boydell Press, 1989.

0074   St. Patrick, A.D. 493-1993. *Ed.* David N. Dumville with Lesley Abrams ... [et al]. Pp 334. Woodbridge: Boydell Press, 1993. (Studies in Celtic history, vol. 13).

0075   Stair na Gaeilge: in ómós do Pádraig Ó Fiannachta. *Ed.* Kim McCone ... [et al]. Pp xxiv, 905. Maigh Nuad: Roinn na Sean-Ghaeilge, Coláiste Phádraig, 1994.

STANCLIFFE (Clare), ed. See *St Cuthbert* (1989).

STONE (Lawrence), ed. See *An imperial state at war* (1993).

STOREY (Patricia J.), ed. See *Constitutions and national identity* (1993).

STOVER-LEIDIG (Helgard), ed. See *Reading Swift* (1993).

0076   Strong words, brave deeds: the poetry, life and times of Thomas O'Brien: volunteer in the Spanish civil war. *Ed.* H. Gustav Klaus. Pp 271. Dublin: O'Brien Press, 1994.
Thomas O'Brien, 1914-1974.

TEICH (Mikulás), ed. See *The national question in Europe in historical context* (1993).

0077   Three nations - a common history?: England, Scotland and Ireland and British history, c.1600-1920. *Ed.* Ronald G. Asch. Pp 298. Bochum: Brockmeyer, 1993. (Veröffentlichung, Arbeitskreis Deutsche England- Forschung, 23,).

0078   Tipperary county: people and places: an anthology of county Tipperary, some historical events and the history of the principal towns in the county. *Ed.* Michael Hallinan. Pp 176. Dublin: Kincora Press, 1993.

0079   Trade union century. *Ed.* Donal Nevin. Pp 473. Dublin: Mercier Press in association with Irish Congress of Trade Unions & Radio Telefís Éireann, 1994. (The Thomas Davis Lecture series).

0080   Traditional architecture in Ireland and its role in rural development and tourism. *Ed.* Bairbre Ní Fhloinn, Gabriel Dennison. Pp 94. Dublin: University College Dublin, Environmental Institute, 1994.

Uí MHORÓNAIGH (Eibhlín), ed. See *Ó ghlúin go glúin* (1993).

UÍBH EACHACH·(Vivian), ed. See *Féile Zozimus vol 3: Two Dubliners* (1994).

0081   Ulster 1641: aspects of the rising. *Ed.* Brian Mac Cuarta. Pp xv, 238. Belfast: Institute of Irish Studies, Queen's University of Belfast, 1993.

0082   The United Irishmen: republicanism and rebellion. *Ed.* David Dickson, Dáire Keogh and Kevin Whelan. Pp xii, 378. Dublin: Lilliput Press, 1993.

URQUHART (Diane), ed. See *Coming into the light* (1994).

0083   La Vendée dans l'histoire: actes du colloque tenu a La Roche-sur-Yon en Avril 1993. *Ed.* Alain Gerard, Thierry Heckmann. Pp x, 482. Paris: Perrin, 1994.

0084   Visualizing Ireland: national identity and the pictorial tradition. *Ed.* Adele M. Dalsimer. Pp. vi, 230. London: Faber, 1993.

WALL (Richard), ed. See *Poor women and children in the European past* (1994).

WALLER (David), comp. See The *Longman guide to sources in contemporary British history* (1994).

WENTKER (Hermann), ed. See *Föderalismus im deutsch-britischen Meinungsstreit* (1993).

WHELAN (Kevin), ed. See *The United Irishmen* (1993).

WHITE (Harry), ed. See *Music and the church* (1993).

0085   Wicklow: history and society: interdisciplinary essays on the history of an Irish county. *Ed.* Ken Hannigan, William Nolan. Pp 1005. Dublin: Geography Publications, 1994.

WIEGANDT (Ellen), ed. See *Roots of rural ethnic mobilisation* (1993).

WILLIAMS (T. Desmond), ed. See *The great famine* (1994).

WILLIAMSON (Jeffrey G.), ed. See *Migration and the international labor market* (1994).

0086   With warmest love: lectures for Kate O'Brien, 1984-93. *Ed.* John Logan. Pp vii, 171. Limerick: Mellick Press for the Kate O'Brien Weekend Committee, 1994.
       Kate O'Brien, 1897-1974.

WOOD (Ian S.), ed. See *Scotland and Ulster* (1994).

WORSLEY (Giles), ed. See *The role of the amateur architect* (1994).

0087   Writers, raconteurs and notable feminists: two monographs by Alf MacLochlainn and Andrée Sheehy Skeffington. Pp 52. Dublin: National Library of Ireland Society, 1993.

0088   AALEN (F.H.A.). Vernacular rural dwellings of the Wicklow mountains. In *Wicklow*, pp 581-624 (1994).

0089   ADAMS (Jack). Cullybackey 'yin nought yin': memories of an Ulster village. Pp 80. Ballymena: Adams Enterprises, 1993.

       ADAMS (Valerie). See *An Irish genealogical source* (1994)

0090   ADAMSON (Ian). The Ulster-Scottish connection. In *Scotland and Ulster*, pp 1-21 (1994).

0091   AHERN (Michael). Clonmel grammar school. In *Tipp. Hist. Jn.*, pp 128-34 (1993).

0092   AHLQVIST (Anders). Litriú na Gaeilge. In *Stair na Gaeilge*, pp 23-59 (1994).

0093   AKENSON (Donald Harmon). The Irish diaspora: a primer. Pp ix, 319. Toronto: P. Meany; Belfast: Institute of Irish Studies, Queen's University of Belfast, 1993.

0094   ALLEN (Andrew W.). Old Ballyclug, transcribed by Andrew W. Allen; foreword by Brian O'Hara. Pp 17. Ballymena: Ballymena Borough Council, [1994]. (Ballymena borough gravestone series).

0095   ALLEN (Gregory). Policemen in your family tree. In *Aspects of Irish genealogy*, pp 9-16 [1993].
       Police records, RIC etc

0096   Along the Black Pig's dyke: folklore from Monaghan and south Armagh. *Ed.* Brian Sherry and Raymond McHugh Pp [7], 232. Castleblayney: Castleblayney Community Enterprise, [1993?].

0097   ANDERSON (Amy). The manor of Ballygalget. In *Upper Ards Hist. Soc. Jn.*, i, 2-3 (1977).

0098   ANDERSON (Robert). The port of Coleraine. In *The Bann Disc*, i, 35-8 (1994).

0099   ANDREWS (J.H.). Mullingar. In *Irish country towns*, pp 179-190 (1994).

0100   The annals of Clonmacnoise: being annals of Ireland from the earliest period to A.D. 1408: translated into English A.D. 1627 by Conell Mageoghagan and *ed.* by Denis Murphy. Pp ix, 393. Felinfach: Llanerch, 1993.
       Facsimile of ed. originally published by Dublin University Press, 1896.

0101   ANNESLEY (Patrick G.) [et al]. St Mary's Church of Ireland church Castletownroche. In *Mallow Field Club Jn.*, xii, 63-75 (1994).

0102   Archaeological inventory of County Cork: vol 2: east and south Cork: comprising the baronies of Barrymore, Cork, Courceys, Imokilly, Kerrycurrihy, Kinalea, Kinnatalloon & Kinsale. Compiled by Denis Power with Elizabeth Byrne ... [et al]. Pp xii, 432. Dublin: Stationery Office, 1994.

0103   ASCH (Ronald G.). 'Obscured in whiskey mist and misery': the role of Scotland and Ireland in British history. In *Three nations - a common history?*, pp 9-48 (1993).

0104   ASSOCIATION OF CRICKET STATISTICIANS. Irish cricketers, 1855-1980. Pp 40. Cleethorpes: Association of Cricket Statisticians, [1980].

0105   'As time goes by ...': a pictorial record of Kingscourt and its environs. Vol. 1. Compiled by Kingspan and Kingscourt Community Council. Pp 100. [Kingscourt, Co. Cavan]: [Kingspan and Kingscourt Community Council], 1994.

0106   ATHLONE COUNTRY WOMEN'S ASSOCIATION. Athlone: glimpses and gleanings. Pp 62. [Athlone]: [Athlone's Country Women's Association], [1993]

0107   AUGHNEY (John, P.P.). Brett of Craanluskey and Ballygowan. In *Carloviana*, xl, 18-19 (1992/93).

0108   AVERY (Michael) and ROSE (Petra). GIS, Irish grid references and the Northern Ireland sites and monuments record. In *U.J.A.*, lvi, 163-78 (1993).

0109   AYLMER (Richard J.). The Aylmers of Donadea. In *Oughterany*, i, no. 1, pp 5-17 (1993).

0110   BAILEY (John), DOCKRELL (Morgan), ed. St Columba's cricket: not out 150. Pp 32. [Dublin]: [St Columba's College], 1993

0111   BAILYN (Bernard). Introduction: Europeans on the move 1500-1800. In *Europeans on the move*, pp 1-5 (1994).

0112   BAKER (Augustine F.). The Bakers of Lismacue: a family chronicle. In *Tipp. Hist. Jn.*, pp 115-28 (1994).

0113   BAKER (John Austin). Ireland and Northern Ireland. In *The Furrow*, xxxiii, 13-21 (1982).

0114   BALLARD (Linda). Aspects of the history and development of Irish dance costume. In *Ulster Folklife*, xl, 62-7 (1994).

0115   BALLARD (Linda). Irish lace: tradition or commodity. In *Folk Life*, xxxi, 43-56 (1992/93).

0116   BALLARD (Linda M.). Some Christmas customs. In *Arch. Ire.*, iii, 132-5 (1989).

0117   Ballynoe cemetery: a guide and brief history. Pp 119. [Ballynoe, Co. Cork]: [Ballynoe Cemetery Committee], [1993?].

0118   BARKLEY (John M.). 1690 and all that: a Presbyterian perspective. In *Presb. Hist. Soc. of Ire. Bull.*, xxi, 11-16 (1992).

0119   BARNARD (Toby). Art, architecture, artefacts and ascendancy. In *Bullán*, i, no 2, pp 17-34 (1994).

0120   BARRETT (Evelyn). Rathbeale hall. In *Swords Voices*, i, no. 2, pp 6-9 (1994).
       Rathbeale hall, built 1710, memories of growing up there in the early years of this century.

0121   BARRY (Ann). Public records and archival sources for genealogical research in Cork. In *O'Mahony Jn.*, xii, 38-42 (1982).

0122   BARRY (Deirdre). Local place names. In *The Other Clare*, i, 16 (1977).

0123   BARTON (Roy L.). Roscommon in history. In *Roscommon Hist. Soc. Jn.*, v, 6-10 (1994).

0124   BARY (Valerie). Houses of Kerry, illustrations Stephanie Walsh. Pp 294. Whitegate, Co. Clare: Ballinakella Press, 1994.

0125   BATES (Nora). Up the Down street. Pp 80. Banbridge: Adare, c.1994. Saintfield.

0126   BEATTIE (Sean). Ancient monuments of Inishowen, north Donegal. Pp 64. Carndonagh, Co. Donegal: Lighthouse Publications, 1994.

0127   BEAUMONT (Pauline), MAGINNIS (Hilary). Princess Gardens School: a goodly heritage. Pp 508. Belfast: MW Publications, 1993.

       BEEDHAM (Katharine). See *Royal Historical Society annual bibiliography of British and Irish history* (1994).

0128   BEHAN (A.P.). Up Harcourt Street from the Green. In *Dublin Hist. Rec.*, xlvii, 24-45 (1994).
       A review of notable people and events connected with Harcourt Street.

0129   BELCHEM (John). The Irish in Britain, United States and Australia: some comparative reflections on labour history. In *The Irish in British labour history*, pp 19-28 (1993).

0130   BELL (Desmond). Culture and politics in Ireland: postmodern revisions. In *Hist. Europ. Ideas*, xvi, 141-6 (1993).

0131   BELL (J. Bowyer). The gun in politics: an analysis of Irish political conflict, 1916-1986. Pp x, 371. New Brunswick, N.J.: Transaction Books, 1987.

0132   BELL (Robert). The book of Ulster surnames. Pp [10], 285. Belfast: Blackstaff Press, 1994.
       First pub.: 1988.

Beneath the granite throne. See Sandyford, Dundrum, Ballawley [1993?].

0133   BENNETT (Douglas). A Dublin anthology. Pp xvi, 288. Dublin: Gill and Macmillan, 1994.

0134   BENNETT (J.). Sliabh Chairbre (Carn Hall). In *Teathba*, i, no 1, p 17 (1969).

0135   BENSON (Asher). Jewish genealogy in Ireland. In *Aspects of Irish genealogy*, pp 17-27 [1993].

0136   BIELENBERG (Andy). Locke's distillery, 1757-1992: a history. Pp vi, 122. Dublin: Lilliput Press, 1993.

0137   BIELENBERG (Andy). The Locke family and the distilling industry in Kilbeggan. In *Hist. Ire.*, i, no 2, pp 46-50 (1993).
           The distillery operated from 1757-1958.

0138   BIRMINGHAM (Hubert). The Augustinians and Dunmore. In *Galway Roots*, ii, 94-7 (1994).

0139   BIRTHISTLE (Dorcas). Lime and lime-kilns. In *Old Kilkenny Rev.*, xlvi, 75-7 (1994).

0140   BLAIR (May). Once upon the Lagan: the story of the Lagan canal. Pp ix, 129. Belfast: Blackstaff Press, 1994.
           First pub.: 1981.

0141   BLAIR (S. Alexander). S. Alex Blair's County Antrim characters: 'portraits from the past' which first appeared in the Ballymena Guardian, compiled by Eull Dunlop, prefaces by Maurice O'Neill and Irene P.M. Grant. Pp 96. Ballymena: Mid-Antrim Historial Group, 1993. (Mid Antrim Historical Group, 19).

0142   BLUETT (Anthony). Things Irish. Pp 156. Cork; Dublin: Mercier, 1994.

0143   BOLAND (Matthew). The decline of the O'Kennedys of Ormond. In *Tipp. Hist. Jn.*, pp 129-41 (1994).

0144   BOSWORTH (C. Esmond). Irish and British contributions to Arabic and Islamic studies since 1800. In *The Edward Hincks bicentenary lectures*, pp 178-94 (1994).

0145   BOURKE (Cormac). Carved stones from Donaghenry and Stewartstown. In *The Bell*, v, 60-65 (1994).

0146   BOURKE (Cormac). Finds from the river Blackwater. In *Curr. Archeaol.*, xii, no 134, pp 63-4 (1993).

0147   BOURKE (Edward J.). Shipwrecks of the Irish coast, 1105-1993. Pp 240. Dublin: Edward J. Bourke, 1994.

0148   BOURKE (Marcus). Tipperary: the cradle of the GAA. In *Tipperary county*, pp 53-62 (1993).

0149   BOURKE (Marie). The Irish landscape through the eyes of the painter. In *Decoding the landscape*, pp 133-48 (1994).

0150   BRADLEY (John) and DUNNE (Noel). A crannog at Loughnaneane, Roscommon town. In *Roscommon Hist. Soc. Jn.*, iii, 34-6 (1990).

0151   BRADSHAW (Brendan). Revising Irish history. In *Reconsiderations of Irish history and culture*, pp 27-41 (1994).

0152   BRADY (Anne). Blackrock. In *Dun Laoghaire Jn.*, iii, 12-20 (1993).

0153   BRANNON (Nick). Archaeological excavations at Cathedral Hill, Downpatrick, 1987. In *Lecale Miscellany*, vi, 3-9 (1988).

0154   BRANNON (Nick). Recent discoveries at Down cathedral and Quoile Castle. An interim report. In *Lecale Miscellany*, v, 3-9 (1987).

0155   BRANNON (Nick). A souterrain in Spittle Quarter townland, Co. Down. In *Lecale Miscellany*, viii, 39-41 (1990).

0156   BREATHNACH (Diarmuid) and NÍ MURCHÚ (Máire). Beathaisnéis: 1882-1982. Pp 191. Baile Átha Cliath: An Clóchomhar, 1994.

0157   BREATNACH (Deasún). Chugat an púca. Pp ix, 266. Baile Átha Cliath: An Clóchomhar, 1993.

0158   BREATNACH (Liam). An Mheán-Ghaeilge. In *Stair na Gaeilge*, pp 221-333 (1994).

0159   BREATNACH (Pádraig A.). Bernard Bischoff (d. 1991), the Munich school of medieval Latin philology, and Irish medieval studies. In *Camb. Med. Celtic Stud.*, xxvi, 1-14 (1993).

0160   BREEN (Eleanor). "Kilarny grange": but what's in a name. In *In the Shadow of the Steeple*, iv, 115-25 (1994).

0161   BRENNAN (John). Jenkinstown oratory. In *Old Kilkenny Rev.*, iv, 1159-63 (1993).

0162   BREW (Frank). A farm hearth in Tubber. In *The Other Clare*, xvii, 44 (1993).

0163   BRINDLEY (Anna L.), KILFEATHER (Annaba). Archaelogical inventory of County Carlow. Pp x, 128. Dublin: Stationery Office, 1993.

0164   BRODERICK (Eugene). Review article: Waterford history and society. In *Decies*, xlvii, 52-7 (1993).
        Review of *Waterford: history and society*, edited by W. Nolan and T.P. Power, Dublin 1992.

0165   BRODERICK (Mary). History of Cobh (Queenstown) Ireland. 2nd ed. Pp 175. [s.l.]: [s.n.], 1994.
        Previous ed. pub.: 1989 with title History of Cobh.

0166   BROOKE (Peter). Ulster Presbyterianism: the historical perspective 1610-1970. Pp 208. Belfast: Athol Books, 1994.

0167   BROPHY (Liam). The Royal Hospital, Kilmainham: the restoration. In *Blackrock Soc. Proc.*, ii, 56-63 (1993/94).

0168   BROPHY (P.J.). A view of the Barrow's west bank. In *Carloviana*, xxxiii, 6-8 (1985/86).

0169   BROWNE (Bernard). Old Ross - the town that never was: a community biography. Pp 133. [Wexford?]: Sean Ros Press, 1993.

0170   BRYAN (Dominic). Interpreting the Twelfth. In *Hist. Ire.*, ii, no 2, pp 37-41 (1994).

0171   BRYCE (John). Folklore: "The fairies of Piping Rock". In *Lecale Miscellany*, v, 20-1 (1987).

0172   BRYCE (John A.). The village blacksmith. In *Lecale Miscellany*, xi, 57-8 (1993).

0173   BUCHANAN (R.H.). Downpatrick. In *Irish country towns*, pp 35-46 (1994).

0174   BURKE (Bob). These be thine arms forever: 35 centuries of Burkes. Pp [3], 63. Oklahoma City: Commonwealth Press, 1993.

0175   BURKE (Freddie). Saint Senan's well at Doonass. In *Sliabh Aughty*, v, 17-18 (1994).

0176   BURKE (Helen). The Royal Hospital Donnybrook: a heritage of caring, 1743-1993. Pp 10, 378. Dublin: Royal Hospital Donnybrook and Social Science Research Centre, University College Dublin, 1993.

0177   BURNSIDE (Sam). Within and without the magic circle: the literary heritage of Derry city. In *The glow upon the fringe*, pp 1-29 (1994).

0178   BURTCHAELL (Jack). The geography of Deise surnames. In *Decies*, l, 37-59 (1994).

0179   BUTLER (David). Spain and the Butlers. In *Butler Soc. Jn.*, iii, 479-83 (1994).

0180   Butlers of Grallagh and Boytonrath [family tree]. In *Butler Soc. Jn.*, iii, 582-3 (1994)

0181   By the sign of the Dolphin: the story of Dolphin's Barn. *Ed.* Catherine Scuffil. Pp vi, 149. Dublin: Dophin's Barn Historical Society, 1993.

        BYRNE (Elizabeth). See *Archaeological inventory of county Cork* (1994).

0182   BYRNE (Michael), ed. Durrow in history: a celebration of what has gone before. Pp xx, 304. Tullamore: Esker Press, 1994.

0183   CADOGAN (Jim). Surnames of county Cork. In *Ir. Roots*, 1994, no 3, pp 14-15 (1994).

0184   CAHILL (Mary). Mr Anthony's bog oak case of gold antiquities. *R.I.A. Proc.*, sec c, xciv, 53-109 (1994).

0185   CAMP (Anthony). Sources for Irish genealogy at the Irish Society of Genealogists. In *Aspects of Irish genealogy*, pp 28-43 [1993].

0186   CAMPBELL (Colm). Emergency law in Ireland, 1918-1925. Pp xxiii, 429. Oxford: Clarendon Press, 1994.

0187   CANAVAN (Bernard). Story-tellers and writers: Irish identity in emigrant labourers' autobiographies, 1870-1970. In *The creative migrant*, pp 154-69 (1994).

0188   CANAVAN (Kitty). "Old St Peter's" Athlone 1795-1937. In *Roscommon Hist. Soc. Jn.*, iv, 70 (1992).

0189   CANAVAN (Tony). Newry: the frontier town. In *Ir. Roots*, 1992, no 2, pp 19-22 (1992).

0190   CANNY (Nicholas). In search for a better home?: European overseas migration 1500-1800. In *Europeans on the move*, pp 263-83 (1994).

0191   CARLOW COUNTY LIBRARY. Local history holdings of Carlow interest and recent acquisitions. In *Carloviana*, xli, 25 (1993/94).

0192   CARR (Kathleen). The Turas (Sts Peter & Paul). In *Donegal Annual*, xlvi, 114-16 (1994).

0193   CARSON (John T.). 'From Thomas Cartwright to John Howe; some Puritans who came among us'. In *Presb. Hist. Soc. of Ire. Bull.*, xix, 3-28 (1990).

0194   CASEY (Christine) and ROWAN (Alistair). North Leinster: the counties of Longford, Louth, Meath and Westmeath. Pp 576, [64]. London: Penguin, 1993. (The buildings of Ireland, vol. 2).

0195   CASSIDY (Herbert). Armagh Public Library. In *Dúiche Néill*, viii, 133-9 (1993).

0196   Catalogue of books in the Henry library, St Nicholas' Collegiate Church Galway. *Ed.* Treasa Moore. 170 leaves. [Galway]: St Nicholas' Collegiate Church, [1993].

0197   CATHCART (Rex). In the shadow of St. Patrick's. In *Dublin Hist. Rec.*, xlvii, 71-6 (1994).
        The Cathedral Choir School and the Cathedral Grammar School.

0198   Cavan town roots: exploring family origins and old Cavan town. Pp 48. [Cavan]: [The Anglo-Celt], [1993?].

0199   Cemetery inscriptions in Cavan parish. In *Breifne*, vi, 408-17 (1986).

0200 CHALLIS (S.D.). Galway postal history. In *Galway Arch. Soc. Jn.*, xlv, 155-7 (1993).

0201 CHAPMAN (Barbara). Newtownbutler: the story of a local community. Pp iv, 80. Newtownbutler: Newtownbutler Local History Project Committee, 1993.

0202 The Church of Ireland: a critical bibliography, 1536-1992. Part I, 1536-1603, by James Murray. Part II: 1603-41, by Alan Ford. Part III: 1641-90,by J.I. Maguire. Part IV: 1690-1800, by S.J. Connolly. Part V: 1800-1870, by Fergus O'Ferrall. Part VI: 1870-1992, by Kenneth Milne. In *I.H.S.*, xxviii, 345-84 (1993).

0203 CLAFFEY (John A.). History of Moylough-Mountbellew part I: from the earliest times to 1601. Pp 168. [Tuam]: [J. Claffey], 1983.

0204 CLARK (Mary). Sources for Irish freemen. In *Aspects of Irish genealogy*, pp 44-53 [1993].

CLARK (Mary). See *Directory of historic Dublin guilds* (1993).

0205 CLARK (Wallace). Rathlin: its island story. 3rd ed. Pp 194, [2]. Coleraine: Impact Printing, 1993.
First pub. with the title Rathlin: disputed island. Portlaw: Volturna Press, 1971.

0206 CLARKE (Peter). The Royal Canal 1789-1993. In *Dublin Hist. Rec.*, xlvi, 46-52 (1993).

CLARKE (R.S.J.). See *Gravestone inscriptions county Down*.

0207 CLEARY (Jimmy). Wicklow Head lighthouses. In *Wicklow Hist. Soc. Jn.*, i, no. 6, pp 47-52 (1993).

0208 COAKLEY (John) and ENGLISH (Richard). Select bibliography of publications on Irish politics during 1992. In *Ir. Political Stud.*, viii, 215-26 (1993).

0209 COAKLEY (John) and ENGLISH (Richard). Select bibliography of publications on Irish politics during 1993. In *Ir. Political Stud.*, ix, 247-56 (1994).

0210 COFFEY (Thomas). The parish of Inchicronan (Crusheen). Pp xii, 233, xxiii. Whitegate (Co. Clare): Ballinakella Press, 1993.
Crusheen, Co. Clare.

0211 COLL (Tom). Dunlewey by the lakes. In *Donegal Annual*, xlvi, 34-42 (1994).

0212 COLLINS (Brenda). Flax to fabric: the story of Irish linen. Pp 36. Lisburn: Irish Linen Centre & Lisburn Museum, 1994. (An Irish Linen Centre & Lisburn Museum publication).

0213 COLLINS (Peter). The making of Irish linen: historic photographs of an Ulster industry. Pp vi, 90. Belfast: Friar's Bush Press, 1994.

0214   COLLINS (Timothy). Some Irish women scientists. In *Review-UCG*, i, 39-53 (1992).

0215   COLMER (Albert W.K.). A King's castle - in name only. In *Lecale Miscellany*, vii, 42-4 (1989)
King's castle, Ardglass.

0216   COLMER (Albert W.K.), Lecale Miscellany 1983-1987 index. In *Lecale Miscellany*, vi, 46-8 (1988).

0217   COOKE (Jim). Ireland's premier coachbuilder: John Hutton & Sons, Summerhill Dublin, 1779-1925. Pp 64. Dublin: Jim Cooke, [1993?].

0218   COLWELL (Stella). Records of the Irish in the British army. In *Aspects of Irish genealogy*, pp 54-74 [1993].

CONCANNON (Kieran), ed. See *Inishbofin through time and tide* (1993).

CONDRON (Patricia). See DRENNAN (John).

0219   CONLAN (Maureen). Working the charm: Tyrone folk cures. In *Dúiche Néill*, ix, 128-37 (1994).

0220   CONN (W. Clark). The Scottish and Irish background of the Rev. Hugh Conn of the colonial clergy of Maryland. In *Familia*, ii, no. 10, pp 39-55 (1994).

0221   Connemara [a map]. In *Connemara*, i, no. 1, pp 48-9 (1993).

0222   CONNOLLY (Al). Ballykinler and Tyrella. In *Lecale Miscellany*, ix, 32-4 (1991).

0223   CONNOLLY (Al). Tabula memorum. In *Lecale Miscellany*, xi, 67-75 (1993).
Abstracts of the names of Catholic clergy who were born in Lecale or who ministered in Lecale, 1595-1895.

0224   CONNOLLY (Al). Tabula memorum. In *Lecale Miscellany*, xii, 56-76 (1994).

0225   CONNOLLY (Sean). The Bandon river: from source to sea. Pp 100. [S.l.]: [s.n.], [1993?].

0226   CONNOLLY (Seán). The laneways of Bandon. In *Bandon Hist. Jn.*, ix, 29-34 (1993).

CONNOLLY (S.J.). See *Church of Ireland: a critical bibliography* (1993).

0227   COONEY (D.A. Levistone). Methodism in Cloughjordan. In *Cloughjordan Heritage*, i, 16-19 (1985).

GENERAL

0228   CORBETT (William). Thurles: the cathedral town. In *Tipperary county*, pp 143-50 (1993).

0229   CORCORAN (Moira). 800 years of Drogheda. In *Old Drogheda Soc. Jn.*, ix, 5-6 (1994).

0230   The Cork anthology. *Ed.* Seán Dunne. Pp xiii, 434. Cork: Cork University Press, 1993.
Biography, literature, history. Includes translations of Irish texts.

0231   COUNIHAN (Martin J.). Ireland and the scientific tradition. In *The creative migrant*, pp 28-43 (1994).
Pelagius, Eriguena, Peter of Ireland, Bernard O'Connor.

0232   COUNTY WICKLOW HERITAGE PROJECT. The last county: the emergence of Wicklow as a county, 1606-1845. Pp 80. [S.l.]: [County Wicklow Heritage Society], [1993].

0233   COWMAN (Des). Dating the mines at Ardmore; illustrations [by] Rosaleen Garbett & John Geaney. In *Ardmore Jn.*, x, 22-30 (1993).

0234   COX (Liam). Placenames of Westmeath: the baronies of Clonlonan and Kilkenny West. Pp 115. Moate: Moate Historical Society, 1994. (Moate Historical Society occasional paper, no. 7).

0235   COX (Robert R.). Source material for a parish history in the diocese of Connor and the united diocese of Down and Dromore. In *Ulster Local Studies*, iii, no. 2, pp 10-21 (1977).

0236   COYLE (Aidan). Surnames in the locality. In *The Bell*, v, 3-6 (1994).

0237   COYLE (Liam). A parish history of Kilglass, Slatta, Ruskey. Pp 559. Kilglass, Co. Roscommon: Kilglass Gaels, [1994].

0238   CRANGLE (Josie). St Patrick's church Portaferry. In *Upper Ards Hist. Soc. Jn.*, i, 24 (1977).

0239   CRAWFORD (W.H.). The handloom weavers and the Ulster linen industry. 2nd ed. Pp [8], 95. Belfast: Ulster Historical Foundation, 1994.
Previous ed. pub.: 1972, with title Domestic industry in Ireland: the experience of the linen industry.

0240   CRAWFORD (W.H.). Lurgan. In *Irish country towns*, pp 97-107 (1994).

0241   CREALEY (Aidan H.). An Irish almanac: notable events in Ireland from 1014 to the present. Pp 196. Cork; Dublin: Mercier Press, 1993.

0242   CREIGHTON (Seamus). The Lloyds of Crogan house. In *Roscommon Hist. Soc. Jn.*, iii, 15-17 (1990).

0243   CROOKS (D.W.T.). In the footsteps of Saint Baithin: a history of the parishes of Taughboyne with Craigdooish, All Saints, Newtowncunningham, Christ Church, Burt and Killea, Carrigans. Pp viii, 94. [S.l]; [s.n.], [1993].

23

0244   CROOKSHANK (Anne). Notes on the cleaning and framing of pictures in Trinity College, Dublin. In *Art is my life*, pp 57-65 (1991).

0245   CROOKSHANK (Anne) and GLIN (Knight of). The watercolours of Ireland: works on paper in pencil, pastel and paint, c.1600-1914. Pp 328. London: Barrie & Jenkins, 1994.

0246   CROSKERY (Thomas), WITHEROW (Thomas). Life of the Rev. A.P. Goudy D.D.; introduction by Eull Dunlop; illustrations by Graham Mawhinney. Pp [2], 182. Draperstown, Co. Londonderry: Moyola Books; Ballymena: Braid Books, 1994. (Ascona series).
       Facsimile of ed. pub. Dublin: Humphrey and Armour, 1887.

0247   CROTTY (Raymond). Ireland and Japan: a comparative study. In *Comparative aspects of Irish and Japanese economic and social history*, pp 1-37 (1993).

0248   CROWLEY (Seamus). The abbey: Bantry's Franscican friary. In *Bantry Hist. Soc. Jn.*, i, 2-16 (1991).

       CROWLEY (Walter). See FARRINGTON (Mrs).

0249   CRUMLISH (Richard). Tullaghobegley church and graveyard excavation report. In *Donegal Annual*, xlv, 42-51 (1993).

0250   CULLEN (Mary). History women and history men: the politics of women's history. In *Hist. Ire.*, ii, no. 2, pp 31-6 (1994).

0251   CULLEN (Mary). History women and history men: the politics of women's history. In *Reconsiderations of Irish history and culture*, pp 113-33 (1994).

0252   CULLETON (Brendan). Treasures of the landscape: County Wexford's rural heritage. Townland names Séamas S. de Vál. *Ed.* Edward Culleton for the Natural Resources Development Centre, Trinity College, Dublin. Pp 260. [Wexford]: Wexford Organisation for Rural Development, 1994.

       CULLETON (Edward). See CULLETON (Brendan).

       CULLETON (Edward). See *Traces of County Wexford's past* (c.1994).

0253   CULLINANE (John P.). Irish dance world-wide: Irish migrants and the shaping of traditional Irish dance. In *The creative migrant*, pp 192-220 (1994).

0254   CULLINANE (Joseph B.). Saint Mary's Church Aughnacloy. In *Dúiche Néill*, ix, 109-27 (1994).

0255   CUNNINGHAM (John B.). Castle Caldwell, County Fermanagh. Pp 28. Belleek: St Davog's Press, [1993?].

       CUNNINGHAM (John B.). See O'DONOVAN (John).

0256   CURTIS (Liz). The cause of Ireland: from the United Irishmen to partition. Pp viii, 436. Belfast: Beyond the Pale Publications, 1994.

0257   DALLAS (George). Is Irish unity possible? In *The Furrow*, xxxiii, 540-5 (1982).

0258   DALLAT (Cahal). Ballycastle and the heart of the glens. Pp 91. Donaghdee: Cottage Publications, 1994.

0259   DALLAT (Cahal). Deep rivers, dry houses: some radical writers from the north west. In *The glow upon the fringe*, pp 67-75 (1994).

0260   DALLAT (Cahal). Placenames in the Ballyclare area. In *The Glynns*, xxii, 51-2 (1994).

0261   DALLAT (Cahal). Placenames in the parish of Derrykeighan. In *The Glynns*, xxi, 77-8 (1993).

0262   DALLAT (Cahal). Place-names in the parish of Layd. In *The Glynns*, viii, 41-4 (1980).

0263   DALLAT (Cahal). Some local links with Scotland. In *Ulster Local Studies*, xvi, no. 1, pp 54-62 (1994).

0264   DALLAT (Cahal). The teaching of local history in post-primary schools in Northern Ireland. In *Ulster Local Studies*, iv, no. 2, pp 20-9 (1978).

0265   DALTON (Brigid). Kavanagh clan - 500 years of change. In *Gateway to the past*, i, no. 2, pp 74-9 (1994).

0266   DALY (Katherine). The archaeological survey of Co. Tipperary. In *Tipp. Hist. Jn.*, pp 155-61 (1994).

0267   DALY (Marie E.). Genealogical research in the United States of America. In *Aspects of Irish genealogy*, pp 83-98 [1993].

0268   DALY (Marie E.). The Irish collection at the New England Historic Genealogical Society. In *Aspects of Irish genealogy*, pp 75-82 [1993].

0269   DAVIES (Mary). Belvedere House, Co. Westmeath. In *Ir. Garden*, i, no. 3, pp 8-10 (1992)

0270   DAVIES (Mary). Bray. In *Irish country towns*, pp 131-41 (1994).

0271   DAVIES (Mary). Killruddery Co. Wicklow: a timeless garden with a sense of peace. In *Ir. Garden*, i, no. 1, pp 8-10 (1992).

0272   DAVIES (Mary). A setting for a jewel. In *Ir. Garden*, iii, no. 1, pp 10-11 (1994).
        Emo Court, Co. Laois.

0273   DAVIS (Bill). An introduction to Irish research: Irish ancestry: a beginner's guide. 2nd ed. Pp v, 100. Birmingham: Federation of Family History Societies, 1994.
        Previous ed.: 1992.

DAVISON (Stephen). See *Northern Ireland and Canada* (1994).

0274   DEAN (J.A. Kimmitt). The gate lodges of Ulster: a gazetteer. Pp xxv, 168. Belfast: Ulster Architectural Heritage Society, 1994.

De FRÉINE (Seán). See O'DONNELL (Jim).

0275   DENIAU (Jean-Martin). Quelques idées sur le theme de la faim dans la littérature Anglo-Irlandaise. In *Alumnus*, 3-4 (1994).
Outline of the author's thesis-in-progress,

De VÁL (Séamas S.). See CULLETON (Brendan).

0276   DEVENNEY (Donnchadh). Footprints through the Rosses. Pp vi, 166. Dublin: [the author], 1993.
        Co. Donegal.

DEVLIN (Kate). See *Lough Derg* (1993).

0277   DEVLIN (Polly). All of us there. Pp 172. Belfast: Blackstaff Press, 1994.
        Co. Tyrone.

0278   The Dialann Staire. In *Teathba*, i, no. 1, pp 62-73 (1969).
A list of historical events relating to Longford arranged by month.

DILLON (Eilís). See MERCIER (Vivian).

0279   Directory of historic Dublin guilds. *Ed.* Mary Clark and Raymond Refaussé. Pp 65. Dublin: Dublin Public Libraries, 1993.

0280   Directory of Irish Archives. *Ed.* Seamus Helferty, Raymond Refaussé. 2nd ed. Pp 154. Blackrock, Co. Dublin: Irish Academic Press, 1993.
Previous ed.: 1988.

0281   DOBSON (David). Irish emigrants in North America. Part 1. Pp 28. St. Andrews, Fife: D. Dobson, 1994.

DOCKRELL (Morgan). See BAILEY (John).

0282   DODDY (Martin). Reading Ennis: its history as written in its streets. In *The Other Clare*, xvii, 13-17 (1993).

0283   DOHERTY (Charles). Saint Maedoc and Saint Molaisse. In *Breifne*, vi, 363-74 (1986).
Saints lives in literature and tradition.

0284   DOHERTY (Jenni), DOHERTY (Liz). That land beyond: folklore of Donegal. Pp vi, 48. Londonderry: Guildhall Press, 1993.

DOHERTY (Liz). See DOHERTY (Jenni).

0285   DOHERTY (Philip). The last pawnshops of Dublin city. In *Dublin Hist. Rec.*, xlvii, 87-94 (1994).

0286   DOLAN (Brigid). Genealogical sources at the Royal Irish Academy. In *Aspects of Irish genealogy*, pp 99-104 [1993].

         DONALD (Sanders). See HENRY (Henry).

0287   Donegal local studies. In *Donegal Annual*, xlv, 113-7 (1993).

0288   DONLON (Billie). Strokestown: comments and connundrums. In *Roscommon Hist. Soc. Jn.*, iii, 31-3 (1990).

0289   DONNELLY (B.). From grand jury to county council: an overview of local administration in Wicklow 1605-1898. In *Wicklow*, pp 855-93 (1994).

0290   DONNELLY (Brian). Archives report. Irish Manuscripts Commission survey of business records; [and] Public Record Office of Northern Ireland: recent accessions of interest to the social and economic historian. In *Ir. Ec. & Soc. Hist.*, xx, 72-5 (1993); xxi, 72-5 (1994).

0291   DONNELLY (Mary). The last post: Glasnevin cemetery: being a record of Ireland's heroic dead in Dublin city and county, also places of historic interest. Pp 93, [1]. Dublin National Graves Association, (1994).

0292   DONNELLY (Peter). Bishops and violence: a response to Oliver Rafferty. In *Studies*, lxxxiii, 331-40 (1994).

0293   DONOHOE (Tony). O'Donnells of Newport and Killeen. In *North Mayo Hist. Jn.*, iii, no. 1, pp 74-6 (1992/93)

0294   DORAN (Patrick F.). 50 treasures from the Hunt collection; with a foreword by the Knight of Glin. Pp [117]. Limerick: Hunt Museum Executive, 1993.
         Foreword gives a history of Limerick custom house 1761- .

0295   The Down Survey maps of Co. Waterford. Part 3. The barony of Upper Third. In *Decies*, xlvii, 29-41 (1993).
         Contined from xlv (1992).

0296   DOYLE (David Noel). Review article: Small differences? The study of the Irish in the United States and Britain. In *I.H.S.*, xxix, 114-9 (1994).

0297   DRENNAN (John). Cannonballs and croziers: a history of Maynooth. *Ed.* Patricia Condrum, Muireann Ní Bhrochláin, Dominic Nylan. Pp 133. Maynooth: Maynooth Community Council, 1994.

0298   Drum and its hinterland. Pp 368. [S.l.]: [Drum Heritage Group], 1994.
         South Roscommon.

0299   Dublin. *Ed.* John Graby and Deirdre O'Connor. Pp 165. London: Phaidon, 1993.
         Architecture guide book.

0300   DUFF (C.). Windmills around Portaferry & district. In *Upper Ards Hist. Soc. Jn.*, i, 13-15 (1977).

0301   DUFFY (Godfrey). Clonmahy parish. In *Dun Laoghaire Geneal. Soc. Jn.*, ii, 64-6 (1993).

0302　　DUFFY (Patrick J.) & KEENAN (James). Landscapes of south Ulster: a parish atlas of the diocese of Clogher. Pp viii, 131. Belfast: Institute of Irish Studies, Queen's University of Belfast in association with the Clogher Historical Society, 1993.
Placenames etc.

0303　　DUKES (Fred E.). Campanology in Ireland: a study of bells, bell-founding, inscriptions and bell-ringing. Pp 256. Blackrock, Co. Dublin: Samton in association with the Royal Dublin Society, 1994.

0304　　DUN LAOGHAIRE GENEALOGICAL SOCIETY. Memorial inscriptions of Deansgrange cemetery, Blackrock, Co. Dublin. Vol. 1: south west section. Pp 122. Dun Laoghaire: Dun Laoghaire Genealogical Society, 1994.

0305　　Dunboyne, Kilbride and Clonee: a picture of the past. *Ed.* Denis Kenny. Pp 142. Dunboyne, Co. Meath: Old Dunboyne Society, [1993].

0306　　DUNGAN (Myles). Distant drums: Irish soldiers in foreign armies. Pp viii, 184. Belfast: Appletree Press, 1993.
American Civil War to Vietnam War.

0307　　DUNLOP (Eull). Antiquarian library catalogued. In *The Glynns*, xxi, 79-80 (1993).
Noting the publication of the catalogue of the antiquarian library of St. Macnissi's College, Garron tower.

DUNLOP (Eull). See BLAIR (S. Alexander).

DUNLOP (Eull). See CROSKERY (Thomas).

DUNLOP (Eull). See McNEILL (Hugh).

0308　　DUNN (Joseph). No lions in the hierarchy: an anthology of sorts. Pp 326. Dublin: Columba Press, 1994.

DUNNE (Noel). See BRADLEY (John).

DUNNE (Seán). See *The Cork anthology* (1993).

0309　　DUNPHY (Richard). Culture and identity. Article in review. In *Times Change*, iii (autumn/winter), 26-8 (1994).

0310　　EAGLETON (Terry). Form and ideology in the Anglo-Irish novel. In *Bullán*, i, no. 1, pp 17-26 (1994).

0311　　EDWARDS (Owen Dudley). Scotland, Ulster and you. In *Scotland and Ulster*, pp 172-82 (1994).

0312　　EDWARDS (Owen Dudley). The stage Irish. In *The creative migrant*, pp 83-114 (1994).

0313　　EGAN (Michael J.S.). Dublin city and county graveyards. Vol. 6. Pp 228. Dublin: [the author?], 1993.
Cover title 'Memorials of the dead'.

0314   EGAN (Patrick K.). The parish of Ballinasloe: its history from the earliest times to the present century. Pp xiv, 355. Galway: Kenny Bookshops, 1994. Facsimile of ed. pub.: Dublin: Clonmore & Reynolds, 1960.

0315   EGAN (Sheila). Ballycotton. In *The book of Cloyne*, pp 201-15 (1994).

0316   ELLIOTT (Bruce). Canadian sources for Irish genealogy. In *Aspects of Irish genealogy*, pp 105-22 [1993].

0317   ELVERT (Jurgen). Geschichte Irlands. Pp 525. Munchen: DTV, 1993.

        ENGLISH (Barbara). See *Royal Historical Society annual bibliography of British and Irish history* (1993), (1994).

0318   ENGLISH (N.W.). Notes on Mosstown House, Kenagh. Its sieges, the Newcomens, Kingstons and a tombstone in Bath, England. In *Teathba*, i, no. 1, pp 29-33 (1969).

        ENGLISH (Richard). See COAKLEY (John).

0319   ERSKINE (John G.W.). Select list of writings relating to Irish Presbyterianism: items appearing in 1988. In *Presb. Hist. Soc. of Ire. Bull*, xviii, 27-30 (1989); in 1989, xix, 43-8 (1990); in 1990, xx, 32-8 (1991); in 1991, xxi, 31-5 (1992); in 1992, xxii, 31-9 (1993).

0320   EVERARD (Richard H.A.J.). The family of Everard. parts iv-v: Everard of Randlestown. In *Ir. Geneal.*, viii, 575-601 (1993); ix, 43-72 (1994). [concluded].

0321   Excavations bulletin 1977-1979: Summary account of archaeological excavations in Ireland. In *Jn. Ir. Archaeol.*, iv, 65-79 (1987/88).

0322   FAGAN (Terry) and SAVAGE (Ben). Down by the dockside: reminiscences from Sheriff Street. Pp 45. Dublin: North Inner City Folklore Project, 1994.

        FAGAN (Terry). See SAVAGE (Ben).

0323   FAHY (Gerard). The English perception of Ireland and the Irish: a geographical analysis and explanation. In *Geographical Viewpoint*, xvii, 24-38 (1988/89).

0324   FALLON (Brian). Irish art: 1830-1990. Pp 208. Belfast: Appletree Press, 1994.

0325   FARRELL (Hugh). Farrell clan: a brief history, compiled by Hugh Farrell; with the assistance of the Farrell clan research committee. Pp 29, [3]. [S.l.]: [s.n.], [1993?].

0326   FARRELLY (Peter V.). 600 years of theatre in Kilkenny, 1366-1966. Pp 180. Kilkenny: P.V. Publications, [1994].

0327   FARRINGTON (Mrs). The ambit of Cook Street; presented by Fr. Walter Crowley, OFM. In *Dublin Hist. Rec.*, xlvii, 138-54 (1994).
        Mrs Farrington, president of Third Order Sisters, d. 17 May 1964.

0328 FAULKNER (Padraig). The clergy of the parish of Dunleer. In *Louth Arch. Soc. Jn.*, xxiii, no 2, pp 218-30 (1994).

0329 FEE (Aidan). St Mary's R.C. church, Stewartstown. In *The Bell*, v, 66-72 (1994).

0330 FEEHAN (John), et al. The book of Aran: the Aran Islands Co. Galway; *ed.* John Waddell .. [et al]. Pp 334. Kinvara, Co. Galway: Tír Eolas, 1994.

0331 FEHENEY (John P.M.). Limerick O'Shaughnessys: an overview. In *Ir. Family Hist.*, ix, 10-16 (1993).

0332 FELHMANN (Guy). An historical survey. In *The big house in Ireland*, pp 15-18 (1991).

0333 FERGUS (Howard A.). Montserrat: a history of a Caribbean colony. Pp x, 294. London: Macmillan, 1994.
Irish references.

0334 FINEGAN (John). Dublin's lost theatres. In *Dublin Hist. Rec.*, xlvii, 95-9 (1994).

FINN (Ann). See *The lives of rural women* (1993).

0335 FITZGERALD (Joe). Ballykinler. In *Lecale Miscellany*, xi, 55 (1993).

0336 FITZGERALD (Michael). Frankfort and its castle. In *Old Kilkenny Rev.*, iv, 1166-9 (1993).

0337 The Fitzmaurices: lords of Kerry and barons of Lixnaw. *Ed.* Helen O'Carroll. Pp 74. [Lixnaw, Co. Kerry]: Oidhreacht Leac Snámhna, [1994?].

0338 FITZPATRICK (David). The Irish in Britain: settlers or transients? In *The Irish in British labour history*, pp 1-10 (1993).

0339 FITZPATRICK (Helen). Historical aspect of Kilmore House. In *Review*, v, no. 3, pp 16-17 (1986/87).

0340 FLANAGAN (Deirdre) and FLANAGAN (Laurence). Irish place names. Pp 271. Dublin: Gill & Macmillan, 1994.

FLANAGAN (Laurence). See FLANAGAN (Deirdre).

0341 FLEMING (W.E.C.). Communications in Clancan. In *Review*, v, no. 3, pp 14-15, 18 (1986/87).
Travel over the centuries in the area south of Lough Neagh.

0342 FLOWER (Robin). The Irish tradition. Pp xi, 180. Dublin: Lilliput Press, 1994.
Originally pub.: Oxford University Press, 1947.

0343 FOLEY (Brian). Butler testamentary records in Cádiz. In *Butler Soc. Jn.*, iii, 484-99 (1994).

0344   FOLEY (Claire). Preliminary report on archaeological work in the River
        Quaile at Inch abbey, 1991-2. In *Lecale Miscellany*, xii, 40-5 (1994).

0345   For God or king: the history of Mountshannon, Co. Clare 1742-1992. *Ed.*
        Gerard Madden. Pp 222. Tuamgraney, Co. Clare: East Clare Heritage, 1993.

        FORD (Alan). See *The Church of Ireland: a critical bibliography* (1993).

        FORDE (Catherine). See *The lives of rural women* (1993).

0346   FOSTER (R.F.). Paddy and Mr Punch: connections in Irish and English
        history. Pp xvii, 382. London: Alan Lane, 1993.

        FOY (Geoffrey). See HEMPSTEAD (Frank).

0347   FRAHER (William). MacGrath's Castle, Abbeyside, Dungarvan. In *Decies*,
        xlix, 38-44 (1994).

0348   FRÉCHET (René). Histoire de l'Irlande. 6th ed. Pp 127. Paris: Presses
        Universitaires de France, 1992. (Que sais-je?; 394).

0349   FRENCH (Noel E.). Meath ancestors: a guide to sources for tracing your
        ancestors in Co. Meath. Pp 68. Trim, Co. Meath: Trymme Press, 1993.

0350   FRENCH (Noel). Surnames of county Meath. In *Ir. Roots*, 1992, no 2, pp
        14-15 (1992).

0351   The French connection. In *A window on the Past*, [i], 14-15 (1987).
        Chevers family of Macetown, originally from Normandy.

0352   FRY (Malcolm F.) and MARTIN (Alan). Conservation and copying:
        logboats, horizontal mills and other large archaeological timbers from the
        North of Ireland. In *Ulster Local Studies*, xvi, no. 1, pp 7-30 (1994).

0353   A further bibliography of the history of the Irish in Britain. In *An Pobal
        Éirithe*, v, 13-18 (1991).

0354   GAFFNEY (Ben). Inscriptions from Denn old cemetery. In *Breifne*, viii,
        497-512 (1994).

0355   GALLAGHER (John). Connacht: a heritage to explore. Pp 144. [Castlebar,
        Co. Mayo]: Fiona Books, 1994.

        GALLAGHER (William). See *Glenveagh Castle* (1993).

0356   GALLOGLY (Dan). Kilmore churches. In *Breifne*, viii, 389-444 (1994).

        GARBETT (Rosaleen). See PRENDERGAST (Des).

0357   GARRY (James). Donore inscriptions. In *Old Drogheda Soc. Jn.*, ix, 129-71
        (1994)

0358   GARVIN (Wilbert), O'RAWE (Des). Northern Ireland: scientists and
        inventors. Pp [56]. Belfast: Blackstaff Press, 1993.

0359   General alphabetical index to the townlands and towns, parishes and baronies of Ireland. Based on the census of Ireland for the year 1851. Pp xii, 968. Baltimore (Md.): Genealogical Publishing Co., 1984.
Originally pub.: Dublin, 1861.

0360   GIFFORD (Dick). Education in Downpatrick. In *Lecale Miscellany*, vii, 13-17 (1989).

0361   GILLESPIE (Raymond). Explorers, exploiters and entrepreneurs: early modern Ireland and its context, 1500-1700. In *An historical geography of Ireland*, pp 123-57 (1993).

0362   GILLESPIE (Raymond). Irish funeral monuments and social change 1500-1700: perceptions of death. In *Ireland*, pp 155-68 (1994).

0363   GILLESPIE (Raymond). The sacred in the secular: religious change in Catholic Ireland, 1500-1700: the fifth annual lecture in Catholic studies, sponsored by the Edmundite trust fund for Catholic Studies and Ministry at St. Michael's College, 21 April 1993. Pp 30. Colchester, Vermont: Saint Michael's College, 1993.

0364   GILMORE (Hilary). The thistle as a source of design. In *The Other Clare*, ii, 7-9 (1978).

0365   GILVARRY (James). The story of Frank Walsh of Ballymachola. In *North Mayo Hist. Jn.*, iii, no. 1, pp 62-8 (1992/93).

0366   GLENNON (Liam). Irish music: historical background. In *Teathba*, i, no. 1, pp 24-8 (1969).

0367   Glenveagh castle, [written by William Gallagher]. Pp 47. Dublin: Stationery Office, 1993.

GLIN (Knight of). See CROOKSHANK (Anne).

GLIN (Knight of). See DORAN (Patrick F.).

0368   GOLDEN (Richard). 'Down the old bog road': two bog trackways in Creggane, Co. Roscommon close to the Lung river. In *Roscommon Hist. Soc. Jn.*, iv, 41-2 (1992).

0369   GOLDING (Patrick). The Kirwans. In *Galway Roots*, ii, 56-60 (1994).

0370   GOODBODY (Olive). Old Dun Laoghaire and neighbourhood. In *Dun Laoghaire Jn.*, ii, 3-11 (1991/92).
An edited precis by Colin Scudds of a paper read to the Old Dublin Society November 1966.

0371   GOODBODY (Rob). On the borders of the Pale: a history of Kilgobbin, Stepaside and Sandyford area. Pp xi, 132. Bray, Co. Wicklow: Pale Publishing, 1993.

0372   GORMLEY (Mary). Elphin: a proud past - a promising future. In *Roscommon Hist. Soc. Jn.*, iv, 66-9 (1992).

0373 GOSLING (Paul). Archaeological inventory of County Galway. Vol. 1: west Galway (including Connemara and the Aran islands). Pp xii, 242. Dublin: Stationery Office, 1993.

0374 GOSLING (Paul). From Dun Delca to Dundalk: the topography and archaeology of a medieval town, c.1187-1700. Pp 135. Dundalk: Co. Louth Archaeological and Historical Society, 1993.

GRABY (John). See *Dublin* (1993).

0375 GRACE (Daniel). The parish of Cloughjordan. In *Cloughjordan Heritage*, i, 3 (1985).

0376 GRAHAM (B.J.), and PROUDFOOT (L.J.). A perspective on the nature of Irish historical geography. In *An historical geography of Ireland*, pp 1-18 (1993).

GRANT (Irene P.M.). See BLAIR (S. Alexander).

0377 Gravestone inscriptions. County Down, vol. 21: old families of Downpatrick & district from gravestone inscriptions, wills and biographical notes. *Ed.* R.S.J. Clarke. Pp xii, 195. Belfast: Ulster Historical Foundation, 1993.

0378 GRAY (Tony). Ireland this century. Pp xii, 371. London: Little Brown, 1994.

0379 GRAY (Victor). The Scots church: Presbyterian church in Carlow. In *Carloviana*, xli, 23-4 (1993/94).

0380 GREHAN (Ida). Irish family histories. Pp xxiv, 262. Schull, Co. Cork: Roberts Rinehart, 1993.

0381 GRENHAM (John). Clans and families of Ireland: the heritage and heraldry of Irish clans and families. Pp 188. Dublin: Gill and Macmillan, 1993.

0382 GRIFFIN (David J.), LINCOLN (Simon). Drawings from the Irish Architectural Archive, with an introduction by Nicholas Robinson. Pp 79. Dublin: The Irish Architectural Archive, 1993.

0383 GROGAN (Eoin), HILLERY (Tom). A guide to the archaeology of County Wicklow. Pp 55. [Wicklow]: Wicklow County Tourism, 1993.

0384 GUIFFAN (Jean). Histoire de l'Irlande. Pp 272. Paris: Hatier, 1992.

0385 GUTHRIE-JONES (Winston). The Wynnes of Sligo & Leitrim. Pp 112. Manorhamilton, Co. Leitrim: Drumlin Publications, 1994.

0386 HACKETT (Michael Benedict). The Irish Augustinians in England and Scotland, 1539-1992: the Irish province-restorer of its Anglo-Scottish mother province. In *The Irish Augustinians in Rome*, pp 57-81 (1994).

0387 HACKETT (Mike). Youghal's fading footsteps: the humour, history & people of east Cork and west Waterford. Pp 79. Blarney, Co. Cork: On Stream Publications, 1994.

0388 HADFIELD (Andrew). Rocking the boat: a response to Hiram Morgan. In *The Ir. Rev.*, xiv, 15-19 (1993).

HADFIELD (Andrew). See *Strangers to that land* (1994).

0389 HALL (Michael). Drangan's places of worship down through the years. In *Souvenir of the re-dedication of Church of the Immaculate Conception, Drangan*, pp 18-22 (1993).

0390 HALL (Michael). Ulster's European heritage. Pp 32. Newtownabbey: Island Publications, 1994. (Island pamphlets, 8).

0391 HALL (Michael). Ulster's Scottish connection. Pp 32. Newtownabbey: Island Publications, 1993. (Island pamphlets, 3).

0392 HALL (Michael). Ulster's shared heritage. Pp 32. Newtownabbey: Island Publications, 1993. (Island pamphlets, 6).

0393 HALPIN (Thomas B.). Kilkenny U.S.A. In *Old Kilkenny Rev.*, xlvi, 20-2 (1994).

0394 HAREN (Michael). Lough Derg, the continent of Europe and the recesses of the mind. In *Donegal Annual*, xlvi, 107-14 (1994).

0395 HARKNESS (D.W.). The constitutions of Ireland and the development of national identity, 1919-1984. In *Constitutions and national identity*, pp 304-16 (1993).

0396 HARRIS (Walter). The history and antiquities of the city of Dublin, from the earliest accounts compiled from authenick memoirs ... Pp [8], 509, [1]. Ballynahinch: Davidson Books, 1994.
Facsimile of ed. pub.: Dublin: printed for Laurence Flinn and James Williams, 1766.

0397 HARRISON (Jennifer). Irish research in Australia. In *Aspects of Irish genealogy*, pp 138-49 [1993].

0398 HARTNETT (Margaret). Sea lore. In *The book of Cloyne*, pp 229-41 (1994).
Ship wrecks.

0399 HARTY (J.J.). Agriculture. In *The book of Cloyne*, pp 145-58 (1994).

0400 HATTON (Helen E.). The largest amount of good: Quaker relief in Ireland, 1654-1921. Pp xi, 367. Kingston, Ontario: McGill - Queen's University Press, 1993.

0401 HAYDEN (Tadhg). The Haydens in Tipperary: a 700-year history. In *Tipp. Hist. Jn.*, pp 142-54 (1994).

0402 HAYES (William J.). Holy Cross: Tipperary's famed religious site. In *Tipperary county*, pp 108-13 (1993).

0403 HAYES (William J.). O Meaghar, Meagher and Maher - and their disposal in Tipperary. In *Tipp. Hist. Jn.*, pp 160-6 (1993).

0404 HEALY (Elizabeth). Literary tour of Ireland. Pp 272. Dublin: Wolfhound Press, 1994.

0405 HEALY (James). Hunger strikes: other ethical reflections. In *Milltown Studies*, xv, 83-102 (1985).

0406 HEANEY (Seamus). A sense of the past. In *Hist. Ire.*, i, no. 4, pp 33-7 (1993).

0407 HEAVENER (Robert). Credo: Dunganstown: an age-old parish with a living message for everyman today. Pp xiv, 146. Jordanstown, Co. Antrim: Cromlech Books, 1993.
Dunganstown, Co. Wicklow.

HELFERTY (Seamus). See *Directory of Irish archives* (1993).

0408 HEMPSTEAD (Frank). A life in the flood plain of the River Shannon. *Ed.* Geoffrey Foy. Pp 46. [S.l.]: [F. Hempstead and G. Foy], 1994.

0409 HENRY (Henry). An address to the people of Connor, containing a clear and full vindication of the Synod of Ulster from the aspersions of the people called convenanters. Written in the name of Sanders Donald, late sexton of Connor. Pp 25. Ballymena: Mid Antrim Historical Group, 1994. (Mid Antrim Historical Group).

0410 'Hermitage House', Ballinagare. In *Roscommon Hist. Soc. Jn.*, iv, 23 (1992).

0411 HIGGINBOTHAM (Michael). The Office of Public Works survey of thatched houses. In *Traditional architecture in Ireland*, pp 32-42 (1994).

0412 HIGGINS (Jim). The iconography of a post-medieval headstone at Burriscarra, Co. Mayo. In *Cathair na Mart*, xiv, 65-8 (1994).

0413 HILL (Christopher) and JENNINGS (Jill). Belfast. Pp 112. Belfast: Blackstaff Press, 1994.

HILLERY (Tom). See GROGAN (Eoin).

0414 HIPPSLEY (Paul). Derry's walls. Rev. ed. Pp 44. Derry: Guildhall Press, 1994.
Previous ed.: 1988.

0415 Historians' guide to early British maps: a guide to the location of pre-1900 maps of the British Isles preserved in the United Kingdom and Ireland. *Ed.* Helen Wallis. Pp ix, 465. London: Royal Historical Society, 1994. (Royal Historical Society guides and handbooks, 18).

0416 Historical survey of Wellington Square and surrounding area. 7 leaves. [Cork]: [the Community History Co-op], [1993].

0417 HODGINS (John). The Fetherston family of Ardagh. In *Teathba*, ii, no. 1, pp 17-32 (1980).
Ardagh House - inspiration for Goldsmith's 'She stoops to conquer'.

0418 HODKINSON (Brian). Excavations at Cormac's chapel, Cashel, 1992 and 1993: a preliminary statement. In *Tipp. Hist. Jn.*, pp 167-74 (1994).

0419 HOLM (Paul). Between apathy and antipathy: the Vikings in Irish and Scandinavian history. In *Peritia*, viii, 151-69 (1994).

HOLMES (Michael). See WHELAN (Bernadette).

0420 HORNER (Arnold). Maynooth. In *Irish country towns*, pp 59-70 (1994).

0421 HOURIHAN (Kevin). The evolution and influence of town planning in Cork. In *Cork*, pp 941-61 (1993).

0422 HOURIHAN (Kevin). Rural settlement and change near Bantry 1600-1845. In *Bantry Hist. Soc. Jn.*, i, 44-53 (1991).

0423 HOWLEY (James). The follies and garden buildings of Ireland. Pp ix, 251. New Haven: Yale University Press, 1993.

0424 HOYNE (Liam). The Shee family of Garrandarragh. In *Old Kilkenny Rev.*, iv, 1208-14 (1993).

0425 HUBERT (Henri). The history of the Celtic people. Pp xxix, 315, xvi, 313. London: Bracken Books, 1993.
Originally published in 1934 as, The rise of the Celts and, The greatness and decline of the Celts.

0426 HUGHES (A.J.). Land acquisition by Gaelic bardic poets: insights from place-names and other sources. In *Ainm*, vi, 74-102 (1994/95).

0427 HUGHES (Art). Gaeilge Uladh. In *Stair na Gaeilge*, pp 611-60 (1994).

0428 HUGHES (John). A city lights up. In *Dun Laoghaire Jn.*, i, [11-12] (1990). Public lighting from 1616 to the present.

0429 HUGHES (Michael). Ireland divided: the roots of the modern Irish problem. Pp xiii, 143. Cardiff: University of Wales Press, 1994. (The past in perspective).

0430 HUNT (Christine). St Nicholas' Church. In *Galway Roots*, [i], 48-9 (1993).

0431 HUNT (Thomas A.). The Irish Augustinians in Australia, 1839-1992: Australia remembers St. Patrick's College, Rome. In *The Irish Augustinians in Rome*, pp 139-53 (1994).

0432 HUNTER (Dean J.). The Church of the Latter-day Saints and Irish records. In *Aspects of Irish genealogy*, pp 162-7 [1993].

0433 HURLEY (Maurice). Recent archaeological investigations in Waterford city. In *Arch. Ire.*, ii, 17-21 (1988).

HUTTENBERGER (Peter). See WITZ (Cornelia).

0434 IGOE (Vivien). A literary guide to Dublin: writers in Dublin: literary associations and anecdotes. Pp xxi, 361. London: Methuen, 1994.

0435   Inishbofin through time and tide. *Ed.* Kieran Concannon for the Inishbofin Heritage Project. Pp xiv, 129. Dublin: FÁS, 1993.

0436   Ireland: photographs 1840-1930, introduction J.J. Lee, text Carey Schofield, compiler Sean Sexton. Pp 208. London: Laurence King, 1994.

0437   Irish Congress of Trade Unions appendices. In *Trade union century*, pp 433-51 (1994).
        Membership 1894-1994; Congress executives 1894-1994; Northern Ireland committee chairpersons, 1945-94; trade union banners.

0438   Irish Congress of Trade Unions bibliography of trade unions and trade unionism in Ireland. In *Trade union century*, pp 452-72 (1994).
        Including locations of archives and records.

0439   An Irish genealogical source: a guide to church records. *Ed.* Valerie Adams. Pp xix, 279. Belfast: Ulster Historical Foundation, 1994.

0440   The Irish language in Inishowen north Donegal. In *Donegal Annual*, xlv, 29-42 (1993).

0441   IRWIN (Liam). Begley's diocese of Limerick: a review article. In *North Munster Antiq. Jn.*, xxxv, 76-80 (1993/94).

0442   IRWIN (Liam). Some excavations in Co. Clare. In *The Other Clare*, i, 9-10 (1977).

0443   JAMES (Simon). Exploring the world of the Celts. Pp 192. London: Thames & Hudson, 1993.

0444   JAMES (W.V.). Strangford: past imperfect, future indefinite. In *Lecale Miscellany*, xi, 5-15 (1993).

0445   JEFFERY (Keith). The great war in modern Irish memory. In *Men, women and war*, pp 136-57 (1993).
        1914-1918.

0446   JEFFERY (William H.). The Furlongs of County Wexford. In *Old Wexford Soc. Jn.*, vi, 73-9 (1976/77).

0447   JEFFREY (David). Four plants for 400 years. In *Ir. Garden*, i, no. 2, pp 12-13 (1992).
        Celebrating Trinity College's Botanic Garden Herbaruim and their connection with botanical research.

0448   JENKINS (William). Oldtown: a chapel-village of north County Dublin. In *Baile*, pp 28-33 (1992).
        Oldtown chapel built 1770 on the outskirts of Eyre Coote's estate.

        JENNINGS (Jill). See HILL (Christopher).

0449   JOHNSON (James H.). The human geography of Ireland. Pp xi, 221. New York: Wiley, 1994.

0450   JOHNSON (Nuala C.). Sculpting heroic histories: celebrating the centenary of the 1798 rebellion in Ireland. In *Inst. Brit. Geog. Trans.*, n.s., xix, 78-93 (1994).

0451   JOHNSTON (Alan). A history of Kilclief church. In *Lecale Miscellany*, vi, 17-21 (1988).

         JONES (John). See O'REGAN (Carol).

         JONES (John). See *Moylough* (1993).

0452   JORDAN (Donald E.). Land and popular politics in Ireland: County Mayo from the plantation to the land war. Pp xiv, 369. Cambridge: Cambridge University Press, 1994. (Past and Present publications).

0453   JOYCE (John). Graiguenamanagh: a town and its people: an historical and social account of Graiguenamanagh & Tinnahinch. Pp 198. Graiguenamanagh: Graigue Publications, 1993.

0454   JUDGE (Leo). The story of Kells. Pp 376. Kells: Kells Publishing Company Ltd., 1993.

0455   JUPP (Belinda) and NEILL (Marie). Recycling raths. In *Ulster Local Studies*, xvi, no. 1, pp 43-53 (1994).

0456   KAVANAGH (Art). In the shadow of Mount Leinster: a history of the Ui Cinnsealaigh from the earliest times up to 1650, with special emphasis on the Kavanaghs, plus extensive notes on the leading Gaelic families of the district and copious references to the Anglo-Norman and English families who found their way here between 1170 and 1650. Pp 217. [S.l.]: [the author], [1993?].

0457   KAVANAGH (Art) and MURPHY (Rory). The Wexford gentry. Vol. 1. Pp 239. Bunclody, Co. Wexford: Irish Family Names, 1994.

0458   KAVANAGH (Joan). A select bibliography of County Wicklow. In *Wicklow*, pp 953-65 (1994).

0459   KAVANAGH (Michael). Kavanagh - Caomhanach. In *Gateway to the Past*, i. no. 2, pp 70-3 (1994).

0460   KAVANAGH (P.J.). Voices in Ireland: a traveller's literary companion. Pp viii, 354. London: John Murray, 1994.

0461   KAY (Billy). The Scots ower the Sheuch. In *Scotland and Ulster*, pp 88-96 (1994).
         Scottish culture.

0462   KEANEY (Marian). Surnames of County Westmeath. In *Ir. Roots*, 1992, no. 4, pp 20-1 (1992).

0463   KEARNEY (Patrick). Granard. In *Teathba*, i, no. 1, pp 18-23 (1969).

0464   KEARNEY (Richard). Postmodernity, nationalism and Ireland. In *Hist. Europ. Ideas*, xvi, 147-55 (1993).

KEENAN (James). See DUFFY (Patrick J.).

0465   KELLEHER (George D.). Gunpowder to guided missiles: Ireland's war industries. Pp xvi, 400. Inniscarra (Co. Cork): John F. Kelleher, 1993.

0466   KELLEHER (George D.). The gunpowder mill at Ballincollig: an extract from Gunpowder to guided missiles: Ireland's war industries. Pp 76. Inniscarra (Co. Cork): John F. Kelleher, 1993.

0467   KELLEHER (Thomas). Bishops and abbots of Cloyne. In *The book of Cloyne*, pp 60-7 (1994).
        560-1835.

0468   KELLEHER (Thomas). The Catholic church since the Reformation. In *The book of Cloyne*, pp 101-17 (1994).

0469   KELLEHER (Thomas). Parish priests of Cloyne. In *The book of Cloyne*, pp 118-9 (1994).

0470   KELLY (A.A.). Irish women travel writers: an overview. In *Linen Hall Rev.*, x, no. 1, pp 4-8 (1993).

0471   KELLY (Eamonn P.). Treasure-hunting in Ireland: its rise and fall. In *Antiquity*, lxvii, 378-81 (1993).

KELLY (Stephen). See *The life, the times, the people* [1993].

0472   KEMMY (Jim). The Granary. In *Old Limerick Jn.*, xxix, 5-6 (1992).

0473   KEMMY (Jim). Limerick stone and stonemasons. In *Old Limerick Jn.*, xxxi, 21-5 (1994).

0474   KENNEDY (Brian P.). Irish painting. Pp 141. Dublin: Town House and Country House, 1993.

0475   KENNEDY (Brian P.). The traditional Irish thatched house: image and reality, 1793-1993. In *Visualizing Ireland*, pp 164-79 (1993).

0476   KENNEDY (Liam). People and population change: a comparative study of population change in Northern Ireland and the Republic of Ireland. Pp vii, 68. Dublin: Co-operation North, 1994.
        1900-1991.

0477   KENNEDY (W.E.). Oldcourt chapel, Strangford. In *Lecale Misc.*, xii, 3-5 (1994).

0478   KENNY (Colum). King's Inns and Henrietta Street chambers. In *Dublin Hist. Rec.*, xlvii, 155-68 (1994).

KENNY (Denis). See *Dunboyne, Kilbride and Clonee* [1993].

0479   KENNY (James G.). Lore of the linen "Lords" and others. In *The Glynns*, xxi, 58-64 (1993)

0480   KENNY (Michael J.). Saint Kieran's church and graveyard, Ballymaglasson, Co. Meath. In *Ríocht na Midhe*, ix, no. 1, pp 61-9 (1994/95).

0481   KERBER (Walter). The politically motivated hunger strike: towards a verdict in moral theology. In *Milltown Studies*, xv, 65-81 (1985).

0482   KERNOHAN (J.W.). The parishes of Kilreagh and Tamlaght O'Crilly: a sketch of their history, with an account of Boveedy congregation. Pp 80. [Kilrea]: [Kilrea Local History Group], [1993].

0483   KERR (Peter). Families and holdings in the townland of Innishatieve, Carrickmore. In *Seanchas Ardmhacha*, xv, no. 2, pp 151-235 (1993).

0484   KIBERD (Declan). Post-colonial Ireland - "being different". In *Reconsiderations of Irish history and culture*, pp 94-112 (1994).

0485   KIERNAN (Victor). The British Isles: Celt and Saxon. In *The national question in Europe in historical context*, pp 1-34 (1993).

0486   KILBRIDE-JONES (Howard E.) and RYNNE (Etienne). The Hunt collection: a review article. In *North Munster Antiq. Jn.*, xxxv, 24-8 (1993/94).

0487   KILCOYNE (Anthony). Achill. Pp 31. [Keel, Achill Island]: [Sister of the Little Company of Mary], [1993].

         KILFEATHER (Annaba). See BRINDLEY (Anna L.).

0488   KILFEATHER (Siobhán). Origins of the Irish female gothic. In *Bullán*, i, no. 2, pp 35-45 (1994).

0489   KILLEEN (Richard). A short history of Ireland. Pp 71. Dublin: Gill and Macmillan, 1994.

0490   KINANE (Vincent). A history of the Dublin University Press, 1734-1976. Pp xx, 386. Dublin: Gill and Macmillan, 1994.

0491   KING (A.C.). British and Irish archaeology: a bibliographical guide. Pp xii, 324. Manchester: Manchester University Press, 1994.
         History and related disciplines select bibliographies.

0492   KING (Heather A.). Irish memorial brasses to 1700. In *R.I.A. Proc.*, xciv, sec. c, 111-40 (1994).

0493   KING (Philip). Monasterboice heritage: a centenary celebration: a compilation of fact & folklore history to celebrate Tenure church centenary. Pp 352. [Monasterboice, Co. Louth]: [Parish of Monasterboice], 1994.

0494   KINMOUTH (Claudia). Irish country furniture, 1700-1950. Pp x, 248. Newhaven: Yale University Press, 1993.

0495   KINSELLA (Anna). The windswept shore: a history of Courtown district. 2nd ed. Pp 205. [s.l.]: [Anna Kinsella?], 1994.
         Previous ed.: 1982.

0496   KINSELLA (Sean). The cult of violence and the revolutionary tradition in Ireland. In *Studies*, lxxxiii, 20-9 (1994).

0497   KIRWAN (John). The Robbins family of Ballyduff and Firgrove, Co. Kilkenny: a preliminary study. In *Old Kilkenny Rev.*, xlvi, 122-35 (1994).

        KISSANE (Noel). See *Treasures from the National Library of Ireland* (1994).

0498   KNOCKAINEY G.A.A. Bord na nÓg. Rambling through Knockainey: the history of the Gaelic Athletic Association in Knockainey and Patrickswell, with other tales of sporting, social and historical life of the parish.   Pp 118. Knockainey (Limerick): Knockainey G.A.A. Bord na nÓg, 1993.

0499   KNOX (R. Buick). The Westminster Assembly of divines. In *Presb. Hist. Soc. of Ire. Bull.*, xxii, 5-15 (1993).

0500   KRUGER (Chuck). Cape Clear: island magic: a photographic, historical & dramatic account of Clear Island, Ireland.   Pp xvi, 112, [2].   Cork: Collins Press, 1994.

0501   LACY (Brian). The archaeology of clay pipes and local history. In *Ulster Local Studies*, iv, no. 2, pp 17-19 (1978).

0502   LAFFAN (Moira). The Barringtons of Glendruid: a talk ... Pp 16. [Foxrock, Dublin]: Foxrock Local History Club, [1990]. (Publication (Foxrock Local History Club), no. 33).

0503   LAMB (Keith). A shelf of garden history. In *Ir. Garden*, i, no. 3, pp 22-4 (1992).
        A survey of some source material.

0504   LANE (Pádraig G.). The Gonne-Bell estate at Streamstown, Co. Mayo: a record of property vicissitudes. In *Cathair na Mart*, xiii, 82-9 (1993).

0505   LAVELLE (Des). The Skellig story: ancient monastic outpost. Updated ed. Pp 105. Dublin: O'Brien Press, 1993.
        Previous ed. published as: Skellig: island outpost of Europe, 1976.

0506   LAVERTY (Donal). Early settlements around Creeve Lough, Stewartstown. In *The Bell*, v, 7-17 (1994).

0507   LAW (Edward J.). The presentation plate of the Corporation of the City of Kilkenny 1684-1834. In *Old Kilkenny Rev.*, xlvi, 57-74 (1994).

0508   LAW (Edward J.). The "Gardeners" cottage, Bishopslough.   In *In the Shadow of the Steeple*, iv, 19-24 (1994).

0509   Leabharliosta. In *Stair na Gaeilge*, pp 795-825 (1994).

        LEE (J.J.). See *Ireland* (1994).

0510   LEERSSEN (Joep). The western mirage: on the Celtic chronotope in the European imagination. In *Decoding the landscape*, pp 1-11 (1994).

0511   LENIHAN (Edmund). The holy wells of Doora-Barefield parish. In *The Other Clare*, xviii, 43-8 (1993).

0512   LESLIE (J.B.). Clergy of Connor: from Patrician times to the present day, based on the unpublished succession lists compiled by J.B. Leslie. Pp xi, 672. Belfast: Ulster Historical Foundation; Library Committee of the dioceses of Down, Connor & Dromore, 1993.
        Includes memoir of Canon J.B. Leslie, 1865-1952 by H.W. Lowe.

0513   LEYDEN (Maurice). Boys and girls come out to play: a collection of Irish singing games. Pp 152. Belfast: Appletree Press, 1993

0514   LIECHTY, (Joseph). Roots of sectarianism in Ireland: chronology and reflections. Pp 51. Belfast: Dr Joseph Liechty, 1993.

0515   The life, the times, the people ...: [Clonbullogue, Bracknagh, Walsh Island]. [*Ed*. Stephen Kelly .. et al]. Pp [7], 415. [s.l.]: [s.n.], [1993?].
        Co. Offaly.

0516   LIGGETT (Michael). A district called Ardoyne: a brief history of a Belfast community. Pp 51. Belfast: Glenravel Publications, 1994.

        LINCOLN (Simon). See GRIFFIN (David J.).

0517   The lives of rural women in the Republic of Ireland, Northern Ireland and Great Britain: an annotated bibliography; edited by the Rural Women's Research Project; researched by Anne Finn and Catherine Forde. Pp 80. Cookstown, Co. Tyrone: Rural Development Council for Northern Ireland, 1993.

0518   Lixnaw heritage trail. *Ed*. Helen O'Carroll. Pp 49. [Lixnaw, Co. Kerry]: Oidhreacht Leac Snámha, [1994?].

0519   Local history in college theses. In *Local History Rev.*, vi, 15-29 (1993).

0520   LOGAN (Patrick). Irish folk medicine. In *Teathba*, ii, no. 1, 41-6 (1980).

0521   LOHAN (Rena). Guide to the archives of the Office of Public Works. Pp 307. Dublin: Stationery Office, 1994. ([Catalogue lists] Ireland Stationery Office).

0522   LONG (Bill). Bright light, white water: the story of Irish lighthouses and their people. Pp 224. Dublin: New Island Books, 1993.

0523   LONG (Frank). Glasthule. In *Dun Laoghaire Jn.*, iii, 37-9 (1993).

0524   LONGFORD (Elizabeth). Wellington and the Irish connection. In *Ríocht na Midhe*, ix, no. 1, pp 50-60 (1994/95).

0525   LONGLEY (Edna). The living stream: literature and revisionism in Ireland. Pp 302. Newcastle upon Tyne: Bloodaxe Books, 1994.

0526   Lough Derg: the westside story. *Ed*. Kate Devlin ... et al; cartographer Geraldine O'Daly. Pp 8. Dublin: FÁS, 1993.
        Map compiled by Woodford Heritage Indexation Project.

GENERAL

0527   LUCAS (A.T.).   Magic.   In *North Munster Antiq. Jn.*, xxxv, 98-103 (1993/94).

0528   LUDLOW (Charles G.).   Salt politics: the Corporation of Salt Makers of Bandonbridge. In *Bandon Hist. Jn.*, x, 21-8 (1994).

0529   LUNNEY (Linde).   Ulster attitudes to Scottishness: the eighteenth century and after. In *Scotland and Ireland*, pp 56-70 (1994).

0530   LUSTICK (Ian).   Unsettled states, disputed lands: Britain and Ireland, France and Algeria, Israel and the West Bank-Gaza. Pp xiv, 576. Ithaca (N.Y.); London: Cornell University Press, 1993.   (The Wilder House series in politics, history and culture).
         Ireland, 1800- .

0531   LUTTON (S.C.) The inland port of Portadown. In *Review*, v, no. 3, pp 18-22 (1986/87).

0532   LYNCH (Anne) and MANNING (Conleth).   Dublin Castle: the archaeological project. In *Arch. Ire.*, iv, 65-68 (1990).

0533   LYNCH (Christopher). Bunratty Castle: a short history. In *The Other Clare*, i, 17-18 (1977).

0534   LYNCH (David).   The Warrens and the Johnsons. In *A Window on the Past*, iii, 51-4 (1993).

0535   LYNCH (Geraldine).   The holy wells of County Wicklow: traditions and legends. In *Wicklow*, pp 625-48 (1994).

0536   LYNCH (Helen).   The bishop's palace. In *The book of Cloyne*, pp 139-42 (1994).

0537   LYNCH (Helen).   Folklore of the parish. In *The book of Cloyne*, pp 254-8 (1994).

0538   LYNCH (Kevin).   Derrywaddreen-Derrynagun (The Derry-Hortland islands). In *Oughterany*, i, no 1, p 23 (1993).

0539   LYNCH (Kevin).   Kilcock churchyard (old). In *Oughterany*, i, no. 1, pp 65-76 (1993).

0540   LYNN (Chris).   Navan fort: new light on the Irish epics. In *Current Archael.*, xii, 44-9 (1993).

0541   LYNN (C.J.) and McDOWELL (J.A.).   Two unrecorded monuments near Navan, County Armagh? In *Emania*, iii, 22-7 (1987).
         Tirgarriff mound and Legarhill pillar-stone.

0542   LYSAGHT (Patricia).   Bealtaine: Irish Maytime customs and reaffirmation of boundaries. In *Boundaries & thresholds*, pp 28-43 (1993).

0543   LYSAGHT (Patricia).   Of death and the banshee. In *Roscommon Hist. Soc. Jn.*, iv, 11-12 (1992).

43

0544   LYSAGHT (Patricia). Vernacular rural dwellings in Ireland. In *Traditional architecture in Ireland*, pp 8-20 (1994).

0545   McALISTER (Jacqueline). Investigating Mountsandel cottage. In *The Bann Disc*, i, 7-9 (1994).

0546   Mac an ULTAIGH (Críostóir). Urney: a portrait of an Irish parish. Pp 145. [Strabane?]: [Urney G.A.A. Club], [1994].

0547   Mac AODHA (Breandán). The big house in western Ireland. In *The big house in Ireland*, pp 19-29 (1991).

0548   Mac AODHA (Breandán). Distribution, function and architecture. In *The big house in Ireland*, pp 43-57 (1991).

0549   Mac AODHA (Breandán). Some aspects of the toponymy of the Ballintempo district, Co. Fermanagh. In *Ainm*, vi, 56-73 (1994/95).

0550   MacBRADAIGH (Seán Ó Raghallaigh). The Mac Bradaigh chiefs of Teallach Cearbhuill. In *Breifne*, vi, 355-62 (1986).

0551   McCABE (Brian). St David's Church, Naas. In *Ir. Family Hist.*, ix, 39-54 (1993).

0552   McCAFFREY (Lawrence J.). The Catholic and urban profile of Irish America. In *The Ir. Rev.*, xiv, 1-9 (1993).

McCARTHY (Muriel). See *'Mighty monsters in Marsh's'* (1993).

0553   McCARTHY (Philomena). Kenmare and its storied glen: from the cursing stones to the Christian chanticleer. Pp [7], 166. Kenmare: [the author], 1993.

0554   McCARTHY (Timothy J.) and ROSS (Noel). Gravestone inscriptions in Haynestown. In *Louth Arch. Soc. Jn.*, xxiii, 127-33 (1993).

0555   McCARTHY (Tony). The Irish roots guide. Reprinted with corrections. Pp ix, 116, [2]. Dublin: Lilliput Press, 1993.
       First pub.: 1991.

0556   McCARTNEY (Dónal). History revisions: good and bad. In *Reconsiderations of Irish history and culture*, pp 134-56 (1994).

0557   McCARTNEY (Jean). Portaferry Presbyterian church. In *Upper Ards Hist. Soc. Jn.*, i, 19-23 (1977).

0558   McCAVERY (Trevor). Newtown: a history of Newtownards. Pp 221. Belfast: The White Row Press, 1994.

0559   McCLURE (Robert David). Serendipity and the crooked griddle: an account of research on the McClure family. In *Familia*, ii, no. 10, pp 72-87 (1994).

0560   McCOLLUM (John K.). The aristocrat of fibres and an Ulster scutch mill. In *The Bann Disc*, i, 21-5 (1994).

Mac CON IOMAIR (Liam). See ROBINSON (Tim).

0561   McCONE (Kim). An tSean-Ghaeilge agus a Réamhstair. In *Stair na Gaeilge*, pp 61-219 (1994).

0562   McCONMARA (Michael). Kilquane graveyard Parteen. In *Sliab Aughty*, v, 42-8 (1994).

0563   McCONNELL (Charles).   Carrickfergus: a stroll through time.   Pp 66. [Carrickfergus]: Carrickfergus Publications, 1994.

0564   McCORMACK (W.J.). Dissolute characters: Irish literary history through Balzac, Sheridan Le Fanu, Yeats and Bowen.   Pp xi, 260.   Manchester: Manchester University Press, 1993.

0565   McCORMACK (W.J.). From Burke to Beckett: ascendancy, tradition and betrayal in literary history. Pp ix, 470. Cork: Cork University Press, 1994.
        First published in 1985 as: Ascendancy and tradition in Anglo-Irish literary history from 1789 to 1939.

0566   MacCORMAIC (Éamonn). South County Longford: its farming patterns and customs. In *Teathba*, ii, no. 1, pp 61-2 (1980).

0567   McCORRY (Francis Xavier). Lurgan: an Irish provincial town, 1610-1970. Pp vi, 194. Lurgan: Inglewood Press, 1993.

0568   McCOTTER (Paul). The Carews of Cork. In *Cork Hist. Soc. Jn.*, xcviii, 61-74 (1993); part 2, xcix, 66-82 (1994).

0569   McCOTTER (Paul). The Fitzgeralds of Imokilly. In *The book of Cloyne*, pp 79-100 (1994).

0570   McCOTTER (Paul). The townlands of Cloyne. In *The book of Cloyne*, pp 29-44 (1994).
        Placenames.

0571   McCRAITH (L.M.). Cahir. In *Tipperary county*, pp 73-9 (1993).
        Chapter is based on article originally published 1912, revised and updatetd by editor Michael Hallinan.

0572   MacCURTAIN (Margaret). Ennistymon. In *Irish country towns*, pp 109-19 (1994).

0573   McCUTCHEON (W.A.). Industrial archaeology: a case study in Northern Ireland. In *World Archaeol.*, xv, 161-72 (1983).

0574   McDAID (Mary). History of land ownership and agrarian structure of the estate of William Connolly. In *Donegal Annual*, xlvi, 53-60 (1994).

0575   McDONNELL (Finola J. Keyes). Folklore and customs. In *Bandon Hist. Jn.*, ix, 11-15 (1993).

0576   McDONNELL (Hector). Agnews and O'Gnímhs In *The Glynns*, xxi, 13-53 (1993).

0577   [McDONNELL (Hector)]. An Agnew/O Gnímhs postscript. In *The Glynns*, xxii, 24-7 (1994).

0578   McDONOGH (Steve). The Dingle peninsula: history, folklore and archaeology. Pp 256. Dingle (Co. Kerry): Brandon, 1993.

McDOWELL (J.A.). See LYNN (C.J.).

0579   McEVOY (John). Carlow College: two hundred years of education. In *Carloviana*, xl, 2-8 (1992/93).

0580   McEVOY (John). Carlow College 1793-1993: the ordained students and teaching staff of St. Patrick's College, Carlow. Pp 300. Carlow: St. Patrick's College, 1993.

0581   McGETTERICK (Thomas). Trees, bushes, shrubs - even weeds. In *Irish Family History*, i, no. 1, pp 15-16 (1993).
        Place-name components.

0582   McGINN (Brendan). Some more place names. In *Benbradagh*, xii, 3-4 (1982).

0583   McGINN (Brian). Ché Guevara's Irish blood: the Lynch family of Argentina. In *Ir. Roots*, 1993, no. 2, pp 11-14 (1993).

0584   McGOWAN (Eileen). Surnames of County Roscommon. In *Ir. Roots*, 1993, no. 1, pp 20-1 (1993).

0585   McGOWAN (Joe). In the shadow of Benbulben. Pp 336. [Mullaghmore, Co. Sligo]: Aeolus, 1993.
        History of the Mullaghmore area, Co. Sligo.

0586   McGRATH (Margaret). Extradition: another Irish problem. In *N. Ire. Legal Q.*, xxxiv, 292-314 (1983).

McGUIRE (J.I.). See *The Church of Ireland: a critical bibliography* (1993).

0587   McGUINNE (Dermot). Irish types in the U.S.A. In *Bibliog. Soc. America Papers*, lxxxviii, 227-34 (1994).
        Survey of Irish printing typefaces with especial reference to the U.S.A.

0588   McHENRY (P.J.). The history of a house. In *Upper Ards Hist. Soc. Jn.*, i, 29-30 (1977).
        No. 8 Ferry Street, Portaferry.

0589   McHENRY (P.J.). The Irish in our place-names. In *Upper Ards Hist. Soc. Jn.*, i, 25 (1977)

McHUGH (Raymond). See *Along the Black Pig's dyke* [1993?].

0590   McINERNEY (Bill). Cratloe. In *The Other Clare*, ii, 12 (1978).

0591   MACIVER (J.). Origins of the surname Maciver. In *The Glynns*, xxii, 28-32 (1994).

0592   McKAY (Bertie). The role of the commerical fisherman in fisheries management. In *The Bann Disc*, i, 15-21 (1994).

0593 McKAY (Pat). The *Tuath* - names of the baronies of Toome, Co. Antrim. In *Ainm*, vi, 107-14 (1994/95).

0594 McKENDRY (Eugene). Presenting the Irish language in the Ulster context. In *Linen Hall Rev.*, xi, no. 1, pp 10-11 (1994).

0595 McKIERNAN (Francis J.). Kilmore priests. In *Breifne*, vi, no. 24, pp 308-19 (1986).

0596 McKIERNAN (Francis J.). The O'Reillys of Corlattyannan and their relations. In *Breifne*, viii, 489-96 (1994).

0597 MacLARAN (Andrew). Dublin: the shaping of a capital. Pp xiii, 242. London: Bellhaven Press, 1993. (World cities series).

0598 MacLAUGHLIN (Dan). Notes on the origin of Portstewart. In *The Bann Disc*, i, 66-7 (1994).

0599 Mac LAUGHLIN (Jim). Historical and recent Irish emigration: a critique of core-periphery and behavioural models. Pp 54. London: University of North London, Irish Studies Centre, 1994. (Irish Studies Centre occasional papers series, no.5).
   19th-20th centuries.

0600 Mac LAUGHLIN (Jim). Ireland: the emigrant nursery and the world economy. Pp 88. Cork: Cork University Press, 1994. (Undercurrents series).

0601 MacLOUGHLIN (Guillermo). The Irish in South America. In *Aspects of Irish genealogy*, pp 172-6 [1993].

0602 MacMAHON (Bryan). The story of Ballyheigue. Pp 264. Baile Uí Thaidgh, Co. Chiarraí: Oidhreacht, 1994.
   Co. Kerry.

0603 McMANUS (Damian). An Nua-Ghaeilge chlasniceach. In *Stair na Gaeilge*, pp 335-445 (1994).

0604 McNAMARA (Pakie). Marriage customs in east Clare. In *Sliabh Aughty*, v, 9-11 (1994).
   From the Irish Folklore Commission 1938 east Clare school reports.

0605 McNEILL (D.B.). Slip carriages in Ireland. In *Ir. Railway Rec. Soc. Jn.*, xviii, 425-30 (1994).

0606 McNEILL (Hugh). The annals of the parish of Derrykeighan: from A.D. 453 to A.D. 1890; introduced by Eull Dunlop. Pp 81. Ballymena: Mid Antrim Historical Group, 1993.

0607 Mac PÓILIN (Aodán). 'Spiritual beyond the ways of men': images of the Gael. In *The Ir. Rev.*, xvi, 1-22 (1994).

0608 Mac RAOIS (Breandán). Ar bhruacha na Life: stair Átha Cliath go dtí an bhliain 1803. *Ed.* Vivian Uíbh Eachach. Pp 214. Baile Átha Cliath: An Clóchomhar, 1994. (Leabhair thaighde, 78).
   History of Dublin till 1803.

0609   McROBERT (John). Inch abbey. In *Lecale Miscellany*, ix, 66-70 (1991).

0610   MacSIOMÓIN (Tomás). The colonised mind: Irish language and society. In *Reconsiderations of Irish history and culture*, pp 42-71 (1994).

    McTERNAN (John C.). See *Sligo: sources of local history* (1994).

0611   MacTHOMÁIS (Éamonn). Me jewel and darlin' Dublin, illustrated by Michael O'Brien. 4th rev. ed. Pp 186. Dublin: O'Brien Press, 1994.
        Previous ed.: 1977.

    McVEAGH (John). See *Strangers to that land* (1994).

0612   MACKEY (J.P.), ed. The cultures of Europe: the Irish contribution. Pp 197. Belfast: Institute of Irish Studies, Queen's University of Belfast, 1994.

0613   MADDEN (Gerard). Shameful neglect of a historic place Tuamgraney. In *Sliabh Aughty*, v, 5-8 (1994).

    MADDEN (Gerard). See *For God or King* (1993).

0614   MAGEE (Sean). Dublin poll books and registers of electors. In *Dun Laoghaire Geneal. Soc. Jn.*, ii, 5-12 (1993).

    MAGEOGHAGAN (Conell). See *The annals of Clonmacnoise* (1993).

    MAGINNIS (Hilary). See BEAUMONT (Pauline).

0615   MAHER (Michael). Sunday in the Irish church. In *Ir. Theol. Quart.*, lx, 161-84 (1994).

0616   MAG RIABHAIGH (Seán). Mainistir na Búille. Tús agus turnamh. In *An t-Ultach*, lxxi, no. 10, pp 4-11 (1994).
        Boyle Abbey, Co. Roscommon.

0617   MAGUIRE (Martin). Select bibliography of writings on Irish economic and social history published in 1992. In *Ir. Ec. & Soc. Hist.*, xx, 84-106 (1993).

0618   MAGUIRE (Martin). Select bibliography of writings on Irish economic and social history published in 1993. In *Ir. Ec. & Soc. Hist.*, xxi, 84-111 (1994).

0619   MAGUIRE (W.A.). Belfast. Pp 208. Keele: Keele University Press, 1993. (Town and city histories).

0620   Mahony of Cullina: [pedigree]. In *O'Mahony Jn.*, xii, 10-11 (1982).

0621   Major accessions to repositories relating to Irish history, 1992. In *I.H.S.*, xxix, 120-1 (1994).

0622   MALONE (Emer). Dalkey: medieval manor and seaport. 1 pack. [Dun Laoghaire Borough Heritage Society, 1993].
        Contains 3 pamphlets - castles, seaport, manor.

0623   MALONEY (Dan). Gortmore House. In *Gateway to the Past*, i, no. ii, pp 59-60 (1994).

0624   MANNING (Conleth). A possible sweathouse in Cloghkeating. In *Cloughjordan Heritage*, i, 24-5 (1985).

        MANNING (Conleth). See LYNCH (Ann).

0625   MARNANE (Denis G.). Surnames of County Tipperary. In *Ir. Roots*, 1994, no. 2, pp 25-6 (1994).

0626   MARNANE (Denis G.). Tipperary: the town of the well. In *Tipperary county*, pp 133-41 (1993).

        MARTIN (Alan). See FRY (Malcolm F.).

0627   MARTIN (Elaine). Ballinagare. In *Roscommon Hist. Soc. Jn.*, iv, 18-20 (1992).

0628   MARTIN (F.X.). The Irish Augustinians in Rome, 1656-1994. In *The Irish Augustinians in Rome*, pp 5-55 (1994).

0629   Master Rath a powerful rector. In *A window on the past*, [i], 24-5 (1987).
        Church at Rathfeigh, county Meath, c.1400- ; Richard Rath rector c. 1413.

0630   MATTHEWS (Séamus). Under the hill of Donore. In *Old Drogheda Soc. Jn.*, ix, 118-28 (1994).

        MAWHINNEY (Graham). See CROSKERY (Thomas).

        MAWHINNEY (Graham). See Ó CEALLAIGH (Seamus).

0631   MAYES (Frank). The Donaghenry coin hoard. In *The Bell*, v, 41-3 (1994).

0632   MAYES (Frank). What's in a name? Part II: the townlands of Donaghenry. In *The Bell*, v, 48-59 (1994).
        Continued from iii (1989).

0633   MEAGHER (Jim). The history and legends of Ballyhoura mountains. In *The history and legends of Ballyhoura mountains*, pp 32-40 (1993).

0634   MERCIER (Vivian). Modern Irish literature: sources and founders. *Ed.* and presented by Eilís Dillon. Pp xvii, 381. Oxford: Clarendon Press, 1994. 1798- .

0635   MERRIGAN (M.). Number twenty nine. A jewel of Georgian Dublin. In *Dun Laoghaire Geneal. Soc. Jn.*, ii, 21-3 (1993).
        29 Lower Fitzwilliam Street, Dublin.

0636   MESSENGER (John C.). St Patrick's day in "The other Emerald Isle". In *Éire-Ireland*, xxix, no. 1, pp 12-23 (1994).
        Colony of Irish extraction on Montserrat, West Indies.

0637   'Mighty monsters in Marsh's': an exhibition of early natural history books in Marsh's Library. Compiled by Muriel McCarthy and Caroline Sherwood-Smith. Pp 72. Dublin: Archbishop Marsh's Library, 1993.

0638　MILLER (Kerby) and WAGNER (Paul). Out of Ireland: the story of Irish emigration to America. Pp 132. London: Aurum Press, 1994.

MILNE (Kenneth). See *The Church of Ireland: a critical bibliography* (1993).

0639　MITCHELL (Brian). Derry: a city invincible. Pp 98. Eglinton, Co Londonderry: Grocers' Hall Press, 1994. First pub.: 1990.

0640　MITCHELL (Brian). Historic Eglinton: a thriving ornament. Pp 94. Eglinton, Co. Londonderry: Grocers' Hall Press, 1994.

0641　MITCHELL (Frank). A geological letter from John Jackson. In *Mizen Jn.*, i, 5-7 (1993).

0642　MITCHELL (Frank) and TUITE (Breeda). The great bog of Ardee. In *Louth Arch. Soc. Jn.*, xxiii, 7-95 (1993).

0643　MITCHELL (Frank). The Victor Clarke geological collection in the Millmount Museum. In *Old Drogheda Soc. Jn.*, ix, 106-07 (1994).

0644　MOLLAN (Charles). 'The Irish national inventory and one of its "discoveries".' In *Making instruments count*, pp 443-53 (1993).

0645　MOLLAN (Charles) and UPTON (John). The scientific apparatus of Nicholas Callan and other historic instruments. Pp 304. Maynooth: St. Patrick's College; Blackrock, Co. Dublin: Samton, 1994. (Catalogues of historic scientific instruments in Irish collections, no. 1).

0646　MOLONEY (Aonghus) [et al]. Excavations at Clonfinlough County Offaly. In *Ir. Archaeological Wetland Unit Trans*, ii, pp i-x, 1-131 (1993).

0647　MOLONEY (Aonghus) [et al]. Survey of the raised bogs of county Longford. In *Ir. Archaeological Wetland Unit Trans*, i, pp i-vii, 1-120 (1993).

0648　MOLONEY (Bernie), ed. Times to cherish: Cashel and Rosegreen parish history. Pp 224. Cashel: Parish of Cashel and Rosegreen, 1994.

0649　MONTGOMERY (Michael). The lexicography of Hiberno-English. In *The Scotch-Irish and Hiberno-English language and culture*, pp 20-36 (1993).

0650　MOORE (Desmond F.). Dublin's yesterdays. Pp 224. Portlaoise: Nomad Books, [1994?]

MOORE (Treasa). See *Catalogue of books in the Henry Library* (1993).

0651　MORAN (James M.). Stepping on stones: local history of the Ballinturly/Correal valley in the Suck lowlands, Roscommon mid-west. Pp 146. [Athleague, Co. Roscommon]: James M. Moran, 1993.

0652　MORGAN (Danny). A glimpse of the maritime tradition of the Glens. In *The Glynns*, xxii, 45-50 (1994).

0653　MORGAN (Hiram). Empire-building an uncomfortable Irish heritage. In *Linen Hall Rev.*, x, no. 2, pp 8-11 (1993).

0654   MORONEY (Nora) and O'CONNOR (Jim). Skenakilla history. In *Mallow Field Club Jn.*, xi, 23-35 (1993).

0655   MORRIS (H.F.). The Reynett family of Waterford. In *Decies*, xlviii, 33-48 (1993).

0656   MOULDEN (John). Thousands are sailing: a brief song history of Irish emigration. Pp 44. Portrush: Ulstersongs, c.1994.

0657   Moylough: a people's heritage. *Ed.* Carol O'Regan and John Jones. Pp ix, 137. [Moylough]: [Moylough Community Council, [1993].
        Moylough, north County Galway.

0658   MULCAHY (John). The Church of Ireland in Blarney. In *Old Blarney*, iii, 42-54 (1993).

0659   MULCAHY (John). Gynes Castle, Cloghroe. In *Old Blarney*, iii, 57-68 (1993).

0660   MULLIGAN (Padraig). Corn mills of Leitrim. In *Breifne*, viii, 359-85 (1992/93).

0661   MULLIN (T.H.). Bannfield over four centuries. In *The Bann Disc*, i, 10-14 (1994).

0662   MULVEEN (Jack). Galway goldsmiths, their marks and ware. In *Galway Arch. Soc. Jn.*, xlvi, 43-64 (1994).

0663   MUNCK (Ronnie). The Irish economy: results and prospects. Pp xvii, 177. London: Pluto Press, 1993.

0664   MURPHY (Brian P.). The canon of Irish cultural history: some questions concerning Roy Foster's *Modern Ireland*. In *Studies*, lxxxii, 171-84 (1993).

0665   MURPHY (Brian P.). Past events and present politics: Roy Foster's 'Modern Ireland'. In *Reconsiderations of Irish history and culture*, pp 72-93 (1994).

        MURPHY (Denis). See *The annals of Clonmacnoise* (1993).

        MURPHY (Donal A.). See MURPHY (Nancy).

0666   MURPHY (Hilary). Byrnes and Wickams of Wexford. In *Ir. Family Hist.*, ix, 55-8 (1993).

0667   MURPHY (Hilary). Surnames of County Wexford. In *Ir. Roots*, 1992, no. 3, pp 20-1 (1992).

0668   MURPHY (John A.). Cork: anatomy and essence. In *Cork*, pp 1-14 (1993).

0669   MURPHY (Kevin H.). Echoes of Caher. Pp 84. [s.l.]:[s.n.], [1994?].
        Cahirsiveen.

0670   MURPHY (Nancy). Nenagh castle: chronology and architecture. Pp 8. Nenagh: Relay, 1993.

0671   MURPHY (Nancy) & MURPHY (Donal A.). Walkabout Nenagh. Pp 139. Nenagh: Relay Publications, 1994.

MURPHY (Nancy). See TREACY (Brendan).

0672   MURPHY (Paula). The politics of the street monument. In *Ir. Arts Rev. Yearbk*, pp 202-08 (1994).

MURPHY (Rory). See KAVANAGH (Art).

0673   MURPHY (Sean). Irish septs and surnames. In *Ir. Roots*, 1993, no. 3, pp 24-5 (1993).

0674   MURPHY (Sean). The Moravians of Dublin 1746-1980. In *Ir. Roots*, 1994, no. 2, p 12 (1994).

0675   MURPHY (Sean). The Murphy septs. In *Ir. Roots*, 1994, no. 4, pp 28-9 (1994).

0676   MURPHY-LAWLESS (Jo). The silencing of women in childbirth or let's hear it for Bartholemew and the boys. In *Irish women's studies reader*, pp 9-19 (1993).
        Male midwives in the Rotunda Hospital, Dublin.

MURRAY (James). See *The Church of Ireland: a critical bibliography* (1993).

0677   MURRAY (James P.). Galway: a medico-social history. Pp 266. Galway: Kenny's Bookshop and Art Gallery, 1994.

0678   MURRAY (Peter). A sectarian skeleton in the Gaelic League's cupboard? 'Roy Foster, Brian Murphy and the case of George A. Birmingham'. In *Studies*, lxxxii, 481-6 (1993).

0679   MURTAGH (Ben). Archaeological investigations at Dysart, Co. Kilkenny 1989-1994: an interim report. In *Old Kilkenny Rev.*, xlvi, 78-94 (1994).

0680   MURTAGH (Ben). The Kilkenny castle archaeological project 1990-1993: interim report. In *Old Kilkenny Rev.*, iv, 1101-17 (1993).

0681   MURTAGH (Harman). Athlone. In *Irish country towns*, pp 154-65 (1994).

0682   MURTAGH (Harman). Athlone. Pp 16. Dublin: Royal Irish Academy, 1994. (Irish historic town atlas, no. 6).

0683   Náisuín, stát agus pobal. Eoin Ó Murchú agus Deasún Fennell ag caint le hOghma. In *Oghma*, 2, pp 47-57 (1990).

0684   NEAL (Frank). English-Irish conflict in the north-east of England. In *The Irish in British labour history*, pp 59-85 (1993).

0685   NEESON (Eoin). Aspects of parallelism in Japanese and Irish character and culture. In *Comparative aspects of Irish and Japanese economic and social history*, pp 71-122 (1993).

0686　NEILL (Kathleen). How to trace family history in Northern Ireland. Updated and expanded [ed.]. Pp 150. Belfast: Irish Heritage Association, 1993. First pub.: 1986.

　　　　NEILL (Marie). See JUPP (Belinda).

0687　NEWMANN (Kate). Dictionary of Ulster biography. Pp 278. Belfast: Institute of Irish Studies, Queen's University of Belfast, 1993.

0688　NEWMANN (Kate). The dictionary of Ulster biography. In *Ulster Local Studies*, xvi, no. 2, pp 40-4 (1994).

0689　Newmarket court (1725-1994). By Tionscnamh Oidreachta Duthalla = Duhallow Heritage Project. Pp 88. [Newmarket, Co. Cork]: Duhallow Heritage Project, 1994.

　　　　Ní BHROCHLÁIN (Muireann). See DRENNAN (John).

　　　　Ní MHURCHÚ (Máire). See BREATHNACH (Diarmuid)

0690　Ní RIAIN (Nóirín). The nature and classification of traditional religious songs in Irish: with a survey of printed and oral sources. In *Music and the church*, pp 190-253 (1993).

0691　Nic EOIN (Máirín). An Ghaeilge i gCill Chainnigh. Pp (various pagings). Baile Átha Cliath: Comhar na Múinteoirí Gaeilge, 1993.

0692　Nic GIOLLA BHRÍDE (Cáit). Gaoth Dobhair, sean agus nua. In *An t-Ultach*, lxx, no. 5, pp 12-14 (1993).

0693　NOLAN (Patrick M.). Tipperary Historical Journal: index 1988-1992. In *Tipp. Hist. Jn.*, pp 1-18 (1993).

0694　NOLAN (William). Castlecomer. In *Irish country towns*, pp 121-30 (1994).

0695　North of Ireland Family History Society, Belfast Branch. Carved in stone: a record of memorials in the ancient graveyard around the Church of the Holy Evangelists (Church of Ireland) at Carnmoney, Newtownabbey, County Antrim. Pp 138. Belfast: North of Ireland Family History Society, Belfast Branch, 1994.

0696　Northern Ireland and Canada: a guide to Northern Ireland sources for the study of Canadian history, c.1705-1992. *Ed.* Stephen Davison. Pp vii, 144. Belfast: Queen's University of Belfast, Centre of Canadian Studies and the Public Record Office of Northern Ireland, 1994.

0697　NUGENT (Martin). A historical and social study of Gurkaderra a Clare townland. In *Sliabh Aughty*, iv, 8-11 (1993).

　　　　NYLAND (Dominic). See DRENNAN (John).

0698　Ó BAOIGHILL (Pádraig). Cuimhní ar Dhochartaigh Ghleann Fhinne. Pp 43. Baile Átha Cliath: Coiscéim, 1994.
　　　　　　Ó Dochartaigh family, Co. Donegal.

0699   O'BRIEN (Barry). Macroom castle and estate once owned by Judge Bernard. In *Bandon Hist. Jn.*, ix, 19-23 (1993).

0700   O'BRIEN (Conor). The Byrnes of Ballymanus. In *Wicklow*, pp 305-39 (1994).

0701   O'BRIEN (Conor Cruise). Ancestral voices: religion and nationalism in Ireland. Pp 197. Dublin: Poolbeg Press, 1994.

0702   O'BRIEN (Gearoid). Childrens literature from County Longford 1760-1960. In *Teathba*, ii, no. 1, pp 47-56 (1980).

0703   O'BRIEN (Hugh B.). St Michael's, Cootehill: a brief history of the church, its buildings, its people. Pp 124. Cootehill: [s.n.], 1993.

0704   O'BRIEN (John). Mountcashel tower house and its colourful inhabitants throughout history. In *The Other Clare*, ii, 13-14 (1978).

0705   O'BRIEN (Madeline). Excavations at Barrack Street - French's Quay, Cork. In *Cork Hist. Soc. Jn.*, xcviii, 27-49 (1993).

0706   O'BRIEN (Patrick). Fenloe: a graveyard and a legend. In *The Other Clare*, ii, 5-6 (1978).

0707   O'BRIEN (Sean). Bloody ambassadors. Pp 194. Swords, Co. Dublin: Poolbeg Press, 1993.
        Irish people tried for murder abroad.

0708   O'BRIEN (William). Our mining past: the metal-mining heritage of Cork. Pp 23. Cork: Cork Public Museum, 1994.

0709   Ó BROIN (Liam). Drogheda: a personal view. Pp [12], 108. Drogheda: Liam Ó Broin Gallery & Studio, 1993.

0710   Ó CANANN (Tomás G.). A pair of toponyms from Clann Mhic Giolla Dhé. In *Ainm*, vi, 38-45 (1994/95).
        Ballykildea, County Clare and Ballykilladea, County Galway.

0711   O'CARROLL (Cian). Shannon/Tradaree historical background. In *The Other Clare*, ii, 31-4 (1978).

        O'CARROLL (Helen). See *The Fitzmaurices* (1994).

        O'CARROLL (Helen). See *Lixnaw heritage trail* (1994).

0712   Ó CASAIDE (Peadar). Logainmneacha i bhFearnmhaigh. Pp [5], 38. [s.l.]: Clo Fhearnmhai Farney, [1993?].
        Placenames of Farney, Co. Monaghan; text in English and Irish.

0713   Ó CEALLAIGH (Colm). Ár gcomharsannaí thiar nainn. In *Connemara*, i, no. 1, pp 25-7 (1993).
        Contacts with emigrants in Newfoundland and Nova Scotia.

0714   Ó CEALLAIGH (Daltún). Reconsiderations. In *Reconsiderations in Irish history and culture*, pp 5-26 (1994).

0715   Ó CEALLAIGH (Séamus). Gleanings from Ulster history; major contributions from Niamh Whitfield and Nollaig Ó Muraile, compiled by Graham Mawhinney. Pp xlv, 197. Draperstown: Ballinascreen Historical Society, 1994.
        Originally published: Cork University Press, 1951. Séamus Ó Ceallaigh, 1879-1954.

0716   O'CLEIRIGH (Nellie). Clonmel. In *Tipperary county*, pp 95-100 (1993).

0717   Ó COFAIGH (Tomás F.). Punt sa sparán. In *Náisiún na hÉireann*, pp 18-33 (1993).
        Irish currency.

0718   Ó CONAIRE (Breandán). Na Protastúnaigh, an Ghaeilge agus Dubhghlas de híde. In *Seanchas Ardmhacha*, xv, no 2, pp 130-50 (1993).

0719   Ó CONCHÚIR (M.F.). Úna Bhán. Pp 245. Indreabhán, Conamara: Cló Iar-Chonnachta, 1994. (Na hAmhráin Mhóra, 1).
        Text in Irish with passages in English; Irish literature, folklore and song.

0720   O'CONNELL (Deirdre). A bibliography of Irish labour history, 1991-1992. In *Saothar*, xviii, 110-25 (1993).

0721   O'CONNELL (Deirdre). A bibliography of Irish labour history, 1992-1993. In *Saothar*, xix, 159-72 (1994).

        O'CONNOR (Deirdre). See *Dublin* (1993).

        O'CONNOR (Jim). See MORONEY (Nora).

0722   O'CONOR DON (The). Monkstown castle. In *Dun Laoghaire Jn.*, iii, 2-5 (1993).

0723   Ó CORRÁIN (Donnchadh). Corcu Loígde: land and families. In *Cork*, pp 63-81 (1993).

0724   Ó CORRÁIN (Donnchadh). Early Ireland: directions and redirections. In *Bullán*, i, no. 2, pp 1-15 (1994).

0725   Ó CRÓINÍN (Micheal). A dó is a dó sin a cúig. An cás ar son cultúr eolaíchta in Éirinn. In *Oghma*, 2, pp 68-74 (1990).

0726   Ó DÁLAIGH (Art P.). Huntsmen of the Blackwater basin. In *Dúiche Néill*, viii, 140-59 (1993).

        O'DALY (Geraldine). See *Lough Derg* (1993).

0727   Ó DOIBHLIN (Diarmaid). The glow upon the fringe of a great flame: north west Ulster's writers in Irish. In *The glow upon the fringe*, pp 53-63 (1994).

0728   Ó DIOBHLIN (Diarmaid). Laoithe ar phár agus léann na muintire. In *Náisiún na hÉireann*, pp 1-17 (1993).
        Oral and written sources.

0729   O'DONNELL (Declan). Aspects of the flora and fauna of west Cork. In *Mizen Jn.*, i, 11-17 (1993).

0730   O'DONNELL (Jim) and De FRÉINE (Seán). Ireland: the great little answer book. Pp vii, 152. Dublin: Torc, 1994.

0731   O'DONNELL (M.J.). The Pakenhams - earls of Longford. In *Teathba*, i, no. 1, pp 34-40 (1969).

0732   O'DONOGHUE (Dan). Ballyporeen. Pp 86. [s.l.]: [s.n.], [1994?].

0733   O'DONOVAN (John). John O'Donovan's letters from County Fermanagh (1834): letters containing information relative to the antiquities and families and places collected during the ordnance survey in 1834. *Ed.* John B. Cunningham. Pp 107. Belleek: St Davog's Press, 1993.
Cover title: The letters of John O'Donovan from Fermanagh.

0734   O'DOWD (Mary). Sligo. In *Irish country towns*, pp 142-53 (1994).

0735   O'DOWD (Peadar). Down by the Claddagh. Pp viii, 200. Galway: Kennys' Bookshop and Arts Galleries, 1993.
History of the fishing community of Galway city.

0736   O'DOWD (Peadar). A family heritage in stone. In *Galway Roots*, [i], 6-8 (1993).
Monumental records of the Tribes of Galway.

0737   Ó DUIGNEÁIN (P.). Sweat house. In *Teathba*, i, no. 1, pp 52-3 (1969).

0738   Ó DUINN (Seán). Gnasanna na Marbh. In *Irisleabhar Mhá Nuad*, pp 118-31 (1994).

0739   O'DWYER (Michael). Rothe House: owners, leases and tenants. In *Old Kilkenny Rev.*, xlvi, 10-19 (1994).

0740   Ó FIAICH (Tomás). Eoghan Ruadh i saol na hÉireann 1649-1942, [Athchló ar alt le Tomás Ó Fiaich, nach maireann as *Ard Macha*, Meitheamh 1943]. In *Alt t-Ultach*, lxx, no 6, pp 14-17 (1993).

0741   Ó GADHRA (Nollaig). Oidhreacht Chonradh na Gaeilge, 1983-1993. (Bunaithe ar nótaí a ullmhaíodh don Léacht Tionscnaimh a thug an t-údar Nollaig Ó Gadhra ag Éigse Uladh i nGaoth Dobhair, 5 Marta, 1993). In *Alt t-ÚHtach*, lxxi, no. 4, pp 4-13 (1994).

0742   O'MAHONY (Frank). Kilcrohane and the holy ground. *Bantry Hist. Soc. Jn.*, i, 26-40 (1991).

0743   Ó MAININ (Micheál B.). Place-names of Northern Ireland vol 3: County Down III: the Mournes. *Ed.* Gerard Stockman. Pp xxi, 246. Belfast: Institute of Irish Studies, Queen's University of Belfast, 1993.

0744   Ó MEACHAIR (Mícheál). An scrioptúr i mbeathaí naomh na hEireann. In *Irisleabhar Mha Nuad*, pp 82-9 (1993).

0745   Ó MÓRDHA (Pilip). Early schools and school teachers in Clones. In *Clogher Rec.*, xv, no. 1, pp 48-50 (1994).

0746   Ó MÓRDHA (Pilip). The Griffiths of Laurelhill, County Monaghan and associated families. In *Clogher Rec.*, xiv, no. iii, pp 111-24 (1993).
        Raises the possibility that this was the family of Arthur Griffith.

0747   Ó MORÓNAIGH (Seán). Oola's name & Cluggin's fame. In *Oola Past & Present*, i, 13-14 (1992).

0748   Ó MURAILE (Nollaig). Recent publications relating to Irish place-names. In *Ainm*, vi, 115-22 (1994/95).

        Ó MURAILE (Nollaig). See Ó CEALLAIGH (Séamus).

0749   Ó MURCHADHA (Diarmuid). Clann Taidhg Ruaidh na Scairte. In *Cork Hist. Soc. Jn.*, xcix, 32-46 (1994).

0750   Ó MURCHADHA (Diarmuid). Mag Cetne and Mag Ene. In *Éigse*, xxvii, 35-46 (1993).
        A note on the conflation of two placenames which appear in the annals.

0751   Ó MURCHADHA (Diarmuid). Memorial inscriptions of Irish interest from Somerset. In *Ir. Geneal.*, ix, no. 1, pp 5-13 (1994).

0752   Ó MURCHADHA (Diarmuid). O Mahony's around Dunmanus Bay. In *O Mahony Jn.*, xvi, 36-9 (1993).

0753   Ó MURCHADHA (Diarmuid). A reconsideration of some place-names from *The Annals of Connacht*. In *Ainm*, vi, 1-31 (1994/95).

0754   Ó MURCHADHA (M.K.). Music in Saint Nicholas' Collegiate Church Galway 1480-1912. In *Galway Arch. Soc. Jn.*, xlv, 29-43 (1993).

0755   Ó MURCHADHA (Seán). Diseart Tola and its environs. In *The Other Clare*, xvii, 36-42 (1993); xviii, 20-22 (1994).
        Continued from xvi (1992).

0756   O'NEILL (Kevin). Looking at the pictures: art and artfulness in colonial Ireland. In *Visualizing Ireland*, pp 55-70 (1993).

0757   O'NEILL (Mary). A story in stone from south Carlow. In *Carloviana*, xxxiii, 11-13 (1985/86).
        A resumé of some work done on the cemetery inscriptions of Carlow.

        O'NEILL (Maurice). See BLAIR (S. Alexander).

0758   Ó NÉILL (Pádraig). History of Knockbridge. Pp 587. [s.l]: [Pádraig Ó Neill], 1994.
        Knockbridge, Co. Louth.

0759   O'NEILL (Rose). A rich inheritance: Galway Dominican nuns, 1644-1994. Pp 200, [1]. Galway: Dominican Sisters, 1994.

0760   O'NEILL (Seán). The O'Neills of Nagh dá chonn. In *Carloviana*, xli, 8-21 (1993/94).

0761   O'NEILL (T.P.). Freemen and voters. In *Galway Roots*, [i], 38-9 (1993).

0762   O'NEILL (T.P.). Surnames of County Galway. In *Ir. Roots*, 1994, no. 1, pp 26-8 (1994).

0763   O'RAHILLY (Celie). Recent research in Limerick city. In *Arch. Ire*, ii, 140-4 (1988).

        O'RAWE (Des). See GARVIN (Wilbert).

0764   Ordnance Survey of Ireland, Place Names Branch. Liostaí logainmneacha Contea Chill Chainnigh: County Kilkenny. Pp xiv, 94. Baile Átha Cliath: Oifig an tSoláthair, 1993.

0765   Ordnanace Survey of Ireland, Place Names Branch. Liostái logainmneacha Contae Uíbh Fhailí: County Offaly. Pp xiv, 76. Baile Átha Cliath: Oifig an tSoláthair, 1994.

0766   O'REGAN (Carol) and JONES (John). The O'Rorkes of Moylough. In *Galway Roots*, ii, 65-9 (1994).

        O'REGAN (Carol). See *Moylough* (1993).

0767   O'REILLY (Hugh). The O'Reillys of Annagh. In *Breifne*, vi, 395-407 (1986).

0768   Ó RIAIN (Pádraig). 'To be named is to exist': the instructive case of Achadh Bolg (Aghabulloge). In *Cork*, pp 45-61 (1993).
        History of church c.830-1750.

0769   O RÓNÁIN (Liam). Donegal local publications, 1994. In *Donegal Annual*, xlvi, 125-9 (1994).

0770   O'ROURKE (Kevin) and POLAK (Ben). Documents and sources: Property transactions in Ireland, 1708-1988: an introduction. In *Ir. Ec. & Soc. Hist.*, xxi, 58-71 (1994).

0771   O'Rourke strongholds of west Breifne and some other chieftaincies: photographs with historic notes and maps. Pp 74. [s.l.]: [s.n.], [1993].

0772   ORR (Jack). The Church of Ireland parish of Ballyphilip. In *Upper Ards Hist. Soc. Jn.*, i, 31 (1977).

0773   OSBOROUGH (W.N.). Puzzles from Irish law reporting history. In *The life of the law*, pp 89-111 (1993).

        Ó SEARCAIGH (Cathal). See *Tulach Beaglaoích inne agus ínníu* (1994).

0774   O'SHEA (Stephen). The O'Mahonys of Dunloe and Cullina. In *O'Mahony Jn.*, xii, 4-10 (1982)

0775   Ó SUILLEABHAIN (Seán). Surnames of County Leitrim. In *Ir. Roots*, 1994, no 4, pp 15-16 (1994).

0776   O'SULLIVAN (Michael). Monumental inscriptions at the abbey, Kilculliheen, Ferrybank, Co. Waterford. Part I: nos 1-88 (letters A-D). In *Decies*, xlix, 2-22 (1994); Part II, nos 89-165 (letters E to J) *Decies* l, 25-36 (1994).

0777   O'SULLIVAN (Patrick). Introduction: the creative migrant. In *The creative migrant*, pp 1-27 (1994).

0778   O'SULLIVAN (Patrick). The Irish joke. In *The creative migrant*, pp 57-82 (1994).

0779   O'TOOLE (Bridget). Sunlight falling across Annish: some writers of Derry and Inishowen. In *The glow upon the fringe*, pp 33-49 (1994).

0780   O'TOOLE (Jimmy). The Carlow gentry: what will the neighbours say! Pp xv, 234. Carlow: Jimmy O'Toole, 1993.

0781   PACK-BERESFORD (Susan E.). Christchurch, Carrowdore: 'the wee church on the hill'. Pp ix, 116. [s.l.]: [the author], [1994].
        County Down.

PALMER (J.J.N.). See *Royal Historical Society annual bibliography of British and Irish history* (1993, 1994).

0782   The parish of Skryne. In *A Window on the Past*, [i], 28-31 (1987).

0783   Parish registers database. In *Dublin Heritage Group. Annual Report*, v, 2-10 (1993); vi, 1-6 (1994).

0784   PARKINSON (Danny). Donnybrook graveyard c. 800-1993. Pp 66. Dublin: Dublin Family History Society, 1993. (Dublin Family History Society series).

0785   PARKINSON (Edward). Downpatrick. Paper read by Edward Parkinson before Down Y.M.C.A. on 24th March 1893. In *Lecale Miscellany*, v, 48 (1987).
        Continued from iv.

0786   PARSONS (Aisling). The early history of Tuam. In *Galway Roots*, ii, 86-8 (1994).

0787   PATTON (Marcus). Central Belfast: an historical gazetteer. Pp xiii, 354. Belfast: Ulster Architecural Heritage Society, 1993.

POLAK (Ben). See O'ROURKE (Kevin).

POWER (Denis). See *Archaeological inventory of County Cork* (1994).

0788   POWER (Dermot). The street where you live: Waterford placenames their origin and meaning. Pp 24. Waterford: Scoláire Bocht, 1993.

0789   POWER (Pat). Redcross - County Wicklow. In *Arklow Hist. Soc. Jn.*, pp 27-33 (1992/93).

0790   POWER (Patrick). A survey: some Wicklow maps 1500-1888. In *Wicklow*, pp 723-60 (1994).

0791   POWER (Patrick C.). Carrick-on-Suir. In *Tipperary county*, pp 80-8 (1993).

0792   PRENDERGAST (Des) and GARBETT (Rosaleen). Monumental inscriptions at Kilrossanty old graveyard Co Waterford. In *Decies*, xlviii, 17-32 (1993).

0793   PRENDERGAST (Mae). A short visit to the U.S.A. and the Irish connection. In *Galway Roots*, ii, 79-85 (1994).
        Includes extracts from *Tombstones of the Irish born* by Joseph Silinonte.

0794   PROCTER (Margaret). The Irish community in north-west England: a guide to local archive sources. Pp 31. Liverpool: Merseyside Record Office/University of Liverpool, Institute of Irish Studies, 1993.

0795   PROUDFOOT (L.J.). Dungarvan. In *Irish country towns*, pp 166-78 (1994).

        PROUDFOOT (L.J.). See GRAHAM (B.J.).

0796   Public Record Office of Northern Ireland. Guide to church records: an Irish genealogical source. Pp xix, 279. Belfast: Ulster Historical Foundation on behalf of [the] Public Record Office of Northern Ireland, 1994.

0797   Public Record Office of Northern Ireland. Guide to educational records. Pp 110. Belfast: Public Record Office of Northern Ireland, 1993.

0798   Public Record Office of Northern Ireland. Guide to sources for women's history. Pp 144. Belfast: Public Record Office of Northern Ireland, 1993.

0799   PYBURN (Jennifer). A history of the church at Crookhaven, Co. Cork, now called St Brendan the Navigator in the diocese of Cork. In *Mizen Jn.*, i, 60-70 (1993).

        QUINN (Brendan). See QUINN (J.F.).

0800   QUINN (J.F.). History of Mayo vol I. *Ed.* Brendan Quinn. Pp xvii, 447. Ballina (Co. Mayo): Brendan Quinn, 1993.
        Compilation of articles first published in *Western People*, 1931-1939.

0801   QUINN (Mary Kelly). The evolution of forestry in County Wicklow from prehistory to the present. In *Wicklow*, pp 823-54 (1994).

0802   RAFFERTY (Oliver P.). The Catholic bishops and revolutionary violence in Ireland. Some 19th and 20th century comparisions. In *Studies*, lxxxiii, 30-42 (1994).

0803   RAFFERTY (Oliver P.). Catholicism in Ulster, 1603-1983: an intrepretative history. Pp xiv, 306. London: Hurst, 1994.

0804   RAI (Milan). Columbus in Ireland. In *Race & Class*, xxxiv, no. 4, pp 25-34 (1993).
        Parallels between the effect of Columbus in the Americas and the British in Ireland.

0805   REECE (Bob). Introduction. In *Irish convict lives*, pp 1-12 (1993).

REES (Nicholas). See WHELAN (Bernadette).

0806   REEVES-SMYTH (Terence). Irish country houses. Pp 96. Belfast: Appletree, 1993. (Appletree guides).

0807   REFAUSSÉ (Raymond). Church of Ireland parish registers in the Representative Church Body Library, Dublin. In *Ir. Geneal.*, ix, 73-5 (1994).

REFAUSSÉ (Raymond). See *Directory of historic Dublin guilds* (1993).

REFAUSSÉ (Raymond). See *Directory of Irish archives* (1993).

0808   REGAN (Siobhan). Castlemore. In *Roscommon Hist. Soc. Jn.*, iv, 14 (1992).

0809   REID (Noel) ed. A table of Church of Ireland parochial records and copies. Pp 108. Naas: Irish Family History Society, 1994.

0810   REID (Noel). Timahoe graveyard [inscriptions]. In *Oughterany*, i, no. 1, pp 57-64 (1993).

0811   REILLY (Terry). Dear old Ballina. Pp 442. [s.l.]: [the author], 1993.

0812   REILLY (Tom). Some minutes from times past. In *Old Drogheda Soc. Jn.*, ix, 108-17 (1994).

0813   RENEHAN (Dan). Basket jobs. In *Ir. Railway Rec. Soc. Jn.*, xviii, 418-24 (1994).
Working conditions from 1919 onwards on the Irish railways.

0814   RIDLEY BARKER (J.K.S.). Cloyne cathedral. In *The book of Cloyne*, pp 49-54 (1994).

0815   ROBERTSON (June O'Carroll). A long way from Tipperary. Pp 256. Upton-upon-Severn: Images, 1994.
Carrol family, Tipperary.

0816   ROBINS (Joseph). Custom House people. Pp xiii, 206. Dublin: Institute of Public Administration, 1993.
'Portraits of fifty personalities ... associated with the Custom House' 1781-1992.

ROBINSON (Nicholas). See GRIFFIN (David J.).

0817   ROBINSON (Philip). Carrickfergus. In *Irish country towns*, pp 47-58 (1994).

0818   ROBINSON (Tim). Spas, am, Conamara, aistriú Gaeilge a rinne Liam Mac Con Iomair ar Space, time and Connemara le Tim Robinson (as a leabhar Connemara part 1: introduction and gazetter). Pp [4], 32. Baile Átha Cliath: Coscéim, 1993.

0819   ROCHE (Richard) and WILLIAMS (Tom). Tales of the Wexford coast: with a list of shipwrecks and groundings. Pp ix, 137. Enniscorthy: Duffry Press, 1993.

0820   ROCKETT (Kevin). The Irish migrant and film. In *The creative migrant*, pp 170-91 (1994).

0821   RODGER (Richard). Research in urban history: a classified survey of doctoral and masters' theses. Pp vii, 271. Aldershot, Hants: Scolar Press, 1994.

0822   ROGERS (Nuala). Ballymote: aspects through time. Pp 31. [s.l.]: [s.n.], 1993; 2nd ed. Pp 40, 1994.

0823   ROLSTON (Bill). The training ground: Ireland, conquest and decolonisation. In *Race & Class*, xxxiv, no. 4, pp 13-24 (1993).

0824   ROOM (Adrian). A dictionary of Irish place-names. Rev. ed. Pp 136. Belfast: Appletree Press, 1994.
          Previous ed.: 1986.

0825   Roscommon: an independent diocese and a separate kingdom. In *Roscommon Hist. Soc. Jn.*, iv, 51-3 (1992).

        ROSE (Petra). See AVERY (Michael).

0826   ROSS (Cecil). Dungiven parish church: 175th anniversary celebrations. In *Benbradagh*, xxiii, 3 (1993).

0827   ROSS (Marion). Crossing the seven streams: writers from Foyle to Erne. In *The glow upon the fringe*, pp 79-103 (1994).

0828   ROSSITER (Ann). Bringing the margin into the centre: a review of aspects of Irish women's emigration. In *Irish women's studies reader*, pp 177-202 (1993).

0829   ROSSITER (Nicky). A Wexford miscellany. Pp 160. Wexford: Wexford Historical Publications, 1994.

        ROWAN (Alistair). See CASEY (Christine).

0830   ROWAN (Ann Martha). A database of Irish architects 1700-1950. In *Ir. Georgian Soc. Bull.*, xxxvi, 75-7 (1994)

0831   Royal Arch Purple Order, Research Group. History of the Royal Arch Purple Order. Pp 213. [Belfast]: [Royal Arch Purple Order], [1993?].
          1690-1993.

0832   Royal Historical Society annual bibliography of British and Irish history: publications of 1992. *Ed.* Barbara English and J.J.N. Palmer. Pp x, 327. Oxford: Oxford University Press, 1993.

0833   Royal Historical Society annual bibliography of British and Irish history publications of 1993. *Ed.* Katharine Beedham, Barbara English, J.J.N. Palmer. Pp xi, 305. Oxford: Oxford University Press, 1994.

0834   RUANE (Kevin M.). The Patrician brothers in Mallow ... 1879 to 1994. In *Mallow Field Club Jn.*, xii, 5-28 (1994).

0835   RYAN (Brendan). A land by the river of God: a history of Ferbane parish: from earliest times to c.1900. Pp [6], xiii, 348. [s.l.]: St Mel's Diocesan Trust, 1994.

0836   RYAN (Christopher). Ballinteer: a new family history branch. In *Irish Family History*, i, no. 1, pp 24-8 (1993).
        Brief history of Ballinteer.

0837   RYAN (Frank). A history of coopering. In *Arch. Ire.*, vii, no. 2, pp 27-30 (1993).

0838   RYAN (Hazel A.) An ecclesiastical site at Cloontogher, Kilteevan. In *Roscommon Hist. Soc. Jn.*, iv, 45-7 (1992).

0839   RYAN (James). St Mary's church, Thurles. [Gravestone inscriptions]. In *Ir. Family Hist.*, x, 77-119 (1994).

0840   RYAN (Liam). The GAA - 'part of what we are': a centenary assessment. In *The Furrow*, xxxv, 752-64 (1984).

0841   RYAN (Martin). Magh Adhair, inauguration place of the kings of Thomond. In *The Other Clare*, i, 11-12 (1977).

0842   RYAN (Michael), ed. Irish archaeology illustrated. Pp 224. Dublin: Country House, 1994.
        Originally published 1991 as 'The illustrated archaeology of Ireland'.

0843   RYAN (Patrick M.). The Ryans - who are they? In *Oola Past & Present*, ii, 33-5 (1993).

0844   RYNNE (Colin). The archaeology of Cork city and harbour: from the earliest times to industrialisation. Pp viii, 110. Cork: Collins Press, 1993.

        RYNNE (Etienne). See KILBRIDE-JONES (Howard E.).

0845   SALTER (Mike). Castles and stronghouses of Ireland. Pp 160. Malvern (Worcs): Folly Publications, 1993.

0846   Sandyford, Dundrum, Ballawley - and surrounding areas from times past [compiled by Local history group, Sandyford ICA guild, Irish Countrywomen's Association]. Pp 68. [Sandyford, Co. Dublin]: [Sandyford ICA Guild], [1993?].
        Cover title: Beneath the granite throne.

0847   SAVAGE (Ben) and FAGAN (Terry). All around the Diamond. Pp 47. Dublin: North Inner City Folklore Project, [1994?].
        Gloucester Diamond, Dublin city.

        SAVAGE (Ben). See FAGAN (Terry).

0848   SAWYER (Roger). 'We are but women': women in Ireland's history. Pp xix, 210. London: Routledge, 1993.

0849   SCHNAULBELT (Joseph C.). The Irish Augustinians in North America, 1794-1992: the Irish Augustinian mission to the United States of America. In *The Irish Augustinians in Rome*, pp 83-111 (1994).

SCHOFIELD (Carey). See *Ireland* (1994).

0850   SCOTT (C.W.). History of the Fastnet Rock lighthouses. Pp [8], 56. Ballydehob, Co. Cork: Schull Books, 1993.
     Facsimile reprint of 1906 edition.

SCUFFIL (Catherine). See *By the sign of the Dolphin* (1993).

SEXTON (Sean). See *Ireland* (1994).

0851   SHAW (William). Cullbackey and district. Pp 16. Ballymena: Ballymena Borough Council, 1993. (Ballymena Borough research series).
     Reproduced from the magazine of the Cullybackey United Free Church, 1912.

0852   SHEEDY (Kieran). The Clare elections. Pp 886. Dun Laoghaire: Bauroe Publications, 1993.

0853   SHEEHAN (C.) et al. The city wall at 118-119 Parade Quay, Waterford. In *Decies*, 1, 8-16 (1994).

SHERRY (Brian). See *Along the Black Pig's Dyke* [1993?].

SHERWOOD-SMITH (Caroline). See *"Mighty monsters in Marsh's"* (1993).

0854   SHIELDS (Hugh). Narrative singing in Ireland: lays, ballads, come-all-yes and other songs. Pp ix, 283. Blackrock, Co. Dublin: Irish Academic Press, 1993.

0855   SHIELDS (Hugh). The woodcuts of Irish ballad sheets, 1626-1960. In *Images, identities and ideologies*, pp 207-26 (1994).

0856   SHINE (Michael). Ballybeg priory. Parts 1-2. In *Mallow Field Club Jn.*, xi, 84-112 (1993); xii, 89-114 (1994).

0857   SIGGINS (Albert). Co. Roscommon's holy wells. In *Roscommon Hist. Soc. Jn.*, iv, 76-7 (1992).

0858   SIGGINS (Albert). Heads and tails of stone. In *Roscommon Hist. Soc. Jn.*, iii, 45-8 (1990).
     Sheela-na-Gigs and stone heads 'hitherto unrecorded.'

0859   SIMMS (Anngret). Kells. In *Irish country towns*, pp 21-33 (1994).

0860   SIMMS (Anngret). The origin of Irish towns. In *Irish country towns*, pp 11-20 (1994).

0861 SIMPSON (Lesley). Down County Museum: a source for local history. In *Lecale Miscellany*, xi, 28-30 (1993).

0862 SIMPSON (M. Lesley). Some tobacco pipes in Down Museum. In *Lecale Miscellany*, vii, 50-52 (1989).
Pipes from the 17th to 19th centuries.

0863 SKEHAN (Walter G.). Cashel & Emly heritage. Pp vi, 463. [Thurles, Co. Tipperary]: Abbey Books, 1993.

0864 Sligo: sources of local history: a catalogue of the local history collection, with an introduction and guide to sources. *Ed.* John C. McTernan. New ed. Pp xxii, 257. Sligo: Sligo County Library, 1994.
Previous ed.: 1988.

0865 SMAL (Chris) ed. Ancient Rathdown and St Crispin's cell: a uniquely historic landscape. Pp 48. Greystones, Co. Wicklow: the Friends of Historic Rathdown, 1993.

0866 SMITH (Albert). A brief history of Kells, Co. Kilkenny. Pp 24. [s.l.]: [the author], [1993].

0867 SMITH (Geoff). Theses and dissertations on British and Irish labour history. In *Labour History Rev.*, lviii, no. 2, pp 9-13 (1993).

0868 SMITH (Geoff). Theses and dissertations on British and Irish labour history 1993. In *Labour History Rev.*, lix, no. 2, pp 3-9 (1994).

0869 SMITH (Graeme). My love is in America: migration and Irish music. In *The creative migrant*, pp 221-36 (1994).

0870 SMYTH (Hazel P.). The town of the road: the story of Booterstown. [2nd ed.]. Pp [6], 111. Bray: Pale Publishing, 1994.
Previous ed.: 1971.

0871 SMYTH (Jim). The making and undoing of a confessional state: Ireland 1660-1829. [Review article]. In *Jn. Eccles. Hist.*, xliv, 506-13 (1993).

0872 SMYTH (Jim). Nationalist nightmares and postmodernist utopias: Irish society in transition. In *Hist. Europ. Ideas*, xvi, 157-63 (1993).

0873 SMYTH (John). A short history of the Irish National Foresters. In *Carloviana*, xl, 10-11 (1992/93).

0874 SMYTH (William J.). The making of Ireland: agendas and perspectives in cultural geography. In *An historical geography of Ireland*, pp 399-438 (1993).

0875 SNODGRASS (Lee). Kilmoe church. In *Mizen Jn.*, ii, 41-4 (1994).

0876 SPEERS (Arthur). 300 years of the Brookes and other ascendancy familes at Lough Eske. In *Donegal Annual*, xlv, 94-103 (1993).

0877 'A special correspondent'. Bibliophiles diary number five. The history of the book from an Irish perspective. In *Long Room*, xxxviii, 5-14 (1993).

0878   STEVENS (David). The Protestant idea of liberty - three pamphlets. In *The Furrow*, xxxvii, 12-20 (1986).
Three Field Day pamphlets by Marianne Elliot, Robert McCartney and Terence Brown.

STOCKMAN (Gerard). See Ó MAININ (Michéal B.).

0879   Strangers to that land: British perceptions of Ireland from the Reformation to the famine. *Ed.* Andrew Hadfield and John McVeagh. Pp xii, 315. Gerrards Cross: Colin Smythe, 1994. (Ulster editions and monographs, 5).

0880   Surnames of County Down. In *Ir. Roots*, 1993, no. 2, pp 30-1 (1993).

0881   SWEENEY (Loughlin). Clann tSuibhne. In *Dun Laoghaire Geneal. Soc. Jn.*, ii, 113-24 (1993).

0882   SWIFT (Cathy). John O'Donovan and the framing of early medieval Ireland in the nineteenth century. In *Bullán*, i, no. 1, pp 91-103 (1994).
John O'Donovan employed by the Ordnance Survey of Ireland, 1830-42.

0883   SWORDS (Liam). The Irish continental colleges. In *O'Mahony Jn.*, xii, 14-18 (1982).

0884   TAYLOR (Alice). The night before Christmas. Pp 153. Dingle: Brandon, 1994.

0885   TAYLOR (Dolores). Taylors and Fosters. In *Gateway to the Past*, i, no 3, pp 145-9 (1994).

0886   TAYLOR (Serina). My ancestral home - Marlay Park. In *Irish Family History,* i, no. 1, pp 17-19 (1993).

0887   THACKER (Christopher). The genius of gardening: the history of gardens in Britain and Ireland. Pp 352. London: Weidenfeld & Nicolson, 1994,

0888   THOMAS (Timothy). Sources for Irish genealogy in the India Office records. In *Aspects of Irish genealogy*, pp 177-89 [1993].

0889   THUILLIER (David). Profile of Millstreet town. In *Ir. Roots*, 1992, no. 1, pp 19-22 (1992).

0890   TIERNEY (Mark). Dom Columba Marmion: a biography. Pp 283. Blackrock, Co. Dublin: Columba Press, 1994.

0891   TONER (Gregory). An eilimint *íneán i logainmneacha Reachlainne. In *Ainm*, vi, 32-7 (1994/95).
Placenames on Rathlin Island.

0892   Traces of county Wexford's past. [*Ed.* Mary Tubridy and Edward Culleton]; [text *ed.* Michael Tubridy]. Pp 94. [s.l.]: [Wexford Organisation for Rural Development], c. 1994.

0893   TREACY (Brendan) and MURPHY (Nancy). Nenagh yesterday. Pp 144. Nenagh: Relay Publications, 1993.

0894   Treasures from the National Library of Ireland. *Ed.* Noel Kissane. Ppx, 243. [Drogheda]: Boyne Valley Honey Company, 1994.

0895   TRODD (Valentine). Midlanders: chronicle of a midland parish. Pp vi, 226. Banagher: Scéal Publications, 1994.
    Banagher, Co. Offaly.

0896   TROHY (Anthony). Holy Trinity Church: (parish of Kilkeevan, Castlerea). In *Roscommon Hist. Soc. Jn.*, v, 18 (1994).

0897   TROY (B.). The cemetery, Church of Our Lady of the Most Holy Rosary, Midleton, Co. Cork gravestone inscriptions. Pp [4], 224. [Midleton, Co.Cork]: [the author], 1994.

    TUBRIDY (Mary). See *Traces of county Wexford's past* (c1994).

    TUBRIDY (Michael). See *Traces of county Wexford's past* (c1994).

    TUITE (Breeda). See MITCHELL (Frank).

0898   Tulach Beaglaoích ínne agus ínníu = Tullaghbegley past and present. [Research and text Cathal Ó Searcaigh]. Pp 68. [Fál Carrach]: [Cumann Staire], [1993?].
    Falcarragh, Co. Donegal; parallel text in English and Irish.

0899   TURNER (Brian S.). The Methodist connexion: Downpatrick and the story of two men called Smith. In *Lecale Miscellany*, ix, 2-7 (1991).

0900   TURPIN (John). Irish art and design education. In *Ir. Arts Rev. Yearbk.*, pp 209-16 (1994).

0901   TWEED (Carol Robinson). Taney: portrait of a parish: a social and historical profile of the parish of Taney in Dublin. Pp 136. Dublin: Select Vestry, Taney Parish, 1994.

0902   Two holy wells in County Roscommon: their relation to the festival of Lughnasa. In *Roscommon Hist. Soc. Jn.*, iv, 56-9 (1992).

0903   Ua SÚILLEABHÁIN (Seán). Gaeilge na Mumhan. In *Stair na Gaeilge*, pp 479-538 (1994).

    UÍBH EACHACH (Vivian). See Mac RAOIS (Breandán).

0904   Ulster Architectural Heritage Society: Hillsborough Castle. Pp 48. [Belfast]: Ulster Architectural Heritage Society, 1993. (Ulster houses series).

    UPTON (John). See MOLLAN (Charles).

0905   VANCE (Norman). Presbyterian culture and revival. In *Presb. Hist. Soc. of Ire. Bull.*, xxii, 16-19 (1993).

    WADDELL (John). See FEEHAN (John).

    WAGNER (Paul). See MILLER (Kerby).

0906   WALKER (Simon). Hillsborough: an illustrated history and companion. Pp 91. Donaghadee: Cottage Publications, 1994.

0907   WALL (Mervyn). Some memories of the borough. In *Dun Laoghaire Jn.*, i, [13-21] (1990).

0908   WALLACE (Martin). A little history of Ireland. Pp 60. Belfast: Appletree Press, 1994.

        WALLIS (Helen). See *Historian's guide to early British maps* (1994).

0909   WALSH (Brendan M.). Wage convergence and integrated labour markets: Ireland and Britain, 1841-1991. Pp 21, [3]. Dublin: University College Dublin, Department of Economics, 1994. (Working paper (University College Dublin Centre for Economic Research) WP 94/6).

0910   WALSH (Gerry). Preliminary report on the archaeological excavations on the summit of Croagh Patrick, 1994. In *Cathair na Mart*, xiv, 1-10 (1994).

0911   WALSH (Micheline Kerney). The Irish College of Madrid. In *Seanchas Ardmhacha*, xv, no. 2, pp 39-50 (1993).

0912   WALSH (Micheline Kerney). Ulster families on the continent. In *Ulster Local Studies*, xv, no. 2, pp 22-33 (1993).

0913   WALSH (Pat). Irish republicanism and socialism: the politics of the republican movement 1905 to 1994. Pp 280. Belfast: Athol Books, 1994.

        WALSH (Stephanie)., See BARY (Valerie).

0914   WALSH (Thomas P.). Dunbrody through the ages. In *Old Wexford Soc. Jn.*, vi, 18-37 (1976/77).
        Cistercian abbey in Co. Wexford.

0915   WALTON (Julian C.). Surnames of County Waterford. In *Ir. Roots*, 1992, no. 1, pp 14-16 (1992).

0916   WARD (Alan). Models of government and Anglo-Irish relations. In *Albion*, xx, 19-42 (1988).

0917   WARD (Alan J.). The Irish constitutional tradition: responsible government and modern Ireland, 1782-1992. Pp viii, 412. Blackrock, Co. Dublin: Irish Academic Press, 1994.

0918   WARD (Margaret). 'Suffrage first - above all else!': an account of the Irish suffrage movement. In *Irish women's studies reader*, pp 20-44 (1993).

0919   WARD (Michael). Limekilns and lime usage. In *Old Drogheda Soc. Jn.*, ix, 42-7 (1994).

0920   WARNER (Richard). The 'prehistoric' Irish annals: fable or history? In *Arch. Ire.*, iv, 30-33 (1990).

0921   WATSON (Seosamh). Gaeilge na hAlban. In *Stair na Gaeilge*, pp 661-702 (1994).

0922   WEAVER (Jack W.). Sociolinguistics of Scotch-Irish speech in Appalachia. In *The Scotch-Irish and Hiberno English language and culture*, pp 12-19 (1993).

0923   WEBSTER (Gillian). Descent of the Mahons of Cavetown, Co. Roscommon. In *Roscommon Hist. Soc. Jn.*, iii, 42-3 (1990).

0924   WEIR (Anthony). Potency and sin: Ireland and the phallic continuum. In *Arch. Ire.*, iv, 52-6 (1990).

0925   WEIR (Hugh W.L.). O'Connor: people and places. Pp 99. Whitegate, (Co. Clare): Ballinakella Press, 1994.

0926   WEIR (Mary). Clay pipes. In *The Bell*, v, 38-9 (1994).

0927   WHELAN (Bernadette), HOLMES (Michael), REES (Nicholas). Ireland and the third world: a historical perspective. In *Ir. Stud. in International Affairs*, v, 107-19 (1994).

0928   WHELAN (Kevin). The bases of regionalism. In *Culture in Ireland - regions*, pp 5-62 (1993).

0929   WHELAN (Kevin). Clio agus Caitlín Ní Uallacháin. In *Oghma*, 2, pp 9-19 (1990).

0930   WHELAN (Kevin). Enniscorthy. In *Irish country towns*, pp 71-82 (1994).

0931   WHELAN (Kevin). The geography of hurling. In *Hist. Ire.*, i, no.1, pp 27-31 (1993).

0932   WHELAN (Kevin). The recent writing of Irish history. In *U.C.D. Hist. Rev.*, v, 27-35 (1991).

0933   WHELAN (Kevin). Settlement patterns in the west of Ireland in the pre-famine period. In *Decoding the landscape*, pp 60-78 (1994).

0934   WHITE (Harry). Church music and musicology in Ireland: an afterword. In *Music and the church*, pp 333-7 (1993).

       WHITEFIELD (Niamh). See Ó CEALLAIGH (Séamus).

0935   WHOLLEY (Diarmuid). A conducted tour of Timoleague Friary on Monday June 20th 1983. In *Timoleague Hist. Soc. Newsheet*, ii, [1-8] (1986).

0936   WHYTE (Edward). Parish priests of Cloughjordan. In *Cloughjordan Heritage*, i, 5-7 (1985).

0937   WILLIAMS (Fionnuala). The Black Pig and linear earthworks. In *Emania*, iii, 12-19 (1987).
       Folklore of the Black Pig in relation to linear earthworks and other physical features.

0938   WILLIAMS (Miriam). Kilfane Church of Ireland. In *In the Shadow of the Steeple*, iv, 8-18 (1994).

0939   WILLIAMS (Nicholas). An Mhanainnis. In *Stair na Gaeilge*, pp 703-44 (1994).

0940   WILLIAMS (Nicholas). Na canúintí a theacht chun solais. In *Stair na Gaeilge*, pp 447-8 (1994).

        WILLIAMS (Tom). See ROCHE (Richard).

0941   WILLIAMSON (David). American presidents of Irish descent. In *Aspects of Irish genealogy*, pp 190-200 [1993].

0942   WILSON (Anthony M.). Index to Lecale Miscellany vols. 1 to 10, 1983-1992. In *Lecale Miscellany*, xi, 45-50 (1993).

0943   WILSON (Anthony M.). Some Downpatrick maps. In *Lecale Miscellany*, viii, 27-36 (1990).

        WITHEROW (Thomas). See CROSKERY (Thomas).

        WITHERS (Bente). See WITHERS (Paul).

0944   WITHERS (Paul) & WITHERS (Bente). British coin-weights: a corpus of the coin-weights made for use in England, Scotland and Ireland. Pp 359. Llanfyllin, Powys: Galata Print, 1993.

0945   WITZ (Cornelia). and HÜTTENBERGER (Peter). Grossbritannien-Ploetz: Geschichte Grossbritanniens und Irlands zum Nachschlagen. 3rd ed. Pp 223. Freburg im Breisgau: Ploetz, 1993.
        History of Great Britain and Ireland for reference.

0946   Woodford Heritage Indexation Project. Gráig na Muilte Iarainn = Woodford: a guide to its sights. Pp 19. [Woodford, Co. Galway]: Woodford Heritage Indexation Project, [1994?].

0947   WOODS (C.J.). Theses on Irish history completed in Irish universities, 1992. In *I.H.S.*, xxviii, 440-1 (1993).

0948   WOODS (C.J.). Theses on Irish history completed in Irish universities, 1993. In *I.H.S.*, xxix, 250-1 (1994).

0949   WREN (Jimmy). Crinan-Dublin: a history of 13 north inner city streets. Pp [4], 85. Dublin: North Inner City Folklore Project, 1993.

0950   WYLIE (Mona). Saint Patrick's churchyard, Clonfeacle. In *Dúiche Néill*, viii, 78-118 (1993).
        Includes list of gravestone inscriptions compiled by George and Mona Wylie.

0951   WYLIE (Mona). St Patrick's Church, Clonfeacle. In *Dúiche Néill*, viii, 67-77 (1993).

0952   Yesterday once more: a stroll down memory lane: Fermanagh, - Donegal, - Germany. Pp 131. [Enniskillen?]: [Fermanagh District Council?], [1994?].

0953   ALLEN (J. Romilly). Celtic art in pagan and christian times. Pp xviii, 315.
        London: Studio Editions, 1993.
        Facsimile reprint of 1904 edition.

0954   BATTAGLIA (Frank). A common background to "Lai de Graelent" and
        "Noínden Ulad"? In *Emania*, xi, 41-8 (1993).

0955   BOURKE (Cormac). Antiquities from the river Blackwater II, Iron age
        metalwork. In *U.J.A.*, lvi, 109-13 (1993).

0956   BOURKE (Edward). Glass vessels of the first nine centuries A.D. in Ireland.
        In *R.S.A.I. Jn.*, cxxiv, 163-209 (1994).

0957   BRADLEY (John). Excavations at Moynagh Lough, Co. Meath. In *Ríocht na
        Midhe*, ix, no. 1, pp 158-69 (1994/95).

0958   BREEN (Martin). The finding of prehistoric stone artifacts in the Doolin area.
        In *The Other Clare*, xvii, 43 (1993).

0959   BRENNAN (J.H.). A guide to megalithic Ireland. Pp 202. London:
        Aquarian/Thorsons, 1994.

0960   BRIGGS (Stephen). The discovery and description of trench mines at
        Derricarhoon Td, Co. Cork, in 1846. In *Jn. Ir. Archael.*, ii, 33-9 (1984).

0961   BRINDLEY (Anna). Irish prehistory: an introduction. Pp 47. Dublin:
        Country House in association with the National Museum of Ireland, 1994.

        BUCKLEY (Victor M.). See CONDIT (Tom).

0962   BUDD (P.) [et al]. The sources for prehistoric bronze production in Ireland.
        In *Antiquity*, lxviii, 518-24 (1994).

0963   BURL (Aubrey). From Carnac to Callanish: the prehistoric stone rows and
        avenues of Britain, Ireland and Brittany. Pp xvi, 286. New Haven: Yale
        University Press, 1993.

0964   CAHILL (Mary). Some unrecorded bronze age gold ornaments from Co.
        Limerick. In *North Munster Antiq. Jn.*, xxxv, 5-23 (1993/94).

0965   CAULFIELD (Séamus). Forest clearance and land use in Mayo around 3000
        B.C. In *Ir. Forestry*, xxxviii, 92-100 (1981).

0966   CHARLES-EDWARDS (T.M.). Early Irish and Welsh kinship. Pp xvi, 597.
        Oxford: Clarendon Press, 1993.

0967   CLINTON (Mark). Souterrain at Loughcrew, near Oldcastle, County Meath.
        In *R.S.A.I. Jn.*, cxxiii, 120-6 (1993).

0968   COFFEY (Thomas). Field notes. In *The Other Clare*, xviii, 13-14 (1994).

PREHISTORIC

0969   CONDIT (Tom) and BUCKLEY (Victor M.). The 'Doon' of Drumsna - gateways to Connacht. In *Emania*, vi, 12-14 (1989).

CONDIT (Tom). See GROGAN (Eoin).

CONWAY (M.G.). See SIMPSON (D.D.A.).

0970   COONEY (Gabriel) and O'KEEFE (Tadhg). A collection of prehistoric axe heads at St. Patrick's College, Carlow. In *R.S.A.I. Jn.*, cxxiv, 210-13 (1994).

0971   COONEY (Gabriel) and GROGAN (Eoin). Irish prehistory: a social perspective. Pp xiii, 251. Dublin: Wordwell, 1994.

0972   COONEY (Gabriel). A sense of place in Irish prehistory. In *Antiquity*, lxvii, 632-41 (1993).
Response to Peter Woodman's survey article in *Antiquity*, lxvi, 295-314 (1992). Followed by response from Peter Woodman.

0973   DAVIES (K. Mary). A note on the location of the Roman burial site at Bray, Co. Wicklow. In *Arch. Ire.*, iii, 108-09 (1989).

0974   ELLIS (Peter Berresford). Celt and Saxon: the struggle for Britain AD 410-937. Pp 288. London: Constable, 1993.

0975   EOGAN (George) and ROCHE (Helen). A grooved ware wooden structure at Knowth, Boyne valley, Ireland. In *Antiquity*, lxviii, 322-30 (1994).

0976   The excavation of St. Vogue's well & dolmen (site of) at Carnsore, Co. Wexford. In *Old Wexford Soc. Jn.*, vi, 55-60 (1976/77).

0977   FRAHER (Willie). The megalithic tomb at Mine Head. In *Ardmore Jn.*, x, 7-9 (1993).

GIBBONS (Michael). See HIGGINS (Jim).

0978   GIBSON (Alex) [et al]. Excavations at the Sarn-y-bryn-caled cursus complex, Welshpool, Powys, and the timber circles of Great Britain and Ireland. In *Proc. Prehistoric Soc.*, lx, 143-223 (1994).

0979   GREEN (Miranda). Pagan Celtic religion: archaeology and myth. In *Cymmrodorian Soc. Trans*, pp 13-28 (1990).

0980   GROGAN (Eoin) and CONDIT (Tom). The later prehistoric landscape of south-east Clare. In *The Other Clare*, xviii, 8-12 (1994).

GROGAN (Eoin). See COONEY (Gabriel).

0981   HALL (Michael). The Cruthin controversy. Pp 32. Newtownabbey: Island Publications, 1994. (Island pamphlets, 7).
Picts in Ulster.

0982   HARVEY (Anthony). The Ogham inscriptions and the Roman alphabet: two traditions or one? In *Arch. Ire.*, iv, 13-14 (1990).

0983   HERITY (Michael). Motes and mounds at royal sites in Ireland. In *R.S.A.I. Jn.*, cxxiii, 127-51 (1993).

0984   HIGGINS (Jim) and GIBBONS (Michael). Prehistoric find on Omey Island. In *Connemara*, i, no. 1, pp 50-3 (1993).

0985   HODGERS (Dan). The Salterstown surface collection project. In *Louth Arch. Soc. Jn.*, xxiii, no. 2, pp 240-68 (1994).

0986   KELLY (Dorothy). Cross at Ogulla, County Roscommon. In *R.S.A.I. Jn.*, cxxiv, 213-4 (1994).

0987   KELLY (Dorothy). Some remains of high crosses in the west of Ireland. In *R.S.A.I. Jn.*, cxxiii, 152-63 (1993).

0988   KENNEDY (Gerry). Ancient Ireland: the user's guide. Pp 112. Killala, Co. Mayo: Morrigan Books, 1994.

0989   KILBRIDE-JONES (Howard). Metalworking practices in early Ireland. In *Arch. Ire.*, viii, no. 3, pp 19-21 (1994).

0990   KING (John). The Celtic druid's year: seasonal cycles of the ancient Celts. Pp 240. London: Blandford, 1994.

0991   LAWLESS (Christy). Carrowmacloughlin ancient settlement, Turlough, Co. Mayo, cashel, ringfort and hut sites. In *Cathair na Mart*, xiii, 53-71 (1993).

0992   LAWLESS (Christy). Primitive stone tools and fulachta fiadh in the Cashel/Lack valley, Turlough, Co. Mayo. In *Cathair na Mart*, xiv, 16-26 (1994).

0993   LENNON (Anne-Marie). Excavation of a ringfort, Raheens 1, near Carrigaline, Co. Cork. In *Cork Hist. Soc. Jn.*, xcviii, 75-89 (1993).

0994   LENNON (Anne-Marie). Summary report on excavation of ringfort, Raheens no. 2, near Carrigaline, Co. Cork. In *Cork Hist. Soc. Jn.*, xcix, 47-65 (1994).

0995   LOHAN (Máire). A hilltop cairn on Benlevy, near Clonbur, Co. Galway. In *Galway Arch. Soc. Jn.*, xlv, 157-60 (1993).

0996   LOHAN (Máire). Moytura Conga: a mythical and ritual landscape. In *Cathair na Mart*, xiii, 16-31 (1993).

0997   LYNCH (Ann) and Ó DONNABHÁIN (Barra). Poulnabrone portal tomb. In *The Other Clare*, xviii, 5-7 (1994).

0998   LYNN (Chris). Navan Fort - home of gods and goddesses? In *Arch. Ire.*, vii, no. 1, pp 17-21 (1993).

0999   LYNN (C.J.). A bibliography of northern linear earthworks. In *Emania*, vi, 18-21 (1989).

1000   LYNN (C.J.). Hostels, heroes and tales: further thoughts on the Navan mound. In *Emania*, xii, 5-20 (1994).

1001   LYNN (C.J.). House-urns in Ireland? In *U.J.A.*, lvi, 70-7 (1993).

1002   LYNN (C.J.). An interpretation of "The Dorsey". In *Emania*, vi, 5-10 (1989).
         A group of earthworks in Co. Armagh.

1003   LYNN (C.J.). Lagore, County Meath and Ballinderry No. 1, County Westmeath crannogs: some possible structural reinterpretations. In *Jn. Ir. Archaeol.*, iii, (1985/86).

1004   LYNN (C.J.). Linear earthworks in Drummiller, Co. Down and Goragh, Co. Antrim. In *Emania*, vi, 15-16 (1989).

1005   LYNN (C.J.). Some 'early' ring-forts and crannogs. In *Jn. Ir. Archaeol.*, i, 47-58 (1983).

1006   McCORMICK (Finbar). Excavations at Iona 1988. In *U.J.A.*, lvi, 78-108 (1993).

1007   McHUGH (Anna). Caherlistrane, long, long before our time. In *Galway Roots*, ii, 6-8 (1994).

1008   MacMAHON (Michael). A wedge-tomb and other monuments near Lough Graney in N.E. Clare. In *Galway Arch. Soc. Jn.*, xxxviii, 88-9 (1981/82).

1009   McMANN (Jean). Forms of power: dimensions of an Irish megalithic landscape. In *Antiquity*, lxviii, 525-44 (1994).

1010   McMANN (Jean). Loughcrew: the cairns: a guide to an ancient Irish landscape. Pp 48. Oldcastle: After Hours Books, 1994.

1011   MALLORY (J.P.). The fort of the Ulster tales. In *Emania*, xii, 28-38 (1994).

1012   MALLORY (J.P.). The origins of the Irish. In *Jn. Ir. Archaeol.*, ii, 65-9 (1984).
         Summary of opinion expressed at a seminar held by the Irish Association of Professional Archaeologists.

1013   MALLORY (J.P.). Trial excavations at Haughey's Fort. In *Emania*, iv, 5-20 (1988).

1014   MEIGHAN (I.G.) [et al.]. Trace element and isotopic provenancing of north Antrim porcellanites: Portrush-Tievebulliagh-Brockley (Rathlin Island). In *U.J.A.*, lvi, 25-9 (1993).

1015   MONK (M.A.). Evidence from macroscopic plant remains for crop husbandry in prehistoric and early historic Ireland: a review. In *Jn. Ir. Archael.*, iii, 31-6 (1985/86).

         MOORE (D.). See SIMPSON (D.D.A.).

1016   MORRIS (Henry). The Belladooan skeleton. In *North Mayo Hist. Jn.*, iii, no. 1, pp 69-72 (1992/93).

1017   MOUNT (Charles). Aspects of ritual deposition in the late neolithic and beaker periods at Newgrange, Co. Meath. In *Proc. Prehistoric Soc.*, lx, 433-43 (1994).

1018   NAPIER (J.C,). Sodisinam. In *Lecale Miscellany*, vi, 24-5 (1988).
        An old Irish gloss in the Ravenna cosmiography.

1019   NAPIER (James Christopher). Claudius Ptolomaeus and the Picts. In *Lecale Miscellany*, v, 31-3 (1987).
        An early description of Ireland.

1020   The Navan landscape. In *Curr. Archaeol.*, xii, 53-5 (1993).

        NORTHOVER (Peter). See SHERIDAN (Alison).

1021   O'BRIEN (Elizabeth). Iron age burial practices in Leinster: continuity and change. In *Emania*, vii, 37-42 (1990).

1022   O'BRIEN (William). Altar tomb and the prehistory of Mizen. In *Mizen Jn.*, i, 19-26 (1993).

1023   O'BRIEN (William). Bronze age copper mining on Mount Gabriel. In *Mizen Jn.*, ii, 27-32 (1994).

        Ó DONNABHÁIN (Barra). See LYNCH (Ann).

1024   O'DONOVAN (Patrick). An Cladh Ruadh, a travelling earthwork from Co. Kerry. In *Emania*, iii, 20-21 (1987).

1025   Ó DUIBHIR (Siomon). Music of the late bronze age in Ireland. In *Arch. Ire.*, ii, 135-6 (1988).

1026   Ó FLOINN (Raghnall). A bog burial from Derrymaquirk and other related finds from County Roscommon. In *Roscommon Hist. Soc. Jn.*, iv, 71-2 (1992).

        O'KEEFE (Tadhg). See COONEY (Gabriel).

1027   O'LEARY (Paddy). The Cape Clear passage tomb. In *Mizen Jn.*, ii, 37-40 (1994).

1028   O'LEARY (Paddy) and TWOHIG (Elizabeth Shee). A possible iron age pillarstone on Cape Clear, Co, Cork. In *Cork Hist. Soc. Jn.*, xcviii, 133-40 (1993).

1029   O LOCHLAINN (Mícheál). Society structures in ancient Ireland. In *An Aisling*, iii, 61-2 (1991).

1030   O'SULLIVAN (Muiris). Megalithic art in Ireland. Pp 46. Dublin: Town House and Country House, 1993.

1031   O'SULLIVAN (Muiris). Recent investigations at Knockroe passage tomb. In *R.S.A.I. Jn.*, cxxiii, 5-18 (1993).

1032   O'SULLIVAN (Muiris). A stylistic revolution in the megalithic art of the Boyne valley. In *Arch. Ire.*, iii, 138-42 (1989).

1033   POWELL (Andrew B.). Newgrange: science or symbolism. In *Proc. Prehistoric Soc.*, lx, 85-96 (1994).

1034   POWER (Catryn). Reconstructing patterns of health and dietary change in Irish prehistoric populations. In *U.J.A.*, lvi, 9-17 (1993).

1035   RAFTERY (Barry). Pagan Celtic Ireland: the enigma of the Irish iron age. Pp 240. London: Thames & Hudson, 1994.

1036   RAMSDEN (Peter G.). Prehistoric archaeology in the Burrin river valley Carlow, Ireland. In *Carloviana*, xxxix, 18-21, 27 (1991/92).

1037   The rich history of royal Tara. In *A window on the past*, [i], 2-4 (1987).

ROCHE (Helen). See EOGAN (George).

1038   ROCHE (John). The influence of Ireland on Roman Britain ... cursus unicus? In *Arch. Ire.*, vii, no. 1, pp 7-9 (1993).

RONAYNE (Margaret). See TWOHIG (Elizabeth Shee).

1039   RYAN (Gerard). Archaeological monuments of south Clare. In *The Other Clare*, i, 3-8 (1977).

1040   RYAN (Michael). Metal craftsmanship in early Ireland. Pp 47. Dublin: Town House and Country House, 1993.

1041   SHERIDAN (Alison) and NORTHOVER (Peter). A beaker period copper dagger blade from the Sillees river near Ross Lough, Co. Fermanagh. In *U.J.A.*, lvi, 61-9 (1993).

1042   SIMPSON (D.D.A.), CONWAY (M.G.) and MOORE (D.). The excavation of a shell midden at Minnis North, Co. Antrim. *U.J.A.*, lvi, 114-9 (1993).

1043   SIMPSON (D.D.A.). Stone artifacts from the Lower Bann valley. In *U.J.A.*, lvi, 31-43 (1993).

1044   SPEARS (Arthur). The Galician rock-art of County Donegal and elsewhere with some thoughts about it. In *Ulster Local Studies*, xvi, no. 2, pp 71-90 (1994).

1045   STOUT (Geraldine). Wicklow's prehistoric landscape. In *Wicklow*, pp 1-40 (1994).

1046   SWAN (D.L.). Excavations at Kilpatrick, Killucan Co. Westmeath, evidence for bone antler and iron working. In *Riocht na Midhe*, ix, no. 1, pp 1-21 (1994/95).

1047   TWOHIG (Elizaeth Shee), RONAYNE (Margaret). Past perceptions: the prehistoric archaeology of south-west Ireland. Pp 183. Cork: Cork University Press, 1993.

TWOHIG (Elizabeth Shee). See O'LEARY (Paddy).

1048   VAN HOEK (M.A.M.) Addenda to the prehistoric rock art of County Donegal. In *U.J.A.*, lvi, 179-80 (1993).

1049   VAN HOEK (Maarten A.M.). The prehistoric rock art of the Bohen stone, Co. Mayo. In *Cathair na Mart*, xiii, 1-15 (1993).

WADDELL (J.). See WATERMAN (D.M.).

1050   WADDELL (John). Excavation at 'Dathi's Mound', Rathcroghan, Co. Roscommon. In *Jn. Ir. Archaeol.*, iv, 23-36 (1987/88).

1051   WADDELL (John). Past imperfect: women in ancient Europe. In *Arch. Ire.*, iv, no. 3, 12-14 (1990).

1052   WADDELL (John). Rathcroghan: a royal site in Connacht. In *Jn. Ir. Archaeol.*, i, 21-46 (1983).

1053   WADDELL (John). A tale of two landscapes: the Irish sea in prehistory. In *Decoding the landscape*, pp 35-47 (1994).

1054   WAILES (B.). Dún Ailinne: a summary excavation report. In *Emania*, vii, 12-21 (1990).
        Dún Ailinne - Knockaulin, Co. Kildare.

1055   WALSH (Aidan). Excavating the Black Pig's Dyke. In *Emania*, iii, 5-11 (1987).

1056   WARNER (R.B.). The 'Ernean House'. In *Emania*, xii, 21-7 (1994).
        An archaeological 'three-walled' house - reflected in a tale written down in the 12th century.

1057   WARNER (R.B.) [et al]. Irish early iron age sites: a provisional map of absolute dated sites. In *Emania*, vii, 46-50 (1990).

1058   WARNER (R.B.). Tree-rings, catastrophes and culture in early Ireland: some comments. In *Emania*, xi, 13-19 (1993).

1059   WATERMAN (D.M.) and WADDELL (J.). A bronze age cist cemetery at Stranagawilly, Co. Tyrone. In *U.J.A.*, lvi, 44-60 (1993).

1060   WEIR (D.A.). Pollen analysis of a small basin deposit, Tievebulliagh, Co. Antrim. In *U.J.A.*, lvi, 18-24 (1993).

1061   WEIR (David A.). Dark ages and the pollen record. In *Emania*, xi, 21-30 (1993).

WOODMAN (Peter). See COONEY (Gabriel).

1062   AITCHISON (N.B.). Armagh and the royal centres in early medieval Ireland: monuments, cosmology and the past. Pp x, 356. Woodbridge: Boydell and Brewer for Cruithne Press, 1994.

1063   AITCHISON (N.B.). Kingship, society and sacrality: rank, power and ideology in early medieval Ireland. In *Traditio*, xlix, 45-75 (1994).

1064   AITCHISON (Nicholas B.). The Ulster cycle: heroic image and historical reality. In *Jn. Medieval History*, xiii, 87-116 (1987).

        ALLEN (J. Romilly). See 0953

1065   BARRY (T.B.). The medieval moated sites of County Wexford. In *Old Wexford Soc. Jn.*, vi, 5-17 (1976/77).

        BASTABLE (Patrick). See PATRICK (Saint).

        BATTAGLIA (Frank). See 0954.

1066   Beatha Barra: Saint Finbarr of Cork: the complete life. *Ed.* Pádraig Ó Riain. Pp xvii, 322. London: Irish Texts Society, 1994.

1067   BREATHNACH (Edel). Killeshin: an Irish monastery surveyed. In *Camb. Med. Celt. Stud.*, xxvii, 33-47 (1994).

1068   BIELER (Ludwig). Two observations concerning the *Navigatio Brendani*. In *Celtica*, xi, 15-17 (1976).

        BIELER (Ludwig). See PATRICK (Saint).

1069   BITEL (Lisa M.). Isle of the saints: monastic settlement and Christian community in early Ireland. Pp xiv, 268. Cork: Cork University Press, 1993. Originally pub.: Cornell University Press, 1990.

1070   BITEL (Lisa M.). Women's monastic enclosures in early Ireland. In *Jn. Medieval History*, xii, 15-36 (1986).

1071   BOURKE (Cormac). The chronology of Irish crucifixion plaques. In *The age of migrating ideas*, pp 175-81 (1993).

1072   BOURKE (Cormac). On the 'crozier' of Glendalough. In *Arch. Ire.*, iv, no 4, pp 10-11 (1990).

1073   BOURKE (Cormac). Patrick: the archaeology of a saint. Pp 61. Belfast: HMSO, 1993.

1074   BOURKE (Cormac). Notes on the relics of St. Patrick. In *Lecale Miscellany*, vii, 5-10 (1989).

        BOURKE (Edward). See 0956.

1075   BRADLEY (John). The archaeology and history of Saint Patrick: a review article. In *North Munster Antiq. Jn.*, xxxv, 29-44 (1993/94).

1076   BRADLEY (John). Killaloe: a pre-Norman borough? In *Peritia*, viii, 170-9 (1994).

1077   BRADLEY (John). Moynagh Lough: an insular workshop of the second quarter of the 8th century. In *The age of migrating ideas*, pp 64-73 (1993). Co. Meath.

1078   BRADLEY (John) and HALPIN (Andrew). The topographical development of Scandinavian and Anglo-Norman Cork. In *Cork*, pp 15-44 (1993).

BRADLEY (John). See 0957.

BRADLEY (Thomas). See WALSH (John R.).

1079   BRANNON (Nick). Archaeological excavations at Cathedral Hill, Downpatrick, 1986. In *Lecale Miscellany*, v, 37-40 (1987).

1080   BRANNON (Nick). Not just a load of old bones: the human and animal remains from the Cathedral Hill excavations, Downpatrick. In *Lecale Miscellany*, vii, 18-22 (1989).

1081   BREEZE (Andrew). Andrew Sall (+1682), Andrew Sall (+1686) and the Irish bible. In *Eigse*, xxviii, 100-02 (1994).

1082   BRIGGS (C. Stephen). On the Viking-age silver hoards from Co. Galway. In *Galway Arch. Soc. Jn.*, xxxviii, 79-82 (1981/82).

1083   BROWN (Michelle P.). Echoes: the Book of Kells and southern English manuscript production. In *The Book of Kells*, pp 333-43 (1994).

1084   BROWN (Michelle P.). The Lindisfarne scriptorium from the seventh to the early ninth century. In *St. Cuthbert*, pp 151-63 (1989).

1085   BROWN (Michelle P.). 'Paten and purpose', the Derrynaflan paten inscriptions. In *The age of migrating ideas*, pp 162-7 (1993).

1086   BRUCE-MITFORD (R.). The Durham-Echternach calligrapher. In *St. Cuthbert*, pp 175-88 (1989).

1087   BRYNE (F.J.) and FRANCIS (Pádraig). Two lifes of Saint Patrick: "Vita Secunda" and "Vita Quarta". In *R.S.A.I. Jn.*, cxxiv, 5-117 (1994).

1088   CAHILL (Therese). The round tower. In *The book of Cloyne*, pp 68-74 (1994).

1089   CAINS (Anthony). The surface examination of skin: a binder's note on the identification of animal species used in the making of parchment. In *The Book of Kells*, pp 172-4 (1994).

1090   CAMPBELL (Ewan) and LANE (Alan). Celtic and Germanic interaction in Dalriada: the 7th-century metalworking site at Dunadd. In *The age of migrating ideas*, pp 52-63 (1993).

1091   CAREY (John). A new introduction to Lebor Gabála Érenn: The Book of the taking of Ireland edited and translated by R.A. Stewart Macalister. Pp [2], 21. Dublin: Irish Texts Society, 1993.

1092   CHARLES-EDWARDS (T.M.). A contract between king and people in early medieval Ireland? 'Crítt Gabhlach' on kingship. In *Peritia*, viii, 107-19 (1994).

1093   CHARLES-EDWARDS (T.M.). Palladius, Prospex and Leo the Great: mission and primatial authority. In *St. Patrick*, pp 1-12 (1993).

1094   CHARLES-EDWARDS (T.M.). The social background to Irish *Peregrinatio*. In *Celtica*, xi, 443-59 (1976).

        CHARLES-EDWARDS (T.M.). See 0966.

1095   CLANCY (Finbarr G.). The Irish penitentials. In *Milltown Studies*, xxi, 87-109 (1988).

1096   CLANCY (Thomas Owen) and MÁRKUS (Gilbert). Iona: the earliest poetry of a Celtic monastery. Pp x, 271. Edinburgh: Edinburgh University Press, 1994.
        Text in English, Irish and Latin.

1097   CLAYTON (Mary). Centralism and uniformity versus localism and diversity: the Virgin and native saints in the monastic reform. In *Peritia*, viii, 96-106 (1994).

        CONNEELY (Daniel). See PATRICK (Saint).

        CONWAY (M.G.). See 1042.

1098   CORLETT (Chris) and McGUINNESS (David). An unrecorded cross-slab from Kiltiernan, County Dublin. In *R.S.A.I. Jn.*, cxxiv, 217-8 (1994).

1099   CORLETT (Chris). Previously unrecorded cross-slab from Feenure in the barony of Murrisk, County Mayo. In *R.S.A.I. Jn.*, cxxiii, 169-70 (1993).

1100   CRAMP (Rosemary). A reconsideration of the monastic site of Whitby. In *The age of migrating ideas*, pp 64-73 (1993).

1101   CURRAN (Michael). Cathedral and monastic office in Ireland. In *Milltown Studies*, ii, 42-57 (1978).

1102   DARGAN (Pat). The morphology of Irish towns. Part 1 - urban genesis. In *Geographical Viewpoint*, xxii, 49-60 (1994).

1103   DAVIES (R.R.). Presidential address: the peoples of Britain and Ireland 1100-1400. In *Royal Hist. Soc. Trans.*, 6th series, iv, 1-20 (1994).

1104   De PAOR (Liam). Saint Patrick's world: the Christian culture of Ireland's apostolic age. Pp 335. Blackrock, Co. Dublin: Four Courts Press, 1993.

1105   DUFFY (Sean). Pre-Norman Dublin: capital of Ireland? In *Hist. Ire.*, i, no.4, pp 13-8 (1993).

1106   DUMVILLE (David). Language, literature, and law in medieval Ireland: some questions of transmission. [Review article]. In *Camb. Med. Celt. Stud.*, ix, 91-8 (1985).

1107   DUMVILLE (David N.). 'Acta Palladii' preserved in Patrician hagiography. In *St. Patrick*, pp 65-84 (1993).

1108   DUMVILLE (David N.). The afterlife of *Liber angeli*. In *St. Patrick*, pp 253-4 (1993).

1109   DUMVILLE (David N.). The Armagh list of 'coarbs of St. Patrick'. In *St. Patrick*, pp 273-8 (1993).

1110   DUMVILLE (David N.). Auxilius, Iserninus, Secundinus and Benignus. In *St. Patrick*, pp 89-105 (1993).

1111   DUMVILLE (David N.). Bishop Palladius's computus. In *St. Patrick*, pp 85-8 (1993).

1112   DUMVILLE (David N.). Church-government and the spread of christianity in Ireland. In *St. Patrick*, pp 179-81 (1993).

1113   DUMVILLE (David N.). Coroticus. In *St. Patrick*, pp 107-15 (1993).

1114   DUMVILLE (David N.). The date 432. In *St. Patrick*, pp 39-43 (1993).

1115   DUMVILLE (David N.). The dating of the tripartite life of St. Patrick. In *St. Patrick*, pp 255-8 (1993).

1116   DUMVILLE (David N.). The death-date of St. Patrick. In *St. Patrick*, pp 29-33 (1993).

1117   DUMVILLE (David N.). Emain Macha, Ard Macha. In *St. Patrick*, pp 147-52 (1993).

1118   DUMVILLE (David N.). The floruit of St. Patrick - common and less common ground. In *St. Patrick*, pp 13-18 (1993).

1119   DUMVILLE (David N.). The form of St. Patrick's 'Confessio' in the *Book of Armagh*. In *St. Patrick*, pp 191-202 (1993).

1120   DUMVILLE (David N.). Muirchú's life of St. Patrick from the Book of Armagh. In *St. Patrick*, pp 203-19 (1993).

1120A   DUMVILLE (David N.). Patrick senior and junior. In *St. Patrick*, pp 59-64 (1993).

1121   DUMVILLE (David N.). Picti apostatae (que). In *St. Patrick*, pp 129-31 (1993).

1122   DUMVILLE (David N.). St. Patrick and fifth-century Irish chronology: the kings. In *St. Patrick*, pp 45-50 (1993).

1123   DUMVILLE (David N.). St. Patrick and fifth-century Irish chronology: the saints. In *St. Patrick*, pp 51-7 (1993).

1124   DUMVILLE (David N.). St. Patrick and the christianisation of Dál Riata. In *St. Patrick*, pp 183-9 (1993).

1125   DUMVILLE (David N.). St. Patrick and the Scandinavians of Dublin. In *St. Patrick*, pp 259-64 (1993).

1126   DUMVILLE (David N.). St. Patrick and his 'first synod'. In *St. Patrick*, pp 175-8 (1993).

1127   DUMVILLE (David N.). St. Patrick in the *Historia Brittonum*: three texts. In *St. Patrick*, pp 221-32 (1993).

1128   DUMVILLE (David N.). St. Patrick's missing years. In *St. Patrick*, pp 25-8 (1993).

1129   DUMVILLE (David N.). Verba militibus mittenda Corotici: an analysis of St. Patrick's tract on the crimes of Coroticus. In *St. Patrick*, pp 117-27 (1993).

1130   EDWARDS (Nancy). Review article: The iconography of the Irish high crosses: Carolingian influence in Ireland in the ninth century. In *Early Med. Eur.*, iii, no. 1, pp 63-71 (1994).

1131   EISENLOHR (Erika). The puzzle of the scribes: some palaeographical observation. In *The Book of Kells*, pp 196-208 (1994).

    ELLIS (Peter Berresford). See 0974.

1132   ETCHINGHAM (Colmán). Bishops in the early Irish church: a reassessment. In *Studia Hibernica*, xxviii, 35-62 (1994).

1133   ETCHINGHAM (Colmán). Evidence of Scandinavian settlement in Wicklow. In *Wicklow*, pp 113-38 (1994).

1134   ETCHINGHAM (Colmán). The implications of paruchia. In *Ériu*, xliv, 139-62 (1993).

    The excavation of St Vogue's well. See 0976.

1135   FANNING (Thomas). Viking age ringed pins from Dublin. Pp xi, 140. Dublin: Royal Irish Academy, 1994. (Medieval Dublin excavations 1962-81. Ser. B).

1136   FARR (Carol A.). Textual structure, decoration, and interpretive images in the Book of Kells. In *The Book of Kells*, pp 437-49 (1994).

1137   FISHER (Ian). The monastery of Iona in the eighth century. In *The Book of Kells*, pp 33-47 (1994).

1138   FITZPATRICK (Liz). Raiding and warring in monastic Ireland. In *Hist. Ire.*, i, no. 3, pp 13-18 (1993).

1139   FITZSIMONS (Eilis). Saint Torannan of Ballyhornan. In *Lecale Miscellany*, xi, 53-4 (1993).

1140   FLACHENECKER (Helmut). Schottenkloster: Irische Benediktinetkonvente in hochmittelalterlichen Deutschland. Pp 401, Faderbom: Schoningh, 1994. (Quellen und Forschungen aus am Gebiat der Geschichte; neue Folge, 18).
'Scottish' monasteries: Irish Bendedictine convents in Germany in the high middle ages.

1141   FLANAGAN (Marie Therese). Historia Gruffud vab Kenan and the origins of Balrothery, Co. Dublin. In *Camb. Med. Celt. Stud.*, xxviii, 71-94 (1994).

1142   FORBES (Will). The first recorded archaeological find at Emain Macha. In *Emania*, vii, 443-5 (1990).
Entry in *Chronicum Scottorum* for the year meant to be 1115 AD.

FRANCIS (Pádraig). See BYRNE (F.J.).

1143   FREEMAN (Philip M.). Visions from the dead in Herodotus, Nicander of Colophon, and the "Táin Bó Cuailnge". In *Emania*, xii, 45-8 (1994).

1144   FUCHS (Robert) and OLTROGGE (Doris). Colour material and painting technique in the Book of Kells. In *The Book of Kells*, pp 133-71 (1994).

1145   GARRIGUES (Marie-Odile). L'auteur de la 'Visio Tnugdali'. In *Studia Monastica*, xxix, 19-62 (1987).

1146   GEARY (Patrick J.). Insular religion [review article]. In *Jn. British Studies*, xxxii, no. 1, pp 71-6 (1993).

GIBBONS (Michael). See HIGGINS (Jim).

1147   GILLESPIE (Fergus). Irish genealogy and pseudo-genealogy. In *Aspects of Irish genealogy*, pp 123-37 [1993].

1148   GRABOWSKI (Kathryn). The historical overview of Dún Ailinne. In *Emania*, vii, 32-6 (1990).

1149   GRAHAM (B.J.). Early medieval Ireland: settlement as an indicator of economic and social transformation, c.500-1100. In *An historical geography of Ireland*, pp 19-57 (1993).

1150   GRAHAM (B.J.). The high middle ages: c.1100 to c.1350. In *An historical geography of Ireland*, pp 58-98 (1993).

1151   GRAHAM (B.J.). Urban genesis in early medieval Ireland. In *Jn. Hist. Geog.*, xiii, 3-16 (1987).

1152   GUILMAIN (Jacques). An analysis of some ornamental patterns in Hiberno-Saxon manuscript illumination in relation to their Mediterranean origins. In *The age of migrating ideas*, pp 92-103 (1993).

1153   GWYNN (Aubrey). Some notes on the history of Ardmore. In *Ardmore Jn.*, x, 13-16 (1993).

1154   HALL (Mark E.). A hacksilver find from Dysart, Thomastown. In *Old Kilkenny Rev.*, iv, 1164-5 (1993).
Uncertain date, but probably 9th century.

1155 HALLIDEN (Patrick). Saint Colman of Cloyne. In *The book of Cloyne*, pp 45-9 (1994).

HALPIN (Andrew). See BRADLEY (John).

1156 HARBISON (Peter). The bronze crucifixion plaque said to be from St John's (Rinnagan), near Athlone. In *Jn. Ir. Archaeol.*, ii, 1-17 (1984).

1157 HARBISON (Peter). The Derrynaflan ladle: some parallels illustrated. In *Jn. Ir. Archaeol.*, iii, 55-8 (1985/86).

1158 HARBISON (Peter). Early Irish pilgrim archaeology in the Dingle peninsula. In *World Arch.*, xxvi, 90-103 (1994).

1159 HARBISON (Peter). A high cross base from the Rock of Cashel and a historical reconsideration of the 'Ahenny group' of crosses. In *R.I.A. Proc.*, xciii, section c, 1-20 (1993).

1160 HARBISON (Peter). High crosses and the Book of Kells. In *The Book of Kells*, pp 266-9 (1994).

1161 HARBISON (Peter). Irish high crosses: with the figure sculptures explained. Pp viii, 109. Drogheda: Boyne Valley Honey Compay, 1994.

1162 HEIST (W.W.). Over the writer's shoulder: Saint Abban. In *Celtica*, xi, 70-84 (1976).

1163 HERBERT (Máire). Charter material from Kells. In *The Book of Kells*, pp 60-77 (1994).

1164 HERBERT (Máire). The Irish Sex aetates mundi: first editions [review article]. In *Camb. Med. Celt. Stud.*, xi, 97-112 (1986).

1165 HERITY (Michael). Early Irish hermitages in the light of the Lives of Cuthbert. In *St. Cuthbert*, pp 45-63 (1989).

1166 HERITY (Michael). The forms of the tomb-shrine of the founder saint in Ireland. In *The age of migrating ideas*, pp 188-95 (1993).

1167 HERITY (Michael). Les premiers ermitages et monasteres en Irlande 400-700 A.D. In *Cahiers de Civilisation Mediévale*, xxxvi, 219-61 (1993).

HERITY (Michael). See 0983.

1168 HIGGINS (Jim). A chi-rho decorated pebble from Kilcorban, County Galway. In *R.S.A.I. Jn.*, cxxiii, 164-5 (1993).

1169 HIGGINS (Jim) and GIBBONS (Michael). Early Christian monuments at Kilgeever, Co. Mayo. In *Cathair na Mart*, xiii, 32-44 (1993).

1170 HIGGINS (Jim). An early Christian site on Saint's Island, Lough Mask, Co. Mayo, and its cross-slabs. In *Cathair na Mart*, xiii, 45-52 (1993).

1171 HIGGINS (Jim). Further medieval sculpture at Carran church, County Clare and its significance. In *The Other Clare*, xviii, 16-19 (1994).

1172 HIGGITT (John). The display script of the Book of Kells and the tradition of insular decorative capitals. In *The Book of Kells*, pp 209-33 (1994).

1173 HOURIHAN (Colm). The mason and his craft in medieval Ireland. In *Bantry Hist.Soc. Jn.*, i, 66-73 (1991).

HOWLETT (D.R.). See PATRICK (Saint).

1174 HUDSON (Benjamin). William the Conqueror and Ireland. In *I.H.S.*, xxix, 145-58 (1994).

1175 HUDSON (Benjamin T.). Kings and church in early Scotland. In *Scottish Hist. Rev.*, lxxiii, 145-70 (1994).

1176 KARKOV (Catherine). The chalice and cross in insular art. In *The ideas of migrating ideas*, pp 237-44 (1993).

1177 KELLY (Dorothy). The relationship of the crosses of Argyll: the evidence of form. In *The age of migrating ideas*, pp 219-29 (1993).

1178 KELLY (Eamonn P.). Early Celtic art in Ireland. Pp 47. Dublin: Town House and Country House in association with the National Museum of Ireland, 1993.

1179 KELLY (Eamonn P.). The Lough Kinale book-shrine. In *The age of migrating ideas*, pp 168-74 (1993).

1180 KELLY (Eamonn P.). The Lough Kinale book shrine: the implications for the manuscripts. In *The Book of Kells*, pp 280-9 (1994).

1181 KELLY (Fergus). The old Irish tree-list. In *Celtica*, xi, 107-24 (1976).

1182 KEOGH (Raymond M.). Does the Armorican forest hold the key to Saint Patrick's excape? In *Studia Hibernica*, xxviii, 145-57 (1994).

1183 KILBRIDE-JONES (H.E.). On some instances of Celtic art patterns inscribed on grave-slabs discovered at Carrowntemple, Co. Sligo, Ireland. In *Board of Celt. Stud. Bull.*, xxxvi, 230-8 (1989).

KILBRIDE-JONES (Howard). See 0989.

1184 KING (Heather). Prophets and evangelists (speaking from stone). In *Arch. Ire.*, viii, no. 2, pp 9-10 (1994).
Cross of scriptures, Clonmacnoise.

1185 KITZINGER (Ernst). Interlace and icons: form and function in early insular art. In *The age of migrating ideas*, pp 3-15 (1993).

LANE (Alan). See CAMPBELL (Ewan).

1186 La NIECE (Susan) and STAPLETON (Colleen). Niello and enamel on Irish metalwork. In *Antiq. Jn.*, lxxiii, 148-51 (1993).

1187 LAPIDGE (Michael). A seventh-century insular Latin debate poem on divorce. In *Camb. Med. Celt. Stud.*, x, 1-23 (1985).

1188   LEERSSEN (Joep). The contention of the bards (Iomarbhágh na bhfileadh) and its place in Irish political and literary history. Pp 72. Dublin: Irish Texts Society, 1994. (Irish Texts Society subsidiary series, 2).

1189   LEHANE (Brendan). Early Celtic christianity. Pp 240. London: Constable, 1994.
        Facsimile of edition published 1968.

1190 . LUDDY (Ailbe J.). Life of St. Malachy. Pp xxiv, 187. Felinfach: Llanerch, 1994.
        Facsimile reprint of ed. originally published: Dublin: M. H. Gill, 1930. St Malachy 1094-1148.

1191   LYNN (C.J.) and McDOWELL (J.A.). Murchú's Armagh. In *Emania*, iv, 42-6 (1988).
        The acquisition of Armagh as an ecclesiastical site.

        LYNN (C.J.). See 1000, 1003, 1005.

1192   McCAFFERTY (John). The Celi De - monastic reforms in 8th and 9th century Ireland. In *U.C.D. Hist. Rev.*, iii, 12-14 (1989).

        MACALISTER (R.A. Stewart). See CAREY (John).

1193   McCARTHY (Daniel). The chronological apparatus of the Annals of Ulster AD 431-1131. In *Peritia*, viii, 47-79 (1994).

1194   McCARTHY (Daniel). The origin of the Latercus Paschal cycle of the insular Celtic churches. In *Camb. Med. Celtic Stud.*, xxviii, 25-49 (1994).

1195   McCONE (Kim R.). Werewolves, cyclopes, díberga and fíanna: juvenile delinquincy in early Ireland. In *Camb. Med. Celt. Stud.*, xii, 1-22 (1986).

        McCORMICK (Finbar). See 1006.

        McDOWELL (J.A.). See LYNN (C.J.).

1196   McGANLEY (Thomas). Early Irish brewing laws. In *U.C.D. Hist. Rev.*, vii, 7-9 (1993).

1197   McGRAIL (Seán). Medieval boat and ship timbers from Dublin. Pp x, 178. Dublin: Royal Irish Academy for the National Museum of Ireland and the Royal Irish Academy, 1993. (Medieval Dublin excavations, 1962-81 ser. B, vol. 3 (1993)).

1198   McGRAIL (Sean). Ships timbers from Wood Quay, Dublin and other medieval sites in Ireland. In *Bullán*, i, no. 1, pp 49-61 (1994).

        McGUINNESS (David). See CORLETT (Chris).

        McGUINNESS (David). See REDMOND (Markus).

1199   McGURK (Patrick). An edition of the abbreviated and selective set of Hebrew names found in the Book of Kells. In *The Book of Kells*, pp 102-32 (1994).

        McHUGH (Anna). See 1007.

1200   Mac LEAN (Douglas). The Book of Kells and the Northumbrian type of classic drapery. In *The Book of Kells*, pp 301-10 (1994).

1201   Mac LEAN (Douglas). Snake-bosses and redemption at Iona and in Pictland. In *The age of migrating ideas*, pp 245-53 (1993).

1202   MacMAHON (Michael). The charter of Clare Abbey and the Augustinian 'province' in Co. Clare. In *The Other Clare*, xvii, 21-8 (1993).

1203   McNAMARA (Martin). Irish gospel texts, Amb.I.61; bible texts and date of Kells. In *The Book of Kells*, pp 78-101 (1994).

1204   McNAMARA (Martin). Monastic schools in Ireland and Northumbria before A.D. 750. In *Milltown Studies*, xxv, 19-36 (1990).

1205   Mac NIOCAILL (Gearóid). The background to the battle of Tarbga. In *Celtica*, xi, 133-40 (1976).

1206   MacRÉAMOINN (Seán). St. Patrick. In *The Furrow*, xxxviii, 162-71 (1987).

1207   MacSHAMHRÁIN (A.S.). The Uí Muiredaig and the abbacy of Glendalough in the eleventh to thirteenth centuries. In *Camb. Med. Celt. Stud.*, xxv, 55-75 (1993).

1208   MacSHAMHRÁIN (A.S.). The 'unity' of Cóemgen and Ciarán: a convent between Glendalough and Clonmacnois in the tenth to eleventh centuries. In *Wicklow*, pp 139-50 (1994).

1209   MAGEE (Philip). In journeyings often. Pp 34. [Kiltegan, Co. Wicklow]: [the author], [1993?]
          On places associated with St. Patrick.

1210   MALLORY (J.P.). The career of Conall Cernach. In *Emania*, vi, 22-8 (1989).

        MALLORY (J.P.). See 1011, 1013.

1211   MANNING (Conleth). Clonmacnoise. Pp 48. Dublin: Stationery Office, 1994.

1212   MANNING (Conleth). The earliest plans of Clonmacnoise. In *Arch. Ire.*, viii, no. 1, pp 18-20 (1994)

1213   MANNING (Conleth). The stonebuilt ringfort entrance at Cahiervagliair, Cappeen, Co. Cork. In *Jn. Ir. Archaeol.*, iv, 37-54 (1987/88).

        MÁRKUS (Gilbert). See CLANCY (Thomas Owen).

1214   MARSHALL (Jenny White) and WALSH (Claire). Illaunloughan: life and death on a small early monastic site. In *Arch. Ire.*, iii, no. 4, pp 24-8 (1994).
          Co. Kerry.

1215   MAUND (K.L.). The second obit of St. Patrick in the Annals of Boyle. In *St. Patrick*, pp 35-7 (1993).

1216   MEEHAN (Bernard). The Book of Kells: an illustrated introduction to the manuscript in Trinity College Dublin. Pp 95. London: Thames and Hudson, 1994.

1217   MEEHAN (Bernard). The division of hands in the Book of Kells. In *The Book of Kells*, pp 183-95 (1994).
       Revision of article originally pub. in *The Books of Kells, MS 58, Trinity College Library Dublin: commentary*, ed. Peter Fox, Luzern, 1990.

1218   MÉRINDOL (Christian de). Du Livre de Kells et du Psautier de Corbie a l'art roman: origine, diffusion et signification du théme des personnages se saisissant a la barbe. In *The Book of Kells*, pp 290-300 (1994).

1219   MICHELLI (Perette). Migrating ideas or migrating craftsmen? the case of the bossed penannular brooches. In *The age of migrating ideas*, pp 182-7 (1993).

1220   MINAHANE (John). The christian druids: on the filid or philosopher-poets of Ireland. Pp [7], 245. Dublin: Sanas Press, 1993.

       MONK (M.A.). See 1015.

       MOORE (D.). See 1042.

1221   MORI (Setsuko).   Irish monasticism and the concept of inheritance: an examination of its legal aspects. In *Comparative aspects of Irish and Japanese economic and social history*, pp 123-47 (1993).

1222   MULLALLY (Evelyn).   Mélanges.   La colonisation de l'Irlande au xii^es. d'apres une chronique Anglo-Normande.   In *Cahiers de Civilisation Mediévale*, xxxvii, 365-70 (1994).
       The song of Dermot and the earl.

1223   MURPHY (Donald). Monasterboice: secrets from the air. In *Arch. Ire.*, viii, no. 3, pp 15-17 (1993).

1224   NEES (Lawrence). Ultan the scribe. In *The age of migrating ideas*, pp 104-5 (1993).

1225   NENK (Beverley S.) [et al]. Medieval Britain and Ireland in 1992. In *Medieval Archaeology*, xxxviii, 240-313 (1993).

1226   NENK (Beverley S.) [et al]. Medieval Britain and Ireland in 1993. In *Medieval Archaeology*, xxxix, 184-293 (1994).

1227   NETZER (Nancy). The origin of the beast canon tables reconsidered. In *The Book of Kells*, pp 322-32 (1994).

1228   NETZER (Nancy). Willibrord's scriptorium at Echternach and its relationship to Ireland and Lindisfarne. In *St. Cuthbert*, pp 203-12 (1989).

1229   NEWMAN (Roger Chatterton). Brian Boru: king of Ireland. Pp 224. Dublin: Anvil Books, 1993.
       First pub.: 1983.

1230   NIEKE (Margaret R.). Penannular and related brooches: secular ornament or symbol of action? In *The age of migrating ideas*, pp 128-34 (1993).

1231 Ní MHEARA (Róisín). In search of Irish saints: the peregrinatio pro Christo. Pp 128. Dublin: Four Courts Press, 1994.
Irish missionaries in Europe.

1232 NOLAN (Tom). Port Lairge: the first sixty-five years? In *Decies*, 1, 3-7 (1994).

1233 Ó CANANN (Tomás G.). Aspects of an early Irish surname: Ua Canannáin. In *Studia Hibernica*, xxvii, 113-44 (1993).

1234 Ó CARRAGÁIN (Éamonn). *'Traditio evangeliorum'* and *'sustantio'*: the relevance of liturgical ceremonies to the Book of Kells. In *The Book of Kells*, pp 398-436 (1994).

1235 Ó CORRÁIN (Donnchadh). The historical and cultural background of the Books of Kells. In *The Book of Kells*, pp 1-32 (1994).

1236 Ó CORRÁIN (Donncha). The Uí Chennselaig kingship of Leinster 1072-1126. Part II. In *Old Wexford Soc. Jn.*, vi, 45-53 (1976/77).

1237 Ó CRÓINÍN (Dáibhí). Is the Augsburg gospel codex a Northumbrian manuscript? In *St. Cuthbert*, pp 189-202 (1989).

1238 Ó FLOINN (R.). A bog body from Meenybraddan bog, Co. Donegal Ireland. In *Donegal Annual*, xlv, 23-8 (1993).

1239 Ó FLOINN (Raghnall). A fragmentary house-shaped shrine from Clonard, Co. Meath. In *Jn. Ir. Archaeol.*, v, 49-55 (1989/90).

1240 Ó FLOINN (Raghnall). Irish shrines & reliquaries of the middle ages. Pp 46. Dublin: Country House in association with the National Museum of Ireland, 1994.

1241 Ó hUIGINN (Ruairí). Fergus, Russ and Rudraige: a brief biography of Fergus Mac Róich. In *Emania*, xi, 31-40 (1993).

1242 Ó hUIGINN (Ruairí). The literature of the Laigin. In *Emania*, vii, 5-9 (1990).
The literature of the Leinster area.

1243 O'KEEFE (Tadhg). Lismore and Cashel: reflections on the beginnings of Romanesque architecture in Munster. In *R.S.A.I. Jn.*, cxxiv, 118-52 (1994).

1244 Ó LAOGHAIRE (Diarmuid). St Virgil and his Irish background. In *Milltown Studies*, xiv, 72-85 (1984).

O LOCHLAINN (Mícheál). See 1029.

1245 O'LOUGHLIN (Thomas). The earliest world maps known in Ireland. In *Hist. Ire.*, i, no. 1, pp 7-10 (1993).

1246 O'LOUGHLIN (Thomas). The library of Iona in the late seventh century: the evidence from Adomnán's *De locis sanctis*. In *Ériu*, xlv, 33-52 (1994).

OLTROGGE (Doris). See FUCHS (Robert).

1247   O'NEILL (Assumpta). Waterford diocese, 1096-1363. Part 5: Religious foundations in the diocese of Waterford. In *Decies*, xlvii, 42-51 (1993); Part 6: appendices, xlix, 23-8 (1994).
Continued from xlvi (1992).

1248   O'NEILL (Timothy). Book-making in early Christian Ireland. In *Arch. Ire.*, iii, 96-100 (1989).

1249   ORCHARD (Andy). Audite omnes amantes: a hymn in Patrick's praise. In *St. Patrick*, pp 153-73 (1993).

1250   O'REILLY (Jennifer). The Book of Kells, folio 114r: a mystery revealed yet concealed. In *The age of migrating ideas*, pp 106-14 (1993).

1251   O'REILLY (Jennifer). Exegesis and the Book of Kells: the Lucan geneaology. In *The Book of Kells*, pp 344-97 (1994).

        Ó RIAIN (Padraig). See BEATHA (Barra).

1252   O'SULLIVAN (Aidan). An early historic period fishweir on the Fergus estuary, Co. Clare. In *North Munster Antiq. Jn.*, xxxv, 52-61 (1993/94).

1253   O'SULLIVAN (Aidan). Harvesting the waters. In *Arch. Ire.*, viii, no. 1, pp 10-12 (1994).
Fishweirs from early Christian period.

1254   O'SULLIVAN (William). The palaeological background to the Book of Kells. In *The Book of Kells*, pp 175-82 (1994).

1255   PARIS (Madame la Comtesse de). Saint Laurent O'Toole et Henri II. In *Cahiers de Civilisation Mediévale*, xxxvii, 111-14 (1994).

1256   PATRICK (Saint). Liber epistolarum Sancti Patricii episcopi = The book of letters of Saint Patrick the bishop. *Ed.* D.R. Howlett. Pp 135. Blackrock, Co. Dublin: Four Courts Press, 1994. (Celtic studies).
Text in Latin and English.

1257   PATRICK (Saint). Liber epistolarum Sancti Patricii. Introduction, text and commentary by Ludwig Bieler. 2nd ed. Pp [6], 215, [5]. Dublin: Royal Irish Academy, 1993. (Royal Irish Academy dictionary of medieval Latin from Celtic sources. Ancillary publications, 4) (Clavis Patricii, 2).
Previous ed.: 1952. Text in Latin and English.

1258   PATRICK (Saint). St Patrick's letters: a study of their theological dimension by Daniel Conneely. *Ed.* Patrick Bastable .. [et al]. Pp 249. Maynooth: An Sagart, 1993.
Latin text of the letters with English and Irish translations and English commentary.

1259   PATTERSON (Nerys). Patrilineal kinship in early Irish society: the evidence from the Irish law texts. In *Board Celt. Stud. Bull.*, xxxvii, 133-65 (1990).

1260   PATTERSON (Nerys Thomas). Cattle-lords and clansmen: the social structure of early Ireland. 2nd ed. Pp xv, 425. Notre Dame: University of Notre Dame Press, 1994.
Previous ed.: 1991.

1261   PONTFARCY (Yolande de). Pre-reformation pilgrimages to St. Patrick's Purgatory. In *Ulster Local Studies*, xv, no. 2, pp 7-21 (1993).

1262   POWER (Catryn). Diet and disease: evidence from the human dental remains in two medieval Irish populations. In *Jn. Ir. Archaeol.*, iii, 49-53 (1985/86). Dublin and Waterford.

1263   POWER (Rosemary). Magnus Barelegs, the War Hollow and Downpatrick. In *Ulster Local Studies*, xv, no. 2, pp 40-54 (1993).

1264   REDMOND (Markus) and McGUINNESS (David). An unrecorded tau cross at Dalkey, county Dublin. In *R.S.A.I. Jn.*, cxxiii, 167- 9 (1993).

        The rich history of royal Tara. See 1037

1265   RICHARDSON (Hilary). Remarks on the liturgical fan, flabellum or rhipidon. In *The age of migrating ideas*, pp 27-34 (1993).

1266   RICHTER (Michael). The formation of the medieval west: studies in the oral culture of the barbarians. Pp xv, 292. New York: St. Martin's Press, 1994. Pp 181-231 on Ireland.

1267   RICHTER (Michael). Two centenaries: St. Vergil of Salzburg (+784) and St. Methodius (+885). In *Milltown Studies*, xvi, 85-96 (1985).

1268   ROE (Helen M.). Monasterboice and its monuments. 2nd ed. Pp 78. Dundalk: County Louth Archaeological and Historical Society, 1993. Previous ed.: 1981.

1269   RYAN (Michael). The Book of Kells and metalwork. In *The Book of Kells*, pp 270-9 (1994).

1270   RYAN (Michael). Early Christian metalwork: new evidence from Ireland. In *Churches built in ancient times*, pp 313-24 (1994).

1271   RYAN (Michael). The menagerie of the Derrynaflan chalice. In *The age of migrating ideas*, pp 151-61 (1993).

1272   RYAN (Michael). Ten years of early Irish metalwork. In *Ir. Arts Rev. Yearbk.*, pp 153-6 (1994).

        RYAN (Michael). See 1040.

1273   RYNNE (Colin). Archaeology and the Irish watermill. In *Arch. Ire.*, iii, 110-14 (1989).

1274   RYNNE (Etienne). Drolleries in the Book of Kells. In *The Book of Kells*, pp 311-21 (1994).

1275   SAYERS (William). Supernatural pseudonyms. In *Emania*, xii, 49-60 (1994). Naming in early medieval Irish literature.

1276   SAYERS (William). Vífull - captive Gael, freeman settler, Icelandic forbear. In *Ainm*, 46-55 (1994/95). Irish slave freed in Iceland during the Saga age.

1277   SCALLY (Brendan). A quiet place in south Kilkenny. In *Local History Rev.*, vi, 30-1 (1993).
Celtic cross of 10th/12th centuries.

1278   SCOTT (B.G.). An early Irish law tract on the blacksmith's forge. In *Jn. Ir. Archaeol.*, i, 59-62 (1983).
8th century *Blai ord indeoin* (the exemption of the hammer and anvil).

1279   SHEEHAN (John). A Merovingian background for the Ardmoneel stone? In *Cork Hist. Soc. Jn.*, xcix, 23-31 (1994).

1280   SHELDON-WILLIAMS (I.P.). Eriugena and Citeaux. In *Studia Monastica*, xix, 75-92 (1977)

SIMPSON (D.D.A.). See 1042.

1281   Skryne's link with St Mary's Abbey. In *A Window on the Past*, [i], 11-13 (1987).

1282   SMITH (Peter). Aimirgein glúngel tuir tend: a middle Irish poem on the authors and laws of Ireland. In *Peritia*, viii, 120-50 (1994).

1283   SMYTH (Alfred P.). Kings, saints and sagas. In *Wicklow*, pp 41-111 (1994).

1284   SOMERVILLE (Orna). Kite-shaped brooches. In *R.S.A.I. Jn.*, cxxiii, 59-101 (1993).

1285   SPEARMAN (R. Michael). The mounts from Crieff, Perthshire, and their wider context. In *The age of migrating ideas*, pp 135-42 (1993).

1286   STALLEY (Roger). Ireland and Europe in the Middle Ages: selected essays on architecture and sculpture. Pp [5], ii, 335. London: Pindar Press, 1994.

1287   STALLEY (Roger). Scribe and mason: the Book of Kells and the Irish high crosses. In *The Book of Kells*, pp 256-65 (1994).

STAPLETON (Colleen). See La NIECE (Susan).

1288   STEVENSON (Robert B.K.). Further thoughts on some well known problems. In *The age of migrating ideas*, pp 16-26 (1993).

1289   STEVICK (Robert D.). The earliest Irish and English bookarts: visual and poetic forms before A.D. 1000. Pp xiv, 282. Philadelphia: University of Pennsylvania Press, 1994. (Middle Ages series).

1290   STEVICK (Robert D.). Page design of some illuminations in the Book of Kells. In *The Book of Kells*, pp 243-56 (1994).

1291   SWAN (D.L.). Kells and its book. In *The Book of Kells*, pp 48-59 (1994).

1292   SWEETMAN (David). Archaeological excavation at the Cross of Cloonshanville, Co. Roscommon. In *Galway Arch. Soc. Jn.*, xxxviii, 83-7 (1981/82).

1293   A tale of two monasteries. In *A Window on the Past*, [i], 5-7 (1987).
The Augustinian monastery on the hill of Skryne and an undentified one near the graveyard of Trevet.

1294   TARZIA (Wade). No trespassing: border defence in the Táin Bó Cuailnge. In *Emania*, iii, 28-33 (1987).

1295   TIETZSCH-TYLER (Daniel). The Augustinian priory of Kells, Co. Kilkenny: an exploration: a visitor's guide and explanation. Pp [42]. [s.l.]: K.R.E.T.E (Kells Region Economic & Tourism Enterprise Ltd), 1993.

1296   TONER (Gregory). Emain Macha in the literature. In *Emania*, iv, 32-5 (1988).

1297   VAN HOEK (M.A.M.). Early Christian rock art at Clehagh, Co. Donegal. In *U.J.A.*, lvi, 139-47 (1993).

1298   VAN STONE (Mark). Ornamental techniques in Kells and its kin. In *The Book of Kells*, pp 234-42 (1994).

1299   VEREY (Christopher D.). The gospel texts at Lindisfarne at the time of St. Cuthbert. In *St. Cuthbert*, pp 143-50 (1989).

WADDELL (John). See 1052.

WALSH (Claire). See MARSHALL (Jenny White).

1300   WALSH (John R.) and BRADLEY (Thomas). A history of the Irish church, 400-700 AD. 2nd ed. Pp viii, 160. Blackrock, Co. Dublin: Columba Press, 1993.
Previous ed.: 1991.

1301   WAMERS (Egon). Insular art in Carilingian Europe: the reception of old ideas in a new empire? In *The age of migrating ideas*, pp 35-44 (1993).

WEIR (David A.). See 1061.

1302   WERNER (Martin). Crucifixi, sepulti, suscitati: remarks on the decoration of the Book of Kells. In *The Book of Kells*, pp 450-88 (1994).

1303   WHITFIELD (Niamh). The filigree of the Hunterston and 'Tara' brooches. In *The age of migrating ideas*, pp 118-27 (1993).

1304   WHITFIELD (Niamh). The sources of gold in early Christian Ireland. In *Arch. Ire.*, vii, no. 4, pp 21-3 (1993).

1305   WILSON (Anthony M.). John de Courcy and the battle of Down. In *Lecale Miscellany*, vii, 46-9 (1989).

1306   WOOD (Juliette). Another island close at hand: the Irish immramma and the travelogue. In *Boundaries & thresholds*, pp 54-64 (1993).
'.. the nature of foreign in medieval cosmology...'

1307   ARTHURSON (Ian). The Perkin Warbeck conspiracy, 1491-1499. Pp xii, 244. Stroud, Gloucs.: Alan Sutton, 1994

1308   BARRY (T.B.). Late medieval Ireland: the debate on social and economic transformation, 1350-1550. In *An historical geography of Ireland*, pp 99-122 (1993).

        BARRY (T.B.). See 1065.

1309   BEAUSANG (Seamus). The pipe roll of Cloyne (Pipa Colmann). In *The book of Cloyne*, pp 76-8 (1994).
        1364.

        BITEL (Lisa M.). See 1069.

1310   BOIVIN (Jeanne-Marie). L'Irlande au moyen age: Giraud de Barri et la Topographica Hibernica (1188). Pp 414. Paris: Champion, 1993. (Nouvelle bibliotheque du moyen age, 18).
        Includes a French translation of Giraldus Cambrensis 'Topographia Hibernica'.

1311   BOURKE (Cormac). An enamelled cruet from Grangewalls, Co. Down. In *Lecale Miscellany*, vi, 38-43 (1988).

1312   BOURKE (Cormac). A medieval helmet from Lough Henney, Co. Down. In *Lecale Miscellany*, viii, 5-7 (1990).

1313   BRADLEY (Helene). Anglo-Norman settlement in County Louth. In *Baile*, pp 34-7 (1992).

1314   BRADLEY (Helene). The Sinnots of Co. Wexford 1169-1650. In *Baile*, pp 7-9 (1989).

        BRADLEY (John). See 1076, 1078.

        BRANNON (Nick). See 1080.

1315   BRANNON (Patrick). The search for the Celtic rite: the TCD Sarum divine office MSS reassessed. In *Music and the church*, pp 13-40 (1993).
        15th century.

1316   BREATNACH (Caoimhín). The historical context of Cath Fionntrágha. In *Eigse*, xxviii, 138-55 (1994).

        BREEN (Martin). See Ua CRÓINÍN (Risteárd).

        BYRNE (F.J.). See 1087.

1317   BYRNE (Martin E.). The results of a resistivity survey undertaken at Clonmines, Co. Wexford. In *Wexford Hist. Soc. Jn.*, xv, 67-73 (1994/95).

1318   CABALL (Marc). Bardic poetry & and the analysis of Gaelic mentalities. In *Hist. Ire.*, ii, no. 2, pp 46-50 (1994).

1319   Calendar of entries in the papal registers relating to Great Britain and Ireland. Papal letters, vol. 17, Part 1: Alexander VI (1492-1503). Lateran registers part 2: 1495-1503. *Ed.* Anne P. Fuller. Pp lxvii, 926. Dublin: Irish Manuscripts Commission, 1994.

1320   CARROLL (Finbarr). A famous bishop from the banks of the Bandon. In *Bandon Hist. Jn.*, ix, 3-6 (1993).
        Thaddeus McCarthy, fl. 1482, bishop of the dioceses Cork, Cloyne and Ross.

1321   CHERRY (Stella). Sheela-na-gigs from County Cork. In *Cork Hist. Soc. Jn.*, xcviii, 107-12 (1993).

1322   CLARKE (Howard B.). The 1192 charter of the liberties and the beginnings of Dublin's municipal life. In *Dublin Hist. Rec.*, xlvi, 5-14 (1993).

1323   CLEARY (Rose M.). Medieval town wall at Emmet Street, Clonmel. In *Tipp. Hist. Jn.*, pp 194-8 (1993).

1324   CLYNE (Miriam). A medieval pilgrim: from Tuam to Santiago de Compostela. In *Arch. Ire.*, iv, no. 3, pp 21-2 (1990).

1325   COLMER (Albert W.K.). A romantic view of Inch Abbey, monastic site on the banks of the Quoile. In *Lecale Miscellany*, vi, 32-3 (1988).

1326   CONNOLLY (Philomena). Select document xliv: An attempted escape from Dublin Castle: the trial of William and Walter de Birmingham, 1332. In *I.H.S.*, xxix, 100-08 (1994).

1327   COSGROVE (Art). Marriage in medieval Ireland. In *Hist. Ire.*, ii, no. 3, pp 16-20 (1994).

1328   COTTER (Francis J.). The Friar's minor in Ireland: from their arrival in 1400. *Ed.* Roberta A. McKelvie. Pp xii, 264, [8]. St. Bonaventure (N.Y.): Franciscan Institute, St. Bonaventure University, 1994. (Franciscan Institute publications, history series, no. 7).

1329   CULLEN (Seamus). The Pale in the Donadea area. In *Oughterany*, i, no. 1, pp 18-22 (1993).

        DAVIES (R.R.). See 1103.

1330   DUMVILLE (David). On editing and translating medieval Irish chronicles: the Annals of Ulster [review article]. In *Camb. Med. Celt. Stud.*, x, 67-86 (1985).

1331   DUNBOYNE (Lord). Who wrote Glanville?. In *Butler Soc. Jn.*, iii, 500-01 (1994).
        12th century treatise on the laws of England, possibly written by a member of the Butler family.

1332   ELLIS (William). Ratheadon, parish of Leighlin. In *Carloviana*, xli, 16-17 (1993/94).
        Ruin of Ratheadon church - with feature dating to the 11th/12th century.

1333   FANNING (Thomas). Decorated medieval paving tiles in Ireland. In *Arch. Ire.*, ii, 101-04 (1988).

1334   FLANAGAN (Marie Therese). Anglo-Norman change and continuity: the castle of Telach Cail in Delbna. In *I.H.S.*, xxviii, 385-9 (1993).

FLANAGAN (Marie Therese). See 1141.

1335   FRAME (Robin). 'Les Engleys nées en Irlande': the English political identity in medieval Ireland. In *Royal Hist. Soc. Trans.*, iii, 83-103 (1993).

FRANCIS (Pádraig). See 1087.

FULLER (Anne P.). See *Calendar of entries in the papal registers relating to Great Britain and Ireland* (1994).

1336   GLOVER (Winifred). Mexican 'axe-money' in Ireland - the Spanish connection. In *Arch. Ire.*, iv, no. 4, 15-17 (1990).

1337   GOODBODY (Rob). Pale ditch in south County Dublin. In *Arch. Ire.*, vii, no. 3, pp 24-5 (1993).

GRAHAM (B.J.). See 1150.

GWYNN (Aubrey). See 1153.

HALPIN (Andrew). See 1078.

HARBISON (Peter). See 1161.

1338   HAREN (Michael J.). Bishop Gynwell of Lincoln, two Avignonese statutes and Archbishop Fitzralph of Armagh's suit at the Roman curia against the friars. In *Archiv. Hist. Pont.*, xxxi, 275-92 (1993).

1339   HARTWELL (B.N.). The experimental firing of a replica double-flued kiln based on an excavated medieval example from Downpatrick. In *U.J.A.*, lvi, 152-62 (1993).

HERITY (Michael). See 1165.

1340   HICKEY (Elizabeth). Skryne and the early Normans: papers concerning the medieval manors of the de Feypo family in Ireland in the 12th and early 13th centuries. Pp 218. [Tara]: Meath Archaeological and Historical Society, 1994.

1341   HIGGINS (Jim). Georgian and other merchants' marks. A side-light in heraldry and genealogy of the 15th-17th centuries. In *Galway Roots*, [i], 21-7 (1993).

1342   HIGGINS (Jim). Lost late medieval woodwork from Priory Lane, Galway. In *Galway Arch. Soc. Jn.*, xlv, 163-4 (1993).

1343   HIGGINS (Jim). Some missing and rescued pieces of family history in stone from Galway. In *Galway Roots*, ii, 49-51 (1994).

HIGGINS (Jim). See 1171.

1344   HODKINSON (Brian J.). A fifteenth century precentor of Limerick. In *North Munster Antiq. Jn.*, xxxv, 72-5 (1993/94).

1345   HOLLAND (Patrick). Anglo-Norman Galway: rectangular earthworks and moated sites. In *Galway Arch. Soc. Jn.*, xlvi, 203-11 (1994).

1346   HOLLAND (Patrick). Late medieval structures in Clonmel: further remarks. In *Tipp. Hist. Jn.*, pp 175-7 (1994).

1347   HOLLAND (Patrick). The thirteenth-century remains at Cahir Castle, Co. Tipperary. In *North Munster Antiq. Jn.*, xxxv, 62-71 (1993/94).

        HOURIHAN (Colm). See 1173.

1348   JEFFERIES (Henry A.). The church courts of Armagh on the eve of the Reformation. In *Seanchas Ardmhacha*, xv, no. 2, pp 1-38 (1993).

1349   JENKINS (William). Ballyboughal. In *Baile*, pp 19-20 (1991). The origin of the name.

1350   KIRWAN (John). A portrait of James Butler 9th Earl of Ormond. In *Butler Soc. Jn.*, iii, 512-3 (1994).

1351   LENNON (Colm). The foundation charter of St. Sythe's guild, Dublin, 1476. In *Archiv. Hib.*, xlviii, 3-12 (1994). Transcript and translation of document.

1352   LONG (Harry). Three settlements of Gaelic Wicklow 1169-1600: Rathgall, Ballinacor and Glendalough. In *Wicklow*, pp 237-65 (1994).

1353   LYDON (James). Alexander Bicknor: archbishop and peculator. In *Hist. Ire.*, i, no. 2, pp 14-17 (1993).

1354   LYDON (J.F.). Medieval Wicklow: 'a land of war'. In *Wicklow*, pp 151-89 (1994).

1355   LYNCH (Anthony). Thomas Fleming, O.F.M., bishop of Leighlin (1432-c.58), cited to a provincial council at Ferns. In *Collect. Hib.*, xxxiv/xxxv, 7-9 (1992/93).

1356   LYONS (Mary Ann). Sidelights on the Kildare ascendancy: a survey of Geraldine involvement in the church, c.1470-c. 1520. In *Archiv. Hib.*, xlviii, 73-87 (1994).

1357   Mac an t'SAOI (Máire). Ar thóir Ghearóid Iarla. In *Oghma*, 2, pp 20-33 (1990).

1358   McCAFFERTY (John). Defamation and the church courts in early sixteenth-century Armagh. In *Archiv. Hib.*, xlviii, 88-99 (1994).

1359   McCARTHY (C.J.F.). Norman times. Bridgetown Priory of the Canons of St Victor (Beate Marie virginis de Villa Pontis, ordinis sancti Augustini Clonensis diocesis). In *Mallow Field Club Jn.*, xii, 134-52 (1994).

1360   Mac EITEAGAIN (Darren). Peasant revolt in Gaelic Ireland. In *U.C.D. Hist. Rev.*, viii, 26-30 (1994).

1361   Mac EITEAGAIN (Darren). Wine and whiskey: a taste of the Irish Renaissance. In *U.C.D. Hist. Rev.*, vii, 38-43 (1993).

McGRAIL (Sean). See 1197, 1198.

1362   McKEE (James). Niall O Neill and the twilight of Emain Macha. In *Dúiche Néill*, ix, 83-95 (1994).

McKELVIE (Roberta). See COTTER (Francis J.).

1363   MacMAHON (Michael). The charter of Clare Abbey and the Augustinian 'province' in Co. Clare. In *The Other Clare*, xvii, 21-8 (1993).

1364   McNAMEE (Colm). The Bruce invasions of Ireland. In *Hist. Ire.*, i, no. 1, pp 11-16 (1993).

1365   McNEILL (T.E.). Church building in 14th century Ireland and the "Gaelic revival". In *Jn. Ir. Archaeol.*, iii, 61-4 (1985/86).

1366   McNEILL (T.E.). Early castles in Leinster. In *Jn. Ir. Archaeol.*, v, 57-64 (1989/90).

1367   McNEILL (T.E.). Trim Castle, Co. Meath: the first three generations. In *Archaeol. Jn.*, cxlvii, 308-36 (1990).

McNEILL (T.E.). See MURPHY (E.M.).

MacSHAMHRÁIN (A.S.). See 1207.

1368   MAGEEAN (Anne). The Ardclinis or Glenarm crozier. In *The Glynns*, viii, 34-6 (1980).

1369   MAHER (Denise). Derrynaflan: the medieval grave slabs. In *Tipp. Hist. Jn.*, pp 162-6 (1994).

MALLORY (J.P.). See 1210.

1370   MANNING (Conleth). A 16th-century rothe in stone. In *Arch. Ire.*, vii, no. 2, pp 12-13 (1993).

1371   MANNING (Conleth). Two medieval grave slabs with French inscriptions from Parliament Street, Kilkenny. In *Old Kilkenny Rev.*, iv, 1141-45 (1993).

1372   MARTIN (B.K.). The Órlám episode in the medieval Irish Táin Bó Cúailnge. In *Medieval codicology, icongraphy, literature, and translation*, pp 194-205 (1994).

1373   MITCHELL (James). Mayor Lynch of Galway: a review of the tradition. In *Galway Arch. Soc. Jn.*, xxxviii, 31-44 (1981/82).

1374   MOONEY (Linne R.). An English record of the founding of a university in Dublin in 1358. In *I.H.S.*, xxviii, 225-7 (1993).

1375   MORGAN (Hiram). Reform and reaction in sixteenth-century Ulster. In *Nordirland in Geschichte und Gegenwart*, pp 13-26 (1994).

MULLALLY (Evelyn). See 1222.

1376   MURPHY (E.M.) and McNEILL (T.E.). Human remains excavated at Doonbought Fort, Co. Antrim, 1969. In *U.J.A.*, lvi, 120-38 (1993).

NENK (Beverley S.). See 1225, 1226.

1377   NICHOLLS (Kenneth). The development of lordship in County Cork 1300-1600. In *Cork*, pp 157-211 (1993).

Ní MHEARA (Róisín). See 1231.

1378   The Norman invasion. In *A window on the past*, [i], 8-10 (1987).

1379   O'BRIEN (A.F.). Politics, economy and society: the development of Cork and the Irish south-coast region c.1170 to c.1583. In *Cork*, pp 83-154 (1993).

1380   O'BRIEN (Caimin). A 13th-century hall house at Clohaskin, Co. Tipperary. In *North Munster Antiq. Jn.*, xxxv, 104-06 (1993/94).

1381   O'BRIEN (Elizabeth). Excavations at Dundrum Castle, Dundrum, Co. Dublin. In *Arch. Ire.*, iii, 136-7 (1989).

1382   O'BRIEN (John). Tower houses in south Clare. In *The Other Clare*, i, 19-23 (1977).

1383   Ó CANNAN (Tomás G.). A poem on the rights of the coarb of Saint Molaisse. In *Clogher Rec.*, xv, no. 1, pp 7-24 (1994).

Ó CANNAN (Tomás G.). See 1233.

1384   Ó CONCHEANAINN (Tomás). The scribe of the Irish astronomical tract in RIA B.II.1. In *Celtica*, xi, 158-67 (1976).

1385   Ó CONCHUBHAIR (Mícheál). Smaointe fáin ar leagha Éireann. In *Irisleabhar Mha Nuad*, pp 195-216 (1993).

1386   O'DOWD (Peadar). A baselard-knife from Annaghkeen. In *Galway Arch. Soc. Jn.*, xlv, 161-2 (1993).

Ó FLOINN (R.). See 1238.

Ó hUIGINN (Ruairí). See 1241, 1242.

1387   O'KEEFE (Tadhg). The archaeology of Norman castles in Ireland. Part 1: mottes and ringworks. In *Arch. Ire.*, iv, no. 3, pp 15-17 (1990); part 2: stone castles, iv, no 4, pp 20-22 (1990).

1388   O'LOUGHLIN (Thomas). Medieval papal letters: a source for local history. In *Hist. Ire.*, i, no. 3, pp 56-8 (1993).

O'NEILL (Assumpta). See 1247.

1389   PALMER (William). Borderlands and colonies: Tudor Ireland in the perspective of colonial America. In *Éire-Ireland*, xxix, no. 3, pp 37-51 (1994).

1390   PALMER (William). The problem of Ireland in Tudor foreign policy, 1485-1603. Pp 161. Woodbridge: Boydell Press, 1994.

1391   PALMER (William). That "insolent liberty": honor, rites of power, and persuasion in sixteenth-century Ireland. In *Renaissance Quarterly*, xlvi, 308-27 (1993).

1392   PARKER (Ciaran). Local government in County Waterford in the thirteenth and fourteenth centuries. Part I: the office of sheriff, c.1208-1305. In *Decies*, l, 17-24 (1994).

1393   PARKER (Ciaran). The Ostmen in post-Norman Waterford. In *Decies*, xlix, 29-37 (1994).

1394   PARKER (Ciaran). The social and ethnic distribution of crime in County Waterford, 1295-1325. In *Ir. Jurist*, xxviii/xxx, 264-9 (1993/95).

1395   PHILLIPS (J.R.S.). The remonstrance revisited: England and Ireland in the early fourteenth century. In *Men, women and war*, pp 13-27 (1993).

1396   PHILLIPS (Seymour). The medieval background. In *Europeans on the move*, pp 9-25 (1994).

PONTFARCY (Yolande de). See 1261.

POWER (Catryn). See 1262.

1397   RAMBO (Elizabeth). Colonial Ireland in medieval English literature. Pp 160. Selinsgrove, Pa.: Susquehanna University Press, 1994.

1398   RANKIN (Fred). The Down petition. In *Lecale Miscellany*, ix, 47-51 (1991).
        Includes transcript of E/36/1744 Public Record Office, London.

1399   RYAN (Gerard). The Normans in Thomond. In *The Other Clare*, ii, 10-11 (1978).

1400   SIMPSON (Linzi). Anglo-Norman settlement in Uí Briúin Cualann 1169-1350. In *Wicklow*, pp 191-235 (1994).

Skryne's link with St Mary's Abbey. See 1281.

1401   SMITH (Brendan). A county community in early fourteenth century Ireland: the case of Louth. In *Eng. Hist. Rev.*, cviii, 561-88 (1993).

1402   SMITH (Brendan). The De Pitchford family in thirteenth-century Ireland. In *Studia Hibernica*, xxvii, 29-43 (1993).

1403   SMITH (Philip). On the fringe and in the middle. The MacDonalds of Antrim and the Isles 1206-1586. In *Hist. Ire.*, ii, no. 1, pp 15-20 (1994).

1404   STACEY (Robin Chapman). The road to judgement: from custom to court in medieval Ireland and Wales. Pp xvi, 342. Philadelphia: University of Pennsylvania Press, 1994. (Middle Ages series).
        Personal suretyship.

A tale of two monasteries. See 1293.

TONER (Gregory). See 1296.

1405   Ua CRÓINÍN (Risteard). Recently discovered carving at Kilnaboy. In *The Other Clare*, xviii, 15 (1994).

1406   Ua CRÓINÍN (Risteárd) and BREEN (Martin). Some obscure tower house sites in the Corofin area. In *The Other Clare*, xvii, 5-12 (1993); xviii, 23-7 (1994).

1407   WILLIAMS (Bernadette). The annals of Friar John Clyn: provenance and bias. In *Archiv. Hib.*, xlvii, 65-77 (1993).

1408   WILLIAMS (Bernadette). The sorcery trial of Alice Kyteler. In *Hist. Ire.*, ii, no. 4, pp 20-4 (1994).

1409   WILSON (Anthony M.). Lords of Downpatrick 1512-1617. In *Lecale Miscellany*, ix, 59-65 (1991).

1410   WRIGHT (Charles D.). The Irish tradition in old English literature. Pp xii, 321. Cambridge: Cambridge University Press, 1993. (Cambridge studies in Anglo-Saxon England, 6).

1411   ZALESKI (Carol G.). St Patrick's Purgatory: pilgrimage motifs in a medieval otherworld vision. In *Jn. Hist. Ideas*, xlvi, 467-85 (1985).

1412   ABBOTT (William M.). James Ussher and 'Ussherian' episcopacy, 1640-
1656: the Primate and his Reduction manuscript. In *Albion*, xxii, 237-59
(1990).

1413   AHERN (Mary). The Fitzgerald harp. In *The Book of Cloyne*, pp 174-6
(1994).
Made in 1621.

1414   AHERN (Michael). Our Tipperary-born martyrs. In *Tipperary county*, pp 23-
36 (1993).
Dermot O'Hurley, Archbishop of Cashel, 1530-1585; John Kearney, 1619-
1653; Terence O'Brien, Bishop of Emly, 1601-1651.

1415   Aibidil gaoidheilge & caiticiosma: Seaán (sic) Ó Cearnaigh's Irish primer of
religion published in 1571. *Ed.* Brian Ó Cuív. Pp x, 246. Dublin: Institute
for Advanced Studies, 1994.
Text in English and Irish with a complete facsimile of the 'Aibidil ...'.

1416   ARNOLD (L.J.). The restoration land settlement in County Dublin, 1660-
1688: a history of the administration of the Acts of settlement and explanation.
Pp 211. Blackrock, Co. Dublin: Irish Academic Press, 1993.

1417   BAKER (David J.). Off the map: charting uncertainty in Renaissance Ireland.
In *Representing Ireland*, pp 76-92 (1993).

BARBOUR (Bill). See *The Irvine baronetcy*.

1418   BARNARD (T.C.). Athlone, 1685; Limerick, 1710: religious riots or
charivaris. In *Studia Hib.*, xxvii, 61-75 (1993).

1419   BARNARD (T.C.). The Hartlib circle and the cult and culture of improvement
in Ireland. In *Samuel Hartlib and universal reformation*, pp 281-97 (1994).

1420   BARNARD (T.C.). Lawyers and the law in later seventeenth-century Ireland.
In *I.H.S.*, xxviii, 256-82 (1993).

1421   BARNARD (T.C.). The political, material and mental culture of the Cork
settlers, c.1650-1700. In *Cork*, pp 309-65 (1993).

1422   BARNARD (T.C.). Protestants and the Irish language c. 1675-1725. In *Jn.
Eccles. Hist.*, xliv, 243-72 (1993).

1423   BARNARD (Toby). 1641: a bibliographical essay. In *Ulster 1641*, pp 173-
86 (1993).

BARRY (T.B.). See 1308.

1424   BELL (Robert). 'Sheep stealers from the north of England': the Riding clans
in Ulster. In *Hist. Ire.*, ii, no. 4, pp 25-9 (1994).

1425   BENNIS (Emilie M.). The Quakers in Limerick, 1657-1707. In *Old Limerick Jn.*, xxx, 4-6 (1993).

1426   BOOMER (William). Boyle's Island, Donegal. In *R.S.A.I. Jn.*, cxxiii, 166-7 (1993).

BRADLEY (Helene). See 1314.

1427   BRADLEY (Pamela). When royalist Bandon switched to support of Cromwell. In *Bandon Hist. Jn.*, ix, 7-9 (1993).

1428   BRADSHAW (Brendan). Geoffrey Keating: apologist of Irish Ireland. In *Representing Ireland*, pp 166-90 (1993).

1429   BRADY (Ciaran). The chief governors: the rise and fall of reform government in Tudor Ireland, 1536-1588. Pp xviii, 322. Oxford: Cambridge University Press, 1994. (Cambridge studies in early modern British history).

1430   BREATHNACH (Catherine). Archbishop John Brenan (1625-1693): his life and work. In *Tipp. Hist. Jn.*, pp 148-59 (1993).

1431   BREATNACH (P.A.). The second earl of Tyrconnell, +1642, In *Eigse*, xxviii, 169-71 (1994).
        An account of his death, in Irish with translation.

1432   BREEN (John). The empirical eye: Edmund Spenser's "A view of the present state of Ireland". In *The Irish Review*, xvi, 44-52 (1994).

BREEN (Martin). See Ua CROÍNÍÍN (Ristéard).

1433   BROWNE (Mary Bonaventure). Recollections of an Irish Poor Clare in the seventeenth century: Mother Mary Bonaventure Browne, third abbess of Galway, 1647-1650. *Ed.* Celsus O'Brien. Pp [7], 22. [Galway]: [Poor Clares], [1993].

1434   BUTLER (Toby), ed. Documentary sources for the Butlers of Grallagh and Boytonrath in Co. Tipperary in the 16th and 17th centuries: a calendar of documents copied into the Blake Butler MSS vol II (unpublished). In *Butler Soc. Jn.*, iii, 584-600 (1994).

1435   BUTLER (Toby). 'Vile and ingrate traytors': aspects of rebellion in Munster 1569-1602. In *Butler Soc. Jn.,* iii, 530-40 (1994).

1436   CABALL (Marc). Providence and exile in early seventeenth-century Ireland. In *I.H.S.*, xxix, 174-88 (1994).

CABALL (Marc). See 1318.

1437   CANNY (Nicholas). The attempted anglicization of Ireland in the seventeeth century: an exemplar of British history. In *Three nations - a common history?*, pp 49-82 (1993).

1438   CANNY (Nicholas). English migration into and across the Atlantic during the seventeenth and eighteenth centuries. In *Europeans on the move*, pp 39-75 (1994).

1439   CANNY (Nicholas). Irish resistance to empire? 1641, 1690 and 1798. In *An imperial state at war*, pp 288-321 (1993).

1440   CANNY (Nicholas). The 1641 depositions: a source for social & cultural history. In *Hist. Ire.*, i, no. 4, pp 52-5 (1993).

1441   CANNY (Nicholas). The 1641 depositions as a source for the writing of social history: County Cork as a case study. In *Cork*, pp 249-308 (1993).

CANNY (Nicholas). See ROBINSON (Philip S.).

1442   CAREY (Vincent P.). Collaborator and survivor?: Gerald the eleventh Earl of Kildare and Tudor rule in Ireland. In *Hist. Ire.*, ii, no. 2, pp 13-17 (1994).

1443   CARLIN (Norah). Extreme or mainstream?: the English Independents and the Cromwellian reconquest of Ireland, 1649-1651. In *Representing Ireland*, pp 209-26 (1993).

1444   CARROLL (Clare). Representations of women in some early modern English tracts on the colonization of Ireland. In *Albion*, xxv, 379-93 (1993).

1445   CAVANAGH (Sheila T.). 'The fatal destiny of that land': Elizabethan views of Ireland. In *Representing Ireland*, pp 116-31 (1993).

1446   CLARKE (Aidan). The 1641 rebellion and anti-popery in Ireland. In *Ulster 1641*, pp 139-57 (1993).

COLMER (Albert W.K.). See 1325.

1447   COMERFORD (Patrick). John Comerford of Ballybur (1598-1667): tracing his later life. In *Old Kilkenny Rev.*, xlvi, 23-36 (1994).

1448   CORISH (Patrick J.). The Irish martyrs and Irish history. In *Archiv. Hib.*, xlvii, 89-93 (1993).

1449   COUGHLAN (Patricia). Natural history and historical nature: the project for a natural history of Ireland. In *Samuel Hartlib and universal reformation*, pp 298-317 (1994).

1450   CRAWFORD (Jon G.). Anglicizing the government of Ireland: the Irish Privy Council and the expansion of Tudor rule, 1556-1578. Pp xiv, 508. Blackrock, Co. Dublin: Irish Academic Press in association with the Irish Legal History Society, 1993.

1451   CROUZET (Francois). Massacres d'Irlande 1649, 1789. In *La Vendée dans l'histoire*, pp 227-37 (1994).

1452   CULLEN (L.M.). The Irish diaspora of the seventeenth and eighteenth centuries. In *Europeans on the move*, pp 113-49 (1994).

1453   CULLEN (Séamus) and O'KEEFE (Tadhg). A turreted enclosure at Pitchfordstown, County Kildare. In *R.S.A.I. Jn.*, cxxiv, 215-7 (1994).

CULLEN (Seamus). See 1329.

1454   CUNNINGHAM (Bernadette). A view of religious affiliation and practice in Thomond, 1591. In *Archiv. Hib.*, xlviii, 13-24 (1994).
Transcript of document, probably by Sir Turlough O'Brien of Ennistymon.

DEVINE (T.M.). See SMOUT (T.C.).

1455   DEVLIN (Kieran). The capture of Conor O Devany, martyr. In *Clogher Rec.*, xiv, no. 3, pp 125-8 (1993).
Conchúr Ó Duibheanaigh (c.1530-1612), observant Franciscan and bishop of Down and Connor.

1456   DUMVILLE (David N.). A seventeenth-century Hiberno-Breton hagiological exchange. In *France and the British Isles in the middle ages and Renaissance*, pp 249-54 (1991).
Influence of Irish hagiology on Albert Le Grand, O.P. Lives of the saints of Brittany, 1620s.

1457   An early emigrant family from Seagoe parish to America in 1682. In *Review*, v, no. 3, pp 7-9 (1986/87).

1458   EDWARDS (David). The Butler revolt of 1569. In *I.H.S.*, xxviii, 228-55 (1993).

1459   Extracts from the hearth money rolls, Co. Dublin. In *Dun Laoghaire Genealogical Soc. Jn.*, iii, 35-9 (1994).
Civil parishes of Monkstown, Dalkey, Killiney, Kill and Tullagh 1664-67.

FALVEY (Jeremiah). See GROGAN (Declan).

1460   FAYÇAL (Ei Ghoul). En marge du tricentenaire de la révocation. Un memoir inédit destiné a favoriser l'establissement de Protestants Français en Irelande (1684). In *Annales de Bretagne*, xcii, 403-09 (1985).

1461   FENLON (Jane). 'Her grace's closet': paintings in the Duchess of Ormond's closet at Kilkenny Castle. In *Ir. Georgian Soc. Bull.*, xxxvi, 30-47 (1994).

1462   FENNING (Hugh). Brevis et Summaria Relatio: an unpublished account of Dominican martyrs and exiles, 1656. In *Collect. Hib.*, xxxiv/xxxv, 34-58 (1992/93).

1463   FENNING (Hugh). Irishmen ordained at Lisbon 1660-1739. In *Collect. Hib.*, xxxiv/xxxv, 59-76 (1992/93).

1464   FLANAGAN (Laurence). The Irish legacy of the Spanish Armada. In *Arch. Ire.*, ii, 145-9 (1988).

1465   FLEETWOOD (John). Thomas Proby. In *Blackrock Soc. Proc.*, i, 14-25 (1992/93).
Thomas Proby, 1665-1720.

1466   FLYNN (Thomas S.). The Irish Dominicans, 1536-1641. Pp xxvii, 379. Blackrock, Co. Dublin: Four Courts Press, 1993.

1467   GIBBONS (Erin). Excavation of an underground passage at Bunratty. In *The Other Clare*, xvii, 29-30 (1993).

1468   GILLESPIE (Raymond). Catholic religious practices and payments in seventeenth-century Ireland [documents]. In *Archiv. Hib.*, xlvii, 3-10 (1993).

1469   GILLESPIE (Raymond). Destabilizing Ulster, 1641-2. In *Ulster 1641*, pp 107-21 (1993).

1470   GILLESPIE (Raymond). Documents and sources: plantation and profit: Richard Spert's Tract on Ireland, 1608. In *Ir. Econ. & Soc. Hist.*, xx, 62-71 (1993).

1471   GILLESPIE (Raymond). The murder of Arthur Champion and the 1641 rising in Fermanagh. In *Clogher Rec.*, xiv, no. 3, pp 52-66 (1993).

1472   GILLESPIE (Raymond). Plantations in early modern Ireland. In *Hist. Ire.*, i, no 4, pp 43-7 (1993).

1473   GILLINGHAM (John). The English invasion of Ireland. In *Representing Ireland*, pp 24-42 (1993).

        GLOVER (Winifred). See 1336.

1474   GROGAN (Declan). Bishop Foy and the cause of reform, edited by Jeremiah Falvey. Part 1. In *Decies*, l, 72-84 (1994).

1475   HADFIELD (Andrew). Briton and Scythian: Tudor representations of Irish origins. In *I.H.S.*, xxviii, 390-408 (1993).

1476   HADFIELD (Andrew). English colonialism and national identity in early modern Ireland. In *Éire-Ireland*, xxviii, no. 1, pp 69-86 (1993).

1477   HADFIELD (Andrew) and MALEY (Willy). Introduction: Irish representations and English alternatives. In *Representing Ireland*, pp 1-23 (1993).

1478   HADFIELD (Andrew). Translating the Reformation: John Bale's Irish Vocacyon. In *Representing Ireland*, pp 43-59 (1993).
        Vocacyon of John Bale to the Bishopricke of Ossorie (Wesel, 1553).

1479   HADFIELD (Andrew). Was Spenser's View of the Present State of Ireland censored? a review of the evidence. In *Notes and Queries*, xl, 459-63 (1994).

1480   HARRISON (Alan). Béal eiriciúil as Inis Eoghain: John Toland (1670-1722). Pp 105. Baile Átha Cliath: Coiscéim, 1994.

1481   HARRISON (Richard S.). The Quakers of Bandon and west Cork (1655-1807). In *Bandon Hist. Jn.*, x, 3-9 (1994).

1482   HAYES (William J.). 'The Prior's tomb' in Templemore old church. In *Tipp. Hist. Jn.*, pp 186-8 (1993).

1483   Hearth money rolls (1663). The parish of Tanee. In *Irish Family History*, i, no. 1, pp 29-30 (1993).

1484   HENRY (Gráinne). Ulster exiles in Europe, 1605-1641. In *Ulster 1641*, pp 37-60 (1993).

1485   HERLIHY (Kevin). The Cromwellian government and the transportation to Connacht. In *Cathair na Mart*, xiii, 72-7 (1993).

1486   HIGGINS (Ian). Swift's politics: a study in disaffection. Pp xiii, 232. Cambridge: Cambridge University Press, 1994. (Cambridge studies in eighteenth-century English literature and thought, 20).

1487   HIGGINS (Jim). Some 17th century renaissance style sculpture from Roscommon town. In *Roscommon Hist. Soc. Jn.*, iv, 61-3 (1992).

        HIGGINS (Jim). See 1341, 1343.

1488   HILL (J. Michael). Fire and sword: Sorley Boy MacDonnell and the rise of Clan Ian Mor, 1538-1590. Pp xiii, 321. London: Athlone Press, 1993.
        Scotland and Ulster.

1489   HILL (J. Michael). The origin of the Scottish plantations in Ulster to 1625: a reinterpretation. In *Jn. British Studies*, xxii, no. 1, pp 24-43 (1993).

1490   HILL (Tracey). Humanism and homocide: Spenser's 'A view of the present state of Ireland'. In *Ir. Studies Rev.*, iv, 2-4 (1993).

1491   HOBSON (R.B.). Maurice Cuffe of Ennis and his family. In *The Other Clare*, xviii, 28-31 (1994).

1492   HUGHES (A.J.). A bardic poem by Diarmuid Mac an Bhaird on the destruction of a MacMahon stronghold in Co. Monaghan 1647 AD. In *Clogher Rec.*, xiv, no. 3, pp 67-76 (1993).

1493   IRELAND (Aideen). A seventeenth-century find of gold ornaments. In *Jn. Ir. Archaeol.*, v, 35-6 (1989/90).
        A re-examination of two accounts relating to the discovery and theft of gold in a manuscript in Trinity College Dublin.

1494   IRELAND (John de Courcy). Privateering of Youghal: illustrations [by] Fiona Kelly. In *Ardmore Jn.*, x, 3-6 (1993).

1495   The Irish fiants of the Tudor sovereigns during the reigns of Henry VIII, Edward VI, Philip and Mary, and Elizabeth I with a new introduction by Kenneth Nicholls, preface by Tomás Ó Canann. 4 vols. Dublin: Éamonn de Búrca for Edmund Burke, 1994.
        1521-1603. Originally published 1875-1890.

1496   The Irvine baronetcy, translated by Bill Barbour, with notes by Jack Johnston. In *Clogher Rec.*, xiv, no. 3, pp 47-51 (1993).

1497   JARDINE (Lisa). Encountering Ireland: Gabriel Harvey, Edmund Spenser, and English colonial ventures. In *Representing Ireland*, pp 60-75 (1993).

1498   JOANNON (Pierre). Jacques II et l'expedition d'Irlande d'apres les depeches du Comte d'Avaux, ambassadeur extraordinaire de Louis XIV. In *Études Irlandaises*, xviii, no. 2, pp 93-108 (1993).

        JOHNSTON (Jack). See *The Irvine baronetcy*.

1499   KELLY (Billy). 'Most illustrious cavalier' or 'unkinde desertor'? James Butler, first duke of Ormond. In *Hist. Ire.*, i, no 2, pp 18-22 (1993).

1500   KELLY (James). 'The glorious and immortal memory': commemoration and Protestant identity in Ireland 1660-1800. In *R.I.A. Proc.*, section c, pp 25-52 (1994).

1501   KENNY (Michael). Irish coin hoards of the 17th century: their historical and archaeological significance. In *Jn. Ir. Archaeol.*, iii, 65-7 (1985/86).

1502   KENNY (Michael).   Silver coins of Charles I (1625-49) found at Scurlockstown, Trim. In *Ríocht na Midhe*, ix, no. 1, pp 22-3, (1994/95).

1503   KIDD (Colin). Gaelic antiquity and national identity in enlightenment Ireland and Scotland. In *English Hist. Rev.*, cix, 1197-1214 (1994).

1504   KILROY (Phil). Protestant dissent and controversy in Ireland, 1660-1714. Pp ix, 300. Cork: Cork University Press, 1994.

1505   KILROY (Phil). Protestantism in Ulster, 1610-1641. In *Ulster 1641*, pp 25-36 (1993).

1506   KIRWAN (John). Thomas Butler, 10th Earl of Ormond. His early career and rise to prominence: Part 1. In *Butler Soc. Jn.*, iii, 514-30 (1994).

         KIRWAN (John). See 1350.

1507   KNOX (R. Buick). The 1642 Presbytery: its background and its consequences. In *Presb. Hist. Soc. Bull. of Ire.*, xxi, 4-10 (1992).

         LANDSMAN (N.C.). See SMOUT (T.C.).

1508   LAURIE (Bruce). The life of Richard Kane: Britain's first Lieutenant-Governor of Minorca. Pp 291. Rutherford, N.J.: Fairleigh Dickinson University Press; London: Associated University Presses, 1994.
         Richard Kane, born Duneane, Co. Antrim 1662, died Minorca 1736.

1509   Le GRAND (Albert). La vie de S. Sané: a seventeenth-century life of Saint Senan; translated by Jean-Michel Picard. In *North Munster Antiq. Jn.*, xxxv, 45-51 (1993/94).

1510   LENIHAN (Pádraig). Catholicism and the Irish Confederate armies: for God or King? In *Recusant History*, xxii, 182-98 (1994/95).

1511   LENNON (Colm). Sixteenth-century Ireland: the incomplete conquest. Pp 390. Dublin: Gill & Macmillan, 1994. (New Gill history of Ireland, 2)

1512   LIGGIO (Leonard). 1492 and all that. English origins of American racism. In *Irishways*, i, 23-5 (1991); ii, 25-6 (1992); iii, 19-20 (1992).

1513   LOEBER (Rolf). The geography and practice of English colonisation in Ireland, 1534 to 1609. Pp 82. [Dublin] Group for the Study of Irish Historic Settlement, 1991. (Irish settlement studies, no. 3)

1514   LOEBER (Rolf). Settlers' utilisation of the natural resources. In *Wicklow*, pp 267-304 (1994).

         LONG (Harry). See 1352.

1515   LUPTON (Julia Reinhard).   Mapping mutability; or, Spenser's Irish plot.   In
         Representing Ireland, pp 93-115 (1993).

1516   McCABE (Richard).   Edmund Spenser, poet of exile.   In *Brit. Acad. Proc.*,
         lxxx, 73-103 (1993).

         MacCARTHY (C.J.F.).   See 1359.

1517   McCAVITT (John).   An Irish trilogy: the wars of the seventeenth century and
         the colonisation of Ulster.   In *Nordirland in Geschichte und Gegenwart*, pp
         27-42 (1994).

1518   McCAVITT (John).   The flight of the earls, 1607.   In *I.H.S.*, xxix, 159-73
         (1994).

1519   McCAVITT (John).   The political background to the Ulster plantation, 1607-
         1620.   In *Ulster 1641*, pp 7-23 (1993).

1520   MacLEAN (Rachel).   Eat your greens: an examination of the potential diet
         available in Ireland during the mesolithic.   In *U.J.A.*, lvi, 1-8 (1993).

1521   Mac CUARTA (Brian).   Introduction.   In *Ulster 1641*, pp 1-6 (1993).

1522   Mac CUARTA (Brian).   A planter's interaction with Gaelic culture: Sir
         Matthew de Renzy, 1577-1634.   In *Ir. Econ. & Soc. Hist.*, xx, 1-17 (1993).

1523   Mac CUINNEAGÁIN (Conall).   'Aodh Ruadh Ó Domhnaill - what caused his
         death?'   In *Donegal Annual,* xlvi, 18-22 (1994).

1524   MacDONNELL (Hector).   A noble pretension.   In *The Glynns*, viii, 20-33
         (1980).
         MacDonald family history.

1525   Mac EITEAGAIN (Darren).   Unmasking of Eoghan Ruadh Ó Néill.   In *Hist.
         Ire.*, ii, no. 3, pp 21-5 (1994).

         Mac EITEAGAIN (Darren).   See 1360, 1361.

1526   McGINN (Brian).   How Irish is Montserrat?   In *Ir. Roots* 1994, no. 1, pp
         20-23 (1994); no. 2, pp 15-17 (1994); no. 4, pp 20-21 (1994).

1527   McGINN (Brian).   The Irish in Roanoke Island.   In *Ir. Roots* 1993, no. 3, p.
         21 (1993).

1528   McGINN (Brian).   Virginia's lost Irish colonists.   In *Ir. Roots* 1993, no. 4,
         pp 21-4 (1993).

1529   Mac GLEANNÁIN (Liam).   The 'massacre' at Longford in 1641.   In
         Teathba, ii, no. 1, pp 63-7 (1980).
         Attack on planter families.

1530   McGLEENON (C.F.).   O'Neill's frontier campaign of 1595 in mid Armagh.
         In *Dúiche Néill*, ix, 66-82 (1994).

1531   McGLEENON (C.F.).   Patterns of settlement in the Catholic parishes of
         Ballymore and Mullaghbrack in the 17th and 18th centuries.   In *Seanchas
         Ardmhacha*, xv, no. 2, pp 51-83 (1993).

1532   McGRATH (Bríd).   County Meath from the depositions.   In *Ríocht na Midhe*, ix, no. 1, pp 24-41 (1994/95).

1533   McGURK (J.J.N.).   A survey of the demands made on the Welsh shires to supply soldiers for the Irish War 1594-1602. In *Cymmrodorian. Soc. Trans.*, pp 56-68 (1983).

1534   McKENNY (Kevin).   Charles II's Irish cavaliers: the 1649 officers and the Restoration land settlement. In *I.H.S.*, xxviii, 409-25 (1993).

        MacMAHON (Michael).   See 1363.

1535   McNEILL (Tom).   Belfast's first industrial revolution.   In *Curr. Archaeol*, xii, no. 134, pp 56-7 (1993).

1536   MagGRAITH (Micheál).   *Beatha Aodha Ruaidh Uí Dhomnaill:* Beathaisnéis de chuid an Renaissance. In *Irisleabhar Mhá Nuad*, pp 45-54 (1994).

1537   MAGUIRE (Bill).   Digging up the past: 1690 and all that.   In *Arch. Ire.*, iv, 61-2 (1990).

1538   MALEY (Willy).   A Spenser chronology. Pp xv, 120.   Basingstoke: Macmillan, 1994.
        Author chronologies.

1539   MALEY (Willy).   How Milton and some contemporaries read Spenser's *View*. In *Representing Ireland*, pp 191-208 (1993).

        MALEY (Willy).   See HADFIELD (Andrew).

1540   MANNING (Conleth).   Revealing a private inscription.   In *Arch. Ire.*, viii, no. 3, pp 24-6 (1994).

        MANNING (Conleth).   See 1370, 1371.

1541   MARSHALL (Alan).   Irish spies and plotters in seventeenth-century Europe. In *Ir. Studies Rev.*, ix, 7-12 (1994).

1542   MEAGHER (Jim).   O'Sullivan Beare's rout of the English at Ballyhea.   In *The history and legends of Ballyhoura mountains*, pp 9-15 (1993).

1543   MEAGHER (Jim).   The scene around Ballyhouras in 1641 - desolation.   In *The history and legends of Ballyhoura mountains*, pp 57-63 (1993).

1544   MILLETT (Benignus).   Franciscans in Ireland in 1654.   In *Collect. Hib.*, xxxiv/xxxv, 23-33 (1992/93).

1545   MILLETT (Benignus).   Maurice MacBrien, bishop of Emly, and the confiscation of his baggage, March 1578.   In *Collect. Hib.*, xxxiv/xxxv, 10-14 (1992/93).

1546   MILLETT (Benignus).   Elphin and Ross seek Franciscans as bishops, 1649-51.   In *Collect. Hib.*, xxxiv/xxxv, 18-22 (1992/93).

1547   MILLETT (Benignus).   Walter Cheevers, O.F.M., postulated for Ferns, 1622. In *Collect. Hib.*, xxxiv/xxxv, 15-17 (1992/93).

1548   MORGAN (Hiram). Faith and fatherland or queen and country?: an unpublished exchange between O'Neill and the state at the height of the Nine Years War. In *Dúiche Néill*, ix, 9-65 (1994).

1549   MORGAN (Hiram). Hugh O'Neill and the Nine Years war in Tudor Ireland. In *Hist. Jn.*, xxxvi, 21-37 (1993).

1550   MORGAN (Hiram). 'Lawes of Irelande': a tract by Sir John Davies. In *Ir. Jurist*, xxviii/xxx, 307-13 (1993/95).

1551   MORGAN (Hiram). Tom Lee: the posing peacemaker. In *Representing Ireland*, pp 132-65 (1993).
        Captain Thomas Lee (1594) portrait by Marcus Gheeraedts, the younger.

1552   MORGAN (Hiram). Tyrone's rebellion: the outbreak of the Nine Years War in Tudor Ireland. Pp xi, 250, [London]: Royal Historical Society; Woodbridge (Suffolk); Boydell & Brewer, 1993. (Royal Historical Society studies in history, no. 67)

        MORGAN (Hiram). See 1375.

1553   MORRILL (John). The Britishness of the English revolution 1640-1660. In *Three nations - a common history?*, pp 83-115 (1993).

1554   MOYLAN (Séamus). At the edge of the abyss: poems by Brian MacGiolla Phádraig (*c.*1580-*c.*1652). In *Old Kilkenny Rev.*, iv, 1170-80 (1993).
        A priest-poet, reputedly martyred by the Cromwellians.

1555   MULCAHY (John). Patrick Lavallin and the Popish Plot. In *Cork Hist. Soc. Jn.*, xcix, 83-95 (1994).

1556   MULVEEN (Jack). Galway goldsmiths, their marks and ware. In *Galway Arch. Soc. Jn.*, xlvi, 43-64 (1994).

1557   MURPHY (Andrew). Gold lace and a frozen snake: Donne, Wotton and the Nine Years War. In *Ir. Studies Rev.*, viii, 9-11 (1994).

        MURPHY (Hilary). See WATSON (Edward).

1558   MURPHY (Seán). Irish Jacobitism and freemasonry. In *Eighteenth-century Ireland*, ix, 75-82 (1994).

1559   MURTAGH (Harman). Kilkenny colonels and their regiments in the Jacobite war, 1689-91. In *Old Kilkenny Rev.*, iv, 1215-27 (1993).

1560   MURTAGH (Harman). The Williamite war 1689-91. In *Hist. Ire.*, i, no. 1, pp 39-42 (1993).

        NICHOLLS (Kenneth). See *The Irish Fiants of the Tudor sovereigns* (1994).

        NICHOLLS (Kenneth). See 1377.

1561   Ní MHEARA (Róisín). The Wild Geese in Austria. In *Seanchas Ardmhacha*, xvi, no. 1, pp 76-92 (1994).

        O'BRIEN (A.F.). See 1379.

111

O'BRIEN (Celsus). See BROWNE (Mary Bonaventure).

O'BRIEN (Elizabeth). See 1381.

1562   O'BRIEN (John). The siege of Bunratty. In *The Other Clare*, ii, 15-18 (1978).

O'BRIEN (John). See 1382.

1563   Ó BUACHALLA (Breandán). James our true king: the ideology of Irish royalism in the seventeenth century. In *Political thought in Ireland since the seventeenth century*, pp 7-35 (1993).

1564   O'CALLAGHAN (John). Travelling in Duhallow before 1760. In *Seanchas Duthalla*, ix, 27-46 (1993).

Ó CANANN (Tomas). See *The Irish fiants of the Tudor sovereigns* (1994).

Ó CEARNAIGH (Seaán) (sic). See *Aibidil Gaoidheilge* (1994).

1565   Ó CIARDHA (Éamonn). Tóraíochas is rapairíochas sa seachtú haois déag. In *Hist. Ire.*, ii, no i, pp 21-5 (1994). With a summary in English.

Ó CONCHUBHAIR (Mícheál). See 1385.

1566   O'CONNELL (Patricia). The northern dioceses and the Irish College of Alcalá, Spain. In *Ulster Local Studies*, xv, no. 2, pp 34-9 (1993).

Ó CUÍV (Brian). See *Aibidil Gaoidheilge* (1994).

1567   Ó CUNLUAIN (Proinsias). Documents from Dungannon: some letters of Hugh O Neill. In *Dúiche Neill*, viii, 9-33 (1993).

1568   Ó DÁLAIGH (Brian). Notice of marriage banns of Owen McConsidin and Una Clanchie Ennis 1658. In *The Other Clare*, xviii, 32 (1994).

1569   O'DONNELL (Sean). 1593. In *Ó Domhnaill Abú*, xx, 3-4 (1993).

1570   O'DONOVAN (Michael R.). Notes on Sir William Hull and Leamcon, etc. In *Mizen Jn.*, i, 30-38 (1993).

1571   O'DONOVAN (Uinsin). Brightness & brightness. An account of Aogáin Ó Rahilly. In *Treoir*, xxv, no. 3, pp 15-20 (1993).

1572   Ó DÚSHLÁINE (Tadhg). As an Duibheagán: Dánta Diaga Uladh san 17ú-18ú haois. In *Irisleabhar Mhá Nuad*, pp 55-72 (1994).

1573   Ó FIONNAGÁIN (Proinsias). Conor O'Mahony, S.J. (1594-1656). Separatist. In *O'Mahony Jn.*, xvi, 3-15 (1993).

1574   Ó hANNRACHÁIN (Tadhg). Vatican diplomacy and the mission of Rinuccini to Ireland. In *Archiv. Hib.*, xlvii, 78-88 (1993).

1575   OHLMEYER (Jane H.). The 'Antrim plot' of 1641: a rejoinder. In *Hist. Jn.*, xxxvii, 431-7 (1994).

1576   OHLMEYER (Jane H.). Civil war and restoration in the three Stuart kingdoms: the career of Randal MacDonnell, Marquis of Antrim, 1609-1683. Pp xxiii, 357. Cambridge: Cambridge University Press, 1993. (Cambridge studies in early modern British history)

1577   OHLMEYER (Jane H.). The Marquis of Antrim: a Stuart turn-kilt? In *History Today*, xliii (March), 13-18 (1993).

    O'KEEFE (Tadhg). See CULLEN (Séamus).

1578   OLDEN (Michael). Geoffrey Keating - Seathrún Céitinn: Tipperary priest and scholar, 1570-1649. In *Tipperary county*, pp 14-22 (1993).

1579   Ó MURAILE (Nollaig). Ruaidhrí Ó hUiginn, scribe, of *An Tearmann* (fl. 1680). In *Ainm*, vi, 103-6 (1994/95).

1580   Ó MURCHADHA (Diarmuid). Gaelic land tenure in County Cork: Uíbh Laoghaire in the seventeenth century. In *Cork*, pp 213-48, (1993). Inchigeelagh parish.

1581   O'REGAN (Noel). 'Blessed with the holy Father's entertainment': Roman ceremonial music as experienced by the Irish earls in Rome, 1608. In *Music and the church*, pp 41-61 (1993). Based on Tadhg Ó Cianáin's diary.

1582   Ó RIORDAN (Michelle). The native Ulster mentalité as revealed in Gaelic sources, 1600-1650. In *Ulster 1641*, pp 61-91 (1993).

1583   Ó SIOCHRÚ (Micheál). The Confederation of Kilkenny. In *Hist. Ire.*, ii, no. 2, pp 51-6 (1994).

1584   O'SULLIVAN (Harold). The restoration land settlement in the diocese of Armagh, 1660 to 1684. In *Seanchas Ardmhacha*, xvi, no. 1, pp 1-70 (1994).

    PALMER (William). See 1389, 1390, 1391.

1585   PARKHILL (Trevor). Sources in the Public Record Office of Northern Ireland. In *Hist. Ire.*, i, no. 1, pp 43-6 (1993). Sources relating to the Williamite war.

1586   PATTERSON (Annabel). Reading Holinshed's Chronicles. Pp xviii, 339. Chicago: University of Chicago Press, 1994. Raphael Holinshed, d. 1580? Chronicles of England, Scotland and Ireland.

1587   PERCEVAL-MAXWELL (M.). Debate. The 'Antrim plot' of 1641 - a myth? A response. In *Hist. Jn.*, xxxvii, 421-30 (1994).

1588   PERCEVAL-MAXWELL (M.). Ulster 1641 in the context of political developments in the three kingdoms. In *Ulster 1641*, pp 93-106 (1993).

1589   PHELAN (Margaret M.). The Rothe monument - St Mary's, Kilkenny. In *Old Kilkenny Rev.*, iv, 1228-33 (1993).

    PICARD (Jean-Michel). See Le GRAND (Albert).

    PHILLIPS (Seymour). See 1396.

1590   PRENDERGAST (Ellen).   Images of the Holy Trinity - two new examples.
        In *Old Kilkenny Rev.*, iv, 1186-94 (1993).

1591   RAFFERTY (Celestine).   The Roman Catholic parish registers of Wexford
        town from *c.*1672:   some considerations   of their significance and use in
        historical research.   In *Wexford Hist. Soc. Jn.*, xv, 102-14 (1994/95).

1592   RAMBUSS (Richard).   Spenser's secret career.   Pp xv, 164. Cambridge:
        Cambridge University   Press, 1993.   (Cambridge studies in renaissance
        literature and culture, 3)

1593   REILLY (Stan J.).   The hearth money rolls for the County of Wicklow, 1668.
        In *Wicklow Hist. Soc. Jn.*, i, no. 6, pp 41-6 (1993).

1594   ROBINSON (Philip S.).   The plantation of Ulster: British settlement in an
        Irish landscape, 1600-1700; with an introduction to the reprint by Nicholas
        Canny [1st ed. reprinted].   Pp xxii, 254.   Belfast: Ulster Historical
        Foundation, 1994.
        1st pub.:   Dublin: Gill & Macmillan, 1984.

1595   ROBINSON-HAMMERSTEIN (Helga).   Archbishop Adam Loftus: the first
        provost of Trinity College, Dublin, Trinity Monday discourse, 17 May 1993.
        Pp 28. [Dublin]: [Trinity College, Dublin], [1993].

1596   ROCHE-KELLY (Hubert).   The oil mills at Ballintlea.   In *The Other Clare*, ii,
        19 (1978).

1597   ROSS (Noel).   The site of Warren's Gate, Dundalk.   In *Louth Arch. Soc.
        Jn.*, xxiii, no. 2, pp 214-17 (1994).

1598   Rothe House in 1619.   (From the will of John Roth Fitzpiers of 31 March
        1619).   In *Old Kilkenny Rev.*, xlvi, 37 (1994).
        From Rev. William Healy, *History and antiquities of Kilkenny (county and
        city)*, 1893.

1599   SESSIONS (William K.).   Further Irish studies in early printing history.   I:
        William Penn's tract printing in Cork in 1670 and II: Edward Jones: the
        travelling printer with William III in 1690.   59 leaves.   [York]: Ebor Press,
        1994. (Greenback series, 14)

1600   SIMMS (Hilary).   Violence in County Armagh, 1641.   In *Ulster 1641*, pp
        123-38 (1993).

        SMITH (Philip). See 1403.

1601   SMOUT (T.C.), LANDSMAN (N.C.), and DEVINE (T.M.).   Scottish
        emigration in the seventeenth and eighteenth centuries.   In *Europeans on the
        move*, pp 76-112 (1994).
        Includes research on Ireland.

1602   STRADLING (R.A.).   The Spanish monarchy and Irish mercenaries: the
        Wild Geese in Spain 1618-68.   Pp 219. Blackrock, Co. Dublin: Irish
        Academic Press, 1993.

1603   SWORDS (Liam).   The Jacobite war.   A dispatch from Limerick, 1691.   In
        Seanchas Ardmhacha, xv, no. 1, pp 71-5 (1994).

1604   SWORDS (Liam).   Patrick O'Donnelly, 1649-1719, Bishop of Dromore.
        Material in the notarial files in Paris and the propaganda archives in Rome.   In
        Seanchas Ardmhacha, xv, no. 2, pp 84-97 (1993).

1605   TIERNEY (Ann).   The world outside Kilkenny in 1594.   In *Old Kilkenny
        Rev.*, xlvi, 4-9 (1994).

1606   TIGHE (Joan).   When Dublin had a woman garbage supremo.   In *Dublin
        Hist. Rec.*, xlvii, 110-11 (1994).
        Katherine White - city scavenger, 1634.

1607   Ua CRÓINÍN (Risteárd) and BREEN (Martin).   Some obscure tower house
        sites in the Corofin area.   In *The Other Clare*, xvii, 5-12 (1993).

        Ua CRÓINÍN (Risteard).   See 1405.

1608   WALSH (Paul).   The medieval merchant's mark and its survival in Galway.
        In *Galway Arch. Soc. Jn.*, xlv, 1-28. (1993).

1609   WATSON (Edward).   Memories of Colonel Jonas Watson;   edited by Hilary
        Murphy.   In *Wexford Hist. Soc. Jn.*, xv, 115-18 (1994/95).

1610   WEBSTER (Charles).   Benjamin Worsley: engineering for universal reform
        from the Invisible College to the Navigation Act.   In *Samuel Hartlib and
        universal Reformation*, pp 213-35 (1994).
        Benjamin Worsley (1618-77) went into service of the earl of Strafford in
        Ireland in 1640.

1611   WILLIAMS (B.B.).   A wooden figure found at Lettershendony, County
        Londonderry.   In *U.J.A.*, lvi, 148-51 (1993).

        WILSON (Anthony M.).   See 1409.

1612   WOKECK (Marianne S.).   German and Irish immigration.   In *Amer. Philos.
        Soc. Proc.*, cxxxiii, 128-43 (1989).
        Immigration to Philadelphia from its founding in 1682 until the 1780s.

1613   ADAMS (J.R.R.). The mass distribution of geographical literature in Ulster 1750-1850. In *Geog. Jn.*, cliii, 383-7 (1987).

1614   ANDERSON (Hugh). The hard case of Sir Henry. In *Irish convict lives*, pp 51-79 (1993).
Sir Henry Browne Hayes, 1761-1832, heiress abductor.

1615   ASCH (Ronald G.). Die englische Herrschaft in Irland und die Krise der Stuart-Monarchie im 17. Jahrhundert. In *Hist. Jahrb*, cx, 370-408 (1990).

1616   ASCH (Ronald G.). The Protestant ascendancy in Ireland from the American Revolution to the Act of Union, 1776-1801. In *Three nations - a common history?*, pp 161-90 (1993).

1617   AUBREY (John). Two of John Aubrey's eminent men; presented by Brendan Neary. In *Butler Soc. Jn.*, iii, 550-54 (1994).

1618   AUDLEY (Brian). A newly discovered portrait of Patrick Quin, the harper, *c*.1745-1812. In *Treoir*, xxvi, no. 4, pp 30-32 (1994).

1619   B. (P.P.). St Stephen's Green. In *Dublin Hist. Rec.*, xlvii, 112 (1994).
A play of that name by William Philips, performed in 1699-1700 season.

1620   The Backbone: diaries of a military family in the Napoleonic wars. *Ed.* Alethea Hayter. Pp xi, 343. Edinburgh: Pentland Press, 1993.
Slessor family; section on 1798 rebellion, pp 39-48, plus other Irish references.

1621   BAILEY (Bee). The Brontes' Irish roots. In *Ir. Roots* 1993, no. 2, p. 27 (1993).

1622   BALLHATCHET (Kenneth). The East India Company and Roman Catholic missionaries. In *Jn. Eccles. Hist.*, xliv, 273-88 (1993).

1623   BARNARD (T.C.). Historiographical review. Farewell to old Ireland. In *Hist Jn.*, xxxvi, 909-28 (1993).

BARNARD (T.C.). See 1418, 1421.

1624   BARTLETT (Thomas). The burden of the present: Theobald Wolfe Tone, republican and separatist. In *The United Irishmen*, pp 1-15 (1993).

1625   BARTLETT (Thomas). The Catholic question in the eighteenth century. In *Hist. Ire.*, i, no. 1, pp 17-21 (1993).

1626   BARTLETT (Thomas). 'Masters of the mountains': the insurgent careers of Joseph Holt and Michael Dwyer, County Wicklow, 1798-1803. In *Wicklow*, pp 379-410 (1994).

1627   BARTLETT (Thomas). 'A weapon of war yet untried': Irish Catholics and the armed forces of the crown, 1760-1830. In *Men, women and war*, pp 66-85 (1993).

1628   BELL (Muriel). Notes on the Quakers of mid-Ulster. In *Ulster Local Studies*, xvi, no. 1, pp 63-80 (1994).

1629   BERMAN (David). George Berkeley: idealism and the man. Pp xi, 230. Oxford: Clarendon Press, 1994.

        BENNIS (Emilie M.). See 1425.

1630   BIELENBERG (Andy). The Watt family and the distilling industry in Derry, 1762-1921. In *Ulster Folklife*, xl, 16-26 (1994).

1631   BLACK (Jeremy). Swift and foreign policy revisited. In *Reading Swift*, pp 61-70 (1993).

1632   BLACKSTOCK (Allan). The social and political implications of the raising of yeomanry in Ulster: 1796-8. In *The United Irishmen*, pp 234-43 (1993).

1633   BOOTH (Alan). Liberty or slavery. Irish radicalism in England in the 1790s. In *Ir. Studies Rev.*, ii, 26-8 (1992).

1634   BOYD (Hugh Alexander). An old Ballycastle account book: trade and commerce in the area in the eighteenth century. In *The Glynns*, viii, 13-19 (1980).

1635   BOYDELL (Barra). St Michan's Church, Dublin: the installation of the organ in 1725 and the duties of the organist. In *Dublin Hist. Rec.*, xlvi, 101-20 (1993).

1636   BOYDELL (Brian). Jonathan Swift and the Dublin musical scene. In *Dublin Hist. Rec.*, xlvii, 132-7 (1994).

1637   BOYLE (Darinagh). Half-hanged McNaghten. Pp 51. Derry: Guildhall Press, 1993.
        Criminal, d. 1761.

1638   BRIMS (John). Scottish radicalism and the United Irishmen. In *The United Irishmen*, pp 151-66 (1993).

1639   BROWN (A.W. Geoffrey). Thomas Jackson: minister of Downpatrick, 1700-1708. In *Lecale Miscellany*, ix, 11-20 (1991).

1640   BROWNE (Bernard). John Barry: the forgotten American hero. In *Wexford Hist. Soc. Jn.*, xv, 43-51 (1994/95).

1641   BURKE (Martin). Piecing together a shattered past: the historical writings of the United Irish exiles in America. In *The United Irishmen*, pp 297-306 (1993).

1642   BURKE (Thomas). An Ossory instruction of 1773. *Ed.* Fearghus Ó Fearghail. In *Archiv. Hib.*, xlviii, 25-36 (1994).
        Transcript of document.

1643   BURNETT (Harry). The lead mine at Castleward. In *Lecale Miscellany*, vi, 14-16 (1988).

1644   BURTCHAELL (Jack). Waterford two centuries ago: the *Waterford Herald* for 1792-3. In *Decies*, xlvii, 3-15 (1993).

1645   BUTLER (Toby). The siege of Golden Castle, James Butler of Boytonrath, captain in the Confederate Catholic army, 1642-53. In *Butler Soc. Jn.*, iii, 541-50 (1994).

        BUTLER (Toby). See 1434.

1646   BUTTIMER (Cornelius G.). *Cogadh Sagsana Nuadh sonn*: reporting the American revolution. In *Studia Hib.*, xxviii, 63-101 (1994).

1647   BUTTIMER (Cornelius G.). Gaelic literature and contemporary life in Cork, 1700-1840. In *Cork*, pp 585-653 (1993).

1648   Calendar of Kinsale documents, vol. 3. Compiled by Michael Mulcahy. Pp 103. Kinsale: Kinsale Regional Museum, 1994.
        Kinsale Grand Jury presentments, 1720-1731.

1649   CAMPBELL (Flann). The elusive Mr Ogilvie (1740-1832). In *Familia*, ii, no. 9, pp 3-45 (1993).

1650   CAMPBELL (John L.). Unpublished letters by Edward Lhuyd in the National Library of Scotland. In *Celtica*, xi, 34-42 (1976).

1651   CANAVAN (Thomas L.). Robert Burton, Jonathan Swift and the tradition of anti-puritan invective. In *Jn. Hist. Ideas*, xxxiv, 227-42 (1973).

1652   CANAVAN (Tony). Making a hole in the moon: the rescue of Princess Clementina. In *Hist. Ire.*, i, no. 4, pp 19-22 (1993).

1653   CANAVAN (Tony). The Protestants in eighteenth-century Ireland. In *Nordirland in Geschichte und Gegenwart*, pp 43-52 (1994).

        CANNY (Nicholas). See 1438, 1439.

1654   CANTWELL (Brian J.). Persons who died in 1798, etc. Part 2. In *The Past*, xviii, 45-53 (1992).
        Continued from *The Past*, xvii, 73-6 (1990).

1655   CARROLL (Judith). The excavation of the old Presbyterian Meetinghouse of Ramelton, Co. Donegal. In *Arch. Ire.*, iii, 61-3 (1989).

1656   CASEY (Christine). Architectural line-engraving in Dublin, 1700-1780. In *Long Room*, xxxix, 18-29 (1994).

1657   CASEY (Christine). The restoration of Newman House. In *Ir. Arts Rev. Yearbk*, pp 111-16 (1994).

1658   CHADWICK (Anne). 'Tipperary Joe': Field Marshal Viscount Gough. In *Tipp. Hist. Jn.*, pp 91-5 (1994).
        Viscount Sir Hugh Gough, 1779-1869.

1659   CHAMBERS (George).   Divided loyalties in the business community of Belfast in 1798. In *Familia*, ii, no. 10, pp 13-38 (1994).

CLARK (Gladys L.H.).   See GREENE (John C.).

1660   CLARK (Mary), ed. Dublin city pipe water accounts 1704/5. In *Ir. Geneal.*, ix, no. 1, pp 76-88 (1994).

1661   CLARKSON (L.A.).   Love, labour and life: women in Carrick-on-Suir in the late eighteenth century. In *Ir. Econ. & Soc. Hist.*, xx, 18-24 (1993).

CLARKSON (Leslie A.).   See KENNEDY (Liam).

1662   CLIFFORD (Brendan).   Edmund Burke and the United Irishmen   their relevance in Ireland today: a talk given ... 14 April 1993. Pp 20.   Millstreet, Co. Cork: Aubane Historical Society, 1994.

CLIFFORD (Brendan).   See MORLEY (John).

1663   CLONEY (Sean).   South-west Wexford in 1798. In *Wexford Hist. Soc. Jn.*, xv, 74-97 (1994/95).

1664   COFFEY (R.A.).   The foundation and early history of the Southwell Schools, Downpatrick, 1733-1800.   In *Lecale Miscellany*, viii, 53-64 (1990).

1665   COLEMAN (John).   Evidence for the collecting and display of paintings in mid-eighteenth-century Ireland.   In *Ir. Georgian Soc. Bull.*, xxxvi, 48-62 (1994).

1666   COLLINS (Brenda).   The Irish in Britain, 1780-1921.   In *An historical geography of Ireland*, pp 366-98 (1993).

1667   COLMER (Albert W.K.).   My quest for the Strangford Methodists.   In *Lecale Miscellany*, v, 44-7 (1987).

1668   COMER (Siobhán).   The origins of the gate lodge with specific reference to east Galway. In *Galway Roots*, ii, 13-17 (1994).

1669   CONLAN (Patrick).   Declaration of Emperor Joseph II on the Irish and English Franciscans and Dominicans in the Low Countries, 1782.   In *Collect. Hib.*, xxxiv/xxxv, 116-38 (1992/93).

1670   CONNOLLY (Padraig).   A Roscommon connection with the French Revolution.   In *Roscommon Hist. Soc. Jn.*, iii, 19-20 (1990).

1671   CONNOLLY (S.J.).   Late eighteenth-century Irish politics.   In *Parliamentary Hist.*, xiii, 227-35 (1994).

1672   COONEY (D.A. Levistone).   A pious Dublin printer.   In *Dublin Hist. Rec.*, xlvi, 74-100 (1993).
        Bennet Dugdale (?1756-1826), printer and Methodist.

1673   CORDEN (Arthur E.).   The Earl of Caherlough.   In *Carloviana*, xli, 22 (1993/94).
        A look at some 18th-century holders of this 'Irish' title.

1674   COUGHLAN (A.J.) and O'REILLY (F.D.). Edmund Burke and his kinsfolk in the Blackwater valley as seen through his letters. In *Mallow Field Club Jn.*, xii, 153-76 (1994).

1675   COWIE (Leonard W.). Edmund Burke, 1729-1797: a bibliography. Pp vi, 137. Westport (Conn.): Greenwood Press, 1994. (Bibliographies of British statesmen, no. 19)

1676   COWMAN (D.). The mining community at Avoca 1780-1880. In *Wicklow*, pp 761-88 (1994).

1677   COYLE (Eugene A.). Sir Edward Newenham - the 18th century Dublin radical. In *Dublin Hist. Rec.*, xlvi, 15-30 (1993).

1678   CRAWFORD (W.H.). The Belfast middle classes in the late eighteenth century. In *The United Irishmen*, pp 62-73 (1993).

1679   CRAWFORD (William). Kinship and inheritance in Ulster. In *Ulster Local Studies*, xvi, no. 2, pp 59-70 (1994).

1680   CROMIE (Howard). American presidents of Ulster descent. In *Presb. Hist. Soc. of Ire. Bull.*, xviii, 2-20 (1989).

1681   CROOKSHANK (C.H.). Days of revival: being the history of Methodism in Ireland. 6 vols. Clonmel: Tentmaker Publications, 1994.
Originally published as *History of Methodism* in 3 vols, 1885.

CROUZET (Francois). See 1451.

1682   CULLEN (L.M.). The Blackwater Catholics and County Cork society and politics in the eighteenth century. In *Cork*, pp 535-84 (1993).

1683   CULLEN (L.M.). Caoineadh Airt Uí Laoghaire. The contemporary political context. In *Hist. Ire.*, i, no. 4, pp 23-7 (1993).

1684   CULLEN (L.M.). The contemporary and later politics of 'Caoineadh Airt Uí Laoire'. In *Eighteenth-century Ireland*, viii, 7-38 (1993).
'Caoineadh Airt Uí Laoire' - a poem lamenting the death of Art O'Leary, by his wife Eileen Dubh Ní Chonaill.

1685   CULLEN (L.M.). The internal politics of the United Irishmen. In *The United Irishmen*, pp 176-96 (1993).

1686   CULLEN (L.M.). Politics and rebellion: Wicklow in the 1790s. In *Wicklow*, pp 411-501 (1994).

CULLEN (L.M.). See 1452.

1687   CUNNINGHAM (John). The Caldwells of Quebec. In *Familia*, ii, no. 10, pp 88-114 (1994).

1688   CUNNINGHAM (John). Fermanagh links with the continent in the eighteenth century. In *Ulster Local Studies*, xv, no. 2, pp 55-67 (1993).

1689   CURTIN (Nancy J.). The United Irish organisation in Ulster: 1795-8. In *The United Irishmen*, pp 209-21 (1993).

1690   CURTIN (Nancy J.). The United Irishmen: popular politics in Ulster and Dublin, 1791-1798. Pp vi, 317. Oxford: Clarendon Press, 1994.

1691   DALLAT (Cahal). Some notes on the Fullertons. In *Ulster Local Studies*, xvi, no. 2, pp 38-9 (1994).

1692   D'ARCY (Fergus). Irish trade unions before Congress. In *Hist. Ire.*, ii, no. 2, pp 25-30 (1994).

1693   DAVIES (Mary). Ancestral home of the Irish yew. In *Ir. Garden*, ii, no. 2, pp 10-11 (1993).
        Florence Court, Co. Fermanagh, an eighteenth-century house with garden laid out by William King in 1778-80.

1694   DAVIS (Marie). Child-rearing in Ireland, 1700-1830: an exploration. In *Ireland*, pp 169-83 (1994).

1695   De PORTE (Michael). Swift's horses of instruction. In *Reading Swift*, pp 199-211 (1993).
        Gulliver's travels.

        DEVINE (T.M.). See 1601.

1696   DICKSON (David). Butter comes to market: the origins of commercial dairying in County Cork. In *Cork*, pp 367-90 (1993).
        1680s-1800.

1697   DICKSON (David). Paine and Ireland. In *The United Irishmen*, pp 135-50 (1993).

1698   DOAN (James E.). The Scotch-Irish and the formation of a celtic southern culture in the 18th and 19th centuries. In *The Scotch-Irish and Hiberno-English language and culture*, pp 1-11 (1993).

1699   DOBSON (David). Irish emigrants in North America. Part I. Pp [3], 28. St Andrew's, Fife: D. Dobson, 1994.
        Aphabetical listing of names.

1700   DODD (Liam). William Dodd of Dublin and Westmeath. In *Dun Laoghaire Geneal. Soc. Jn.*, iii, 51-3 (1994).

1701   DONNELLY (Brian). A friend advises in a delicate matter - August 1780. In *Ir. Archives*, pp 22-5 (autumn 1994).
        Letter from W. Gibson to William Pollock on a medical matter.

1702   DORAN (Alan). The Duplicators - traitors of '98? In *Carloviana*, xxxiii, 4-5 (1985/86).

1703   DOYLE (Harry). A religious census of the barony of Cary 1734. In *The Glynns*, xxi, 65-76 (1993).

1704   DOYLE (Harry). A religious census of the barony of Carey [sic] 1734. (The parish of Armoy.) In *The Glynns*, xxii, 53-8 (1994).

1705   DUFFY (Godfrey F.). The Irish in Britain (1798-1916): a bibliography. Pp 12. Dun Laoghaire: Dun Laoghaire Genealogical Society [?1993].

1706 DUFFY (Paul). Some Limerick peruke-makers. In *North Munster Antiq. Jn.*, xxxv, 106 (1993/94).

1707 DUFFY (P.J.). The changing rural landscape 1750-1850: pictorial evidence. In *Ireland*, pp 26-42 (1994).

DUNLOP (Eull). See FERGUSON (Samuel).

DUNLOP (Eull). See *Henry Cooks's centenary* (1993).

1708 DUREY (Michael). The Dublin society of United Irishmen and the politics of the Carey-Drennan dispute, 1792-1794. In *Hist. Jn.*, xxxvii, 89-111 (1994).

1709 ECCLESHALL (Robert). Anglican political thought in the century after the revolution of 1688. In *Political thought in Ireland since the seventeenth century*, pp 36-72 (1993).

1710 ELLIOTT (Marianne). The Defenders in Ulster. In *The United Irishmen*, pp 222-33 (1993).

1711 ELLIOTT (Marianne). The origins and transformation of early Irish republicanism. In *Int. Rev. Soc. Hist.*, xxiii, 405-28 (1978).

1712 ELLIS (Frank H.). 'An argument against abolishing Christianity' as an argument against abolishing the Test Act. In *Reading Swift*, pp 127-39 (1993).

1713 EVANS (Robert Rees). Pantheisticon: the career of John Toland. Pp x, 232. New York: Peter Lang, 1991. (American university studies series 9, History, vol. 98).
John Toland, 1670-1722.

1714 FAGAN (Patrick). An Irish bishop in Penal times: the chequered career of Sylvester Lloyd OFM, 1680-1747. Pp xxvii, 379. Blackrock, Co. Dublin: Four Courts Press, 1993.

1715 FAHIE (Norah). The Huguenot cemetery in Dublin. In *Gateway to the Past*, i, no. 3, pp 143-4 (1994).

1716 FALVEY (J.). Pierce Butler of Coogy. An early eighteenth-century breach of privilege case. In *The Other Clare*, xviii, 33-9 (1994).

1717 FALVEY (Jeremiah). The Church of Ireland episcopate in the eighteenth century: an overview. In *Eighteenth-century Ireland*, viii, 103-14 (1993).

FALVEY (Jeremiah). See 1474.

1718 FAULKNER (Pádraig). Education in the parish of Dunleer. In *Louth Arch. Soc. Jn.*, xxiii, no. 1, pp 97-114 (1993).

1719 FEHENEY (J. Matthew). Aspects of Rice family history. In *A man raised up*, pp 47-66 (1994).

FENLON (Jane). See 1461

1720 FENNING (Hugh). Prayer-books and pamphlets: 1700-1829. In *Seanchas Ardmhacha*, xvi, no. 1, pp 93-9 (1994).

1721   FENNING (Hugh).   The 'Udienze' series in the Roman Archives of Propaganda Fide, 1750-1820. In *Archiv. Hib.*, xlviii, 100-06 (1994).

        FENNING (Hugh). See 1463.

1722   FERGUSON (Samuel).   William Stavely: Samuel Ferguson's 'Brief Biographical Sketch' and other materials on the Ferniskey man (1743-1825) known as the apostle of the Covenanters.   Compiled by Eull Dunlop; foreword by Robert Hanna; afterword by Trevor Magee. Pp 37. Ballymena: Mid Antrim Historical Group, 1993. (Mid Antrim Historical Group)

1723   FEWER (Thomas G.) and NICHOLLS (Kenneth W.), *presenters*.   The will of Robert Forstall of Kilferagh, 1645. In *Decies*, xlviii, 7-16 (1993).

1724   FIGGIS (Nicola).   Henry Trench (*c.*1685-1726), painter and illustrator. In *Ir. Arts Rev. Yearbk.*, pp 217-22 (1994).

1725   FINEGAN (Joanna).   The role of the printed word in Drogheda up to 1815: a case study of print production and consumption in provincial Ireland.   In *Louth Arch. Soc. Jn.*, xxiii, no. 2, pp 181-213 (1994).

1726   FISCHER (John Irwin).   Swift's early odes, Dan Jackson's nose, and 'The character of Sir Robert Walpole': some documentary problems. In *Reading Swift*, pp 225-43 (1993).

1727   FITZGERALD (Sean).   Wolfe Tone and Bantry Bay. In *Bantry Hist. Soc. Jn.*, i, 54-65 (1991).

1728   FITZPATRICK (Liz).   A monument to Archbishop Thomas Walsh in the town of Cashel, Co. Tipperary. In *Butler Soc. Jn.*, iii, 562-4 (1994).

1729   FLATMAN (Richard).   Jamaican memories of Irish interest. In *Ir. Family Hist.*, ix, 20-24 (1993).

        FLEETWOOD (John). See 1465

1730   FOLLIS (Brian A.).   The Brownlow papers. In *Review*, v, no. 3, pp 9-11 (1986/87).
        Outline of the contents of the Brownlow estate papers.

1731   FORREST (Andrew).   The origins, development and administration of French Protestant Charity in Dublin (1692-1794). In *Alumnus*, pp 3-8 (1993).
        Outline of the author's thesis-in-progress.

1732   FOSTER (R.F.).   Commentary. In *Three nations - a common history?*, pp 265-71 (1993).
        On Asch and Krumwiede.

1733   FOSTER (Roy).   The ascendancy mind. In *History Today*, xxxviii, no. 12, pp 20-28. (Dec. 1988).
        An edited extract from his *Modern Ireland, 1600-1972*.

1734   FRANKLING (F.T.).   Brief background for Robinson settlements. In *Mallow Field Club Jn.*, xii, 48-59 (1994).

1735   FRENCH (Noel E.). Bellinter House; illus. by Sandra Caffrey and Susan Priest, plans by Frances Mitchell. Pp 44. Trim, Co. Meath: Trymme Press, 1993.
Near Navan, Co. Meath, home of Preston and Briscoe families. Designed by Richard Castle, *c*.1750.

1736   GACQUIN (William). A south Roscommon parish in the eighteenth century. In *Roscomon Hist. Soc. Jn.*, iii, 50-54 (1990).
Parish of Kilcoom and Cam, census 1749.

1737   GAHAN (Daniel). The military strategy of the Wexford United Irishmen in 1798. In *Hist. Ire.*, i, no. 4, pp 28-32 (1993).

1738   GILDEA (J.). The founding of Australia. In *North Mayo Hist. Jn.*, iii, no. 2, pp 74-90 (1993/94).

1739   GILLESPIE (Raymond). Describing Dublin: Francis Place's visit, 1698-99. In *Visualizing Ireland*, pp 99-117 (1993).

GILLEY (Sheridan). See HOLMES (Colin).

1740   GIRVIN (Brian). The Act of Union, nationalism and religion, 1780-1850. In *Nordirland in Geschichte und Gegenwart*, pp 53-81 (1994).

1741   GIVEN (Anne). A little-known curiosity in County Tyrone. In *Arch. Ire.*, ii, 12-14 (1988).
Acheson Moore, 1685-1770, supporter of the Pretender.

1742   Goldsmith: interviews and recollections. *Ed.* E.H. Mikhail. Pp xvii, 230. New York: St Martin's Press, 1993. (Interviews and recollections)

1743   GOODALL (David). A divided family in 1798: the Grays of Whitefort and Jamestown. In *Wexford Hist. Soc. Jn.*, xv, 52-66 (1994/95).

1744   GOUGH (Hugh). Book imports from continental Europe in late eighteenth-century Ireland: Luke White to the Société Typographique de Neuchâtel. In *Long Room*, xxxviii, 35-48 (1993).

1745   GRAHAM (Thomas). 'An union of power'?: the United Irish organisation. In *The United Irishmen*, pp 244-55 (1993).

1746   GRAHAM (Tommy). Whitelaw's 1798 census of Dublin. In *Hist. Ire.*, ii, no. 3, pp 10-15 (1994).

1747   GREENE (John C.) and CLARK (Gladys L.H.). The Dublin stage, 1720-1745: a calendar of plays, entertainments, and afterpieces. Pp 473. Bethlehem, Pa.: Lehigh University Press, 1993.

1748   GRIBBON (Harry). Linen seals. In *Ulster Folklife*, xl, 56-61 (1994).

1749   GRIFFIN (Brian). 'Mad dogs and Irishmen': dogs and rabies in the eighteenth and nineteenth centuries. In *Ulster Folklife*, xl, 1-15 (1994).

GROGAN (Declan). See 1474.

1750   HAMILTON (Pádraig). Caoineadh ar Dhoncha Mac Cártha, easpag Chorcaí, 1712-1726. In *Bandon Hist. Jn.*, ix, 16-18 (1993).
Lament for Doncha Mac Cártha, bishop of Cork, 1712-26, taken from a manuscript book kept by Daniel Savage, fl. 1828.

1751   HAMMOND (Brean S.). Applying Swift. In *Reading Swift*, pp 185-97 (1993).
Gulliver's travels.

HARRISON (Alan). See 1480.

1752   HARRISON (Jennifer). The Australian share. In *Ir. Roots* 1992, no. 1, p. 7 (1992).

HARRISON (Richard S.). See 1481.

1753   HARVEY (John H.) and KINANE (Vincent). The earliest known printed Irish seed catalogue. In *Long Room*, xxxviii, 49-53 (1993).

1754   HARVEY (Karen J.). Religion and money: Irish Regular Colleges in the Roman Republic, *c.*1798-99. In *Eighteenth-century Ireland*, viii, 73-82 (1993).

1755   HAYES (Francis). John Daniel, Thomas Conolly and the Erne Fisheries, 1796-1799. In *Donegal Annual*, xlvi, 43-52 (1994).

1756   HAYES-McCOY (G.A.). The French campaign in Connacht and north Leinster 1798. In *Teathba*, ii, no. 1, pp 33-40 (1980).

HAYTER (Alethea). See *The Backbone* (1993).

1757   HEMPTON (David). Evangelicalism in English and Irish society, 1780-1840. In *Evangelicalism*, pp 156-76 (1994).

1758   HENIGAN (Julie). 'For want of education': the origins of the hedge schoolmaster songs. In *Ulster Folklife*, xl, 27-38 (1994).

1759   HENRY (Brian). Dublin hanged: crime, law enforcement and punishment in late eighteenth-century Dublin. Pp 222. Blackrock, Co. Dublin: Irish Academic Press, 1994.

1760   HENRY (Brian). Industrial violence, combinations and the law in late eighteenth-century Dublin. In *Saothar*, xviii, 19-33 (1993).

1761   Henry Cooke's centenary. *Ed.* Eull Dunlop, photography Graham Mawhinney. Pp 85. Ballymena, Co. Antrim: Braid Books, 1993. (Ascona series, 10)
Originally published, Belfast, 1888; Henry Cooke, 1788-1868, Presbyterian minister.

1762   HERLIHY (Jim). Davistown and the Davies family. In *Old Blarney*, iii, 32-41 (1993).

1763   HIGGINS (Ian). Swift's politics: a study in disaffection. Pp xiii, 232. Cambridge: Cambridge University Press, 1994. (Cambridge studies in eighteenth-century English literature and thought, 20)

HIGGINS (Ian). See 1486.

1764   HILL (Jacqueline). The politics of Dublin Corporation, 1760-1792. In *The United Irishmen*, pp 88-101 (1993).

1765   HILL (Jacqueline). 1641 and the quest for Catholic emancipation, 1691-1829. In *Ulster 1641*, pp 159-71 (1993).

1766   HOGAN (Patrick M.). The undoing of Citizen John Moore - president of Provisional Government of the Republic of Connacht, 1798. In *Galway Arch. Soc. Jn.*, xxxviii, 59-72 (1981/2).

1767   HOLMES (Colin) and GILLEY (Sheridan). Immigration to Britain. The Irish. In *History Today*, xxxv (June), 16-23 (1985).

1768   HOOD (Susan E.). Sources for the history of eighteenth and nineteenth century estate towns in Ireland. In *Aspects of Irish genealogy*, pp 150-61 [1993].

1769   HOUSTON (C.J.) and SMYTH (W.J.). The Irish diaspora: emigration to the new world, 1720-1920. In *An historical geography of Ireland*, pp 338-65 (1993).

1770   HUNTER (Maureen). Downpatrick's dungeons discovered. In *Lecale Miscellany*, ix, 21-5 (1991).

1771   IRELAND (Aideen). Clancarthy correspondence, 1785-1861. In *Galway Arch. Soc. Jn.*, xlvi, 197-202 (1994).

1772   IRELAND (Aideen). Two Ponsonby letters. In *Old Kilkenny Rev.*, iv, 1181-5 (1993).
        Two letters from Sarah Ponsonby, written from Llangollen, to Andrew Caldwell, barrister, of Rutland Square, Dublin, dated 1799 and 1801.

1773   JACKSON (Patrick N. Wyse) and VACCARI (Ezio). Volcanoes and straw bonnets: the Graydons of Burrishoole. In *Cathair na Mart*, xiii, 90-101 (1993).

1774   JENNINGS (Robert M.) and TROUT (Andrew P.). The Irish tontine (1777) and fifty Genevans; an essay on comparative mortality. In *Jn. European Economic History*, xii, 611-18 (1983).

1775   JOHNSTON (May). Murnin's boat house. In *Lecale Miscellany*, vii, 58-9 (1989).

1776   JONES (Melvyn). Coppice wood management in the eighteenth century: an example from County Wicklow. In *Ir. Forestry*, xliii, 15-31 (1986).

1777   KAVANAUGH (Ann C.). Lord Clare and his historical reputation. In *Hist. Ire.*, i, no. 3, pp 22-6 (1993).

1778   KAVANAUGH (Ann C.). John FitzGibbon, earl of Clare. In *The United Irishmen*, pp 115-23 (1993).

1779   KELLEHER (Daniel V.). Edmund Rice - a timely restorer of faith and hope in Ireland. In *A man raised up*, pp 97-114 (1994).

1780   KELLY (Ann Cline).   The birth of 'Swift'.   In *Reading Swift*, pp 13-23 (1993).

1781   KELLY (James).   The abduction of women of fortune in eighteenth-century Ireland.   In *Eighteenth-century Ireland*, ix, 7-43 (1994).

1782   KELLY (James).   The duel in Irish history.   In *Hist. Ire.*, ii, no. 1, pp 26-30 (1994).

1783   KELLY (James).   Francis Wheatley: his Irish paintings, 1779-83.   In *Visualizing Ireland*, pp 145-63 (1993).

1784   KELLY (James).   Henry Grattan.   Pp [5], 54.   Dundalk: Dundalgan Press for the Historical Association of Ireland, 1993.   (Historical Association of Ireland Life and Times series, no. 1)

1785   KELLY (James).   Parliamentary reform in Irish politics, 1760-90.   In *The United Irishmen*, pp 74-87 (1993).

        KELLY (James).   See 1500.

1786   KELLY (Patrick).   Anne Donnellan: Irish proto-bluestocking.   In *Hermathena*, cliv, 39-68 (1993).
        Eighteenth-century intellectual, who left a legacy to Trinity College Dublin. Copy of her will is appended.

1787   KELLY (Liam).   Defenderism in Leitrim during the 1790s.   In *Breifne*, vi, no. 24, pp 341-54 (1986).

1788   KENNEDY (Liam) and CLARKSON (Leslie A.).   Birth, death and exile: Irish population history, 1700-1921.   In *An historical geography of Ireland*, pp 158-84 (1993).

1789   KENNEDY (Máire).   Antoine D'Esca: first professor of French and German at Trinity College Dublin.   In *Long Room*, xxxviii, 18-19 (1993).

1790   KENNEDY (Máire).   The distribution of a locally-produced French periodical in provincial Ireland: the 'Magazin à la mode', 1777-1778.   In *Eighteenth-century Ireland*, ix, 83-98 (1994).

1791   KENNEDY (W. Edmund).   An ecclesiastical trial.   An examination of the trial, in 1776, of the Rev. Edward Smyth, curate of Ballyculter parish.   In *Lecale Miscellany*, vii, 25-31 (1989).

        KENNY (Adrian).   See Ó CASAIDE (Tomás).

1792   KENNY (James G.).   O'Hara of Craigbilly, Oaklands also.   In *The Glynns*, xxii, 34-43 (1994).
        Also includes a note on the builder of Oaklands, Adam Duffin (1764-1837).

1793   KEOGH (Dáire).   Archbishop Troy, the Catholic church and Irish radicalism: 1791-3.   In *The United Irishmen*, pp 124-34 (1993).

1794   KEOGH (Dáire).   The French disease: the Catholic church and radicalism in Ireland, 1790-1800.   Pp xxvii, 379.   Blackrock, Co. Dublin: Four Courts Press, 1993.

1795   KILLEN (John). An index to the Microscope (1799-1800) and to the Belfast Literary Journal (1816). Pp 117 + 11 microfiche. Belfast: Linen Hall Library, 1994.

KILROY (Phil). See 1504.

1796   KINANE (Vincent). Printers' apprentices in 18th and 19th century Dublin. In *Linen Hall Review*, x, no. 1, pp 11-14 (1993).

KINANE (Vincent). See HARVEY (John H.).

1797   KING (Joseph A.). History and genealogy: the Breens of County Carlow. In *Ir. Roots* 1993, no. 1, pp 24-5 (1993).

1798   KOMLOS (John). A Malthusian episode revisited: the height of British and Irish servants in colonial America. In *Econ. Hist. Rev.*, xlvi, 768-82 (1993).

1799   KRAMER (Dorothy). Examples of mortised headpiece ornaments used by Dublin printers in the eighteenth century. In *Long Room*, xxxviii, 31-4 (1993).

1800   La CASCE (Steward). Swift on medical extremism. In *Jn. Hist. Ideas*, xxxi, 599-606 (1970).

1801   LAFFAN (Pádraig). The 18th century pirates of the Muglins: a talk .... Pp 14. [Foxrock, Dublin]: Foxrock Local History Club, [1989]. (Publications, no. 37)
        Muglans, Dalkey, Co. Dublin.

LANDSMAN (N.C.). See 1601.

1802   La ROCHE (Christopher S.). Jonathan Swift and his influence on eighteenth-century Irish economic historiography. Pp 45. Boston (Mass.): Irish Studies Program, Northeastern University, 1993. (Working papers in Irish studies, 93-2)

LAURIE (Bruce). See 1508.

1803   LAVELLE (Rory). The Mayo rebels of '98 in Connemara. In *Connemara*, i, no. 1, pp 70-75 (1993).

1804   Le BIEZ (Gilles). Irish news in the French press: 1789-98. In *The United Irishmen*, pp 256-68 (1993).

1805   Le GROS (Bernard). Burke et l'Irlande. In *Études Irlandaises*, xviii, no. 2, pp 109-22 (1993).

1806   LEIGHTON (C.D.A.). Catholicism in a Protestant kingdom: a study of the Irish ancien régime. Pp x, 218. London: Macmillan; New York: St Martin's Press, 1994. (Studies in modern history)

1807   LEONARD (John). Dublin and the Duke of Ormonde. In *Butler Soc. Jn.*, iii, 555-60 (1994).

1808   LIGHTBOWN (Mary). Memorial to a poetess: John Flaxman's memorial to Mary Tighe. In *Old Kilkenny Rev.*, iv, 1195-1207 (1993).

1809   LINDLEY (Keith).   Irish adventurers and godly militants in the 1640s.   In *I.H.S.*, xxix, 1-12 (1994).

1810   LINDSAY (Deirdre).   The Fitzwilliam episode revisited.   In *The United Irishmen*, pp 197-208 (1993).

1811   LÖFFLER (Arno).   The Dean and Lady Anne: humour in Swift's Market-Hill poems.   In *Reading Swift*, pp 113-24 (1993).
        Lady Anne Acheson, Market Hill, Co. Armagh.

1812   LONGFIELD (Ada K.).   William Kilburn (1745-1818) and his book of designs.   In *Ir. Georgian Soc. Bull.*, xxiv, 1-28 (1981).
        Irish textile designer.

1813   LOUGHREY (Francis).   The Bray diary 1797-1899.   Pp 199.   [Bray?]: [Francis Loughrey?], 1994.

1814   LOWE (N.F.).   Mary Wollstonecraft and the Kingsborough scandal.   In *Eighteenth-century Ireland*, ix, 44-56 (1994).
        Scandal concerning the family of the Earl of Kingston, one of Ireland's wealthiest peers, in October 1797.

1815   LYALL (Andrew).   The Irish House of Lords as a judicial body, 1783-1800.   In *Ir. Jurist*, xxviii/xxx, 314-60 (1993/95).

1816   McBRIDE (Ian).   Presbyterians in the penal era.   In *Bullán*, i, no. 2, pp 73-86 (1994).

1817   McBRIDE (Ian).   The school of virtue: Francis Hutcheson, Irish Presbyterians and the Scottish enlightenment.   In *Political thought in Ireland since the seventeenth century*, pp 73-99 (1993).

1818   McBRIDE (Ian).   William Drennan and the dissenting tradition.   In *The United Irishmen*, pp 49-61 (1993).

1819   Mac CONMARA (Micheál).   Memorials of the dead in Teampall Muchulla, parish of Clonlara, Co. Clare.   In *Sliabh Aughty*, iv, 45-8 (1993).

1820   McCORMACK (W.J.).   The Dublin paper war of 1786-1788:   a bibliographical and critical inquiry, including an account of the origins of Protestant ascendancy and its 'baptism' in 1792.   Pp 165.   Blackrock, Co. Dublin: Irish Academic Press, 1993.

1821   McCOY (Gerard).   'Patriots, Protestants and Papists':   religion and the ascendancy 1714-1760.   In *Bullán*, i, no. 1, pp 105-18 (1994).

        MacDONNELL (Hector).   See 1524

1822   McDOWELL (R.B.).   Burke and Ireland.   In *The United Irishmen*, pp 102-14 (1993).

1823   Mac EITEAGAIN (Darren).   Earls and Wild Geese.   The Irish experience in Europe, 1600-1750.   In *U.C.D. Hist. Rev.*, vi, 12-20 (1992).

1824   McFARLAND (Elaine W.).   Ireland and Scotland in the age of revolution: planting the green bough.   Pp xii, 272.   Edinburgh: Edinburgh University Press, 1994.

1825   McGINTY (Margaret). Thomas Russell. In *Dúiche Néill*, viii, 119-32 (1993).
1767-1803.

1826   Mac GIOLLA FHINNÉIN (Brian). Pádraig Ó Loingsigh: saol agus saothar. In *Seanchas Ardmhacha*, xv, no. 2, pp 98-124 (1993).

1827   McHUGH (Anna). The Connaught Rangers. In *Galway Roots*, [i], 77-80 (1993).

1828   McLARNON (Douglas S.). Irish 'combinations' and economic activity in the latter half of the eighteenth century. In *Jn. European Economic Hist.*, v, 401-05 (1976).

1829   MacLOUGHLIN (Giullermo). Argentina. The forgotten Irish. In *Ir. Roots* 1993, no. 4, pp 6-7 (1993).

1830   McMINN (Joseph M.). The importance of friendship in Swift's writings. In *Reading Swift*, pp 71-80 (1993).

1831   McMINN (Joseph). Jonathan's travels: Swift and Ireland. Pp 160. Belfast: Appletree Press, 1994.

1832   McPARLAND (Edward). Malton's views of Dublin: too good to be true? In *Ireland*, pp 15-25 (1994).

1833   McPARLAND (Edward). Sir Thomas Hewett and the new junta for architecture. In *The role of the amateur architect*, pp 21-6 (1994).
The new junta's Irish connections particularly Edward Lovett Pearce.

1834   MAIGNANT (Catherine). Représentation du temps et élaboration identitaire (1750-1850). In *Études Irlandaises*, xix, no. 1, pp 109-19 (1994).

1835   MALEY (Willy). Rebels and redshanks: Milton and the British problem. In *Ir. Studies Rev.*, vi, 7-11 (1994).

1836   MARNANE (Denis G.). Samuel Cooper of Killenure (1750-1831) - a Tipperary land agent and his diaries. In *Tipp. Hist. Jn.*, pp 102-27 (1993).

MARSHALL (Alan). See 1541.

1837   MARTIN (Ged), ed. A visitor to Cork in 1775. In *Cork Hist. Soc. Jn.*, xcviii, 141-3 (1993).
Thomas Curtis of Hampshire en route to the Island of St John (later Prince Edward Island).

1838   MASLEN (Keith). George Faulkner and William Bowyer: the London connection. In *Long Room*, xxxviii, 20-30 (1993).

1839   MAYOCK (John), contrib. South Mayo militia papers. (British Public Record Office, Kew, London, Class WO 13 Boxes 3121-40). In *Cathair na Mart*, xiv, 11-15 (1994).

1840   MEAGHER (John H.). Elias Voster: the father of Irish accountancy. In *Cork Hist. Soc. Jn.*, xcix, 111-19 (1994).
Elias Voster (1682-1779) settled in Cork from his native Holland in 1699.

1841   MELVIN (Peter H.).   Burke on theatricality and revolution. In *Jn. Hist. Ideas*, xxxvi, 447-68 (1975).

MIKHAIL (E.H.).   See *Goldsmith*.

1842   MILNE (King).   The Elmes letters.   Part 2.   In *The Past*, xviii, 31-44 (1992).
Continued from *The Past*, xvii, 55-70 (1990).

1843   MONAHAN (Amy).   The letters of Thomas 'Buck' Whaley at Castletown, County Carlow. In *Ir. Georgian Soc. Bull.*, xxxvi, 77-9 (1994).

MOORE (James).   See STEWART (M.A.).

1844   MORLEY (John).   Edmund Burke, introduced by Brendan Clifford.   [New ed.].   Pp 168.   Belfast: Athol Books, 1993.
Previous title: *Burke*.

1845   MORLEY (Vincent).   Aodh Buí Mac Cruitín: file Gaeilge in arm na Fraince. In *Eighteenth-century Ireland*, viii, 39-48 (1993).
An English version of the article 'Hugh MacCurtin: an Irish poet in the French army'; ibid., viii, 49-58 (1993).

1846   MORRIS (H.F.).   Faulkner's Dublin Journal 1766.   Births, marriages and deaths. In *Ir. Geneal.*, ix, no. 1, pp 14-42 (1994).

1847   MOYLAN (Seamus).   Charles Kendal Bushe of Kilmurry. In *In the Shadow of the Steeple*, iv, 51-7 (1994).

1848   MULCAHY (John).   Robert Gordon of Newgrove.   In *Old Blarney*, iii, 69-78 (1993).

1849   MULCAHY (John).   Unwillingly to school: a survey of education in Blarney from the penal days to the famine. In *Old Blarney*, iii, 13-31 (1993).

MULCAHY (Michael).   See *Calendar of Kinsale documents*, vol. 3.

1850   MÜLLENBROCK (Heinz-Joachim).   Swift as a political essayist: the strained medium. In *Reading Swift*, pp 151-8 (1993).

1851   MULLOY (Sheila).   Father Manus Sweeney (1763-1799).   In *Cathair na Mart*, xiv, 27-38 (1994).

MULVEEN (Jack).   See 1556

1852   MURPHY (James H.).   The Wild Geese. In *The Irish Review*, xvi, 23-8 (1994).

1853   MURPHY (Seán).   Charles Lucas: a forgotten artist? In *Hist. Ire.*, ii, no. 3, pp 26-9 (1994).

1854   MURPHY (Seán).   Charles Lucas, catholicism and nationalism.   In *Eighteenth-century Ireland*, viii, 83-102 (1993).
Charles Lucas (1713-71), patriot politician, author and pamphleteer, apothecary and medical doctor.

MURPHY (Seán).   See 1558.

1855   MURPHY (Thomas A.).   Father Nicholas Sheehy, P.P., Clogheen.   In
        Tipperary County, pp 37-40 (1993).
        Hanged 1766.   Originally published in *Clonmel Tercentenary Record* in
        1952.

        NEARY (Brendan).   See AUBREY (John).

1856   NELSON (E. Charles) and PROBERT (Alan).   A man who can speak of
        plants: Dr Thomas Coulter (1793-1843) of Dundalk in Ireland, Mexico and
        Alta California.   Pp viii, 181. Dublin: E. Charles Nelson, 1994.

1857   NEVIN (Monica).   General Charles Vallancey, 1725-1812.   In *R.S.A.I..
        Jn.*, cxxiii, 19-58 (1993).

        NICHOLLS (Kenneth W.).   See FEWER (Thomas G.).

1858   Ní DHÉA (Eilis).   Micheál Ó hAnnracháin agus a chomhscriobhaithe i gCill
        Ruis.   In *The Other Clare*, xvii, 45-7 (1993).

        Ñí MHEARA (Róisín).   See 1561.

1859   NOWLAN (P.F.).   Guns and gunners.   In *An Cosantóir*, li, no. 9, pp 12-14,
        22 (1991).
        Guns and artillery in Ireland *c*.1798.

1860   Ó BRAONÁIN (Micheál).   Príomhshruth Éireann.   Pp 109. Luimneach:
        Bardas Luimnigh, 1994.
        Poem by Roscommon poet on the River Shannon, completed 1794, listing
        30 tributaries and over 300 place-names.

1861   O'BRIEN (Gerard).   The unimportance of public opinion in eighteenth-
        century Britain and Ireland.   In *Eighteenth-century Ireland*, viii, 115-27
        (1993).

1862   O'BRIEN (Ivar).   Rear-Admiral Lucius O'Brien, R.N.   In *Ir. Family
        History*, ix, l02-08 (1993).

1863   O'BRIEN (John B.).   Population, politics and society in Cork, 1780-1900.
        In *Cork*, pp 699-720 (1993).

1864   Ó BUACHALLA (Breandán).   Irish Jacobitism in official documents.   In
        Eighteenth-century Ireland, viii, 128-38 (1993).
        Introduction to and edition of several documents from the P.R.O. and
        P.R.O.N.I.

1865   Ó BUACHALLA (Brendán).   The making of a Cork jacobite.   In *Cork*, pp
        469-97 (1993).
        Fr Dónall Ó Colmáin, author of *Parliament na mBán* (1697) and James
        Cotter, hanged 1720.

1866   Ó CAISIDE (Tomás).   An Caisideach Bán: the songs and adventures of
        Tomás Ó Caiside, translated from the Irish by Adrian Kenny.   Pp 31.
        Ballyhaunis: Greensprint, 1993.

1867   Ó CAITHNIA (Liam P.).   The death of Mrs Edmund Rice.   In *A man raised
        up*, pp 67-78 (1994).
        Died *c*.1789.

1868 Ó CAITHNIA (Liam P.). Edmund Rice and his social milieu. In *A man raised up*, pp 25-46 (1994).

1869 Ó CAITHNIA (Liam P.). The man from Callan. In *A man raised up*, pp 13-24 (1994).
Edmund Rice, 1762-1844.

O'CALLAGHAN (John). See 1564.

1870 Ó CATHÁIN (Diarmaid). An Irish scholar abroad: Bishop John O'Brien of Cloyne and the Macpherson controversy. In *Cork*, pp 499-533 (1993).
John O'Brien, bishop of Cloyne and Ross, 1748-69 and his attack on James Macpherson's *Ossian* in 1764.

1871 Ó CATHAOIR (Brendan). Eamon Ó Mathghamhna: a Munster scribe. In *O'Mahony Jn.*, xii, 24-5 (1982).
Eamon Ó Mathghamhna, d. 1822.

1872 Ó CEARBHAILL (Seán E.). Edmund Rice and Saint Teresa of Avila. In *A man raised up*, pp 115-27 (1994).

1873 Ó CEARNAIGH (Seán). The Irish-English dictionary of Bishop John O'Brien, 1768. In *Linen Hall Review*, x, no. 1, pp 15-17 (1993).

1874 Ó CIOSÁIN (Niall). Highwaymen, tories and rapparees. In *Hist. Ire.*, i, no. 3, pp 19-21 (1993).
Eighteenth-century 'thrillers', and their sources.

1875 Ó CLÉIRIGH (Gearóid). Cerbh é 'Mac an Cheannán'. In *Irisleabhar Mhá Nuad*, pp 7-34 (1993).

1876 O'CONNELL (Maurice R.). Daniel O'Connell, democrat, liberal Catholic and husband. In *Blackrock Soc. Proc.*, ii, 4-17 (1993/94).

O'CONNELL (Patricia). See 1566.

1877 Ó DÁLAIGH (Brian). Flags and emblems of the Ennis Volunteers. In *The Other Clare*, xviii, 40-41 (1994).

1878 Ó DÁLAIGH (Brian). Portrait of Francis Bindon. In *The Other Clare*, xvii, 18-20 (1993).
Francis Bindon, 18th-century Clare artist.

1879 Ó DÁLAIGH (Brian). Students from County Clare at Trinity College Dublin, in the eighteenth century. In *North Munster Antiq. Jn.*, xxxv, 81-91 (1993/94).

1880 Ó DONNCHADHA (Rónán). Mícheál Óg Ó Longáin, file. Pp viii, 199. Baile Átha Cliath: Coiscéim, 1994.
Mícheál Óg Ó Longáin (1766-1837), poet.

1881 O'DONNELL (Ruan). The rebellion of 1798 in County Wicklow. In *Wicklow*, pp 341-78 (1994).

1882 O'DONNELL (Ruan). The Wicklow United Irishmen in New South Wales. Part I. In *Wicklow Hist. Soc. Jn.*, i, no. 7, pp 46-53 (1994).

O'DONOVAN (Uinsin). See 1571.

1883 Ó DUIGNEÁIN (Peadar). Ballinamuck and '98. A talk to the Society. In *Teathba*, i, no. 1, pp 41-6 (1969).

1884 Ó DUIGNEÁIN (Proinnsíos). Hugh O'Donnell of Larkfield - patron of Gaelic literature (1691-1754). In *Breifne*, vi, no. 24, pp 390-94 (1986).

Ó DÚSHLÁINE (Tadhg). See 1572.

1885 O'DWYER (Michael). A Kilkenny printer's will. In *Old Kilkenny Rev.*, xlvi, 120-21 (1994).
Edmund Finn, founder of *Finn's Leinster Journal*, d. 1777.

1886 O'FARRELL (Patrick). [Review article]. In search of the hidden Ireland. In *Jn. Religious Hist.*, xii, 322-30 (1983).

Ó FEARGHAIL (Fearghus). See BURKE (Thomas).

1887 Ó HANNRACHÁIN (Eoghan). Casualties in the ranks of the Clare regiment at Fontenoy. In *Cork Hist. Soc. Jn.,* xcix, 96-110 (1994).

1888 Ó HANNRACHÁIN (Eoghan). The general from Elphin: the life and times of General Jacques Ó Moran. In *Roscommon Hist. Soc. Jn.*, iv, 27-33 (1992).

1889 Ó HANNRACHÁIN (Eoghan). A north Roscommon cavalryman. In *Roscommon Hist. Soc. Jn.*, iv, 55 (1992).
Lieut Bernard McDermott.

1890 O'HEARN (Denis). Innovation and the world-system hierarchy: British subjugation of the Irish cotton industry, 1780-1830. In *Amer. Jn. Sociology*, c, 587-621 (1994/95).

1891 OLIVER (Seán). Irish revolutionary nationalism: Tone to Pearse. In *People power*, pp 94-111 (1993).

1892 Ó LOINSIGH (Pádraig). George Berkeley, Bishop of Cloyne. In *The book of Cloyne*, pp 120-28 (1994).

1893 Ó LOINSIGH (Pádraig). John Brinkley, D.D. (1763-1835). In *The book of Cloyne*, pp 135-8 (1994).

1894 Ó MATHÚNA (Diarmuid). Aodhgán Ó Rathaille agus seann-tsíol chéin. In *O'Mahony Jn.*, xii, 19-23 (1982).

1895 Ó MÓRDHA (Seamas). Charlotte Brooke, her background and achievement. In *Breifne*, vi, no. 24, pp 320-40 (1986).
Text of a lecture.

1896 Ó MUIRITHE (Diarmaid). A natal poem for Daniel O'Connell. In *Éigse*, xxvii, 115-19 (1993).

1897 Ó MURCHADHA (Ciaran). The Moughna affair, 1699, and the bizarre career of Patrick Hurley. In *The Other Clare*, xvii, 48-56 (1993).

1898   O'NEILL (Thomas P.).   Penal laws and convert rolls.   In *Galway Roots*, ii, 70-72 (1994).

O'REILLY (F.D.).   See COUGHLAN (A.G.).

1899   O'REILLY (Stan J.).   Wicklow rebels of 1798.   No. 1:   William Michael Byrne.   In *Wicklow Hist. Soc. Jn.*, i, no. 7, pp 16-18 (1994).

1900   O'SULLIVAN (Patrick).   Greenfield and people associated with it.   In *Seanchas Duthalla*, ix, 9-15 (1993).

1901   O'SULLIVAN (Stephen).   Jonathan Swift and Wexford's spa.   In *Old Wexford Soc. Jn.*, vi, 63-8 (1976/77).

1902   O'SULLIVAN (Tadhg F.).   The impossible diplomatic mission of Giovanni Battista Rinuccini 1645-1649.   In *Études Irlandaises*, xviii, no. 2, pp 87-92 (1993).

1903   O'SULLIVAN (William).   The Irish manuscripts in Case H in Trinity College Dublin - catalogued by Matthew Young in 1781.   In *Celtica*, xi, 229-50 (1976).

1904   PARKE (William K.).   Extracts from the diary of Reverend John Nixon.   In *Clogher Rec.*, xv, no. 1, pp 25-30 (1994).
        Rev. John Nixon, rector of the parish of Inishmacsaint, Co. Donegal, 1765-97.

1905   PARKINSON (Danny).   List of Robinson names which are registered at St Mary's Church (C. of I.), Donnybrook.   In *Irish Family History*, i, no. 1, pp 31-2 (1993).

1906   PHIDDIAN (Robert).   A name to conjure with: games of verification and identity in the Bickerstaff controversy.   In *Reading Swift*, pp 141-50 (1993).

1907   PITTOCK (Murray G.H.).   Poetry and Jacobite politics in eighteenth-century Britain and Ireland.   Pp xiii, 254.   Cambridge: Cambridge University Press, 1994.   (Cambridge studies in eighteenth-century English literature and thought, 23)

1908   POLLARD (M.).   The 'college builder' - Thomas Whitehouse?   In *Long Room*, xxxviii, 17 (1993).

1909   POWER (Patrick C.).   Tipperary courtmartials - 1798-1801.   In *Tipp. Hist. Jn.*, 135-47 (1993).

1910   POWER (Thomas P.).   Land, politics, and society in eighteenth-century Tipperary.   Pp xiv, 376.   Oxford: Clarendon Press, 1993.

PRENDERGAST (Ellen).   See 1590.

PROBERT (Alan).   See NELSON (E. Charles).

1911   PROBYN (Olive T.).   Swift and typographic man: foul papers, modern criticism and Irish dissenters.   In *Reading Swift*, pp 25-43 (1993).

1912 PROUDFOOT (L.J.). Regionalism and localism: religious change and social protest *c*.1700 to *c*.1900. In *An historical geography of Ireland*, pp 185-218 (1993).

1913 PROUDFOOT (L.J.). Spatial transformation and social agency: property, society and improvement, *c*.1700 to *c*.1900. In *An historical geography of Ireland*, pp 219-57 (1993).

1914 QUINLAN (Margaret). The Main Guard, Clonmel. The rediscovery of a seventeenth-century courthouse. In *Ir. Georgian Soc. Bull.*, xxxvi, 4-29 (1994).

1915 RANKIN (Fred). A Downpatrick rental of 1752. In *Lecale Miscellany*, xi, 20-27 (1993); xii, 22-8 (1994).

1916 RANKIN (Fred). Letter from Francis Hutchinson, Bishop of Down and Connor, 1732. In *Lecale Miscellany*, vii, 45 (1989).

1917 Rathfeigh since the penal days. In *A window on the past*, [i], 26-8 (1987).

1918 RAYMOND (Raymond James). A reinterpretation of Irish economic history (1730-1850). In *Jn. European Economic Hist.*, xi, 651-64 (1982).

1919 REAL (Hermann J.). 'A dish plentifully stor'd': Jonathan Swift and the evaluation of satire. In *Reading Swift*, pp 45-58 (1993).

1920 REDDEN (Jennifer). Richard Bourke's views on citizenship and education. In *Old Limerick Jn.*, xxx, 7-17 (1993).

REFAUSSÉ (Raymond). See *Register of the parish of St Thomas, Dublin, 1750-1791*.

1921 Register of the parish of St Thomas, Dublin, 1750-1791. *Ed.* Raymond Refaussé. Pp 162. Dublin: Representative Church Body Library, 1994.

1922 REID (Richard). 'May the Lord in his mercy be kind to Belfast': Thomas Ekenhead's city *c*.1790-1832. In *Familia*, ii, no. 10, pp 1-12 (1994).

ROCHE-KELLY (Hubert). See 1596.

1923 RODINO (Richard H.). 'Splendide Mendax': authors, characters, and readers in *Gulliver's Travels*. In *Reading Swift*, pp 167-84 (1993).

1924 ROSS (Bianca). Of prejudice and predilection: Lady Morgan and her 'Annals of St Grellan'. In *Eighteenth-century Ireland*, ix, 99-113 (1994).

1925 ROSS (Ian Campbell). The Scriblerians and Swift in Ireland. In *Reading Swift*, pp 81-9 (1993).

1926 RYGH (S.). Norwegian captain from Moi Stavanger, was the pioneer for Irish harbour performance. In *Dun Laoghaire Jn.*, iii, 8-11 (1993). Captain Richard Toutcher (1758-1841).

1927 SCHAKEL (Peter J.). 'Friends, side by side': theme, structure, and influence in the Swift-Pope *Miscellanies* of 1727. In *Reading Swift*, pp 103-12 (1993).

1928   SCHELLEKENS (Jona). The role of marital fertility in Irish population history, 1780-1840. In *Econ. Hist. Rev.*, xlvi, 369-78 (1993).

1929   SCHUTTE (Sean). The Palatines. In *Gateway to the past*, i, no. 3, pp 150-58 (1994).

1930   SILKE (John J.). Bishop Coyle's pious miscellany. In *Eighteenth-century Ireland*, ix, 114-28 (1994).
        Anthony Coyle, bishop of Raphoe (1782-1801) author of 'Collectanea sacra: or a pious miscellany in verse and prose' (Strabane,1780).

1931   SINNOTT (T.D.). Kelly of Killane. In *Old Wexford Soc. Jn.*, vi, 69-72 (1976/77).

        SMOUT (T.C.). See 1601.

1932   SMYTH (Denis). Men of liberty - part 2: The life and times and literary works of James Hope, working-class United Irishman, 1764-1847: 'In the cause of the common people'. Pp 54. Belfast: North Belfast History Workshop, 1993.
        Cover title: Jemmy Hope, working-class United Irishman, his life and times.

1933   SMYTH (Jim). 'Like amphibious animals': Irish Protestants, ancient Britons, 1691-1707. In *Hist. Jn.*, xxxvi, 785-97 (1993).

1934   SMYTH (Jim). Freemasonry and the United Irishmen. In *The United Irishmen*, pp 167-75 (1993).

1935   SMYTH (William J.). Social, economic and landscape transformations in County Cork from the mid-eighteenth to the mid-nineteenth century. In *Cork*, pp 655-98 (1993).

        SMYTH (W.J.). See HOUSTON (C.J.).

1936   SNODGRASS (Lee). Survey of graveyard, Crookhaven, Co. Cork. In *Mizen Jn.*, i, 72-9 (1993).

1937   SNYDER (Henry L.). Charges to grand juries: the evidence of the eighteenth-century short-title catalogue. In *Historical Research*, lxvii, 286-300 (1994).

1938   SOLON (John). Interdenominational relations in Connacht in the eighteenth-century. In *Galway Arch. Soc. Jn.*, xlv, 44-69 (1993).

1939   STEWART (A.T.Q.). A deeper silence: the hidden roots of the United Irish movement. Pp xii, 225. London: Faber, 1993.

1940   STEWART (M.A.) and MOORE (James). William Smith (1698-1741) and the Dissenters' book trade. In *Presb. Hist. Soc. of Ire. Bull.*, xxii, 20-27 (1993).

1941   SUTTON (George). Waterford bridge, 1793-1911. In *Decies*, xlviii, 49-53 (1993).

1942   SWORDS (Liam). Calendar of Irish material in the files of Jean Fromont, notary at Paris, May 1701-24 Jan. 1730, in the Archives Nationale, Paris: Part 1, 1701-15. In *Collect. Hib.*, xxxiv/xxxv, 77-115 (1992/93).

1943   SWORDS (Liam). Letter from the northern front. In *Ríocht na Midhe*, ix, no. 1, pp 42-9 (1994/95).
    Testamentary letter from Robert Plunkett a few days before his death in the battle of Malplaquet 1709.

    SWORDS (Liam). See 1604.

1944   TESCH (Pieter). Presbyterian radicalism. In *The United Irishmen*, pp 33-48 (1993).

1945   THOMPSON (Dorothy). Outsiders: class, gender and nation. Pp vi, 186. London: Verso, 1993.
    Extensive references to Irish Chartists and radicals, 1790-1850.

1946   THOMPSON (F. Glenn). The lineage of the Kilkenny Militia. In *Old Kilkenny Rev.*, xlvi, 51-3 (1994).

1947   THUENTE (Mary Helen). The harp re-strung: the United Irishmen and the rise of Irish literary nationalism. Pp x, 286. Syracuse, N.Y.: Syracuse University Press, 1994.

1948   TILLYARD (Stella). Aristocrats: Caroline, Emily, Louisa and Sarah Lennox, 1740-1832. Pp 462. London: Chatto, 1994.
    Louisa, wife of Thomas Conolly; Emily, wife of James Fitzgerald (Lord Kildare) and mother of Lord Edward Fitzgerald.

    TROUT (Andrew P.). See JENNINGS (Robert M.).

    VACCARI (Ezio). See JACKSON (Patrick N. Wyse).

1949   VIGNE (Randolph). 'Le projet d'Irlande': Huguenot migration in the 1690s. In *Hist. Ire.*, ii, no. 2, pp 18-21 (1994).

1950   WALSH (Larry). Richard Crosbie's aerial voyage from Limerick 1786. In *Old Limerick Jn.*, xxxi, 4-10 (1994).
    Transcript of report in the *Limerick Chronicle*.

1951   WALSH (T.J.). Opera in Dublin, 1798-1820: Frederick Jones and the Crow Street Theatre. Pp xiv, 294. Oxford: Oxford University Press, 1993.

1952   WHELAN (Kevin). The United Irishmen, the enlightenment and popular culture. In *The United Irishmen*, pp 269-96 (1993).

1953   WHITE (Stephen K.). Edmund Burke: modernity, politics, and aesthetics. Pp xx, 97. Thousand Oaks, Calif: Sage Publications, *c*.1994. (Modernity and political thought, vol. 5)

    WOKECK (Marianne S.). See 1612.

1954   WOOLLEY (James). The canon of Swift's poems: the case of 'An apology to the Lady Carteret'. In *Reading Swift*, pp 245-64 (1993).
    Probably the work of Patrick Delany.

1955   WOOLLEY (David). *A dialogue upon Dunkirk* (1712) and Swift's '7 penny papers'. In *Reading Swift*, pp 215-23 (1993).

1956   WOZNAK (John F.). James Arbuckle and the 'Dublin Weekly Journal': obstacles to research. In *Jn. Ir. Lit.*, xxii, no. 2, pp 46-52 (1993).

1957   WYNNE (Michael). Thomas Roberts, 1748-1778. In *Ir. Arts Rev. Yearbk*, pp 143-52 (1994).
Eighteeth-century Waterford artist and his travels round Ireland.

1958   YORK (Neil Longley). Neither kingdom nor nation: the Irish quest for constitutional rights 1698-1800. Pp xii, 280. Washington, D.C.: Catholic University of America Press, 1994.

1959   ZACK (Wolfgang). Jonathan Swift and colonialism. In *Reading Swift*, pp 91-9 (1993).

ADAMS (J.R.R.). See 1613.

1960   AHERN (Richard). Liszt in Limerick. In *Old Limerick Jn.*, xxix, 10-12 (1992).

1961   ALLEN (Dennis). The battle of the Somme. In *Ir. Family Hist.*, x, 24-5 (1994).

1962   ALLEN (Donna). Inishbiggle: a challenge. In *Cathair na Mart*, xiii, 145-8 (1993).

1963   ALLEN (Gregory). Policemen in your family tree. In *Dublin Hist. Rec.*, xlvi, 121-8 (1993).

1964   ALLEN (Myrtle). Ballymaloe House. In *The book of Cloyne*, pp 177-82 (1994).

1965   ALOYSIUS of MARY (*Brother*). A journey to Ceylon. In *Carloviana*, xxxiii, 16-18 (1985/86).
        A letter written by James Doyle of Lacken (*Bro.* Aloysius of Mary) to his mother in 1900.

1966   ANDERSON (Audréy). The old barracks, Roscommon. In *Roscommon Hist. Soc. Jn.*, iii, 21-3 (1990).

ANDERSON (Hugh). See 1614.

1967   ANDERSON (W.K.). James Connolly and the Irish left. Pp 200. Blackrock, Co. Dublin: Irish Academic Press in association with National Centre for Australian Studies, Monash University, 1994.

1968   ANDREWS (J.H.). History in the ordnance map: an introduction for Irish readers. 2nd ed. Pp viii, 63. Kerry, Wales: David Archer, 1993.
        Previous ed., 1974.

1969   ANNESLEY (Cressida). The land war in west Cork: the boycott of William Bence Jones. In *Cork Hist. Soc. Jn.*, xcix, 1-22 (1994).

1970   ANTON (Brigitte). Northern voices: Ulsterwomen in the Young Ireland movement. In *Coming into the light*, pp 60-92 (1994).

1971   ANTON (Brigitte). Women of *The Nation*. In *Hist. Ire.*, i, no. 3, pp 34-7 (1993).

1972   ARCHER (Jean). Geological artistry: the drawings and watercolours of George Victor du Noyer in the archives of the Geological Survey of Ireland. In *Visualizing Ireland*, pp 133-44, (1993).
        George Victor du Noyer, 1817-69.

1973   ARNSTEIN (Walter L.).   The Murphy riots: a Victorian dilemma.   In
         Victorian Studies, xix, 51-71 (1975/76).
         William Murphy (1834-82), born in Limerick;   anti-Catholic agitator in
         England.

1974   A.S.   'Mr Val'.   In *Roscommon Hist. Soc. Jn.*, v, 11-17 (1994).
         Val McDonnell, 1884-1973 (entries from his diaries, 1896-1936).

1975   As others saw us: Waterford in Kohl's *Travels in Ireland* (1844).   In *Decies*,
         xlvii, 22-8 (1993).

         The Backbone.   See 1620.

1976   Bagenalstown C.Y.M.S. and the M.P.s billiard table.   In *Carloviana*, xli, 28-
         9 (1993/94).

         BAILEY (Bee).   See 1621.

         BAKER (Allan C.).   See TAYLOR (Patrick).

1977   BAKER (Joe).   The McMahon family and the Belfast troubles 1920-1922.
         Revised international ed.   Pp [87].   Belfast: Glenravel Local History Project,
         1993.

         BALLHATCHET (Kenneth).   See 1622

1978   Ballypatrick Co-operative Dairy Society Ltd.   Ballypatrick Co-operative Dairy
         Society Ltd., 1893-1993, I v. [unpaged].   [Ballypatrick]:   [the society],
         [1993?].
         Co. Tipperary.

1979   BANE (Liam).   The bishop in politics: life and career of John MacEvilly,
         Bishop of Galway 1857-81, Archbishop of Tuam 1881-1902.   Pp viii, 200.
         Westport: Westport Historical Society, 1993.

1980   BARDON (Jonathan).   Belfast at its zenith.   In *Hist. Ire.*, i, no. 4, pp 48-51
         (1993).

         BARTLETT (Thomas).   See 1626, 1627.

1981   BASSETT (John).   The old McClurg house at 'The Shore'.   In *Lecale
         Miscellany*, viii, 12-15 (1990).

1982   BATEMAN (Dilys).   A Corkman and a controversial bible: McNamara and
         the Rhenish notes.   In *Long Room*, xxxix, 32-8 (1994).

1983   BEAN (Philip A.).   The Irish, the Italians and machine politics, a case study:
         Utica, New York (1870-1960).   In *Jn. Urban Hist.*, xx, 205-39 (1993/94).

1984   BEARE (Ellen).   The great famine 1845-1850.   In *Dun Laoghaire
         Genealogical Soc. Jn.*, iii, 139-44 (1994).

         BEARE (Ellen).   See DALY (Tony).

1985   BEAUDOT (William J.K.) and HERDEGEN (Lance J.). An Irishman in the Iron Brigade: the civil war memories of James P. Sullivan, sergt., Company K, 6th Wisconsin Volunteers. Pp [xiv], 189. New York: Fordham University Press, 1993. (Irish in the Civil War, no. 3)

1986   BEAUMONT (H.C.A.). Portadown Bridge 1908. In *Irish Railway Rec. Soc. Jn.*, xviii, no. 122, pp 276-7 (1993).

1987   BEECHER (Seán). An Gaeilge in Cork city: an historical perspective to 1894. Pp 83. Cork: Godly Angel Press, 1993.

1988   BEGLEY (Anthony). The diary of a Ballyshannon lady, 1844-1848. In *Donegal Annual*, xlv, 4-20 (1993).
    Mary Anne Sheil.

1989   BEGLEY (Anthony). Letter from America, 1859. In *Donegal Annual*, xlvi, 83-6 (1994).
    Letter from John Barclay Sheil, born in Ballyshannon, 1797.

1990   BEHAN (A.P.). History from picture postcards. In *Dublin Hist. Rec.*, xlvi, 129-40 (1993).

1991   BELCHEM (John). Republican spirit and military science: the 'Irish brigade' and Irish-American nationalism in 1848. In *I.H.S.*, xxix, 44-64 (1994).

BELL (Muriel). See 1628

1992   BELL (Robert). An academic flower show? A reappraisal of the R.U.I. In *Ir. Studies Rev.*, vii, 19-22 (1994).
    Royal University of Ireland 1879-1908.

1993   BELLEW (Tom). Michael Kieran, 1803-1869, parish priest of Dundalk, 1848-1869, Archbishop of Armagh, 1866-1869. In *Louth Arch. Soc. Jn.*, xxiii, no. 2, 145-80 (1994).

1994   BENSON (Charles). A Dublin printer's strike of 1840-41. In *Long Room*, xxxix, 43-7 (1994).

1995   BERGER (Pamela). The historical, the sacred, the romantic: medieval texts into Irish watercolours. In *Visualizing Ireland*, pp 71-87 (1993).
    Painters Daniel Maclise (1806-70); Frederic William Burton (1816-1900); and Michael Healy (1873-1941).

1996   BEW (Paul). Ideology and the Irish question: Ulster unionism and Irish nationalism 1912-1916. Pp xix, 165. Oxford: Clarendon Press, 1994.

1997   BEW (Paul). The real importance of Sir Roger Casement. In *Hist. Ire.*, ii, no. 2, pp 43-5 (1994).

1998   BHREATHNACH-LYNCH (Síghle). The art of Albert G. Power, 1881-1945: a sculptural legacy of Irish Ireland. In *Ireland*, pp 118-31 (1994).

1999   BHREATHNACH-LYNCH (Síghle). 'Executed': the political commissions of Albert G. Power. In *Eire-Ireland*, xxix, no. 1, pp 44-60 (1994).
    Dublin sculptor Albert Power (1881-1945).

BIELENBERG (Andy). See 1630

2000   BIRDWELL-PHEASANT (Donna). Irish housholds in the early twentieth century: culture, class and historical contingency. In *Jn. Family History*, xviii, 19-38 (1993).

2001   BLACK (Ronald). Four O'Daly manuscripts. In *Éigse*, xxvi, 43-79 (1992).

2002   BLACKER (William) and WALLACE (Robert H.). The formation of the Orange Order, 1795-1798: the edited papers of Colonel William Blacker and Colonel Robert H. Wallace. Pp 166. [Belfast]: Education Committee of the Grand Lodge of Ireland, 1994.
         William Blacker, 1777?-   ; Robert H. Wallace, 1860-1929.

2003   BOLGER (Pat). The village banks in Donegal. In *Donegal Annual*, xlv, 42-75 (1993).
         Set up from 1895 onwards on the same basis as later credit unions.

2004   BOLSTER (Evelyn). A history of the diocese of Cork: the episcopate of William Delany: 1847-1886. Pp xix, 352. Cork: Tower Books, 1993.
         William Delany, 1804-1886.

2005   BOOTH (John). Jack B. Yeats: a vision of Ireland. Pp 128. Nairn: Thomas & Lochar, [1993].

2006   BOOTH (Lionel). History of the Dublin Central Mission, 1893-1993. Pp [20], 60. Dublin: Dublin Central Mission, 1993.
         Irish Methodist church.

2007   BOURKE (Austin). 'The visitation of God'?: the potato and the great Irish famine. *Ed.* for Irish Historical Studies by Jacqueline Hill and Cormac Ó Gráda. Pp x, 230. Dublin: Lilliput Press, 1993.

2008   BOURKE (Fred). Survey of townlands in the parish of Clonlara, 1840-1851. In *Sliabh Aughty*, iv, 41-4 (1993).

2009   BOURKE (Joanna). Avoiding poverty: strategies for women in rural Ireland, 1880-1914. In *Poor women and children in the European past*, pp 292-311 (1994).

2010   BOURKE (Joanna). Husbandry to housewifery: women, economic change, and housework in Ireland, 1890-1914. Pp x, 342. Oxford: Clarendon Press, 1993.

2011   BOURKE (Joanna). Women, economics and power: Irish women 1880-1914. In *Ir. Home Economics Jn.*, i, no. 2, pp 3-16 (1992).

2012   [BOURKE (Marcus)]. Car owners in north Tipperary in 1906. In *Tipp. Hist. Jn.*, p. 66 (1994).

2013   BOURKE (Marie). Frederic William Burton, 1816-1900: painter and antiquarian. In *Eire-Ireland*, xxviii, no. 3, pp 45-60 (1993).

2014   BOURKE (Marie). Rural life in pre-famine Connacht: a visual document. In *Ireland*, pp 61-74 (1994).
         Frederic William Burton, 1816-1900 of Corofin, Co. Clare, and his painting 'The Aran fisherman's drowned child'.

         BOURKE (Tommy). See RYAN (Theresa).

2015 BOWE (Nicola Gordon). A contextual introduction to romantic nationalism and vernacular expression in the Irish arts and crafts movement, *c*.1886-1925. In *Art and the national dream*, pp 181-200 (1993).

2016 BOYCE (D. George). Trembling solicitude: Irish conservatism, nationality and public opinion, 1833-86. In *Political thought in Ireland since the seventeenth century*, pp 124-45 (1993).

2017 BOYCE (George). British politics and the Irish question. In *Nationalism and unionism*, pp 91-105 (1994).

2018 BOYCE (George). Ireland and the First World War. In *Hist. Ire.*, ii, no. 3, pp 48-53 (1994).

2019 BOYD (Hugh Alexander). Olden days in Cushendall and the glens. In *The Glynns*, xxi, 5-12 (1993); continued from *ibid.*, xx, 6-12 (1992); Olden days in Cushendall and the glens *c*.1817, part III. In *ibid.*, xxii, 11-23 (1994).

2020 BOYER (George R.), HATTON (Timothy J.) and O'ROURKE (Kevin). The impact of emigration on real wages in Ireland, 1850-1914. In *Migration and the international labor market, 1850-1939*, pp 221-39 (1994).

2021 BOYLE (Leonard). Fr Joseph Mullooly, O.P. (1812-1880). In *Teathba*, ii, no. 1, pp 3-16 (1980).
Prior of San Clemente and supervisor of excavations.

2022 BRADLEY (John). Canon Charles Quin and the Bessborough Commission. In *Seanchas Ardmhacha*, xvi, no. 1, pp 133-94 (1994).

2023 BRADLEY (John). Fishermen's wives. In *The Bell*, v, 40 (1994).
Tracing the path by which women carried fish in creels from Lough Neagh to Dungannon.

2024 BRADLEY (John) and MURPHY (Eddie). The life and times of Father Bernard Murphy: Termon, Carrickmore 1832-1897. Updated ed. Pp 96. Belfast: Eddie Murphy, 1994.
Previous ed. published as: Fr Bernard Murphy of Termonmaguirk, 1832-1897. In *Seanchas Ardmhacha*, xiii, no. 1 (1988).

2025 BRADY (Margery). The last rose of summer: the love story of Tom Moore and Bessy Dyke. Pp 137. Green Hills (Co. Kilkenny): Green Hills Publications, 1993.
Thomas Moore 1779-1852; Bessy Dyke 1793-1865.

2026 BREEN (Muriel). Liquorice all-sorts: a girl growing up. Pp 174. Dublin: Moytura Press, 1993.
Born Bangor, Co. Down, 1899-

2027 BRENNAN (Helen). Reinventing tradition: the boundaries of Irish dance. In *Hist. Ire.*, ii, no. 2, pp 22-4 (1994).

2028 BRENNAN-HOLOHAN (Mary P.). Catherine A. O'Brien - stained-glass artist (with special reference to her work in Co. Kilkenny). In *Old Kilkenny Rev.*, iv, 968-72 (1992).

2029 BRESNIHAN (Brian). The Powells of Templederry, Co. Tipperary. In *Gateway to the Past*, i, no. 3, pp 134-9 (1994).

BRIGGS (George). See *100 years of the L.F.A.* (1993).

2030 BRITAIN (I.M.). Bernard Shaw, Ibsen and the ethics of English socialism. In *Victorian Studies*, xxi, 381-401 (1977/78).

2031 BROOKE (David). The 'lawless' navvy: a study of the crime associated with railway building. In *Jn. Transport History*, x, no. 2, pp 145-65 (1989).

2032 BROZYNA (Andrea Ebel). 'The cursed cup hath cast her down': constructions of female piety in Ulster evangelical temperance literature, 1863-1914. In *Coming into the light*, pp 154-78 (1994).

2033 BRUNICARDI (Daire). An Irishman at the battle of Jutland. In *An Cosantóir* liii, no. 4, pp 24-5 (1993).
Lieutenant James Morris of Ballinaboy, Co. Mayo, who was aboard the battleship *Saint Vincent*.

2034 BRUNICARDI (Daire). The Royal Navy and 1916. In *An Cosantóir*, li, no. 4, pp 16, 18 (1991).

2035 BUCHANAN (Ian). Magheramore National School. Schools of yesterday (no. 19). In *Benbradagh*, xxiv, 3 (1994).

2036 BUCHANAN (Ian). Termiel (Dromboughel) School. Schools of yesterday (no. 18). In *Benbradagh*, xxiii, 4-6 (1993).

2037 BUCKLAND (Patrick). Carson, Craig and the partition of Ireland. In *Nationalism and unionism*, pp 75-89 (1994).

2038 BUCKLAND (Patrick). The unity of Ulster unionism, 1886-1939. In *History*, lx, 211-23 (1975).

2039 BULL (Philip). The significance of the nationalist response to the Irish land act of 1903. In *I.H.S.*, xxviii, 283-305 (1993).

2040 BURKE (Eimear). 'Our boasted civilisation': Dublin society and the work of the DSPCC, 1899-1922. In *U.C.D. Hist. Rev.*, v, 1-5 (1991).

2041 BURKE (Tim). 1916: A watershed in the evolution of an independent Ireland. In *An Cosantóir*, li, no. 4, pp 9-15 (1991).

2042 BURNETT (Harry). Lead mines in the barony of Lecale. In *Lecale Miscellany*, vi, 22-4 (1988).

BURNETT (Harry). See 1643.

2043 BUSTEED (Mervyn) and HODGSON (Rob). Irish migration and settlement in nineteenth-century Manchester, with special reference to the Angel Meadow district. In *Ir. Geography*, xxvii, 1-13 (1994).

2044 BUTLER (Elizabeth). Autobiography. Pp [6], 281. Sevenoaks: Fisher Press, 1993.
Originally published, 1922. Lady Elizabeth Butler, battle artist, 1846-1933.

2045 BUTLER (Katherine). Centenary of a synagogue: Adelaide Road 1892-1992. In *Dublin Hist. Rec.*, xlvii, 46-55 (1994).

2046   BUTLER (Patricia). A Victorian watercolourist. In *Ir. Arts Rev. Yearbk*, pp 157-62 (1994).
Louisa Anne, Marchioness of Waterford (1818-91) philanthropist and painter.

BUTTIMER (Cornelius G.). See 1647

2047   BYRNE (Declan). A Wicklow family. In *Dun Laoghaire Genealogical Soc. Jn.*, ii, 99-105 (1993).
Kelly family.

2048   BYRNE (Edward). Archbishop Simonds and the Myshall connection. In *Carloviana*, xli, 3 (1993/94).
First native-born Australian bishop - his parents emigrated from Ireland in 1878.

2049   BYRNE (Liam). An Irish soldier remembered. In *An Cosantóir*, li, no. 4, pp 31-3 (1991).
CSM Martin Doyle (1894-1940), recipient of the V.C.; member of the Royal Munster Fusiliers.

2050   BYRNE (Liam). Wireless and the Easter Rising 1916. In *An Cosantóir*, li, no. 4, p. 19 (1991).

2051   BYRNE (Seán). Butlers' Emporium. In *Butler Soc. Jn.*, iii, 569-72 (1994).

2052   CADIGAN (Sean T.). Paternalism and politics: Sir Francis Bond Head, the Orange Order and the election of 1836. In *Canadian Hist. Rev.*, lxxii, 320-47 (1991).

2053   CADOGAN (Tim). Parliamentary politics in Mallow 1870-74. Part 1-2. In *Mallow Field Club Jn.*, xi, 5-21 (1993); xii, 76-88 (1994).

2054   CAHILL (Marie). Mansfield-Bakers-Mallow-Melbourne-Geelong. In *Mallow Field Club Jn.*, xii, 119-33 (1994).

2055   CALLAGHAN (Patrick). Bodyke man transported to New South Wales 1832. The story of an east Clare convict. In *Sliabh Aughty*, v, 39-41 (1994).

2056   CALLAN (Charles). Bookbinders' Consolidated Union banner. In *Labour History News*, ix, 9 (1993).

2057   CALLANAN (Frank). Parnell: the great pretender? In *Hist. Ire.*, i, no. 3, pp 50-55 (1993).

2058   CAMPBELL (Fergus). History or myth? the Irish revolution reconsidered. In *Ir. Studies Rev.*, i, 14-16 (1992).

2059   CAMPBELL (Fergus). Nationalism in transformation: local government in Co. Tipperary, 1912-1920. In *Tipp. Hist. Jn.*, pp 38-47 (1994).

CAMPBELL (Flann). See 1649.

2060   CAMPBELL (Stephen J.). The great Irish famine: words and images from the Famine Museum, Strokestown Park, County Roscommon. Pp 56. [Strokestown, Co. Roscommon]: Famine Museum, 1994.

2061   CANAVAN (Paul). 'Paths for the people'. In *Lecale Miscellany*, vii, 55-7 (1989).

2062   CANNING (Bernard J.). Shay Colm's footsteps trod. In *Ulster Folklife*, xxxix, 41-9 (1993).

2063   CAREY (John). The Irish national origin-legend: synthetic pseudohistory, with a memoir of Edmund Crosby Quiggin by David N. Dumville. Pp xvi, 27. Cambridge: Department of Anglo-Saxon Norse and Celtic, University of Cambridge, 1994. (Quiggin pamphlets on the sources of medieval gaelic history).
Quiggin, Edmund Crosby, 1875-1920.

2064   CARGEEG (George). Michael Dwyer's daughter Mary Ann and her descendants. In *Ir. Family Hist.*, x, 26-8 (1994).

2065   CARR (Peter). The night of the big wind. Pp 155. Belfast: The White Row Press, 1993.
6 Jan. 1839. Originally published as The big wind (1991).

2066   CARROLL (Denis). They have fooled you again: Michael O'Flanagan (1876-1942), priest, republican, social critic. Pp 271. Blackrock, Co. Dublin: Columba Press, 1993.

2067   CARROLL (Frieda). From the archivist's desk. In search of that Smith/Smyth ancestor of County Meath. In *Dun Laoghaire Genealogical Soc. Jn.*, iii, 152-61 (1994).

2068   CARROLL (Frieda). From the archivist's desk. Landholders in County Laois. In *Dun Laoghaire Genealogical Soc. Jn.*, iii, 54-63, 97-106 (1994).

2069   CARROLL (Kathy). Emily Lawless and the Irish question. In *Blackrock Soc. Proc.*, ii, 82-3 (1993/94).

2070   CARTER (J.W.H.). The land war and its leaders in Queen's County, 1879-82. Pp xix, 352. Portlaoise: Leinster Express Newspapers, 1994.

2071   CARVILLE (P.J.), ed. Holy Family parish: centenary celebration 1893-1993. Pp 97. Belfast: Holy Family Parish, [1993].

2072   CASSIDY (Dennis). A path directed: life and times of Belfast city missionary and first world war veteran, James Cassidy (1892-1970). Pp 48. Bangor, Co. Down: Ollav Healer Publications, 1993.

2073   CASSIN (Maeve). Archbishop William Hayden (1868-1936). In *In the Shadow of the Steeple*, iv, 3-7 (1994).
Archbishop of Hobart, Tasmania.

2074   CATHCART (Kevin J.). Edward Hincks (1792-1866): a biographical essay. In *The Edward Hincks bicentenary lectures*, pp 1-29 (1994).

2075   CAWLEY (Mary E.) and Ní SCANNLÁIN (Eibhlín). North-west Connemara: processes and patterns of landscape change during the nineteenth century. In *Decoding the landscape*, pp 99-113 (1994).

CHADWICK (Anne). See 1658.

2076   CHASE (Malcolm). The Teeside Irish in the nineteenth century. In *The Irish in British labour history*, pp 47-58 (1993).

2077   CHEÓINÍN (Seán). Jack Bacach Ó Guairim file agus bádóir. In *Connemara*, i, no. 1, pp 76-80 (1993).
Songs and sayings of a folk poet from Carna, Jack Bacach Ó Guairim, b. c.1843.

2078   CHRISTENSEN (M.). Signalling at Ballynahinch Junction. In *Irish Railway Rec. Soc. Jn.*, xviii, no. 123, pp 337-41 (1994).

2079   CLANCY (Peter). The Irish Augustinians in India, 1834-1841. In *Irish Augustinians in Rome, 1656-1994*, pp 113-37 (1994).

2080   CLARKE (J.A.). A canal from Navan to Dublin. In *A Window on the Past*, iii, 33-7 (1993).

2081   CLARKE (J.A.). Schooling in Rathfeigh. In *A Window on the Past*, iii, 5-10 (1993).

CLARKSON (Leslie A.). See 1788.

2082   CLEARY (Jimmy). Dacket Pier to Kilcoole. In *Wicklow Hist. Soc. Jn.*, i, no. 7, pp 19-21 (1994).
Description of coast with named buildings, c.1900.

2083   CLIFFORD (Brendan). The Irish Civil War: the conflict that formed the state; a speech given to the Duhallow Heritage Centre on 22 April 1992. Pp 23. Millstreet: Aubane Historical Society, 1993.

2084   CLIFFORD (Derek). My native place during the famine. In *Roscommon Hist. Soc. Jn.*, iv, 50 (1992).

2085   COAKLEY (Davis). Oscar Wilde: the importance of being Irish. Pp x, 246. Dublin: Town House and Country House, 1994.

2086   COAKLEY (John). The election that made the first Dáil. In *The creation of the Dáil*, pp 31-46 (1994).
Appendix 1: A note on the results of the general election of 1918, pp 160-63.

2087   COFFEY (Petra). George Victor Du Noyer, 1817-1869, artist, geologist and antiquary. In *R.S.A.I. Jn*, cxxiii, 102-19 (1993).

2088   COHEN (Marilyn). Religion and social inequality in Ireland. In *Jn. Interdisciplinary Hist.*, xxv, 1-21 (1994/95).

2089   COL (Samuel). The Mechanics' Institute. In *Old Wexford Soc. Jn.*, vi, 61-2 (1976/77).

2090   COLDREY (Barry). Brother Jerome Fitzpatrick 1878-1910. An extraordinary pioneer of the Irish language movement. In *Old Limerick Jn.*, xxix, 28-30 (1992).

2091   COLDREY (Barry M.). The scheme: the Christian Brothers and childcare in Western Australia. Pp 464. O'Connor, Western Australia: Argyle-Pacific Publishing 1993.

2092   COLGAN (Brendan). Belfast's original black man: the young earl, 1827-
        1853. Pp 64. Belfast: Phoenix Press, 1994.
        Frederick Richard, earl of Belfast.

2093   COLLINS (B.). The analysis of census returns: the 1901 census of Ireland.
        In *Ulster Local Studies*, xv, no. 1, pp 38-46 (1993).

        COLLINS (Brenda). See 1666.

2094   COLLINS (M.E.). Ireland, 1868-1966. Pp 480. Dublin: Educational
        Company of Ireland, 1993. (History in the making)

2095   COLLINS (Michael). 'Oh! Lord the unrest of soul': the jail journal of
        Michael Collins; edited and introduced by Íosold Ó Deirg. In *Studia Hib.*,
        xxviii, 7-34 (1994).

2096   COLLINS (Peter). The Belfast labour movement 1881-1921. In *Nordirland
        in Geschichte und Gegenwart*, pp 82-98 (1994).

2097   COLLINS (Peter). Irish labour and politics in the late nineteenth and early
        twentieth centuries. In *Nationalism and unionism*, pp 123-53 (1994).

2098   COLLINS (Timothy). The Clare Island survey: an early multidisciplinary
        success story. In *Decoding the landscape*, pp 114-32 (1994).

2099   COLLINS (Timothy). The Galway line in context. Part I. In *Galway Arch.
        Soc. Jn.*, xlvi, 1-42 (1994).
        The Galway transatlantic steamship line.

2100   COLLINS (Timothy). Praeger in the west: naturalists and the antiquarians in
        Connemara and the islands, 1894-1914. In *Galway Arch. Soc. Jn.*, xlv, 124-
        54, plate (1993).

2101   COLMER (Albert). The emigrant's stile. In *Lecale Miscellany*, xii, 46-9
        (1994).
        On the writing of the song, "The Irish emigrant" by Lady Helen Dufferin.

2102   COLMER (Albert). St Dympna's graveyard, Downpatrick. In *Lecale
        Miscellany*, ix, 51-3 (1991).

2103   COLMER (Albert). St John's lighthouse. In *Lecale Miscellany*, xi, 51-2
        (1993).

        COLMER (Albert W.K.). See 1667.

        COMER (Siobhán). See 1668.

2104   The communists and the Irish revolution. Part 1: the Russian revolutionaries
        on the Irish national question, 1889-1924, includes works by Lenin, Trotsky,
        Radek, Chicherin, and statements by the Communists International. Ed. D.R.
        O'Connor Lysaght. Pp [9], 129. Dublin: Literéire Publishers, 1993.

2105   CONLAN (Patrick). A short-title calendar of *Hibernia*, vol. 6 (1888-92), in
        the General Archives of the Friars Minor, Rome. In *Collect. Hib.*,
        xxxiv/xxxv, 190-209 (1992/93).

2106   CONLEY (Carolyn A.). Irish criminal records, 1865-1892. In *Eire-Ireland*, xxviii, 97-106 (1993).

2107   CONLEY (Carolyn A.). No pedestals: women and violence in late nineteenth-century Ireland. In *Jn. Soc. Hist.*, xxviii, 801-18 (1994/95).

2108   CONNELL (Paul). St Finian's College 1802-1994. In *Ríocht na Midhe*, ix, no. 1, pp 135-57 (1994/95).

2109   CONNOLLY (Al). Heaven's command. In *Lecale Miscellany*, xi, 38-44 (1993).
        Elizabeth Anne Sandes (1851-1934) founder of Sandes Soldiers Homes.

2110   CONNOLLY (M. Austin). The death of Brother Edmund Ignatius Rice in the words of an eyewitness. In *A man raised up*, pp 183-92 (1994).
        Br Thomas Hearn, 1797-

        CONNOLLY (Michael). See GRIMES (Seamus).

2111   CONNOLLY (Paddy). Bandon Town Hall. In *Bandon Hist Jn.*, ix, 39-44 (1993).

2112   CONNOLLY (Petra). History of the trades in Galway. In *Galway Roots*, ii, 52-4, map (1994).

2113   CONNOLLY (Ross M.). A rightful place in the sun: the struggle of the farm and rural labourers of County Wicklow. In *Wicklow*, pp 911-25 (1994).

2114   CONNORS (Brendan). A current tale of interest. In *Arch. Ire.*, viii, no. 3, pp 33-5 (1994).
        The Ordnance Survey in Ireland.

2115   CONROY (Jean). Ellen Reilly 1838-1916. In *Ir. Family Hist.*, x, 20-23 (1994).

2116   CONYNGHAM (David Power). The Irish Brigade and its campaigns. *Ed.* with introduction, Lawrence Frederick Kohl. Pp xxx, 616. New York: Fordham University Press, 1994. (Irish in the Civil War, no. 4)
        David Power Conyngham, 1840-83.

2117   COOGAN (Tim Pat). Michael Collins. In *Nationalism and unionism*, pp 155-61 (1994).
        1890-1922.

        COOGAN (Tim Pat). See WOODCOCK (Caroline).

2118   COOK (Scott B.). Imperial affinities: nineteenth century analogies and exchanges between India and Ireland. Pp 162. New Delhi and London: Sage Publications, 1993.

2119   COOKE (Jim). A musical journey, 1890-1993: from Municipal School of Music to Dublin Institute of Technology. Pp vi, 116. Dublin: Dublin Institute of Technology, College of Music, 1994.
        Title on spine: *Coláiste an cheoil, 1890-1993*.

2120   COOKE (Jim). The old township of Pembroke: 1863-1930. Pp v, 42. Dublin: City of Dublin Vocational Education Committee, 1993.

2121 COONEY (D.A. Levistone). An Englishman in Ireland: Arthur Dean Codling. In *Dublin Hist. Rec.*, xlvii, 5-23 (1994).
Arthur Dean Codling (1876-1950), member of the civil service in Ireland, 1900-1944.

2122 COONEY (D.A. Levistone). Momentous days: occasional diaries of Frances Taylor. In *Dublin Hist. Rec.*, xlvii, 77-86 (1994).
Frances Taylor (1890-1993) diaries cover eleven days in 1916 and nine days in 1922.

COONEY (D.A. Levistone). See 1672.

2123 COOPER (Bryan). The Tenth (Irish) Division in Gallipoli. New ed. Pp 155. Blackrock, Co. Dublin: Irish Academic Press, 1993.
Previous ed., London: Herbert Jenkins, 1918.

2124 Cork Archives Institute. Descriptive list of the papers of Liam Ó Buachalla, Banteer, County Cork (1882-1941). Pp iii, 42. Cork: Cork Archives Institute, 1994.

2125 CORRIGAN (Carmel). Household structure in early twentieth-century Ireland. In *Ir. Jn. of Sociology*, iii, 56-78 (1993).

2126 COSNETT (J.E.). An eminent Limerick doctor. Dr William Brooke O'Shaughnessy. In *Old Limerick Jn.*, xxix, 13-16 (1992).

2127 COTTRELL (Michael). Green and orange in mid-nineteenth-century Toronto: the Guy Fawkes' day episode of 1864. In *Canadian Jn. of Irish Studies*, xix, no. 1, pp 12-21 (1993).

2128 COUGHLAN (A.) and O'REILLY (F.D.) Letters of an Irish postman. In *Mallow Field Club Jn.*, xi, 56-66 (1993).
Letters of Anthony Trollope.

2129 COULTER (Carol). The hidden tradition: feminism, women and nationalism in Ireland. Pp vi, 69. Cork: Cork University Press, 1993.

2130 COUSINS (Mel). Social welfare adjudication in Ireland, 1847-1995: a diochronic analysis. In *Ir. Jurist*, xxviii/xxx, 361-82 (1993/95).

2131 COWMAN (Des). Landlords and their minerals *c*.1850: two Waterford case studies. In *Decies*, xlvii, 16-21 (1993).

COWMAN (D.). See 1676.

2132 COX (Ronald C.). Engineering at Trinity: incorporating a record of the School of Engineering. Pp vi, 365. Dublin: Trinity College Dublin, School of Engineering, 1993.

2133 COYNE (F.). The burning of Knockcroghery. In *Roscommon Hist. Soc. Jn.*, 28 (1990).
19 June 1921.

2134 COYNE (F). 19th-century cures and remedies. In *Roscommon Hist. Soc. Jn.*, iv, 75 (1992).

2135   CRADDEN (Terry).   The trade union movement in Northern Ireland.   In
        Trade union century, pp 66-84 (1994).

2136   CRAWFORD (Margaret).   The great Irish famine, 1845-9:   image versus
        reality.   In *Ireland*, pp 75-88 (1994).

2137   CRAWFORD (W.H.).   A handloom weaving community in County Down.
        In *Ulster Folklife*, xxxix, 1-14 (1993).

2138   CRAWFORD (W.H.).   Provincial town life in the early nineteenth century:
        an artist's impressions.   In *Ireland*, pp 43-59 (1994).
        Waterford county in the 1820s.

        CRAWFORD (William).   See 1679.

2139   CREAN (Thomas Neilan).   Labour and politics in Kerry during the First
        World War.   In *Saothar*, xix, 27-39 (1994).

2140   CREMIN (Vicky).   The Liberty Creche, 1893-1993: a hundred years of child
        care in inner city Dublin.   Pp [24], Dublin: Liberty Creche, 1993.

        CROMIE (Howard).   See 1680.

2141   CRONIN (Maura).   Country, class or craft?: the politicisation of the skilled
        artisan in nineteenth-century Cork.   Pp ix, 294.   Cork: Cork University
        Press, 1994.

2142   CRONIN (Maura).   Work and workers in Cork city and county 1800-1900.
        In *Cork*, pp 721-55 (1993).

2143   CROOKES (Gearoid).   Dublin's Eye & Ear: the making of a monument.   Pp
        xii, 211.   Dublin: Town House and Country House, 1993.
        Royal Victoria Eye and Ear Hospital.

        CROOKSHANK (C.H.).   See 1681.

2144   CROSKERY (Eithne).   Denver - a soldier, lawyer, editor.   In *Lecale
        Miscellany*, v, 34-5 (1987).
        Grandson of Patrick Denver who emigrated in 1804.

2145   CROSSMAN (Virginia).   Local government in nineteenth-century Ireland.
        Pp [7], 115.   Belfast: Institute of Irish Studies, Queen's University of Belfast
        for the Ulster Society for Irish Historical Studies, 1994.

2146   CROWLEY (Seamus).   Rebuilding Mallow bridge 1853-1856.   In *Mallow
        Field Club Jn.*, xii, 115-18 (1994).

2147   CULLEN (Elsie).   Cock-a-Rooshkie.   In *Swords Voices*, i, no. 2, pp 14-17
        (1994).
        Memories of Swords and a children's game, Cock-a-Rooshkie.

        CULLEN (L.M.).   See KOSEKI (Takashi).

2148   CULLINGFORD (Elizabeth Butler).   Gender and history in Yeats's love
        poetry.   Pp xv, 334.   Cambridge: Cambridge University Press, 1993.

2149   An Cumann Parnell, 1893-1993.   Pp x, 85.   [Dublin]: [the Club], [1993].

CUMMINS (David). See WALSH (Michael).

2150   CUNNINGHAM (John). Arney brick and the Florencecourt tile, brick and pottery works. In *Ulster Folklife*, xl, 68-73 (1994).

2151   CUNNINGHAM (John). Old graveyards and irregular burials near Pettigo. In *Donegal Annual*, xlvi, 87-90 (1994).

CUNNINGHAM (John). See 1687.

2152   CUNNINGHAM (John B.). Dr Lornbe Atthill and his picture of Fermanagh before the famine. In *Clogher Rec.*, xiv, no. 3, pp 29-41 (1993).

2153   CURRY (Steven). Charles Haddon Spurgeon. In *Ir. Baptist Hist. Soc. Jn.*, xxv, 17-30 (1992/93).

2154   CURTIN (Chris), et al. Replaying the 'Match': marriage settlements in north Galway. In *Ir. Jn. of Sociology*, ii, 85-95 (1992).

2155   CUSACK (Gerard). Early days in the penal colony of Western Australia. In *Breifne*, viii, 354-8 (1992/93).

2156   DALSIMER (Adele M.). 'The Irish peasant had all his heart': J.M. Synge in *The Country Shop*. In *Visualizing Ireland*, pp 200-30 (1993).
    Synge and the painter Jack Butler Yeats, 1871-1957.

2157   D'ALTON (Ian). Keeping faith: an evocation of the Cork Protestant character, 1820-1920. In *Cork*, pp 759-92 (1993).

2158   DALY (Cormac). D.D. Sheehan, B.L., M.P., Mid-Cork, 1901-1918. In *Seanchas Duthalla*, ix, 48-50 (1993).

2159   DALY (Mary E.). The economic ideals of Irish nationalism: frugal comfort or lavish austerity. In *Eire-Ireland*, xxix, no. 4, pp 77-100 (1994).

2160   DALY (Mary E.). Essay in review. Women and labour: margins to mainstream. In *Saothar*, xix, 70-74 (1994).

2161   DALY (Mary E.). Local government and the first Dáil. In *The creation of the Dáil*, pp 123-36 (1994).

2162   DALY (Mary E.). Women and trade unions. In *Trade union century*, pp 106-16 (1994).

2163   DALY (Tony) and BEARE (Ellen). Michael Davitt (1846-1906). In *Dun Laoghaire Genealogical Soc. Jn.*, ii, 81-4 (1993).

2164   DANIELS (Peter T.). Edward Hincks's decipherment of Mesopotamian cuneiform. In *The Edward Hincks bicentenary lectures*, pp 30-57 (1994).

2165   D'ARCY (Fergus). The case of Thaddeus O'Malley. Labour, nationality and religion in nineteenth-century Ireland. In *Old Limerick Jn.*, xxxi, 11-14 (1994).
    Rev. Thaddeus O'Malley 1796-1877.

2166   D'ARCY (Fergus). St Patrick's other island: the Irish invasion of Britain. In *Eire-Ireland*, xxviii, no. 2, pp 7-17 (1993).

D'ARCY (Fergus). See 1692.

2167   D'ARCY (Fergus A.). The Irish trade union movement in the nineteenth century. In *Trade union century*, pp 9-18 (1994).

2168   DAVEY (Peter). Ardglass railway station in the last few years. In *Lecale Miscellany*, xii, 19-21 (1994).

2169   DAVIES (Mary). Augustine Henry, an Irishman who enriched the gardens of the world. In *Ir. Garden*, ii, no. 1, p. 23 (1993).
Augustine Henry, 1857-1930.

DAVIES (Mary). See 1693.

2170   DAVIS (Graham). Talking freedom. The Irish in the Texas revolution. In *Ir. Studies Rev.*, viii, 18-25 (1994).

2171   DAVIS (Graham) and LANDES (Eugenia). 'Talking of paradise'. Irish pioneer settlers in South Texas. In *Ir. Studies Rev.*, v, 10-15 (1993).

DAVIS (Maire). See 1694.

2172   DAVIS (Richard). Victims or initiators? three Irish women convicts of Van Diemen's Land. In *Irish convict lives*, pp 199-230 (1993).
Eliza Callaghan (1802-52), Mary Sullivan (1835-52), Margaret Galvin (--- 1862).

2173   DAVIS (Richard). William Smith O'Brien and the American civil war. In *Canadian Jn. of Irish Studies*, xix, no. 2, pp 45-53 (1993).

DAVIS (Richard). See WILLIAMS (John).

DAY (Angélique). See *Parishes of County Antrim vi, vii, viii, ix, x; Parishes of County Londonderry vii.*

2174   DEANE (Seamus). Land and soil: a territorial rhetoric. In *Hist. Ire.*, ii, no. 1, pp 31-4 (1994).

2175   DEASY (Joe). Big Jim and drink. Temperance and socialism. In *Labour History News*, ix, 8 (1993).

2176   De BHALDRAITHE (Padraig). History in photographs and letters: the Waldron family and Co. Clare. In *The Other Clare*, xvii, 31-5 (1993).

De BHALDRAITHE (Tomás). See Ó SÚILLEABHÁIN (Amhlaoibh).

2177   De COGAN (Donard). Ireland, telecommunications and international politics, 1866-1922. In *Hist. Ire.*, i, no. 2, pp 34-8 (1993).

2178   De hÓIR (Nóra). Éamonn agus Nóra de hÓir: scéal faoi Éirí Amach na Cásca. In *North Munster Antiq. Jn.*, xxxv, 92-7 (1993/94).

2179   De la POER (Nigel K.). As others saw us: Sir Richard Colt Hoare visits the Blackwater Valley, 1806. In *Decies*, xlviii, 3-6 (1993).

2180   DENMAN (Terence). 'The red livery of shame': the campaign against army recruitment in Ireland, 1899-1914. In *I.H.S.*, xxiv, 208-33 (1994).

2181 De PAOR (Máire). Irish antiquarian artists. In *Visualizing Ireland*, pp 119-32 (1993).

2182 DEVALLY (Liam). John McCormack. In *Blackrock Soc. Proc.*, i, 26-9 (1992/93).

2183 De VERE (Aubrey). Christmas holidays. In *Old Limerick Jn.*, xxxi, 20 (1994).
From 'Recollections of Aubrey de Vere', Arnold, New York, 1897.

2184 DILLON (Paul). Irish labour, Irish Soviets and European revolution, 1913-23. In *U.C.D. Hist. Rev.*, vi, 67-80 (1992).

2185 DIXON (Roger). The splendid press of Messrs Marcus Ward & Company. In *Linen Hall Rev.*, xi, no. 2, pp 4-6, (1994).

DOAN (James E.). See 1698.

DOBSON (David). See 1699.

DOBSON (Nóirín). See *Parishes of County Antrim ix, Parishes of County Londonderry vii*.

2186 DOCKRELL (John H.). Blackrock - Town Hall and Baths. Some reflections. In *Blackrock Soc. Proc.*, ii, 18-33 (1993/94).

DODD (Joe). See *100 years of the L.F.A.* (1993)

DODD (Liam). See 1700.

2187 DODD (Luke). The famine on the Strokestown estate, and the Famine Museum at Strokestown Park. In *Roscommon Hist. Soc. Jn.*, iii, 56-7 (1990).

2188 DONNELLY (James S. jr). The great famine: its interpreters, old and new. In *Hist. Ire.*, i, no. 3, pp 27-33 (1993).

2189 DONNELLY (James S. jr). The Marian shrine of Knock: the first decade. In *Eire-Ireland*, xxviii, no. 2, pp 54-99 (1993).

2190 DONNELLY (James S. jr). The Terry Alt movement 1829-31. In *Hist. Ire.*, ii, no. 4, pp 30-35 (1994).

2191 DOOLEY (Terence A.M.). The decline of the Ormonde estate, 1893-1950. In *Old Kilkenny Rev.*, iv, 1118-40 (1993).

2192 DOOLEY (Terence A.M.). Why Monaghan Protestants opposed home rule. In *Clogher Rec.*, xiv, no. 3, pp 42-6 (1993).

2193 DOOLEY (Terence A.M.). From the Belfast boycott to the Boundary Commission: fears and hopes in County Monaghan, 1920-26. In *Clogher Rec.*, xv, no. 1, pp 90-106 (1994).

2194 DOOLEY (Tom). Southern Ireland, historians and the First World War. In *Ir. Studies Rev.*, iv, 5-9 (1993).

2195   DORAN (Liam).   The local gentry and church disestablishment.   In
        Cloughjordan Heritage, i, 31-3 (1985).

2196   DOUGLAS (Wm). The road-menders. In *Benbradagh*, xxiv, 15-16 (1994).

2197   DOWLING (Alan).   Of ships and sealing wax: the introduction of land
        registration in Ireland. In *N. Ire. Legal. Quart.*, xliv, 360-79 (1993).

2198   DOYLE (Ciaran).   Trifylia.   In *Wicklow Hist. Soc. Jn.*, i, no. 6, pp 27-30
        (1993).
        Wreck of the Greek ship 'Trifylia' off Wicklow, 1915.

2199   DOYLE (Joe).   The 'Callan Case' and the national school clerical manager.
        In *Old Kilkenny Rev.*, iv, 1146-58 (1993).

2200   DOYLE (Joe).   Schools in Tullaherin and Kilfane in the 19th century.   In *In
        the Shadow of the Steeple*, iv, 41-9 (1994).

        DOYLE (Maureen).   See *A man from Barnaderg*.

2201   DOYLE (Oliver).   Malahide-Drogheda signalling.   In *Irish Railway Rec.
        Soc. Jn.*, xviii, no. 122, pp 282-93 (1993).

2202   DOYLE (Peter). The first Saturday. In *Lecale Miscellany*, xi, 59-60 (1993).
        Notes from the *Downpatrick Recorder*, Saturday, 2 Jan. 1875.

2203   DOYLE (Tom).   York Road, past and present.   In *Dun Laoghaire Jn.*, iii, 23-
        9 (1993).

2204   Dr Thomas Reid, a convict ship's surgeon, visits Lifford Gaol in 1822.   In
        Donegal Annual, xlv, 76-82 (1993).

2205   DUFFY (Francis). The Cathedral of SS Patrick and Felim, Cavan, 1919-47.
        In *Breifne*, viii, 304-26 (1992/93).

2206   DUFFY (Godfrey).   William Smith O'Brien.   A plea for mercy from the
        people of Ireland. In *Dun Laoghaire Hist. Soc. Jn.*, iii, 74-81 (1994).

        DUFFY (Godfrey F.).   See 1705.

2207   DUFFY (Paul).   Turf, steam and the Stein Browne distillery chimney.   In
        North Munster Antiq. Jn., xxxv, 107-08 (1993/94).

        DUFFY (P.J.).   See 1707.

2208   DUGGAN (John J.).   The Land War in Grenagh.   In *Old Blarney*, iii, 3-12
        (1993).

2209   DUGGAN (J.P.).   1916.   Overall plan: a concept of operations.   In *An
        Cosantóir*, li, no. 4, pp 23-6 (1991).

        DUMVILLE (David N.).   See CAREY (John).

2210   DUNCAN (Mary Frances).   Some New Zealand McBrides.   In *The Glynns*,
        xxi, 54-7 (1993).

2211   DUNLEAVY (John). Michael Davitt. In *Treoir*, xxvi, no. 4, pp 13-15 (1994).

2212   DUNLEVY (Mairead). Dublin in the early nineteenth century: domestic evidence. In *Ireland*, pp 184-206 (1994).

2213   DUNLOP (Eull). Foundation stone of Eskylane meeting-house (1760?) laid in 1842. In *Presb. Hist. Soc. of Ire. Bull.*, xxi, 17-18 (1992).

2214   DUNLOP (Eull). The last of the surviving fathers. In *Presb. Hist. Soc. of Ire. Bull.*, xix, 31-3 (1990).
       Rev. Frederick Buick (1811?-1908).

2215   DUNLOP (Eull). William Arthur: the Methodist leader reared in Kells. Reflections on a recent biography. In *Ulster Local Studies*, xvi, no. 1, pp 81-3 (1994).

       DUNLOP (Eull). See SCOTT (Alfred Russell).

       DUNLOP (Eull). See 1722, 1761.

2216   DWYER (Noel). An Australian family discovers kinship with the 1798 Wicklow chief. In *Ir. Roots* 1994, no. 3, pp 21-4 (1994).

2217   The economic development of Ireland since 1870. *Ed.* Cormac Ó Gráda. 2 vols. Aldershot, Hants: E. Elgar, 1994. (The economic development of modern Europe since 1870, vol. 5) (Elgar reference collection)
       Collection of 39 articles originally published between 1933 and 1991.

2218   ELEBERT (Michael). Recollections of Rapla. In *Cloughjordan Heritage*, i, 9-11 (1985).
       A 'big house' which was burned down by the I.R.A. during the Civil War.

2219   ELLIOTT (Ian). An Irish galaxy. In *Ir. Studies Rev.*, iv, 19-23 (1993).
       Astronomy in Ireland in the 19th century.

       ELLIOTT (Marianne). See 1711.

2220   ELLIS (Peter Berresford). The celtic dawn: a history of Pan celticism. Pp 206. London: Constable, 1993.

2221   ELLIS (William). Milford mills. In *Carloviana*, xli, 12-13 (1993/94).

2222   ELLIS (William). Patrick Fenelon Collier of Myshall. In *Carloviana*, xxxiii, 2-3 (1985/86).
       Patrick Fenelon Collier (1849-1909) publisher in New York.

2223   ELVERT (Jürgen). Der Bruc: Irlands Weg in die zweistaatlichkeit (1916-1921). In *Nordirland in Geschichte und Gegenwart*, pp 128-50 (1994).

2224   EMERSON (Lucius J.). Elizabeth Patterson Bonaparte, from the Baer manuscript. In *Donegal Annual*, xlv, 88-93 (1993).

2225   EMMONS (David M.). The socialization of uncertainty: the Ancient Order of Hibernians in Butte, Montana 1880-1925. In *Eire-Ireland*, xxix, no. 3, pp 74-92 (1994).

2226   ENGLISH (Richard). Green on red: two case studies in early twentieth-century Irish republican thought. In *Political thought in Ireland since the seventeenth century*, pp 161-89 (1993).

2227   EVANS (Alun). The Ralahine horse reaping machine. In *R.S.A.I. Jn.*, cxxiv, 153-62 (1994).

2228   EVANS (John). One of the first recipients of the V.C. In *Roscommon Hist. Soc. Jn.*, iii, 11-13 (1990).
        Luke O'Connor (d. 1915).

2229   An expensive election for Sir Marcus. In *A Window on the Past*, [i], 23 (1987).
        Innkeeper's bill for expenses to Sir Marcus Somerville in 1826 (M.P. for Meath 1800-31).

2230   Extracts from Cork trade directories. In *O'Mahony Jn.*, xii, 43-6 (1982).
        Entries relating to Mahony/O'Mahony.

2231   FAHY (A.M.). Place and class in Cork. In *Cork*, pp 793-812 (1993).

        FAIRBURN (Eleanor). See LYONS (Michael J.).

2232   FAIRHALL (James). James Joyce and the question of history. Pp xiv, 290. Cambridge: Cambridge University Press, 1993.

        FALKINER (Ninian). See WYSE JACKSON (Patrick).

2233   Families of Inishbofin Island. In *Galway Roots* [i], 12 (1993).
        Lists of family names from 1893 and 1993.

2234   FARMAR (Tony). Holles Street 1894-1994: the National Maternity Hospital - a centenary history. Pp xii, 234. Dublin: A.&A. Farmar, 1994.

2235   FARRELL (Brian). The first Dáil and its constitutional documents. In *The creation of the Dáil*, pp 61-74 (1994).
        [Appendix 2 (a-f): The constitution of Dáil Éireann; the democratic programme of the First Dáil; the Johnson draft of the democratic programme; declaration of independence; message to the free nations of the world; check-list of Dáil decrees 1919-1922. Pp 165-77].

2236   FARRELL (Brian). The parliamentary road to independence. In *The creation of the Dáil*, pp 1-13 (1994).

        FAULKNER (Pádraig). See 1718.

2237   FAUSKE (Christopher). A life merely glimpsed: Louis MacNeice at the end of the Anglo-Irish tradition. In *Canadian Jn. of Irish Studies*, xx, no. 1, pp 17-29 (1994).

2238   FAZAKAS (Ray). The Donnelly murders. In *Ir. Roots* 1994, no. i, pp 6-7 (1994)

2239   FEELEY (Pat). The lamentation of James Walsh. In *Old Limerick Jn.*, xxix, 22-4 (1992).

2240   FENNING (Hugh).   Clergy of Elphin diocese 1810-12.   In *Collect. Hib.*,
xxxiv/xxxv, 139-42 (1992/93).

FENNING (Hugh).   See 1720, 1721.

FERGUSON (Samuel).   See 1722.

2241   FERRIS (Tom).   The Irish narrow gauge: a pictorial history.   Vol. 1: from
Cork to Cavan.   Pp 112.   Belfast: Blackstaff Press, 1993.

2242   FERRIS (Tom).   The Irish narrow gauge: a pictorial history.   Vol. 2: The
Ulster lines.   Pp 128.   Belfast: Blackstaff Press, 1993.

2243   FFEARY-SMYRL (S.C.).   Kingstown Congregational Church.   In *Dun
Laoghaire Genealogical Soc. Jn.*, ii, 70-74 (1993).
Part of the baptismal and marriage register - baptisms Mar. 1849-Oct. 1861;
marriages Oct. 1849-June 1851.

2244   FFEARY-SMYRL (Steven C.).   Kingstown Congregational Church.   In *Dun
Laoghaire Genealogical Soc. Jn.*, ii, 31-7 (1993).
Membership roll and index 1849-61.

2245   FFEARY-SMYRL (Steven C.).   Kingstown Congregational Church.   In *Dun
Laoghaire Genealogical Soc. Jn.*, iii, 19-23 (1994).
Baptismal register June 1881 to the last entry of 1911.

2246   FIELDING (Steve).   Class and ethnicity: Irish Catholics in England, 1880-
1939.   Pp xiv, 180.   Ballmoor, Bucks: Open University Press, 1993.
(Themes in twentieth century)

2247   FIELDING (Steve).   Irish politics in Manchester, 1890-1914.   In
International Rev. of Social History, xxxiii, 261-84 (1988).

2248   FINLAY (Andrew).   Sectarianism in the workplace: the case of the Derry shirt
industry 1868-1968.   In *Ir. Jn. Sociol.*, iii, 79-93 (1993).

2249   FINLAY (John).   Wicklow rejects home rule for a republic.   Part III-IV:
After war ... peace.   In *Wicklow Hist. Soc. Jn.*, i, no. 6, pp 31-9 (1993); i,
no. 7, pp 55-60 (1994).
Continued from i, no. 5, pp 25-33 (1992).

2250   FITZGERALD (Desmond).   The Trillick derailment 1854.   In *Clogher Rec.*,
xv, no. 1, pp 31-47 (1994).
Derailment of excursion train from Enniskillen to Derry, 15 Sept. 1854.

2251   FITZGERALD (Desmond) and WEATHERUP (Roger).   The way we were:
historic Armagh photographs from the Allison Collection.   Pp viii, 136.
Belfast: Friar's Bush Press in association with the Public Record Office of
Northern Ireland, 1993.
Herbert T.Allison, 1854-1947 and Herbert Allison, d. 1957.

2252   FITZGERALD (Doireann).   Diplomatic relations between the Irish Republic
and Soviet Russia, 1919-21.   In *U.C.D. Hist. Rev.*, viii, 14-21 (1994).

2253   FITZGERALD (Donal).   The famine in Bantry.   In *Bantry Hist. Soc. Jn.*, i,
83-91 (1991).

2254   FITZGERALD (Michael). Acetylene works in Arklow. In *Arklow Hist. Soc. Jn.*, pp 12-13 (1992/93).

2255   FITZGERALD (Michael). Michael Doheny - the Cork connection. In *Tipp. Hist. Jn.*, pp 72-5 (1993).

2256   FITZMAURICE (James). An article in celebration of '125 years of the I.N.T.O. - nationally and locally'. In *Arklow Hist. Soc. Jn.*, pp 36-8 (1992/93).

2257   FITZPATRICK (David). Emigrant letters. 'I take up my pen to write these few lines'. In *Hist. Ire.*, ii, no. 4, pp 15-18 (1994).

2258   FITZPATRICK (David). Oceans of consolation: personal accounts of Irish migration to Australia. Pp xiv, 649. Cork: Cork University Press, 1994.

FITZPATRICK (David). See LINDSAY (Deirdre).

2259   FITZPATRICK (Georgina). St Andrew's College, 1894-1994: Ardens sed virens. Pp 192. Dublin: St Andrew's College, 1994.

FITZPATRICK (PATRICK). See *A hundred years of Killygarry school* (1994).

2260   FLANNERY (Maeve). Register of voters - 1895. East Wicklow. In *Wicklow Hist. Soc. Jn.*, i, no. 7, pp 61-4 (1994).

2261   FLANNERY (Michael). One hundred years of public health: sanitation to conservation and environmental care. In *Administration*, xxvi, 435-58 (1978).

2262   FLEETWOOD (John F.). Dublin private medical schools in the nineteenth century. In *Dublin Hist. Rec.*, xlvi, 31-45 (1993).

2263   FLYNN (Pat). The general advancement of the country: Clare and the census returns of 1841 and 1851. In *The Other Clare*, xvii, 57-65 (1993).

2264   FOLEY (Denis). Mullinahone Coop: the first one hundred years. Pp 178. [Mullinahone, Co. Tipperary]: Mullinahone Cooperative Dairy Society, [1993].

2265   FOLEY (Timothy P.). D'Arcy Wentworth Thompson: classical scholar and Fenian sympathiser. In *Galway Arch. Soc. Jn.*, xlv, 90-123, plate (1993).

2266   FOLEY (Timothy P.). Thomas Maguire and the Parnell forgeries. In *Galway Arch. Soc. Jn.*, xlvi, 173-96 (1994).

FOLLIS (Brian A.). See 1730.

2267   FORDE (Frank). Shetland incident. In *Arklow Hist. Soc. Jn.*, pp 7-8 (1992/93).

2268   FORDE (Robert). The descendants of an Irish orphan in Australia. In *Mallow Field Club Jn.*, xi, 67-76 (1993).

2269   FORRISTAL (Desmond). The first Loreto sister: Mother Teresa Ball, 1794-1861. Pp 189. Dublin: Dominican Publications, 1994.

2270   FOSTER (Marita). Hurley letters. The Hurley emigrant letters. In *Ir. Roots* 1992, no. 3, pp 30-31 (1992).

2271   FOSTER (R.F.). Parnell and his neighbours. In *Wicklow*, pp 895-910 (1994).

         FOSTER (R.F.). See 1732.

         FOSTER (Roy). See 1733.

2272   FOY (Michael T.). Ulster unionism and the development of the Ulster Volunteer Force before the First World War. In *Nordirland in Geschichte und Gegenwart*, pp 99-127 (1994).

2273   Fr William O'Donnell - 'the Waterloo priest'. In *Ó Domhnaill Abú*, xx, 2 (1993).

         FRANKLING (F.T.). See 1734.

2274   FRASER (Tom). Partitioning Ireland, India and Palestine. In *Nationalism and unionism*, pp 177-86 (1994).

2275   FREITAG (Barbara). Literature rewrites history: James Connolly and James Larkin larger than life. In *Jn. Ir. Lit.*, xxii, no. 2, pp 25-38 (1993).

2276   FRENCH (Ettie). Willie. Pp 106. Holywood, Co. Down: Percy French Society, 1994.
         A memoir of Percy French, 1854-1920 by his daughter.

2277   FULLAM (Brendan). Hurling giants. Pp 256, [10], ill. Dublin: Wolfhound Press, 1994.

2278   FULTON (Eileen). The parish of St Joseph's, Hannahstown, Co. Antrim, 1826-1993. Pp 74. Belfast: Ulster Journals, 1993.

2279   GAGEBY (Patrick). Sellerna: a Connemara mission. In *Connemara*, i, no. 1, pp 32-6 (1993).
         Irish church missions to Catholics in the Clifden area at the time of the Great Famine.

2280   GAMBLE (Norman E.). The D & BJR, 1844-55. Part 4. In *Irish Railway Rec. Soc. Jn.*, xviii, no. 120, pp 169-77 (1993).
         Continued from xviii, no. 119, pp 116-23 (1992).

2281   GARVIN (Tom). The formation of the Irish political élite. In *The creation of the Dáil*, pp 47-60 (1994).

2282   GATENBY (Peter). The School of Physic, Trinity College Dublin: a retrospective view. Pp 76. Dublin: Trinity College Dublin, Faculty of Health Sciences, 1994.
         History of Faculty since 1912.

2283   GAYNOR (Seán). With Tipperary No. 1 Brigade in North Tipperary: 1917-1921. Parts 1-2. In *Tipp. Hist. Jn.*, pp 31-40 (1993); pp 26-37 (1994).

2284   GEOGHEGAN (Vincent).   The emergence and submergence of Irish socialism, 1821-51.   In *Political thought in Ireland since the seventeenth century*, pp 100-23 (1993).

2285   GEOGHEGAN (Vincent).   Socialism, national identities and post-national citizenship.   In *Irish Political Studies*, ix, 61-80 (1994).

2286   GERAGHTY (P.J.).   A heritage in stone: the life and career of architect John Murray.   Pp vi, 66. [Ardee, Co. Louth]: P.J. Geraghty, 1994.
        1807-92.

2287   GERAGHTY (P.J.).   P.J. Dodd of Drogheda, architect and civil engineer.   In *Old Drogheda Soc. Jn.*, ix, 7-37 (1994).
        1845-1891.

2288   German military archives find.   In *An Cosantóir*, li, no. 4, pp 27-9 (1991).
        Material acquired by Lt Col. Duggan (retd).

2289   GIFFORD (Dick).   Downpatrick war memorial.   In *Lecale Miscellany*, xi, 31-4 (1993).

2290   GIFFORD (Dick).   The South Down Militia.   In *Lecale Miscellany*, ix, 42-6 (1991).
        A booklet issued to recruits in the late 19th century.

2291   GILBERT (Elliot L.).   'Tumult of Images': Wilde, Beardsley and *Salome*.   In *Victorian Studies*, xxvi, 117-59 (1982/83).

        GILDEA (J.).   See 1738.

2292   GILLEN (Gerald).   William Telford and the Victorian organ in Ireland.   In *Music and the church*, pp 108-28 (1993).
        Dublin-based organ builder, fl. 1830-66.

        GILLEY (Sheridan).   See 1767.

        GIROUARD (Mark).   See WILLIAMS (Jeremy).

        GIRVIN (Brian).   See 1740.

2293   GLADSTONE (William Ewart).   The Gladstone diaries, with cabinet minutes and prime-ministerial correspondence.   Vol. 12: 1887-1891.   *Ed.* H.C.G. Matthew.   Pp lxxxxvii, 535.   Oxford: Clarendon Press, 1994.

2294   GLAVEY (Michael).   County Mayo Prisoners of War Relief Fund.   Report for the period ending 30th June 1916.   In *Cathair na Mart*, xiv, 97-101 (1994).

2295   GLENDINNING (James).   Ballyclog School.   In *The Bell*, v, 32-7 (1994).

2296   Glimpses of life at sea in the 1880s.   In *Upper Ards Hist. Soc. Jn.*, i, 4-6 (1977).

2297   GLOVER (Winifred).   In the wake of Captain Cook: the travels of Gordon Augustus Thompson (1799-1886).   In *Familia*, ii, no. 9, pp 46-61 (1993).

2298   GOGARTY (Oliver St John).   As I was going down Sackville Street.   Pp 330. Dublin: O'Brien Press, 1994.
Originally published: 1937.

2299   GOLDRING (Maurice).   Exclusion du suffrage: l'émancipation des Catholiques. In *Études Irlandaises*, xix, no. 2, pp 97-105 (1994).

2300   GOLDRING (Maurice).   Irlande: déclassement, reclassement des voleurs nationales. In *Études Irlandaises*, xviii, no. 1, pp 125-32 (1993).

2301   GOLDRING (Maurice).   Pleasant the scholar's life: Irish intellectuals and the construction of the nation-state. Pp 189. London: Serif, 1993.

2302   GOODACRE (John). Valuation and report.   Toratanvally estate, Achill, Co. Mayo, Ireland. The property of John Goodacre Esqre. Decr., 1872.   In *Cathair na Mart*, xiii, 112-16 (1993).
Document in the possession of Duncan Goodacre and submitted by Ian Fisher.

2303   GOODALL (David).   John Greene and the Wexford Independent [Part 1] - Part 2. In *The Past*, xvii, 3-23 (1990); xviii, 3-30 (1992).

GOODALL (David). See 1743.

2304   GORMAN (Liam).   The railway.   An historic outline and some reminiscences. In *Oola Past & Present*, i, 6-10 (1992).

2305   GRACE (Daniel). Dromineer: the port of north-west Tipperary. In *Tipp. Hist. Jn.*, pp 51-62 (1993).

2306   GRAHAM (B.J.) and HOOD (Susan). Town tenant protest in late nineteenth- and early twentieth-century Ireland. In *Ir. Econ. & Soc. Hist.*, xxi, 39-57 (1994).

2307   GRANT (J.R.). Clough Baptist Church, Co. Antrim. In *Ir. Baptist Hist. Soc. Jn.*, n.s., i, 64-5 (1993/94).

2308   GRAY (Jane). Gender and plebian culture in Ulster. In *Jn. Interdisciplinary History*, xxiv, 251-70 (1993/94).

2309   GRAY (Peter). *Punch* and the great famine. In *Hist. Ire.*, i, no. 2, pp 26-33 (1993).

2310   GRAY (Peter). 'Potatoes and providence': British government responses to the great famine. In *Bullán*, i, no. 1, pp 75-90 (1994).

2311   The great Clare gold find of 1854. In *The Other Clare*, ii, 30 (1978).

2312   GREEN (E.R.R.). Agriculture. In *The great famine*, pp 89-128 (1994).

2313   GREENE (Thomas R.).   Michael O'Riordan's *La recente insurrezione in Irlanda*, 1916. In *Eire-Ireland*, xxviii, no. 4, pp 53-73 (1993).

GREINER (Alyson L.). See JORDAN (Terry G.).

2314   GRENE (Nicholas). Synge and Wicklow. In *Wicklow*, pp 693-721 (1994).

GRENE (Nicholas). See *Shaw, Lady Gregory and the Abbey* (1993).

GRIBBON (Harry). See 1748.

2315 GRIFFIN (Brian). An agrarian murder and evictions in Rathcore. In *Ríocht na Midhe*, ix, no. 1, pp 88-103 (1994/95).

GRIFFIN (Brian). See 1749.

2316 GRIFFIN (Seán). Archbishop Murray of Dublin and the episcopal clash on the interdenominational school 'Scripture Lessons' controversy, 1835-1841. In *Recusant History*, xxii, 370-408 (1994/95).

2317 GRIFFIN (Seán). Desegregating the national schools: Archbishop Murray (1823-1852) as a pioneer of church-state cooperation. In *Ir. Educational Studies*, xiii, 46-61 (1994).

2318 Griffith Survey of Dungiven 1858. Valuation of tenements. Parish of Dungiven. In *Benbradagh*, xxiii, 18 (1993). Continued from xxii (1992).

2319 Griffith Survey of Magheramore 1858. Valuation of tenements. Parish of Banagher. In *Benbradagh*, xxiv, 4 (1994).

2320 GRIMES (Seamus) and CONNOLLY (Michael). Emigration from Connemara to America with specific reference to the link between Cois Fharraige and Portland, Maine, 1880s to 1920s. In *Galway Roots*, ii, 40-43 (1994).

2321 GUERIN (Michael). The life of a Limerick dentist, part 1-3. In *Old Limerick Jn.*, xxix, 34-6 (1992); xxx, 47-51 (1993); xxxi, 42-3 (1994).

2322 GUINNANE (Timothy W.). A failed institutional transplant: Raiffeisen's credit cooperatives in Ireland 1894-1914. In *Explorations in Econ. Hist.*, xxxi, 38-61 (1994).

2323 GUINNANE (Timothy W.). The poor law and pensions in Ireland [research note]. In *Jn. Interdisciplinary History*, xxiv, 271-91 (1993/94).

2324 GULLIVER (P.H.) and SILVERMAN (Marilyn). Hucksters and petty retailers in Thomastown, 1880-1945. In *Old Kilkenny Rev.*, iv, 1094-1100 (1993).

2325 HAINES (Keith). Neither rogues nor fools: a history of Campbell College and Campbellians. Pp xx, 377. Belfast: Campbell College, 1993.

2326 HAINES (Robin). Indigent misfits or shrewd operators? Government-assisted emigrants from the United Kingdom to Australia, 1831-1860. In *Population Studies*, xlviii, 223-47 (1994).

2327 HALEY (Bruce). Wilde's 'decadence' and the positivist tradition. In *Victorian Studies*, xxviii, 215-29 (1984/85).

2328 HALL (Michael). Parish priests of Drangan & Cloneen, 1826-1993. In *Souvenir of rededication of Church of the Immaculate Conception, Drangan*, pp 10-14 (1993).

2329   HALL (Michael). Sacrifice on the Somme. Pp 32. Newtownabbey: Island Publications, 1993. (Island pamphlets, 2)

2330   HALL (Norman). A pioneer in agricultural education. In *The Bann Disc*, i, 50-53 (1994).
Agricultural college established in 1827 in Templemoyle, Co. Londonderry.

2331   HALLINAN (Michael). The capture and execution of District Inspector Potter. In *Tipperary County*, pp 157-60 (1993).
Royal Irish constabulary, killed 1921.

2332   HAMILTON (Ian). Cornelius O'Sullivan (1841-1907): his place in 19th-century science. In *Bandon Hist. Jn.*, ix, 35-7 (1993).

2333   HAMILTON (John). Dublin Diocesan Archives: Hamilton Papers (4). *Ed.* Mary Purcell. In *Archiv. Hib.*, xlvii, 11-64 (1993).
Archdeacon John Hamilton (1800-62) for the period 1836-7.

2334   HAMILTON (John). Dublin Diocesan Archives: Hamilton papers (5). *Ed.* Mary Purcell. In *Archiv. Hib.*, xlviii, 37-72 (1994).
Archdeacon John Hamilton (1800-62) for 1838.

HAMILTON (Pádraig). See 1750.

2335   HAMILTON (S.N.). Kilkeel Baptist Church in the Kingdom of Mourne. In *Ir. Baptist Hist. Soc. Jn.*, n.s., i, 49-63 (1993/94).

2336   HANNA (Conac). St Patrick's Catholic Church. In *Lecale Miscellany*, xii, 6 (1994).

2337   HANNAN (Kevin). The County Club. In *Old Limerick Jn.*, xxx, 23-4 (1993).

2338   HANNAN (Kevin). The Limerick watch. In *Old Limerick Jn.*, xxix, 7-9 (1992).

2339   HANNAN (Kevin). Sir Peter Tait. In *Old Limerick Jn.*, xxxi, 26-30 (1994).
Sir Peter Tait 1818-90.

2340   HANNIGAN (Ken). Eye-witness accounts of the famine in Co. Wicklow. In *Wicklow Hist. Soc. Jn.*, i, no. 6, pp 11-26 (1993).

2341   HANNIGAN (Ken). A miscellany of murder: violent death in 19th-century Wicklow. In *Wicklow Hist. Soc. Jn.*, i, no. 7, pp 22-34 (1994).

2342   HANNIGAN (K.). Wicklow before and after the famine. In *Wicklow*, pp 789-822 (1994).

2343   HARKNESS (Dick). The Roman Catholic chapel in Drumbanaway. In *The Bell*, v, 44-5 (1994).

2344   HARRIS (Mary). The Catholic church and the foundation of the Northern Ireland state. Pp xiii, 304. Cork: Cork University Press, 1993.
1912-30.

2345   HARRIS (Ruth-Ann M.). The nearest place that wasn't Ireland: early nineteenth-century Irish labor migration. Pp xvii, 281. Ames: Iowa State University Press, 1994.

2346   HARRISON (Jennifer). 'The very worst class': Irish women convicts at Moreton Bay. In *Irish convict lives*, pp 178-98 (1993).

2347   HARRISON (Jennifer). A willing community. Aspects of Irish immigration to pre-separation Queensland 1848-1852. In *Ir. Roots* 1992, no. 2, pp 28-9 (1992); no. 3, pp 28-9 (1992).

HARRISON (Jennifer). See 1752.

2348   HARRISON (Richard S.). Richard Davis Webb: Dublin Quaker printer (1805-72). Pp ii, 84. [S.l.]: [the author], 1993.

2349   HART (Peter). Class, community and the Irish Republican Army in Cork, 1917-1923. In *Cork*, pp 963-85 (1993).

2350   HARTE (Hilary). Wool carding mill in Cooridorigan. In *Mizen Jn.*, ii, 58-61 (1994).

2351   HASSON (Seamus). The bard of Carntoher. In *Benbradagh*, xii, 5-7, 22-3 (1982).
James O'Kane, 1823-1913.

2352   HASSON (Seamus). A nineteenth-century parochial house - and the men who lived therein. (Parts 8-9) Fr Edward Loughrey, P.P. (1890-1915). In *Benbradagh*, xxiii, 14-16 (1993); xxiv, 11-14 (1994).
Continued from xxii (1992).

2353   HATTON (Timothy J.) and WILLIAMSON (Jeffrey G.). After the famine: emigration from Ireland 1850-1913. In *Jn. Economic History*, liii, no. 3, pp 575-600 (1993).

2354   HATTON (Timothy J.) and WILLIAMSON (Jeffrey G.). International migration, 1850-1939: an economic survey. In *Migration and the international labor market, 1850-1939*, pp 3-32 (1994).

HATTON (Timothy J.). See BOYER (George R.).

2355   HAYES (Alan). The <u>real</u> Maud Gonne. In *Review-UCG*, i, 55-68 (1992).

HAYTER (Alethea). See 1620.

2356   HEALY (James). Notes towards a study of Irish hunger strikes I-II. In *Milltown Studies*, viii, 43-57 (1981); ix, 23-37 (1982).

2357   HEALY (Roisin). The early life and times of Richard J. Healy. In *U.C.D. Hist. Rev.*, iii, 2-4 (1989).

2358   HEALY (T.M.). Portmarnock Golf Club, 1894-1994: a centenary history. Pp iv, 162. Portmarnock, Co. Dublin: Portmarnock Golf Club, 1993.

2359   HEARN (Mona). Below stairs: domestic service remembered in Dublin and beyond 1880-1922. Pp [5], 150. Dublin: Lilliput Press, 1993.

2360   HEGARTY (Dave). John Wayland, musician and revivalist, Mici Cumba and the Australian connection. In *An Aisling*, iii, 115-18 (1991).
John Smithwick Wayland, *c*.1874-1954, buried in Geraldton, Western Australia.

2361   HEGARTY (Dave). Piping in Kerry. In *An Aisling*, iii, 119-31 (1991).

2362   HEGARTY (Lawrence). Drumsurn school. In *Benbradagh*, xii, 10-12 (1982).

HEMPTON (David). See 1757.

2363   HENNESSEY (Thomas), Ulster unionist territorial and national identities 1886-1893: province, island, kingdom and empire. In *Irish Political Studies*, viii, 21-36 (1993).

2364   HENRY (Henry). Letter to Patrick Joseph MacGreevy of Saul. In *Lecale Miscellany*, vii, 10-11 (1989).
Letter written by Henry Henry, subsequently Bishop of Down & Connor, in 1865.

Henry Cooke's Centenary. See 1761

HERDEGEN (Lance J.). See BEAUDOT (William J.K.).

2365   HERLIHY (Jim). Ellis Island - gateway to America - or island of tears. In *Ir. Roots* 1992, no. 4, pp 6-7 (1992).

2366   HERLIHY (Jim). Peter Golden: the voice of Ireland: a biography. Pp xiv, 93. Cork: Peter Golden Commemoration Committee, 1994.
Singer, secretary of the Friends of Irish Freedom, U.S., 1877-1926.

HERLIHY (Jim). See 1762.

2367   HERON (Anastatia). The glamorous Howards.... In *Swords Voices*, i, 2-6 (1992/93).
Memories of Swords.

2368   HERSCOVICI (Steven). The distribution of wealth in nineteenth-century Boston: inequality among natives and immigrants, 1860. In *Explorations in Econ. Hist.*, xxx, 321-35 (1993).

2369   HESKEN (Marie). Kilfane forge. In *In the Shadow of the Steeple*, iv, 90-91 (1994).

2370   HICKEY (Donal). Queen of them all: a history of Killarney Golf and Fishing Club, 1893-1993. Pp 156 [12]. [Killarney]: Killarney Golf and Fishing Club, 1993.

2371   HICKEY (Nora M.). The distribution of the O'Mahonys in Co. Cork. An analysis of Griffith's Valuation, *circa* 1850. In *O'Mahony Jn.*, xvi, 26-35 (1993).

2372   HICKEY (Patrick). Famine, mortality and emigration: a profile of six parishes in the poor law union of Skibbereen, 1846-7. In *Cork*, pp 873-917 (1993).

2373   HICKEY (Patrick).   The visit of the artist James Mahony to west Cork in
        1847. In *O'Mahony Jn.*, xii, 26-32 (1982).

2374   HICKEY (Patrick).   Whiteboys, magistrates and peelers in Mizen Peninsula,
        1813-44. In *Mizen Jn.*, i, 48-59 (1993).

2375   HICKS (Rose).   Recollections of 1916 rebellion.   In *Roscommon Hist. Soc.
        Jn.*, iii, 29 (1990).

        HILL (Jacqueline).   See BOURKE (Austin).

        HILL (Jacqueline).   See 1765.

2376   HILL (Myrtle) and POLLOCK (Vivienne).   Image and experience:
        photographs of Irishwomen, *c*.1880-1920.   Pp ix, 189.   Belfast: Blackstaff
        Press, 1993.

2377   HILL (Myrtle) and POLLOCK (Vivienne).   Images of the past.   Photographs
        as historical evidence. In *Hist. Ire.*, ii, no. 1, pp 9-14 (1994).

2378   History of Kilbride G.A.A. Club, 1887-1992.   *Ed.* John Hunt.   [Kilbride,
        Co. Roscommon]: [Kilbride G.A.A. Club], [1993?].

2379   Hockey in Trinity: the story of Dublin University Hockey Club, 1893-1993.
        Ed. Marcus Webb. Pp viii, 90. Dublin: Trinity Trust and DUCAC, 1993.

2380   HODGINS (Jack).   Sister island: the history of CMS in Ireland, 1814-1994.
        Pp [9], 171, xxiv.   Dunmurry, Co. Antrim: CMS Ireland, 1994.
        Church Missionary Society.

        HODGSON (Rob).   See BUSTEED (Mervyn).

2381   HOGAN (Edmund M.)   The Congregation of the Holy Ghost and the
        evolution of the modern Irish missionary movement. In *Catholic Hist. Rev.*,
        lxx, 1-13 (1984).

2382   HOGAN (Oliver).   Clanna Gael-Fontenoy: the history of Dublin's G.A.A.
        club.   Vol. 1 (1887-1950).   Pp v, 157.   Dublin: Cumann Clanna
        Gael/Fontenoy G.A.A. Club, [1994?].

2383   HOGG (Bill).   Down among the old mills.   In *Dun Laoghaire Genealogical
        Soc. Jn.*, iii, 145-8 (1994).

2384   Hollyford National School, 1891-1991: with background history from 1800.
        Pp 250. [Hollyford, Co. Tipperary]: [Hollyford National School], [1993?].

        HOLMES (Colin).   See 1767.

2385   HOLMES (Janice).   The 'world turned upside down': women in the Ulster
        revival of 1859. See *Coming into the light*, pp 126-53 (1994).

        HOOD (Susan).   See GRAHAM (B.J.).

2386   HOPKINSON (Michael).   Biography of the revolutionary period: Michael
        Collins and Kevin Barry [Review article]. In *I.H.S.*, xxviii, 310-16 (1993).

2387   HOPKINSON (Michael). President Woodrow Wilson and the Irish question. In *Studia Hib,*, xxvii, 89-111 (1993).

2388   HOPPEN (K. Theodore). Grammars of electoral violence in nineteenth-century England and Ireland. In *English Hist. Rev.*, cix, 597-620 (1994).

2389   HORNER (Arnold). Sir Robert Kane's land classification maps - a mid-nineteenth-century cartographic initiative. In *Ir. Geography*, xxvii, 107-21 (1994).

HOUSTON (C.J.). See 1769.

2390   HOWLIN (Phil). Bohemian times: an outline history of Bohemian Football Club & Dalymount Park, 1890-1993. Pp [5], 62. [Dublin]: [the author], [1994?].

2391   HOY (Suellen) and MacCURTAIN (Margaret). From Dublin to New Orleans: Nora and Alice's journey to America 1889. Pp 143. Dublin: Attic Press, 1994.
    Dominican nuns.

2392   HUDELSON (Richard). Jack Carney and the 'Truth' in Duluth. In *Saothar*, xix, 129-39 (1994).

2393   HUGHES (E.W.). The shooting on Brandon. In *Old Kilkenny Rev.*, xlvi, 38-50 (1994).
    Shooting incident between gamekeepers and poachers resulting in two deaths, 7 August 1888.

2394   HULTIN (Neil C.) and OBER (Warren U.). An O'Connellite in Whitehall: Thomas Crofton Croker, 1798-1854. In *Eire-Ireland*, xxviii, no. 3, pp 61-86 (1993).

2395   HUMPHREYS (Madeleine). Quaker principle in the Irish Free State senate. In *U.C.D. Hist. Rev.*, v, 6-10 (1991).

2396   A hundred years of Carrigallen school: a commemorative history celebrating a hundred years of Bredagh School, Carrigallen. Pp 72. [Carrigallen, Co. Leitrim]: [Carrigallen National School], [1993].

2397   A hundred years of Killygarry school: 1894-1994. [*Ed.* Patrick Fitzpatrick]. Pp 96. [Killygarry, Co. Cavan]: [Killygarry Centenary Committee], [1994].

HUNT (John). See *History of Kilbride G.A.A. Club, 1887-1992.*

2398   HUNTER (James). The Gaelic connection: the Highlands, Ireland and nationalism, 1873-1922. In *Scottish Hist. Rev.*, liv, 178-204 (1975).

2399   HURLEY (Frank). St Joseph's Convent of Mercy, Kinsale: a celebration of 150 years, 1844-1994. Pp iv, 156. [Kinsale]: [the author], [1994].

2400   HURLEY (Michael J.). Whaleway tracks. In *Irish Railway Rec. Soc. Jn.*, xviii, no. 122, p. 275 (1993).

2401   HYNES (Christine). A polite struggle: the Dublin seamstresses' campaign, 1869-1872. In *Saothar*, xviii, 35-9 (1993).

2402 HYNES (Rory). History of Clarke Barracks, 1855-1930. Pp 47. [Curragh, Co. Kildare]: [R. Hynes], [1994?]. Curragh, Co. Kildare.

2403 INGLIS (Brian). Roger Casement. Pp 462. Belfast: Blackstaff Press, 1993. Originally published 1974. With new preface.

2404 INGLIS (Henry). A pattern at Maumean. In *Connemara*, i, no. 1, pp 90-93 (1993). Reprinted from Sir Henry Inglis's *Journey through Ireland, 1834*.

2405 INNES (C.L.). Women and nation in Irish literature and society, 1880-1935. Pp 208. Athens, Georgia: University of Georgia Press, 1993.

2406 IRELAND (Aideen M.). The famine. In *Ir. Family Hist.*, x, 44-8 (1994).

IRELAND (Aideen). See 1771, 1772.

2407 Ireland. Oireachtas Dáil. Miontuairisc an chead Dála, 1919-1921 = minutes of proceedings of the first parliament of the Republic of Ireland, 1919-1921: official record. Pp 292. Dublin Stationery Office, 1994. Originally published, 1922?

2408 Irish Congress of Trade Unions. Congress centenary miscellany. In *Trade union century*, pp 171-432 (1994). Presidential addresses (1894-1974); pen portraits of Larkin; poems; songs; ballads; profiles; women; manifestos, etc.

2409 IRVINE (Jimmy). John Larktree. In *The Glynns*, viii, 51-3 (1980).

2410 IRWIN (Liam). The Limerick bishop who said no to papal infallibility. In *Old Limerick Jn.*, xxx, 29-31 (1993). Edward Fitzgerald (1833-1907), bishop of Little Rock, Arkansas.

2411 Is cuimhin linn Kruger. Kruger remembered. *Ed.* Tadhg Ó Dúshláine. Pp 220. Maigh Nuad: An Sagart, 1994. Kavanagh (Muiris, 'Kruger') 1894-1971; text in Irish and English.

2412 JACKSON (Alvin). Irish unionism, 1905-1921. In *Nationalism and unionism*, pp 35-46 (1994).

2413 JACKSON (Alvin). The Larne gun running of 1914. In *Hist. Ire.*, i, no. 1, pp 35-8 (1993).

2414 JACKSON (Alvin). Sir Edward Carson. Pp 74. Dundalk: Dundalgan Press for the Historical Association of Ireland, 1993. (Life and times series, no. 2).

2415 JACKSON (Harold). Memories of an old pupil of Derrycarne School. In *Review*, v, no. 3, pp 5-6 (1986/87).

JACKSON (Patrick N. Wyse). See 1773.

2416 JALLAND (Patricia). A Liberal chief secretary and the Irish question. Augustine Birrell, 1907-1914. In *Hist. Jn.*, xix, 421-51 (1976).

JEFFARES (A. Norman). See McBRIDE (Maud Gonne).

2417   JEFFERY (Keith).   British security policy in Ireland, 1919-21.   In *Nationalism and unionism*, pp 163-75 (1994).

2418   JEFFERY (Keith).   Irish artists and the First World War.   In *Hist. Ire.*, i, no. 2, pp 42-5 (1993).

2419   JEFFERY (Keith).   Irish culture and the Great War.   In *Bullán*, i, no. 2, pp 87-96 (1994).

2420   JENKINS (T.A.).   Hartington, Chamberlain and the unionist alliance, 1886-1895.   In *Parliamentary History*, xi, 108-38 (1992).

2421   JENKINS (William).   The origin and development of creameries in south Tipperary, 1890-1992   In *Baile*, pp 68-9 (1993).

2422   JENNINGS (Catherine).   1880: a distressful year in Connemara.   In *Connemara*, i, no. 1, pp 37-47 (1993).

JENNINGS (Robert M.).   See 1774.

2423   JOCELYN (Robert).   'Marconi express' helped establishment of transatlantic wireless.   In *Connemara*, i, no. 1, pp 12-15 (1993).

2424   JOHNSTON (Jamie).   Victorian Belfast.   Pp 56.   Belfast: Ulster Historical Foundation, 1993. (Using the evidence).

JOHNSTON (May).   See 1775.

2425   JOHNSTON (Sheila Turner).   Alice: a life of Alice Milligan.   Pp 159. Omagh: Colourpoint Press, 1994.
        Alice Milligan, 1866-1953, poetess.

2426   JOHNSTONE (Andrew).   Incongruous organ music in an Irish cathedral.   In *Music and the church*, pp 149-63 (1993).
        St Patrick's Cathedral, 19th century.

2427   JORDAN (Alison).   'Opening the gates of learning': the Belfast Ladies' Institute, 1867-97.   In *Coming into the light*, pp 33-57 (1994).

2428   JORDAN (Bernadette).   Charles Strickland - land agent.   In *Roscommon Hist. Soc. Jn.*, iv, 79-80 (1992).

2429   JORDAN (Kieran).   A photographic history of my ancestors.   In *Ir.Family Hist.*, x, 10-15 (1994).

2430   JORDAN (Terry G.) and GREINER (Alyson L.).   Irish migration to rural eastern Australia: a preliminary investigation.   In *Ir. Geography*, xxvii, 135-42 (1994).

2431   JUDD (Denis).   Radical Joe: a life of Joseph Chamberlain. [2nd ed.].   Pp xvi, 312.   Cardiff: University of Wales Press, 1993.
        Previous ed., 1977.

2432   JUPP (Peter J.) and ROYLE (Stephen A.).   The social geography of Cork city elections, 1801-30.   In *I.H.S.*, xxix, 13-53 (1994).

2433   KAVANAGH (Joan). The case of Eliza Davis. In *Wicklow Hist. Soc. Jn.*, i, no. 7, pp 36-42 (1994).

2434   KAVANAGH (Mary). Local history in Incumbered Estates. Court rentals for County Gaway. In *Galway Roots*, ii, 24-9 (1994).

2435   KAVANAGH (Mary). The photographic collection at Galway county libraries. In *Galway Roots*, [i], 55-9 (1993).

2436   KAVANAGH (Rhoda). Sir William Wilde, M.D., F.R.C.S.I., 1815-1876. In *Roscommon Hist. Soc. Jn.*, iv, 34-8 (1992).

KAVANAUGH (Ann C.). See 1777.

2437   KEANE (Frank S.). Dublin: triumph and failure. In *A man raised up*, pp 128-58 (1994).
Christian Brothers schools 1812-44.

2438   KEARNEY (Patrick). University College, Mungret, 1888-1908. In *Old Limerick Jn.*, xxxi, 37-41 (1994).

2439   KEARNS (Kevin C.). Dublin tenement life: an oral history. Pp 237, [48]. Dublin: Gill & Macmillan, 1994.

2440   KEATING (Joan). The making of the Catholic labour activist, the Catholic Social Guild and Catholic Workers College, 1909-1939. In *Labour History Review*, lix, no. 3, pp 44-56 (1994).

2441   KEE (Robert). The laurel and the ivy: the story of Charles Stewart Parnell and Irish nationalism. Pp xi, 659. London: Hamish Hamilton, 1993.

KELLY (James). See 1782, 1784.

KELLY (John). See YEATS (W.B.).

2442   KELLY (Thos). From 'A list of inhabitants of the united parishes of Kinvara, Duras and Killina, as compiled by Rev. Thos. Kelly' A.D. 1834. In *Galway Roots*, ii, 109-10 (1994).

KENNEDY (Liam). See KING (Carla).

KENNEDY (Liam). See 1788.

2443   KENNEDY (S.B.). Frank McKelvey, R.H.A., R.U.A.: a painter in his time. Pp 96. Blackrock (Co. Dublin): Irish Academic Press, 1993.
1895-1974.

2444   KENNEDY (W.A.). Christian life in Glenravel around 1875. In *Presb. Hist. Soc. of Ire. Bull.*, xviii, 21-6 (1989).

2445   KENNEDY (W.E.). A link with Livingstone. In *Lecale Miscellany*, vi, 36-7 (1988).
Robert Kalloway (1844-1934), sailed as ship's carpenter with H.M. Stanley.

KENNY (James G.). See 1792.

2446   KENNY (Michael). The Fenians: photographs and memorabilia from the National Museum of Ireland. Pp 47. Dublin: Country House in association with the National Museum of Ireland, 1994.

2447   KENNY (Michael). The road to freedom: photographs and memorabilia from the 1916 rising and afterward. Pp 48. Dublin: Town House and Country House, in association with the National Museum of Ireland, 1993.

2448   KEOGH (Brian). John Hornick of Wexford and Sioux city. In *Ir. Roots*, 1994, no. 4, p. 14 (1994).

2449   KEOGH (Dermot). The Catholic church and politics in Ireland. In *People power*, pp 57-79 (1993).

2450   KEOGH (Dermot F.). Foundation and early years of the Irish T.U.C., 1894-1912. In *Trade union century*, pp 19-32 (1994).

2451   KERR (Donal A.). 'A nation of beggars'?: priests, people, and politics in famine Ireland 1846-1852. Pp xiv, 370. Oxford: Clarendon Press, 1994.

2452   KERRIGAN (John). The sad tale of Michael Welsh (the reluctant ribbonman). In *Roscommon Hist. Soc. Jn.*, iii, 8-10 (1990).

2453   KERRIGAN (John). A tale of two rangers: (the Connaught Rangers - a crack British regiment). In *Roscommon Hist. Soc. Jn.*, iv, 24-6 (1992).
Sergeant John Harlow, Private Charles Kerrigan.

2454   KIBBLER (Julia). 1881 census Burton upon Trent registrar's district Staffordshire, England. Irish strays. In *Ir. Family Hist.*, x, 125 (1994).

2455   KIBERD (Declan). Douglas Hyde a radical in Tory clothing. In *Ir. Reporter*, xi, 18-20 (1993).

2456   KIBERD (Declan). The plebians revise the uprising: Seán O'Casey and 1916. In *Féile Zozimus. Vol. 3: Two Dubliners*, pp 29-45 (1994).

2457   KIBERD (Declan). Synge and the Irish language. 2nd ed. Pp xxxiii, 294. London: Macmillan, 1993.
Previous ed.: 1979.

2458   KIELTY (Frances). Jasper Tully, 1858-1938. In *Roscommon Hist. Soc. Jn.*, iii, 59-62 (1990).
Editor of the *Roscommon Herald*.

2459   KIELY (Brendan). The Connerys: the making of a Waterford legend. Pp 145. Dublin: Geography Publications, 1994.
Three brothers transported to Australia in the 1830s for agrarian unrest.

2460   KIELY (David M.). John Millington Synge: a biography. Pp xiii, 305. Dublin: Gill & Macmillan, 1994.
1871-1909.

KILLEN (John). See 1795.

2461   KILLEN (Pat). Haymaking in the early 1900s. In *Lecale Miscellany*, vi, 12 (1988).

KINANE (Vincent). See 1796.

2462   KINEALY (Christine). This great calamity: the Irish famine, 1845-52. Pp xxi, 450. Dublin: Gill & Macmillan, 1994.

2463   KING (Carla) and KENNEDY (Liam). Irish co-operatives. From creameries at the crossroads to multinationals. In *Hist. Ire.*, ii, no. 4, pp 36-41 (1994).

2464   KING (Joseph A.). The Breens of Donner Party. In *Carloviana*, xxxix, 4-9 (1991/92).
The saga of two emigrants from Barnahasken and Rathgeran, Co. Carlow, in the High Sierras of California.

KING (Joseph A.). See 1797.

2465   KINMONTH (Claudia). The last straw? In *Carloviana*, xxxix, 2-3, 9 (1991/92).
Discussion of coiled straw furniture - an example from County Carlow Museum.

2466   KINSELLA (A.). The Rathkeale workhouse incident, November 1921. In *Old Limerick Jn.*, xxix, 18-19 (1992).

2467   KINSELLA (Anna). The spirit of '98 awakened. In *Wexford Hist. Soc. Jn.*, xv, 34-42 (1994/95).

2468   KINZER (Bruce L.). John Stuart Mill and the Irish university question. In *Victorian Studies*, xxxi, 59-77 (1987).

2469   KIRWAN (Elizabeth). From Ardmore to Arabia. The brides of Ardmore. In *Ardmore Jn.*, x, 17-21 (1993).
'The Brides of Ardmore' a novel by Agnes Smith (1843-1926), scholar and novelist.

2470   KLINE (Benjamin). Churchill and Collins 1919-22: admirers or adversaries? In *Hist. Ire.*, i, no. 3, pp 38-43 (1993).

2471   KNOWLTON (Steven E.). The quarrel between Gavan Duffy and John Mitchel: implications for Ireland. In *Albion*, xxi, 581-90 (1989).

2472   KNOX (Melissa). Oscar Wilde: a long and lovely suicide. Pp xxiv, 185. New Haven: Yale University Press, 1994.
1854-1900.

KOHL (Lawrence Frederick). See CONYNGHAM (David Power).

2473   KOSEKI (Takashi). Patrick O'Higgins and Irish Chartism. In *Comparative aspects of Irish and Japanese economic and social history*, pp 148-81 (1993).
Patrick O'Higgins b1790. Comment by L.M. Cullen, pp 178-81.

2474   KOTSONOURIS (Mary). The courts of Dáil Éireann. In *The creation of the Dáil*, pp 91-106 (1994).

2475   KOTSONOURIS (Mary). The Dáil courts in Limerick. In *Old Limerick Jn.*, xxix, 37-40 (1992).

2476 KOTSONOURIS (Mary). Retreat from revolution: the Dáil courts, 1920-24. Pp 172. Blackrock, Co. Dublin: Irish Academic Press, 1994.

2477 KOTSONOURIS (Mary). Revolutionary justice - the Dáil Éireann courts. In *Hist. Ire.*, ii, no. 3, pp 32-6 (1994).

2478 KRAUSE (David). Carleton, catholicism and the comic novel. In *Ir. University Rev.*, xxiv, 217-40 (1994).

2479 KRAUSE (David). The conscience of Ireland: Lalor, Davitt and Sheehy-Skeffington. In *Eire-Ireland*, xxviii, no. 1, pp 7-31 (1993).

2480 KREILKAMP (Vera). Going to the levée as ascendancy spectacle: alternative narratives in Irish painting. In *Visualizing Ireland*, pp 37-54 (1993).
Rose Barton, 1856-1929.

2481 KRUMWIEDE (Sabine). The Home Rule crisis before the first world war. In *Three nations - a common history?*, pp 229-63 (1993).

2482 Labour in art: [representations of labour in Ireland (1870-1970)]. (Essay Fintan O'Toole). Pp [4], 51. Dublin: Irish Museum of Modern Art, 1994.

2483 LACEY (Audrey). Schools of the Claddagh - some extracts. In *Galway Roots*, ii, 32-6 (1994).

2484 LAFFAN (Kathleen). James Scurry (1790-1828): a south Kilkenny scholar. In *Decies*, l, 60-66 (1994).

2485 LAFFAN (Michael). Sinn Féin from dual monarchy to the first Dáil. In *The creation of the Dáil*, pp 15-29 (1994).

2486 LAHERT (Richard). An Maor agus an Meirleach (The Mayor and the outlaw): a postscript to the Carrickshock affray, 1831. In *Decies*, xlix, 45-54 (1994).

LANDES (Eugenia). See DAVIS (Graham).

2487 LANE (Pádraig G.). Agricultural labourers and rural violence, 1850-1914. In *Studia Hib.*, xxvii, 77-87 (1993).

2488 LANE (Pádraig G.). The impact of the Encumbered Estates Court upon the landlords of Galway and Mayo. In *Galway Arch. Soc. Jn.*, xxxviii, 45-58 (1981/82).

2489 LANE (Pádraig G.). The Land and Labour Association, 1894-1914. In *Cork Hist. Soc. Jn.*, xcviii, 90-106 (1993).

2490 LANE (Pádraig G.). Landed encumbrances: a record of the Dillon-Browne estate. In *Cathair na Mart*, xiv, 69-77 (1994).

2491 LANE (Pádraig G.). Lord Plunket and the Partry Mountains: a case study of 1850s landlordism. In *Galway Arch. Soc. Jn.*, xlvi, 156-72 (1994).

2492 LANE (Pádraig G.). Perceptions of agricultural labourers after the great famine, 1850-1870. In *Saothar*, xix, 14-25 (1994).

2493   LANE (Pádraig G.). Some Galway and Mayo landlords of the mid-nineteenth century. In *Galway Arch. Soc. Jn.*, xlv, 70-89 (1993).

2494   LARKIN (John F.), ed. Reports from a lobbyist: two letters from Henry Cooke in London, 1844. In *Presb. Hist. Soc. of Ire. Bull.*, xxi, 21-5 (1992).

2495   LATHAM (Harry). Dalkey Island. 28 March 1912. Purchase from War Office. Decision of Dalkey Urban Council. In *Dun Laoghaire Jn.*, ii, 46-53 (1991/92).

2496   LATHAM (Harry). Saint Patrick's Church of Ireland church and parish, Dalkey, Co. Dublin. Pp 108. Dalkey: [Harry Latham], 1993.
Church's anniversary, 1843-1993.

LAURENCE (Dan H.). See *Shaw, Lady Gregory and the Abbey*.

2497   LAW (Edward J.). The 'Gardener's' cottage, Bishops-lough. In *In the Shadow of the Steeple*, iv, 19-24 (1994).

LAWRENCE (Nicholas). See WHITE (Harry).

2498   LÉCANE (Philip). Deansgrange Cemetery. Casualties from the 1916 Rising. In *Dun Laoghaire Genealogical Soc. Jn.*, iii, 136, 138 (1994).

2499   LEDWIDGE (John). The Brow, the Brothers and the Bogside: a history of the Christian Brothers School, Derry, 1854-1990. Pp 116. Londonderry: Guildhall Press, [1990].

2500   LEE (Joe). The significance of the first Dáil. In *The creation of the Dáil*, pp 137-58 (1994).

2501   LENEHAN (John F.). Memories of Ballinamuck as told to and recorded by John F. Lenehan. In *Teathba*, i, no. 1, pp 47-50 (1969).

2502   LENIHAN (Maurice). Reminiscences of a journalist; selected and edited by Alf Mac Lochlainn. In *Old Limerick Jn.*, xxxi, 15-19 (1994).
Extracts from the *Limerick Reporter* and *Tipperary Vindicator*, 1866-9.

2503   LENNON (Gerard). Ann Morrison - from Downpatrick to Australia. In *Lecale Miscellany*, ix, 35-7 (1991).

2504   LENNON (Gerard). John Kirk - a prisoner of the crown. A case study. In *Lecale Miscellany*, viii, 24-6 (1990).

2505   LENNON (Gerard). Trades and occupations of Portaferry in the mid-l9th century. In *Upper Ards Hist. Soc. Jn.*, i, 26-8 (1977).

2506   LENNON (Gerard). 'Murder most foul - a sequel'. In *Lecale Miscellany*, xi, 3-4 (1993).
Sequel to article in *Lecale Miscellany*, iii (1985).

2507   LENNON (Gerard). 'Murder most foul' further information. In *Lecale Miscellany*, xii, 29-31 (1994).
Continued from ibid., xi (1993).

2508   LEWIS (Gifford). The Yeats sisters and the Cuala. Pp xiv, 199. Blackrock, Co. Dublin: Irish Academic Press, 1994.

LIGHTBOWN (Mary). See 1808.

2509   LINDSAY (Deirdre) and FITZPATRICK (David).   Records of the Irish famine: a guide to local archives, 1840-1855. Pp xii, 75.   Dublin: Irish Famine Network, 1993.

2510   LINEHAN (Thomas P.).   History and development of Irish population censuses. In *Jn. of the Statistical and Social Inquiry Soc. Ire.*, xxvi, no. 4, pp 91-132 (1991/92).

2511   The Lion's tale. In *Carloviana*, xxxiii, 19-20 (1985/86).
        Tale of a pub sign, from the files of *The Nationalist & Leinster Times.*

2512   LITTON (Helen). The Irish famine: an illustrated history. Pp 141. Dublin: Wolfhound Press, 1994.

2513   LLOYD (David).   Anomalous states: Irish writing and the post-colonial moment. Pp x, 174. Dublin: Lilliput Press, 1993.
        Seamus Heaney, Samuel Beckett, W.B. Yeats, James Joyce and violence and the 19th-century novel.

2514   LOGAN (B.J.).   John Ballance, journalist, politician and premier of New Zealand, 1839-1893. In *Ulster Local Studies,* xv, no. 1, pp 80-85 (1993).
        West Antrim.

2515   LOGAN (John). William Phelps's census of Eliogarty, 1821. In *Tipp. Hist. Jn.*, pp 62-71 (1993).

2516   LOHAN (Rena). The archives of the Office of Public Works - their value as a source for local history. In *Ir. Archives*, pp 26-47 (autumn 1994).

        LONGFIELD (Ada K.). See 1812.

        LOUGHREY (Francis). See 1813.

2517   LOWE (W.J.). Policing famine Ireland. In *Eire-Ireland*, xxix, no. 4, pp 47-67 (1994).

2518   LUBENOW (W.C.). Irish home rule and the great separation in the Liberal Party in 1886: the dimensions and parliamentary liberalism.   In *Victorian Studies*, xxvi, 161-80 (1982/83).

2519   LUBENOW (William C.). The Liberals and the national question: Irish home rule, nationalism and the relationship to nineteenth-century liberalism.   In *Parliamentary History*, xiii, 119-42 (1994).

2520   LUCCAN (Nóra).   An bhean tréitheach.   In *Lúise Gabhánach Ní Dhufaigh agus Scoil Bhríde*, pp 8-10 (1993).
        Louise Gavan Duffy.

2521   LUDDY (Maria). Women and the contagious diseases acts, 1864-1886.   In *Hist. Ire.*, i, no. 1, pp 32-4 (1993).

2522   LUDDY (Maria). Women and work in Clonmel: evidence from the 1881 census. In *Tipp. Hist. Jn.*, pp 95-101 (1993).

2523   LYDEN (Michael).   The burning of Clifden, March 17, 1921.   In *Connemara*, i, no. 1, pp 54-9 (1993).
       Eyewitness account by Dr Michael Lyden (1909-85) written for Rory Lavelle and presented by him.

2524   LYNCH (Muireann).   An Irish Rose in Texas.   In *Irish Family History*, i, no. 1, pp 41-5 (1993).
       Letters from Sr Mary Cleophas (Rosie Hurst), b. Dublin 1865, in Texas between 1888 and 1921.

2525   LYNCH (Patrick).   1894-1994: an overview.   In *Trade union century*, pp 159-70 (1994).

2526   LYNCH (Sighle Bhreathnach).   John Hughes: the Italian connection.   In *Ir. Arts. Rev. Yearbk*, pp 195-201 (1994).
       John Hughes (1865-1941), Dublin sculptor.

2527   LYONS (J.B.).   James Joyce and Blackrock.   In *Blackrock Society Proceedings, 1992-3*, pp 30-43 (1993).

2528   LYONS (J.B.).   Surgeon-Major Parke's African journey 1887-89.   Pp xiv, 281. Dublin: Lilliput Press, 1994.
       Thomas H. Parke of Kilmore, Co. Roscommon, 1857-93.

2529   LYONS (J.B.).   William Henry Drummond: poet in Patois.   Pp 217. Markham, Ontario: Fitzhenry & Whiteside, 1994.   (Canadian medical lives, no. 7)
       Physician-poet, born Mohill, Co. Leitrim, 1854, died Canada 1907.

2530   LYONS (Mary Cecilia).   Illustrated incumbered estates: Ireland, 1850-1905: lithographic and other illustrative material in the incumbered estates rentals. Pp li, 247.   Whitegate, Co. Clare: Ballinakella Press, 1993.

2531   LYONS (Michael).   The national struggle, 1913-1921: a pictorial record. Part IV: Bandon, 1920. In *Bandon Hist. Jn.*, ix, 45-52 (1993).

2532   LYONS (Michael).   The national struggle 1913-21: a pictorial record. Part 5: The men of Kilmichael. In *Bandon Hist. Jn.*, x, 11-19 (1994).

2533   LYONS (Michael J.).   Tidal wave at Westport Quay. From notes made by the late Michael J. Lyons about his early experiences in Westport. This extract edited by Eleanor Fairburn. In *Cathair na Mart*, xiii, 135-6 (1993).

2534   LYSAGHT (P.B.) and RYNNE (Etienne).   Old country houses: two comments. In *North Munster Antiq. Jn.*, xxxv, 109-11 (1993/94).

2535   Mac a' GHOILL (Pádraig).   'Cu Uladh' - Peter Toner McGinley 1856-1942. In *Donegal Annual*, xlv, 69-71 (1993).
       Writer and one of the founding members of the Gaelic League.

2536   McALISTER (Helen).   Cushendall Cottage Hospital 1885.   In *The Glynns*, viii, 45-50 (1980).

2537   McALLEN (Bridget).   Thomas Reid's travels.   In *Dúiche Néill*, viii, 40-66 (1993).
       1791-1821.

2538   Mac ANNAIDH (Séamas). Ismael Fitzadam agus Simon Macken - teaghlach liteartha as Achadh hon. In *An t-Ultach*, lxx, no. 2, pp 4-8 (1993).

2539   Mac AONGHUSA (Proinsias). Ar son na Gaeilge: Conradh na Gaeilge 1893-1993: stair Sheanchais. Pp 463. Baile Átha Cliath: Conradh na Gaeilge, 1993.
        Irish language revival.

2540   Mac AONGHUSA (Proinsias). Seán O'Casey and the Gaelic League. In *Féile Zozimus. Vol. 3. Two Dubliners*, pp 11-29 (1994).

2541   MacARTHUR (C.W.P.), ed. James Hack Tuke's narrative of the second, third and fourth weeks of William Forster's visit to some of the distressed districts in Ireland. In *Donegal Annual*, xlvi, 64-82 (1994).

2542   MacARTHUR (C.W.P.), ed. Memoirs of a land agent. Part 1. In *Donegal Annual*, xlvi, 90-107 (1994).
        Autobiography of Daniel Swiney (1826-1915).

2543   MacARTHUR (William P.). Medical history of the famine. In *The Great Famine*, pp 263-315 (1994).

2544   MacATAMNEY (Neil). The great famine in County Fermanagh. In *Clogher Rec.*, xv, no. 1, pp 76-89 (1994).

2545   MacATASNEY (Gerard). The educational views of John McHale. Part 1. In *Cathair na Mart*, xiv, 39-64 (1994).
        John McHale, archbishop of Tuam.

2546   MACAULAY (Ambrose). William Crolly: Archbishop of Armagh, 1835-49. Pp xii, 481. Blackrock, Co. Dublin: Four Courts Press, 1994.

2547   McAULAY (Ambrose). Archbishop Crolly and the development of catholicism in Ulster, 1812-49. In *Familia*, ii, no. 9, pp 75-96 (1993).

2548   MACAULAY (Ambrose). Patrick Dorrian, bishop of Down and Connor, 1865-85. In *Lecale Miscellany*, vii, 23-4 (1989).

2549   McAULIFFE (John). The troubled times in Cloyne. In *The book of Cloyne*, pp 269-72 (1994).
        1920-

2550   McAULIFFE (Nicholas). Caherciveen's musical priest. In *An Aisling*, iii, 48-50 (1991).
        Fr Charles Brennan, 1875-1937.

2551   McBRIDE (Doreen). When hunger stalked the North. Pp 78. Banbridge: Adare, 1994.
        Famine in 19th century.

2552   McBRIDE (Maud Gonne). A servant of the queen: reminiscences. [2nd ed.]. *Ed.* A. Norman Jeffares and Anna MacBride White. Pp xvii, 378. Gerrards Cross: Colm Smythe, 1994.
        Previous ed., London: Gollancz, 1938.

2553   Mac CABA (Anton). Harry Midgley. In *An t-Ultach*, lxx, no. 8, pp 9-10 (1993).

2554 Mac CABA (Anton). Stailc i Muineachán. In *An t-Ultach*, lxx, no. 6, pp 23-4 (1993).

2555 McCABE (Anton). Peadar O'Donnell and the INTO. In *Labour History News*, ix, 10-11 (1993).

2556 McCABE (Anton). 'The stormy petrel of the transport workers': Peadar O'Donnell, trade unionist, 1917-1920. In *Saothar*, xix, 41-51 (1994).

2557 McCABE (Dermot). A famous Clones general. In *Clogher Rec.*, xv, no. 1, pp 122-6 (1994).
General Joseph Finnegan, Confederate States Army (1814-86).

2558 MacCARTHY (C.J.F.). 'The angelic doctor': Denis Charles O'Connor, M.D., LL.D., 1807-1888. In *Bandon Hist. Jn.*, ix, 24-8 (1993).

2559 McCARTHY (Jennie). The educational scene in nineteenth century Bantry. In *Bantry Hist. Soc. Jn.*, i, 75-82 (1991).

2560 McCARTNEY (David James). The milder day or a promise kept. Pp vii, 205. Carrickfergus: Macson Books, 1994.
The McCartney family of Antrim, *c*.1900-

2561 McCARTNEY (Donal). W.E.H. Lecky: historian and politician, 1838-1903. Pp vii, 271. Dublin: Lilliput Press, 1994.

2562 McCLAUGHLIN (Trevor). Horseman pass by: Irish-Australian gravestones. In *Familia*, ii, no. 9, pp 62-74 (1993).

2563 McCONKEY (Kenneth). Sir John Lavery. Pp 232. Edinburgh: Canongate, 1993.

Mac CONMARA (Micheál). See 1819.

Mc CONNELL (James). See O'HARA (James G.).

2564 McCONVILLE (Michael). Lord and Lady de Ros, William Lennox Lasalles Fitzgerald de Ros and Lady Georgina Lennox. In *Lecale Miscellany*, vii, 32-41 (1989).

2565 McCONVILLE (Michael). A short history of 'Our Lady Star of the Sea' Church, Strangford. In *Lecale Miscellany*, vi, 26-31 (1988).

2566 McCONVILLE (Sinéad). 1878 - those were the days. In *Lecale Miscellany*, v, 40 (1987).
Domestic wages list for 1878.

2567 McCORD (M.E.). The sage of Sheepland More. In *Lecale Miscellany*, viii, 37-8 (1990).
Will's Billy Curran (1854-1933).

2568 McCORRY (Frank). Residential stability and population mobility in Lurgan, 1856-64. In *Review*, v, no. 3, pp 27-31 (1986/87).

2569 McCRACKEN (Donal P.). 'Fenians and Dutch carpetbaggers': Irish and Afrikaner nationalisms, 1877-1930. In *Eire-Ireland*, xxix, no. 3, pp 109-25 (1994).

2570   McCRACKEN (J.L.). New light at the Cape of Good Hope: William Porter, the father of Cape liberalism. Pp 160. Belfast: Ulster Historical Foundation, 1993.
Born Limavady 1805, attorney general in the Cape 1839-65, M.P. 1865-73, died 1880.

McCREARY (Alf). See WALKER (Brian).

2571   McCRUM (Elizabeth). Commerce and the Celtic revival: Irish jewelry of the nineteenth century. In *Eire-Ireland*, xxviii, no. 4, pp 36-52 (1993).

2572   McCULLEN (John). The account books of James McCullen, builder, 1817-1877. In *Louth Arch. Soc. Jn.*, xxiii, no. 1, pp 115-26 (1993).

2573   McCULLEN (John). The Drogheda Steam Packet Company. In *Old Drogheda Soc. Jn.*, ix, 48-60 (1994).

2574   McCULLOUGH (Patricia). A unique wedding present. In *Lecale Miscellany*, v, 13-16 (1987).
Lord Dufferin and Clandeboye's gift to Dudley Charles Fitzgerald de Ros and his bride.

2575   MacCURTAIN (Margaret). The real Molly Macree. In *Visualizing Ireland*, pp 9-21 (1993).
Painter Thomas Alfred Jones's (1823-93) depiction of Irish peasantry.

MacCURTAIN (Margaret). See HOY (Suellen).

2576   MacDONAGH (Oliver). Irish emigration to the United States of America and the British colonies during the famine. In *The great famine*, pp 319-88 (1994).

2577   MacDONAGH (Oliver). O'Connell and Parnell. Pp 16. Cambridge: Magdalene College, 1994. (Magdalene College Occasional Papers, no. 11).

2578   McDONALD (B.). The Greenisland loop. In *Irish Railway Rec. Soc. Jn.*, xviii, no. 122, pp 294-8 (1993).

2579   MacDONALD (Brian). Church of Ireland members in the Aghadrumse area in 1823. In *Clogher Rec.*, xv, no. 1, pp 107-21 (1994).

2580   MacDONALD (Brian). A Fermanagh census. In *Clogher Rec.*, xiv, no. 3, pp 77-110 (1993).
From the 'Visiting books' of Rev. William Bredin, for the parishes of Galloon and Sallaghy (*c*.1850-51).

2581   McDONNELL (Finola Keyes). Shopping in the 19th century. In *Bandon Hist. Jn.*, x, 53-6 (1994).

2582   McDONNELL (Pat). From the Lammas Fair to New South Wales: James McGrath of Dromore. In *Irish convict lives*, pp 146-77 (1993).

2583   McDOWELL (Henry). Lord Walter Fitzgerald (1858-1923): genealogist. In *Aspects of Irish genealogy*, pp 168-71 [1993].

2584   McDOWELL (R.B.). Ireland on the eve of the famine. In *The great famine*, pp 3-86 (1994).

2585   McDOWELL (R.B.).   Land & learning: two Irish clubs.   Pp vii, 175.
Dublin: Lilliput Press, 1993.
Kildare Street and University Club.

2586   McELWEE (Richard). The last voyages of the Waterford steamers. Pp 196.
Waterford: The Book Centre, [1993].

2587   McEVOY (Dan). Blacksmiths in Kilkenny: In *Old Kilkenny Rev.*, xlvi, 105-
10 (1994).

2588   McFARLAND (Elaine).   'A mere Irish faction': the Orange Institution in
nineteenth-century Scotland. In *Scotland and Ulster*, pp 71-87 (1994).

McFARLAND (Elaine W.). See 1824.

2589   Mac FHEARGHUSA (Pádraig). 'Queen Scotia's Branch': the Gaelic League
& Kerry. In *An Aisling*, iii, 89-90 (1991).
Article written in Irish.

2590   Mac GABHANN (Séamus).   Salvaging cultural identity: Peter Gallegan
(1792-1860). In *Ríocht na Midhe*, ix, no. 1, pp 70-87 (1994/95).

2591   Mac GAIRBHEITH (Pádraig). Teacht na muice duibhe. In *An t-Ultach*, lxx,
no. 10, pp 4-7 (1993).
The coming of the railway to northwest Donegal, 1902.

2592   McGIFFERT (John). 'Royal Oak'. In *Lecale Miscellany*, xi, 16-19 (1993).
The oldest known rowing racing boat in the world, built *c.*1800.

2593   McGINN (Brendan). [Selections from] O.S. memoirs. In *Benbradagh*, xii,
13-15 (1982).

McGINTY (Margaret). See 1825.

2594   Mac GIOLLA DOMHNAIGH (Gearóid).   Dónall Ó Tuathail sagart na ráite,
1880-1922. In *An t-Ultach*, lxxi, no. 12, pp 8-14 (1994).

Mac GIOLLA FHINNÉIN (Brian). See 1826.

2595   MacGOWAN (Fiona). Robert Lloyd Praeger (1865-1953). In *Gateway to
the Past*, i, no. 2, pp 100-03 (1994).

2596   McGOWAN (Mark G.).   The de-greening of the Irish: Toronto's Irish
Catholic press, imperialism, and the forging of a new identity, 1887-1914. In
Canadian Hist. Assoc. Historical Papers, pp 118-45 (1989).

2597   McGRATH (Sophie). Catholic girls secondary education 1888-1950: a case
study. In *Royal Australian Historical Society Jn.*, lxxix, 33-53 (1993).
School founded by Sisters of Mercy brought out from Kilkenny for that
purpose.

2598   McGUINN (James). Sligo men in the great war, 1914-1918.   Pp [4], 124.
Belturbet, Co. Cavan: Vaughan Press, 1994.

2599   McGUINNE (Dermot). Market testing in the early 19th century: printing the
Bible in the Irish character. In *Long Room*, xxxix, 39-42 (1994).

2600   MacHALE (E.).   Father Michael Conway in Kilfian parish 1826-1839: corrections and additions, 1993. In *North Mayo Hist. Jn.*, iii, no. 2, pp 5-26 (1993/94).

2601   MacHALE (E.).   The Irish Poor Law Act of 1838:   (preparations for).   In *North Mayo Hist. Jn.*, iii, no. 1, pp 5-33 (1992/93).

McHUGH (Anna).   See 1827.

2602   McHUGH (Roger J.).   The famine in Irish oral tradition.   In *The great famine*, pp 391-436 (1994).

2603   McILRATH (R.H.).   Classon Porter.   A short account of the life and work of a nineteenth century non-subscribing minister in Larne.   In *Ulster Local Studies*, xv, no. 1, pp 13-37 (1993).

2604   McINERNEY (Raymond).   Souper school in Tulla.   In *Sliabh Aughty*, iv, 32-3 (1993).

2605   McINTYRE (H.E.).   The old railway station - Portadown.   In *Review*, v, no. 3, pp 12-13 (1986/87).

2606   McKEANE (Ian).   *Saldanha* and that elusive Ulster ancestor.   In *Familia*, ii, no. 10, pp 56-71 (1994).
        Sunk 4 Dec. 1811.

2607   McKERNAN (Anne).   War, gender and industrial innovation: recruiting women weavers in early nineteenth-century Ireland.   In *Jn. Soc. Hist.*, xxviii, 109-24 (1994/95).

2608   McKERROW (Ray E.).   Richard Whately on the nature of human knowledge in relation to ideas of his contemporaries.   In *Jn. Hist. Ideas*, xlii, 439-55 (1981).
        Archbishop of Dublin, 1831-63.

2609   McLERNON (Douglas S.).   Trade union organisation in the south of Ireland in the XIXth century. In *Jn. European Economic Hist.*, x, 145-52 (1981).

2610   Mac LOCHLAINN (Alf).   The portrait artist as a young man: letters of Bernard Mulrenin, 1825-34.   In *Visualizing Ireland*, pp 181-200 (1993).
        Bernard Mulrenin, 1803-68.

2611   Mac LOCHLAINN (Alf).   'Those young men ...':   the National Library of Ireland and the cultural revolution.   In *Writers, raconteurs and notable feminists*, pp 4-33 (1993).

Mac LOCHLAINN (Alf).   See LENIHAN (Maurice).

2612   Mac LOCHLAINN (C.D.).   From Sellerna to Harley Street.   In *Connemara*, i, no. 1, pp 85-9 (1993).
        The career of Sir Peter Johnston Freyer, a Cleggan man, is recalled.

2613   McLOUGHLIN (Ella).   The Kettles.   In *Swords Voices*, i, no. 2, pp 24-7 (1994).

2614   MacLOUGHLIN (Guillermo).   Casey.   An important Irish-Argentine family.   In *Dun Laoghaire Genealogical Soc. Jn.*, ii, 109-10 (1993).

MacLOUGHLIN (Guillermo). See 1829.

2615   MacMAHON (Bryan). A pioneer of Irish traditional music. In *Old Limerick Jn.*, xxix, 25-7 (1992).
        Thomas T. Purcell 1848-1930. Article originally published in *Treoir*, xiv (1982).

2616   McMAHON (Kevin). The time of the Trouble 1919-21. Armagh, south Down and north Louth. Part 2. In *Seanchas Ardmhacha*, xvi, no. 1, pp 195-235 (1994).

2617   MacMAHON (Michael). Agrarian conflict in Clare, 1815-1831. In *The Other Clare*, xviii, 49-56 (1994).

2618   McMEEKIN (Donald). Fairy class, 1902-1992, R.N.I.Y.C.; a short history. Pp 38. [Belfast?]: [Royal North of Ireland Yacht Club], [1994?].

2619   McMILLAN (Norman). Tyndall the philosopher. John Tyndall (1820?-1893). In *Carloviana*, xl, 25-9 (1992/93).

McMULLAN (James). See QUINN (Hugh, jr.).

2620   McNEILL (Ian). The botany of the Stewartstown area. In *The Bell*, v, 18-27 (1994).
        With an appendix on a trip to Roughan Park by members of Belfast Naturalists Field Club in 1907.

2621   McNEILL (Linda). The Sulphate of Amonia Co. Ltd., Carnlough. In *The Glynns*, viii, 37-40 (1980).

2622   McQUILLAN (Jack). The railway town: the story of the Great Northern Railway works and Dundalk. Pp 212. Dundalk: Dundalgan Press, 1993.

2623   MacRAILD (D.M.). Irish culture in an English context. [review essay]. In *Labour History Review*, lviii, no. 2, pp 44-8 (1993).

2624   McVEIGH (Mary T.). Lock-out? Caledon 1919. In *Dúiche Néill*, ix, 96-108 (1994).

MacWILLIAMS (Patrick). See *Parishes of County Antrim, vi, vii, viii, ix, x. Parishes of County Londonderry, vii.*

2625   MADDEN (Gerard). The attempted murder of Philip Reade, Mountshannon, March 17th, 1824, and a Brogan muster in Goulburn, Australia, March 5th, 1988. In *Sliabh Aughby*, iv, 4-7 (1993).

2626   MADDEN (Gerard). The Parkers of Tuamgraney. In *Sliabh Aughty*, v, 21-3 (1994).

2627   MAGEE (Sean). Deserted children in Counties Wicklow & Wexford. In *Dun Laoghaire Genealogical Soc. Jn.*, iii, 118-20 (1994).

2628   MAGUIRE (Albert). 'Accountability in education - an historical perspective'. In *Review*, v, no. 3, pp 24-7 (1986/87).

2629   MAGUIRE (Martin). The organisation and activism of Dublin's Protestant working class, 1883-1935. In *I.H.S.*, xxix, 65-87 (1994).

2630   MAGUIRE (Martin). A socio-economic analysis of the Dublin Protestant working class, 1870-1926. In *Ir. Econ. & Soc. Hist.* xx, 35-61 (1993).

2631   MAGUIRE (W.A.). Banker and absentee landowner: William Tennent in County Fermanagh, 1813-32. In *Clogher Rec.*, xiv, no. 3, pp 7-28 (1993).

2632   MAGUIRE (W.A.). The Verner rape trial, 1813: Jane Barnes v. the Belfast establishment. In *Ulster Local Studies*, xv, no. 1, pp 47-57 (1993).

2633   MAHER (Maureen). Grosse Ile - an end of a sorrowful pilgrimage. In *Treoir*, xxv, no. 3, pp 37-9 (1993).

2634   MAHON (Patrick). From Gort to Australia and a letter home. In *Sliabh Aughty*, v, 15-16 (1994).

2635   MAHONEY (Jim). O'Mahony extractions from the 1901 Census of Ireland. In *O'Mahony Jn.*, xvi, 20-23 (1993).

2636   MAHONEY (Joseph). The immigrant story in the spoken word. In *O'Mahony Jn.*, xii, 47-52 (1982).
        From an interview conducted by Peter Tynan O'Mahony in Manchester, Iowa, in 1981.

        MAIGNANT (Catherine). See 1834.

2637   MALEY (Willy). The Crosshill railway murder of 1840. In *Hist. Ire.*, i, no. 1, pp 24-6 (1993).

2638   A man from Barnaderg (the story of Rickard Jennings). In *Galway Roots*, [i], 14-15 (1993).
        Article by Maureen Doyle from the Australian *Standard*, June 18, 1988.

2639   MANDLE (W.F.). Parnell and sport. In *Studia Hib.*, xxviii, 103-16 (1994).

        MANGAN (James J.). See WHYTE (Robert).

2640   MANNERS (Gerry). An outline history of P.J. Nally. In *Irish Family History*, i, no. 1, pp 37-9 (1993).
        P.J. Nally, 1868-1911, teacher of Irish and traditional musician.

2641   Mantua N.S. 1822-1922: the 100 years connection with the McGlynn family. In *Roscommon Hist. Soc. Jn.*, iv, 48-9 (1992).

2642   MARK (Gordon St George). The Joyces of Merview. Part II. In *Ir. Geneal.*, ix, no. 1, pp 89-113 (1994).
        Continued from viii, p. 392 (1992).

2643   MARNANE (Denis G.). 'To do and to teach': a history of the Christian Brothers in Tipperary town, 1868-1994. Pp 67. Tipperary: The Friends of the Christian Brothers, 1994.

2644   MARNANE (Denis G.). The diary of Frederick Armitage of Noan for 1906. In *Tipp. Hist. Jn.*, pp 48-65 (1994).

2645   MARNANE (Denis G.). John Davis White of Cashel (1820-1893). In *Tipp. Hist. Jn.*, pp 97-104 (1994).

MARNANE (Denis G.). See 1836.

2646   MASHECK (Joseph). Building-art: modern architecture under cultural construction. Pp xv, 298. Cambridge: Cambridge University Press, 1993. (Contemporary artists and their critics)

2647   MATSUO (Taro). The attitudes and activities of the workers in the early years of industrialization. In *Comparative aspects of Irish and Japanese economic and social history*, pp 38-70 (1993).
        Belfast, 1850s-1860s.

MATTHEW (H.C.G.). See GLADSTONE (William Ewart).

2648   MAUME (Patrick). 'Life that is exile': Daniel Corkery and the search for Irish Ireland. Pp ix, 178. Belfast: Institute of Irish Studies, Queen's University of Belfast, 1993.
        1878-1964.

2649   MAUME (Patrick). Lily Connolly's conversion: new evidence on James Connolly's last days. In *Hist. Ire.*, ii, no. 3, pp 31-2 (1994).

2650   MAXWELL (Frank). An attractive cast iron garden seat. In *Lecale Miscellany*, v, 35-6 (1987).
        Work of a Belfast engineering firm.

2651   MAYE (Brian). Why it is time for a new biography of Arthur Griffith. In *Études Irlandaises*, xviii, no. 2, pp 123-9 (1993).

2652   MAYOCK (John). Social and economic conditions in west Mayo with specific reference to the baronies of Murrisk and Burrishoole 1880-1892. In *Cathair na Mart*, xiv, 81-96 (1994).

2653   MEEHAN (Helen). Ethna Carbery - Anna Johnston McManus. In *Donegal Annual*, xlv, 55-65 (1993).
        Ethna Carbery, pen-name of poet Anna Johnston McManus (1864-1902).

2654   MEEHAN (Helen). The McManus brothers. Patrick: 1864-1929; Seumas: 1868-1960. In *Donegal Annual*, xlvi, 5-18 (1994).

2655   MELVILLE (Joy). Mother of Oscar: the life of Jane Francesca Wilde. Pp xi, 308. London: John Murray, 1994.
        Jane Francesca Wilde, 1821?-1896.

2656   Mercy in Rosscarbery, 1894-1994: history, development & reminiscences. Pp xvii, 236. Rosscarbery, Co. Cork: Mount St Michael Centenary Committee, 1994.
        Sisters of Mercy and their school.

2657   MESSENGER (Betty). To be a mill girl. In *Arch. Ire.*, iv, 18-21 (1990).

2658   MINOGUE (Jim). Pre-famine Tipperary and the Clarke murder. In *Cloughjordan Heritage*, i, 12-14 (1985).

2659   MITCHELL (Arthur). JFK and his Irish heritage. Pp 186. Dublin: Moytura Press, 1993.

2660   MITCHELL (Arthur).   Revolutionary government in Ireland: Dáil Eireann, 1919-1921.   Pp xii, 432.   Dublin: Gill & Macmillan, 1993.

2661   MITCHELL (James).   The imprisonment of Wilfrid Scawen Blunt in Galway: cause and consequences.   In *Galway Arch. Soc. Jn.*, xlvi, 65-100 (1994).

2662   MITCHELL (Mary).   History of the Cork Pipers Club.   In *An Aisling*, iii, 93-100 (1991).
        Summary of the Goodman lecture delivered in Ballyheigue in 1989.

2663   MITCHELL (Walter F.).   Belfast Rowing Club, 1880-1982.   Pp [4], 188. Belfast: Belfast Rowing Club, 1994.

2664   MOHR (Paul).   John Birmingham of Tuam: a most unusual landlord.   In *Galway Arch. Soc. Jn.*, xlvi, 111-55 (1994).
        John Birmingham (?1816-1917) scientist and poet.

2665   MOLLOY (David).   Dr Harrison and the Harrison Hall.   In *Roscommon Hist. Soc. Jn.*, iii, 3-6 (1990).
        Dr J.J. Harrison, 1815-90.

2666   MOLLOY (Frank).   'The sigh of thy harps shall be sent o'er the deep':   the influence of Thomas Moore in Australia.   In *The creative migrant*, pp 115-32 (1994).

2667   MOLONEY (Joe).   Are you going the two days?   Tipperary Races at Barronstown Course, 1848-1926.   In *Oola Past & Present*, ii, 25-7 (1993).

2668   MOLONEY (Mick).   Irish music on the American stage.   Pp 39.   Cork: Irish Traditional Music Society, Univeristy College Cork,   1993.   (Ó Riada memorial lecture, 8)
        1833-

2669   MOORE (Treasa).   The Henry family.   In *Galway Roots*, pp 31-2 (1993).

2670   MORAN (Gerard).   An account of Westport and its surroundings from September 1869.   In *Cathair na Mart*, xiv, 78-80 (1994).

2671   MORAN (Gerard).   The Fenians and Tipperary politics, 1868-1880.   In *Tipp. Hist. Jn.*, pp 73-90 (1994).

2672   MORAN (Gerard).   James Daly and the rise and fall of the Land League in the west of Ireland, 1879-82.   In *I.H.S.*, xxix, 189-207 (1994).

2673   MORAN (Gerard).   A radical priest in Mayo: Fr Patrick Lavelle: the rise and fall of an Irish nationalist, 1825-86.   Pp ix, 219.   Blackrock, Co. Dublin: Four Courts Press, 1994.

2674   MORAN (Gerard).   State aided emigration from Ireland to Canada in the 1880s.   In *Canadian Jn. of Irish Studies*, xx, no. 2, pp 1-19 (1994).

2675   MORAN (Maria).   William Mulholland. The Irishman who brought the water to Los Angeles.   In *Ir. Roots* 1993, no. 2, p. 34 (1993).

2676   MORAN (Sean Farrell).   Patrick Pearse and the politics of redemption: the mind of the Easter rising, 1916.   Pp x, 233.   Washington, D.C.: Catholic University of America Press, 1994.

2677   MORGAN (Jack). 'Whistle up the marching tune': the life and times of Thomas W. Sweeny. Pp 32; Fort Lauderdale (Fl.): Nova University, 1994. (Working papers in Irish studies, 94-2).
       Born Dunmanway, Co. Cork 1820, died in New York 1892, soldier in Californian, Civil and Indian wars and leading Fenian in 1866 invasion of Canada.

2678   MORGAN (Kenneth O.). Federalism in the modern United Kingdom: England, Wales, Scotland and Ireland, 1815-1920. In *Föderalismus im deutsch-britischen meinungsstreit*, pp 71-86 (1993).

2679   MORLING (Loreley A.). C.Y. O'Connor and the goldfields water supply. In *Ir. Roots* 1993, no. 3, p. 26 (1993).

2680   MORLING (Loreley A.). The Fulham brothers: Fenians. In *Ir. Roots* 1994, no. 2, pp 6-7 (1994).

2681   MORRISON (George). A photographic glimpse of Ireland in the 1860s and 1870s. In *Blackrock Soc. Proc.*, ii, 66-79 (1993/94).

2682   MORRISON (Kristin). Ancient rubbish and interior spaces: M.A. Butler and M.J. Farrell, dis-covered. In *Visualizing Ireland*, pp 22-35 (1993).
       Mildred Anne Butler (1858-1941) and M.J. Farrell pseudonym for Molly Keane (1904- .

MOYLAN (Seamus). See 1847.

MULCAHY (John). See 1849.

2683   MULHALL (Tom). Bridewell Lane revisited. In *Carloviana*, xxxiii, 21-4 (1985/86).

2684   MULLETT (Killian). Arklow Golf Club. A brief history. In *Arklow Hist. Soc. Jn.*, pp 19-21 (1992/93).

2685   MULLOY (John). Some aspects of trade in Clew Bay. Part III. In *Cathair na Mart*, xiii, 102-11 (1993).

2686   MULVANEY (D.J.). John Graham: the convict as aboriginal. In *Irish convict lives*, pp 109-47 (1993).

2687   MURPHY (Brian). The first Dáil Éireann. In *Hist. Ire.*, ii, no. 1, pp 41-6 (1994).

2688   MURPHY (Charlotte). Some roads and bridges of County Clare, 1827-1835. In *The Other Clare*, i, 24-6 (1977).

2689   MURPHY (Della). The records of F. Barrett & Co., lighthouse engineers, Schoolhouse Lane, Dublin 2. In *Ir. Archives*, pp 48-50 (autumn 1994).

2690   MURPHY (Donal A.). The two Tipperarys: the national and local politics - devolution and self-determination - of the unique 1838 division into two ridings, and the aftermath. Pp xxiv, 342. Nenagh: Relay, 1994.

MURPHY (Eddie). See BRADLEY (John).

2691 MURPHY (Hilary). The Drinagh cement works. In *Old Wexford Soc. Jn.*, vi, 38-44 (1976/77).
Compiled from references in the files of *The People*, 1874-1936.

2692 MURPHY (Hilary). An emigrant's diary (1873). In *Ir. Roots* 1993, no. 1, pp 11-14 (1993).

2693 MURPHY (Hilary). Irish emigration to the province of Ontario. In *Ir. Roots* 1994, no. 3, p. 12 (1994).

2694 MURPHY (Hilary). Martin Doyle, V.C. In *Ir. Roots* 1994, no. 4, pp 27-8 (1994).

2695 MURPHY (Hilary). A 'Wexford' Californian pioneer. In *Ir. Family Hist.*, x, 16-19 (1994).

2696 MURPHY (Hilary). When Wexford workers first united, 1843. In *Wexford Hist. Soc. Jn.*, xv, 98-101 (1994/95).

2697 MURPHY (Ignatius). Building a church in nineteenth century Ireland. In *The Other Clare*, ii, 20-26 (1978).
Kilkee and Kilrush.

2698 MURPHY (Ina). Speaking of Lyre: 1844-1994. Pp xiv, 175. Lyre: Lyre Community Association, 1994.

2699 MURPHY (Roderick P.). Carlow courts and adventures of an Irish R.M. In *Carloviana*, xl, 12-14 (1992/93).

2700 MURPHY (Seán). Who was Molly Malone? In *Hist. Ire.*, i, no. 2, pp 39-41 (1993).
Punctures the myth of the eighteeth-century Molly Malone.

2701 MURPHY (T.). At the seaside in Kilkee in the 1830s and 1840s. In *The Other Clare*, i, 27-32 (1977).

2702 MURPHY (William). The Kilkenny connections of Somerville and Ross - part 1. In *In the Shadow of the Steeple*, iv, 70-89 (1994).

2703 MURRAY (Bernadette C.). The letter from America. In *Ir. Family Hist.*, x, 29-31 (1994).

2704 MURRAY (D.). Mallow to Waterford. In *Irish Railway Rec. Soc. Jn.*, xviii, no. 121, pp 236-51 (1993).

2705 MURRAY (Kevin). Salmon on the strand. In *Dun Laoghaire Jn.*, i, [22-4] (1990).

2706 MURRAY (Paul). A fantastic journey: the life and literature of Lafcadio Hearn. Pp xvii, 379. Folkstone: Japan Library, 1993.
Hearn, Lafcadio, 1850-1904.

2707 MURRAY (Peter). Art institutions in nineteenth-century Cork. In *Cork*, pp 813-72 (1993).

2708   MURRAY (Peter).   Irish cultural nationalism in the United Kingdom state: politics and the Gaelic League 1900-18.   In *Irish Political Studies*, viii, 55-72 (1993).

2709   MYERS (James P.).   'Til their ... bog-trotting feet get talaria':   Henry D. Thoreau and the immigrant Irish.   In *The creative migrant*, pp 44-56 (1994).

2710   MYERS (Seán).   Fossa Rowing Club: a century of history.   Pp 132, ill. [Fossa, Co. Kerry]: Fossa Rowing Club, 1993.

2711   NAUGHTON (Mary).   Judge William Nicholas Keogh.   In *Galway Arch. Soc. Jn.*, xxxviii, 5-30 (1981/82).

2712   NEENAN (Michael).   Martin Burke of the Shelborne Hotel.   in *Tipp. Hist. Jn.*, pp 113-14 (1994).

2713   NEILL (Ian).   The Broighter hoard or how Cavan caught the boat.   In *Arch. Ire.*, vii, no. 2, pp 24-6 (1993).
        Subject of a controversial legal case which lasted from 1897 until 1903.

2714   NEILL (Margaret).   Homeworkers in Ulster, 1850-1911.   In *Coming into the light*, pp 2-32 (1994).

2715   NELLSON (John H.).   Acknowledge the mass graves of Irish on Grosse Ile. In *Treoir*, xxv, no. 2, pp 18-19 (1993).

2716   NELSON (Charles).   Blowing in the wind, Charles Nelson sings the praises of a little-known Victorian gardener from Howth.   In *Ir. Garden*, iii, no. 1, pp 6-8 (1994).
        Mrs Alice Lawrenson (d. 1900) breeder of St Bridgid's anenomes and several roses in Sutton.

2717   NELSON (Charles).   Donard delights.   In *Ir. Garden*, ii, no. 4, pp 14-16 (1993).
        The Slieve Donard Nursery which flourished from the end of the 19th century until 1975.

2718   NELSON (Charles).   On the trail of the big cone pine.   Charles Nelson follows the travels of a botanising doctor from Dundalk.   In *Ir. Garden*, iii, no. 4, pp 30-32 (1994).
        Thomas Coulter (1793-1843), first curator to T.C.D. herborium.

2719   NELSON (Charles).   Orchids for everyman and the Mullingar connection.   In *Ir. Garden*, ii, no. 5, pp 16-18 (1993).
        John Charles Lyons of Mullingar, author of first manual on cultivation of tropical orchids, published 1848.

2720   NELSON (E. Charles).   Mapping plant distribution patterns: two pioneering examples from Ireland published in the 1860s.   In *Archives of Natural History*, xx, 391-403 (1993).
        Frederick James Foot's map of 1862 and David Moone and Alexander Goodman More's map of 1866.

        NELSON (E. Charles).   See 1856.

2721   NESBITT (Ronald).   At Arnotts of Dublin, 1843-1993.   Pp xi, 242.   Dublin: A. & A. Farmar, 1993.

2722   NETZER (Nancy). Picturing one exhibition: James Mahony's watercolors of the Irish Industrial Exhibition of 1853. In *Visualizing Ireland*, pp 88-98 (1993).

NEVIN (Monica). See 1857.

2723   New York bound. In *Galway Roots*, [i], 9-11 (1993).
List of immigrants arriving in New York aboard the *Clarence*, 21 April 1848.

2724   Nic CUMHAILL (Sinead). Lady Hazel Lavery and the pound note controversy. In *U.C.D. Hist. Rev.*, vi, 36-48 (1992).

2725   Ní CHINNÉIDE (Máiréad). Ré órga na gcoláistí Gaeilge. In *An t-Ultach*, lxxi, no. 5, pp 4-7 (1994).

2726   Ní CHINNÉIDE (Máiréad). Máire de Buitléir: bean Athbheochana. Pp viii, 166. Baile Átha Cliath: Comhar Teoranta, 1993.
1873-1920, Irish language revival.

Ní SCANNLÁIN (Eibhlín). See CAWLEY (Mary E.).

2727   NOLAN (J.C.M.). Edward Martyn and guests at Tuliva. In *Ir. Arts Rev. Yearbk*, pp 167-73 (1994).

2728   NOLAN (William). Land and landscape in County Wicklow *c*.1840. In *Wicklow*, pp 649-91 (1994).

2729   NOWLAN (K.B.). The political background. In *The great famine*, pp 131-206 (1994).

2730   Ó BAOIGHILL (Pádraig). Óglach na Rosann: Niall Pluincéad Ó Baoighill. Pp [8], 399. Baile Átha Cliath: Coiscéim, 1994.
Born Donegal 1898; killed in Wicklow by Free State forces, 1923.

2731   O'BEIRNE (Aidan). Blackrock foreshore: part one. In *Blackrock Soc. Proc.*, i, 46-51 (1992/93).
Blackrock before and after 1834.

OBER (Warren U.). See HULTIN (Neil C.).

2732   O'BRIEN (David). Wreck of the African mail steamer 'Armenian'. From the supplement of the *Illustrated London News*, p. 117, Feb. 4th 1865. In *Arklow Hist. Soc. Jn.*, pp 15-16 (1992/93).

2733   O'BRIEN (Hugh B.). The Celtics, 1884-1994: a centenary history of the G.A.A. in Cootehill. Pp 366. [Cootehill]: [s.n.]. [1994?].

O'BRIEN (John B.). See 1863.

2734   O'BRIEN (Nollaig). Bygone days in Lackagh. In *Galway Roots*, ii, 10-12 (1994).

2735   O'BRIEN (Pat). Desmond Arthur 'The Montrose Ghost'. In *Sliabh Aughty*, v, 12-14 (1994).
'Re-appearances' of an early Limerick pilot.

2736   O'BRIEN (Pat).   The famine in Broadford parish.   In *Sliabh Aughty*, iv, 25-6 (1993).

2737   O'BRIEN (Sister Pius).   The Sisters of Mercy of Birr and Nenagh.   Pp 148. [Ennis?]:   Congregation of the Sisters of Mercy, Killaloe Mercy Generalate,1994.

2738   O'BRIEN (Seán).   The tithe war 1831-1838.   In *Carloviana*, xli, 4-10 (1993/94).

2739   O'BRIEN-GRENNAN (Cathleen).   Thomas F. Feigh: philanthropist extraordinary.   In *Old Limerick Jn.*, xxx, 25-8 (1993).

2740   O'BYRNE (Mark).   Jogging my memory: 'The Monks' School', New Ross, in the 1880s.   In *The Past*, xviii, 55-74 (1992).

2741   Ó CAITHNIA (Liam P.).   The provenance of the Carrick portrait of Edmund Rice.   In *A man raised up*, pp 172-82 (1994).
        Carrick-on-Suir, Co. Tipperary, attributed to Robert Kennedy, *c.* 1841.

        Ó CAITHNIA (Liam P.).   See 1868, 1869.

2742   O'CALLAGHAN (Edward P.).   Letters and papers of Archbishop Ignazio Persico, papal commissary to Ireland 1887-8:   part 1.   In *Collect. Hib.*, xxxiv/xxxv, 160-89 (1992/93).

2743   O'CALLAGHAN (Margaret).   Denis Patrick Moran and 'the Irish colonial condition', 1891-1921.   In *Political thought in Ireland since the seventeenth century*, pp 146-60 (1993).

2744   Ó CANANN (Tomás G.).   Gildeas lament: a folksong of emigration.   In *North Mayo Hist. Jn.*, iii, no. 2, pp 49-73 (1993/94).

2745   Ó CARTAIGH (Seán).   S.F. Ó Cianáin, M.B., A scríbhinní i mBunáit na Leabharlainne.   In *Teathba*, i, no. 1, pp 54-61 (1969).
        Notebooks of Dr Keenan of Ballinalea (1861-1945).

2746   Ó CATHAIN (Diarmuid).   The old musicians of north Kerry.   In *An Aisling*, iii, 25-34 (1991).

2747   Ó CATHAOIR (Brendan).   The east Clare by-election of 1917.   In *Sliabh Aughty*, iv, 34-6 (1993).

        Ó CATHAOIR (Brendan).   See 1871.

2748   Ó CATHAOIR (Eva).   The poor law in County Wicklow.   In *Wicklow*, pp 503-79 (1994).

2749   Ó CEARBHAILL (Seán E.).   A memory that lived and charity that died: Edmund Rice and the Mendicity Institute.   In *A man raised up*, pp 159-71 (1994).
        Waterford, 1821-1840

        Ó CEARBHAILL (Seán E.).   See 1872.

2750   Ó CEARNAIGH (Seán). An Stad: croílár na hAthbheochana. Pp [5], 109.
        Baile Átha Cliath: Comhar Teoranta, 1993.
        Irish language revival in Dublin, 1900-1905.

2751   Ó CLÉIRIGH (Nellie), Borris lace. In *Ir. Arts Rev. Yearbk*, pp 140-42
        (1994).

2752   Ó CLÉIRIGH (Nellie). Dublin International Exhibition, 1865. In *Dublin
        Hist. Rec.*, xlvii, 169-82 (1994).

2753   Ó CLÉIRIGH (Nellie Beary). Glimpses of south Tipperary during the great
        famine. In *Tipp. Hist. Jn.*, pp 76-87 (1993).

        Ó CONAIRE (Breandán). See *Tomas an Bhlascaoid* (1992).

2754   Ó CONCHÚIR (Breandán). Thomas Swanton, réamhchonraitheoir in Iar-
        Chairbre. In *Cork Hist. Soc. Jn.*, xcviii, 50-60 (1993).
        Thomas Swanton, 'Protestant Irishman' and supporter of the Irish
        language.

2755   Ó CONLUAIN (Proinsias). Dr George Sigerson and those 'Mountains high'.
        In *Dúiche Néill*, ix, 138-48 (1994).
        1836-1925.

2756   O'CONNELL (Marie). The genesis of convent foundations and their
        institutions in Ulster, 1840-1920. In *Coming into the light*, pp 179-204
        (1994).

        O'CONNELL (Maurice R.). See 1876.

2757   O'CONNOR (David). The demise of the Irish fair, 1853 to the present. In
        Baile, pp 18-24 (1993).

2758   O'CONNOR (Emmet). War and syndicalism 1914-1923. In *Trade union
        century*, pp 54-65 (1994).

2759   O'CONNOR (Patrick J.). All worlds possible: the domain of the Millers of
        Coolybrown. Pp [6], 160. Newcastle West: Oireacht na Mumhan Books,
        1993.
        A County Limerick family, 1825-

        O'CONNOR LYSAGHT (D.R.). See *The communists and the Irish
        revolution*.

2760   O'CONOR NASH (Richard). The life and times of Charles Owen O'Conor
        Don M.P. 1838-1905. In *Roscommon Hist. Soc. Jn.*, v, 19-22 (1994).

2761   Ó DANACHAIR (Caoimhín). Summer pasture in Ireland. In *Folk Life*,
        xxii, (1983/84).

2762   O'DAY (Alan). The political representation of the Irish in Great Britain,
        1850-1940. In *Governments, ethnic groups and political representation*, pp
        31-83 (1993).

2763   O'DAY (Alan). Rural Catholic mobilisation in Ireland, 1850-1922. In *Roots
        of rural ethnic mobilisation*, pp 9-50 (1993).

Ó DEIRG (fosold). See COLLINS (Michael).

2764   Ó DOIBHLIN (Diarmaid). Womenfolk of the Glens of Antrim and the Irish language. In *Seanchas Ardmhacha*, xvi, no. 1, pp 103-24 (1994).

Ó DONNCHADHA (Rónán). See 1880.

2765   O'DONNELL (Declan). Lough Hyne marine nature reserve. In *Mizen Jn.*, ii, 21-6 (1994).

2766   O'DONNELL (E.E.). Father Browne: a life in pictures. Pp 128. Dublin: Wolfhound Press, 1994.
        Francis Browne, S.J. (1880-1960) photographer.

2767   O'DONNELL (Martina). Farm clusters in north-west Inishowen, *c.*1850. In *Ir. Geography*, xxvi, 101-19 (1993).

2768   O'DONNELL (Mona). Nevil Shute in Ireland, his engineering and writing years. In *Dun Laoghaire Jn.*, iii, 43-9 (1993).
        The family lived in Blackrock from 1912-16.

2769   O'DONNELL (Nancy). Four O'Donnells from 'Beautiful Mayo'. In *Ó Domhnaill Abú*, xx, 1 (1993).

2770   O'DONNELL (Ruan). Michael Dwyer: 'the Wicklow chief'. In *Irish convict lives*, pp 13-50 (1993).

O'DONNELL (Ruan). See 1882.

2771   O'DONNELLAN (Sheila). Edward Martyn. In *Galway Roots*, ii, 37-9 (1994).

2772   O'DONOGHUE (Brendan). Bandon's second railway. In *Bandon Hist. Jn.*, x, 29-40 (1994).

2773   O'DONOGHUE (Nicole). Thomas Crowe of Mount Bruis. In *Tipp. Hist. Jn.*, p. 96 (1994).

2774   O'DOWD (Peadar). Family life in the Old Claddagh. In *Galway Roots*, ii, 76-8 (1994).

2775   Ó DRISCEOIL (Proinsias). Placenames as politics: Thurles in 1920. In *Tipp. Hist. Jn.*, pp 59-61 (1993).

2776   O'DRISCOLL (J.). Henry - the tree breeder. In *Ir. Forestry*, xxxviii, 19-26 (1981).
        Augustine Henry (1857-1930), Irish arboriculturalist, co-author of *The trees of Great Britain and Ireland*, 1906-13.

2777   Ó DUBHTHAIGH (Niall). Summer pasture in Donegal. In *Folk Life*, xxii, 42-54 (1983/84).
        An account recorded by Seán Ó hEochaidh in 1943.

2778   Ó DUIBHÍR (Ciarán). Aoidhmín Mac Greagóir 1884-1950. In *An t-Ultach*, lxxi, no. 3, pp 6-14 (1994).

2779   Ó DUIBHIR (Ciarán).   Sinn Féin: the first election, 1908. Pp 127. Manorhamilton: Drumlin Publications, 1993. (North Leitrim history series, no. 4).
Co. Leitrim.

2780   Ó DUIBHIR (Donncha). Litir ghra agus aoir on Gabhailín (1823). In *Tipp. Hist. Jn.*, pp 110-12 (1994).

2781   Ó DÚILL (Gréagóir).   Samuel Ferguson: beatha agus saothar. Pp 256. Baile Átha Cliath: An Clóchomhar, 1993.
Northern Irish poet 1810-86.

2782   Ó DUINN (Seamus).   Monsignor John Hagan 'Watchman of the Gael'. In *Arklow Hist. Soc. Jn.*, pp 25-6 (1992/93).

2783   Ó DÚSHLÁINE (Tadhg).   An tAthair Eoghan Ó Gramhnaigh: fear nó finscéal? In *Irisleabhar Mhá Nuad*, pp 33-44 (1994).

       Ó DÚSHLÁINE (Tadhg). See *Is cuimhin linn Kruger.*

2784   O'FARRELL (Padraic).   The blacksmith of Ballinalee: Seán Mac Eoin. Pp 158. Mullingar: Uisneach Press, 1993.
Previous ed., 1981. 1893-1973.

2785   O'FARRELL (Patrick).   How Irish was New Zealand? In *Ir. Studies Rev.*, ix, 25-30 (1994).

       O'FARRELL (Patrick). See 1886.

2786   O'FERRALL (Fergus).   Daniel O'Connell, the 'Liberator', 1775-1847: changing images. In *Ireland*, pp 91-102 (1994).

2787   O'FERRALL (Fergus). Maria Edgeworth and the local scene: a review. In *Teathba*, ii, no. 1, pp 57-60 (1980).

2788   Ó GLAISNE (Risteárd).   Conradh na Gaeilge, 1893-1993. Conradh na Gaeilge i nDroichead na Bandan. In *Bandon Hist. Jn.*, x, 41-8 (1994).
The Gaelic League in Bandon.

2789   Ó GLAISNE (Risteárd). Douglas Hyde here in Roscommon. Pp 24. Boyle: Roscommon County Council [1993?].

2790   Ó GLAISNE (Risteárd). 'This is no political matter'. In *Studies*, lxxxii, 471-80 (1993).
Douglas Hyde and the Gaelic League.

2791   Ó GLAISNE (Risteárd).   Torna (Tadhg Ó Donnchadha). In *Náisiún na hÉireann*, pp 34-57 (1993).
1874-1949, priest and Irish language activist.

2792   O'GORMAN (Dermot). To hell and back - to heaven and back. In *Oola Past and Present*, ii, 38-43 (1993).
1914-18 war.

2793   O'GORMAN (Dermot). To mass in the gallery. In *Oola Past and Present*, iii, 39-42 (1994).

2794   O'GORMAN (Kevin).   The hunger strike of Terence MacSwiney.   In *Ir. Theological Quarterly*, lix, 114-27 (1993).

2795   O'GORMAN (Michael).   A pride of paper tigers: a history of the great hunger in the Scariff workhouse union from 1839 to 1853. Pp [8], 82.   Tuamgraney, Co. Clare: East Clare Heritage, 1994.

2796   O'GORMAN (Michael).   For whom the bell tolls.   In *Sliabh Aughty*, v, 19-20 (1994).
Mikey Dooley, the last town crier of Scariff.

2797   O'GORMAN (Michael).   National school education in Scariff parish.   In *Sliabh Aughty*, v, 31-5. (1994).

2798   O'GORMAN (Michael).   Scariff flour mills and Charles Walnut.   In *Sliabh Aughty*, iv, 14-16 (1993).

2799   Ó GRÁDA (Cormac).   An Drochshaol: béaloideas agus amhráin. Pp ix, 104. Baile Átha Cliath: Coiscéim, 1994.
Poetry and song relating to the famine.

2800   Ó GRÁDA (Cormac).   Irish agricultural output before and after the famine. In *Jn. European Economic Hist.*, xiii, 149-65 (1984).

2801   Ó GRÁDA (Cormac).   The lumper potato and the famine.   In *Hist. Ire.*, i, no. 1, pp 22-3 (1993).

2802   Ó GRÁDA (Cormac),   [New introduction and bibliography].   In *The great famine*, [new ed.]. Pp xvii-xxvii and 511-16 (1994).

2803   Ó GRÁDA (Cormac).   The wages book of a Fethard farmer, 1880-1905.   In *Tipp. Hist. Jn.*, pp 67-72 (1994).

Ó GRÁDA (Cormac).   See BOURKE (Austin).

Ó GRÁDA (Cormac).   See *The economic development of Ireland since 1870.*

2804   Ó GRÁDA (Diarmuid).   Cath Chéim an Fhia. The background to the song. In *Treoir*, xxvi, no. 1, pp 13-17 (1994).

2805   Ó GRÁDA (Liam).   Drangan Church: a short history.   In *Souvenir of re-dedication of Church of the Immaculate Conception, Drangan*, pp 5-7 (1993).
c.1806-

2806   O'HAGAN (Kevin J.).   The iron mines of Glenravel.   In *The Glynns*, viii, 5-10 (1980).

2807   Ó hALLMHURÁIN (Gearóid).   James Goodman Memorial Lecture: traditional music and society in post-famine Clare. In *An Aisling*, iii, 101-14 (1991).
James Goodman Memorial Lecture delivered in Kerry, May 1991.

2808   O'HALPIN (Eunan).   The army and the Dáil - civil/military relations within the independence movement. In *The creation of the Dáil*, pp 107-21 (1994).

2809   O'HARA (James G.) and McCONNELL (James).   Stoney and the electron.
        Pp 39.   Dublin: Royal Dublin Society, 1993.   (Occasional papers in Irish
        science and technology, no. 8)
        George Johnstone Stoney, 1826-1911.

2810   O'HARE (Colmán).   Who fears to speak?: the Newry proclamation, 1916-
        1984.   In *Eire-Ireland*, xxix, no. 1, pp 7-11 (1994).

        O'HEARN (Denis).   See 1890.

2811   O'KEEFE (Patrick).   My reminiscences of 1914-1923.   In *Oughterany*, i,
        no. 1, pp 42-50 (1993).

2812   O'KELLY (Paula).   Then & now - 130 years on.   Has anything changed?   In
        Ir. Family Hist., x, 53-60 (1994).

2813   Ó LAIGHIN (Pádraig G.).   Éadbhard Ó Dufaigh, 1840-1868.   Pp 127.
        Baile Átha Cliath: Coiscéim, 1994.
        Edward Duffy, Connacht Fenian.

2814   Ó LAOGHAIRE (Donncha).   Three poems in Irish from mid-Cork.   In *Cork
        Hist. Soc. Jn.*, xcix, 120-29 (1994).
        Three poems taken down from seanachai Domhnall Ó hÉalaithe, who died
        in 1934.

2815   O'LEARY (Liam).   Rex Ingram: master of the silent cinema.   Pp x, 224.
        [New ed.]   [Pordenone, Italy]:   Le Giornate del cinema Muto;   London:
        British Film Institute, 1993.
        Rex Ingram, 1893-1950. Previous ed.: Dublin: Academy Press, 1960.

2816   Ó LIONAIN (Fiacra).   The old church in Johnstown.   In *Arklow Hist. Soc.
        Jn.*, pp 50-56 (1992/93).

        OLIVER (Seán).   See 1891.

2817   Ó LOINSIGH (Pádraig).   Famine.   In *The book of Cloyne*, pp 263-8
        (1994).
        1845-7.

2818   Ó LUANAIGH (Dónall).   A gentleman of the press: William J.H. Brayden,
        O.B.E. (1865-1933).   In *Dublin Hist. Rec.*, xlvii, 103-04 (1994).

2819   Ó LUANAIGH (Donall).   Glimpses of the 1916 Rising in Co. Galway.   In
        Galway Roots, ii, 30-31 (1994).

2820   Ó LUANAIGH (Donall).   Inter-church appeal for relief of distress in Galway,
        1831.   In *Galway Roots*, ii, 20-23 (1994).

2821   Ó LUANAIGH (Donall).   A railway pioneer looks at Galway.   In *Galway
        Roots*, ii, 1-5 (1994).
        Extract from work by Sir Cusack Patrick Roney.

2822   Ó LÚING (Seán).   Celtic scholars of Germany: a brief survey.   In *Z.C.P.*,
        xlvi, 249-71 (1994).

2823   O'MAHONY (Canice).   James Barton, engineer.   In *Irish Railway Rec. Soc.
        Jn.*, xviii, no. 122, pp 262-74 (1993).

2824   O'MAHONY (Chris).   Emigration from Tipperary workhouse, 1848-1858.
In *Tipp. Hist. Jn.*, pp 105-09 (1994).

2825   O'MAHONY (Christopher) and THOMPSON (Valerie).   Poverty to promise:
the Mounteagle emigrants 1838-58.   Pp xi, 242.   Sydney: Crossing Press,
1994.
Emigration from Co. Limerick to Australia.

2826   O'MAHONY (Colman).   Fishing in nineteenth-century Kinsale.   In *Cork
Hist. Soc. Jn.*, xcviii, 113-32 (1993).

2827   O'MAHONY (Patsy).   The Ballinvoher forge.   In *The book of Cloyne*, pp
340-48 (1994).
Closed 1957.

2828   O'Mahonys in Thom's Directory, 1872.   In *O'Mahony Jn.*, xvi, 18-19
(1993).

2829   O'MALLEY (William).   Land League days in Ballyconneely.   In *Connemara*,
i, no. 1, pp 28-31 (1993).
Article by William O'Malley M.P. (1853-1939) reprinted from the
Connacht Tribune, 22 May 1909.

2830   O'MEARA (J.).   Three incidents.   In *Irish Railway Rec. Soc. Jn.*, xviii, no.
120, pp 158-64 (1993).

2831   Ó MÓRDHA (Pilib).   Some notes on Clones Workhouse.   In *Clogher Rec.*,
xv, no. 1, pp 74-5 (1994).

2832   Ó MÓRDHA (Pilib B.).   Cumann Peile Thiarnaigh Naofa, Cluain Eois, 1886-
1993.   Pp vii, 215.   [Monaghan]:   [Cumann Peile Thiarnaigh Naofa],
[1994?].
St Tiernach's G.A.A. Club.

2833   Ó MUIRI (Réamonn).   Thomas Gubby *alias* Hughes: informant on the
burning of Wildgoose Lodge.   In *Dúiche Néill*, viii, 34-9 (1993).
Reaghstown, Co. Louth, 30 Oct. 1816.

Ó MUIRITHE (Diarmaid).   See 1896.

2834   Ó MUIRÍ (Damien).   O'Growney - one hundred years on.   In *Ríocht na
Midhe*, ix, no. 1, pp 104-34 (1994/95).

2835   Ó MURCHADHA (Ciarán).   Springfield people: new material on the history
of Springfield College.   In *The Other Clare*, xviii, 63-8 (1994).

2836   Ó MURCHADHA (Diarmuid).   Dughlas de hÍde - Douglas Hyde.   [Review
article].   In *Cork Hist. Soc. Jn.*, xcviii, 148-56 (1993).
Bilingual article.

2837   100 Years of the L.F.A.: Leinster Football Association Centenary Yearbook.
Ed. George Briggs and Joe Dodd.   Pp147. Dublin: Leinster Football
Association, 1993.
1892-1992.

2838   O'NEILL (Assumpta). Nuns and monks at Hennessy's Road: Edmund Rice and the Presentation Sisters in Waterford. In *A man raised up*, pp 79-95 (1994).

2839   O'NEILL (Jenny). The flying Cosgraves. In *Clogher Rec.*, xv, no. 1, pp 126-8 (1994).
Family involved in the entertainment industry in Australia.

2840   O'NEILL (Marie). Dublin Corporation in the troubled times, 1914-1924. In *Dublin Hist. Rec.*, xlvii, 56-72 (1994).

2841   O'NEILL (Marie). The struggle of Irishwomen for the vote. In *Breifne*, viii, 338-53 (1992/93).

2842   O'NEILL (Thomas P.). The organisation and administration of relief, 1845-52. In *The great famine*, pp 209-51 (1994).

2843   O'NEILL (Thomas P.). Rentals of encumbered estates. In *Ir. Family Hist.*, x, 66-8 (1994).

2844   O'REGAN (Brian). North-Cork men in Ottawa Valley. In *Mallow Field Club Jn.*, xii, 60-62 (1994).

2845   O'REGAN (Brian). The stonemason O'Regan. In *Mallow Field Club Jn.*, xi, 125-31 (1993).

O'REILLY (F.D.). See COUGHLAN (A.).

2846   O'REILLY (John Joe). Portobello Bks: reason and insanity with a taste of Joyce. In *An Cosantóir*, li, no. 4, pp 20-22 (1991).
Connections with Portobello Barracks - James Joyce and Francis Skeffington.

2847   O'REILLY-HYLAND (Kathleen). 'The village curate': reflections and recollections. Pp 164. [Oulart, Co. Wexford]: [the author], 1994.
Henry E. Lambert (1878-1964), Co. Wexford, R.C. priest.

2848   Ó RIAIN (Seamus). Maurice Davin (1842-1927): first president of the G.A.A. Pp [8], 236. Dublin: Geography Publications, [1994].

2849   Ó RIAIN (Seán). Dr Douglas Hyde/Dr Ludwig Zamenhof. In *Treoir*, xxv, no. 1, pp 3-4 (1993).

2850   Ó RIAIN (Seán). Pleanáil teanga in Eirinn, 1919-1985. Pp 245. Baile Átha Cliath: Carbad i gcomhar le Bord na Gaeilge, 1994.

2851   Ó RÍORDÁIN (Traolach). Conradh na Gaeilge i gCorcaigh i dtosach a ré. In *Cork Hist. Soc. Jn.*, xcviii, 1-26 (1993).
The Gaelic League in Cork in its early days.

2852   O'ROURKE (Alan). D & SER services, 1914-23. In *Ir. Railway Rec. Soc. Jn.*, xviii, no. 125, pp 431-45 (1994).

2853   O'ROURKE (Kevin). The economic impact of the famine in the short and long run. Pp 18, [10]. Dublin: University College Dublin, Department of Economics, 1993. (Working paper (U.C.D. Centre for Economic Research), WP93/31).

2854   O'ROURKE (Kevin).   Emigration and living standards in Ireland since the
        famine.   Pp 28, [7].   Dublin: University College Dublin, Department of
        Economics, 1994. (Working paper (U.C.D. Centre for Economic Research)).

2855   O'ROURKE (Kevin).   The repeal of the corn laws and Irish emigration.   In
        Explorations in Econ. Hist., xxxi, 120-38 (1994).

        O'ROURKE (Kevin).   See BOYER (George R.).

2856   Ó SAOTHRAÍ (Séamas).   Dr James MacDevitt and 'The Donegal Highlands'.
        In *Ulster Local Studies*, iv, no. 1, pp 4-7 (1978).
        Dr James MacDevitt (1832-79), bishop of Raphoe.

2857   OSBORNE HARPER (W.).   Second Presbyterian Church, Comber, 1838-
        1990.   Pp 221.   Comber, Co. Down: Publications Committee of Second
        Presbyterian Church, Comber, 1992.

2858   O'SHEA (Stephen).   Bequests of Miss Florence O'Mahony of Cullina, in her
        will of 1911.   In *O'Mahony Jn.*, xii, 12-13 (1982).

2859   Ó SIADHAIL (Pádraig).   Stair dhrámáiocht na Gaeilge, 1900-1970.   Pp 239.
        Indreabhán, Conamara: Cló Iar-Chonnachta, 1993.
        History of Irish language theatre.

2860   Ó SÍOCHÁIN (Séamas).   Roger Casement, ethnography and the Putumayo.
        In *Eire-Ireland*, xxix, no. 2, pp 29-41 (1994).

2861   Ó SÚILLEABHÁIN (Amhlaoibh).   The diary of an Irish countryman 1827-
        1835: a translation of Cín lae Amhlaoibh by Tomás de Bhaldraithe.   Pp 139.
        Cork; Dublin: Mercier Press [1993].
        First published with title: The diary of Humphrey O'Sullivan, Cork:
        Mercier, 1979.

2862   O'SULLIVAN (Michael).   Seán Lemass: a biography.   Pp vii, 216.   Dublin:
        Blackwater Press, 1994.
        1899-1971.

2863   O'SULLIVAN (Patrick).   Aspiring to the constabulary and an arms 'find'.   In
        Seanchas Duthalla, ix, 52-4 (1993).

2864   O'SULLIVAN (Patrick).   Civil rights and the [Cork] Constitution of 1825.
        In *Seanchas Duthalla*, ix, 82-4 (1993).

        O'SULLIVAN (Patrick).   See 1900.

        O'TOOLE (Fintan).   See *Labour in Art* (1994).

2865   Ó TUATHAIGH (Gearóid).   Nationalist Ireland, 1912-1922:   aspects of
        continuity and change.   In *Nationalism and unionism*, pp 47-73 (1994).

2866   OWENS (Gary).   Constructing the repeal spectacle: monster meetings and
        people power in pre-famine Ireland.   In *People power*, pp 80-93 (1993).

2867   OWENS (Gary).   Hedge schools of politics.   In *Hist. Ire.*, ii, no. 1, pp 35-
        40 (1994).

2868 OWENS (Gary). Nationalist monuments in Ireland, c.1870-1914: symbolism and ritual. In *Ireland*, pp 103-17 (1994).

2869 OWENS (Rosemary Cullen). Votes for women 1918-1993, 75th anniversary. In *Labour History News*, ix, 15-19 (1993).

2870 PAINE (Derek). Another pictorial history of Greystones, 1870-1990: a collection of old photographs. Pp 208. Blackrock, Co. Dublin: Martello Press, 1994.

2871 PAINE (Derek). A pictorial history of Greystones, 1855 to 1955: a collection of old photographs. Pp vi, 160. Blackrock, Co. Dublin: Martello Press, 1993.

2872 Parishes of County Antrim. VI: 1830, 1833, 1835-8: south-west Antrim. *Ed.* Angélique Day and Patrick McWilliams. Pp xiv, 138. Belfast: Institute of Irish Studies, Queen's University of Belfast in association with the Royal Irish Academy, 1993. (Ordnance Survey Memoirs of Ireland, vol. 19)

2873 Parishes of County Antrim. VII, 1832-8, south Antrim. *Ed.* Angélique Day and Patrick McWilliams. Pp xiii, 139. Belfast: Institute of Irish Studies, Queen's University of Belfast in association with the Royal Irish Academy, 1993. (Ordnance Survey Memoirs of Ireland, vol. 21)

2874 Parishes of County Antrim, VIII, 1831-5, 1837-8, Ballymena and west Antrim. *Ed.* Angélique Day, Patrick McWilliams and Nóirín Dobson. Pp xv, 141. Belfast: Institute of Irish Studies, Queen's University of Belfast in association with the Royal Irish Academy, 1993. (Ordnance Survey Memoirs of Ireland, vol. 23)

2875 Parishes of County Antrim, IX; 1830-2, 1835, 1838-9, north Antrim coast and Rathlin. *Ed.* Angélique Day, Patrick McWilliams and Nóirín Dobson. Pp xiv, 134. Belfast: Institute of Irish Studies, Queen's University of Belfast in association with the Royal Irish Academy, 1994. (Ordnance Survey Memoirs of Ireland, vol. 24)

2876 Parishes of County Antrim, X: 1830-1, 1833-5, 1839-40, east Antrim: Glynn, Inver, Kilroot, and Templecorran. *Ed.* Angélique Day, Patrick McWilliams and Nóirín Dobson. Pp xii, 132. Belfast: Institute of Irish Studies, Queen's University of Belfast in association with the Royal Irish Academy, 1994. (Ordnance Survey Memoirs of Ireland, vol. 26)

2877 Parishes of County Londonderry, VII: 1834-5, north-west Londonderry. *Ed.* Angélique Day, Patrick McWilliams and Nóirín Dobson. Pp xiv, 125. Belfast: Institute of Irish Studies, Queen's University of Belfast, in association with the Royal Irish Academy, 1994. (Ordnance Survey Memoirs of Ireland, vol. 25)

2878 PARKHILL (Trevor). Valuation records in the Public Record Office of Northern Ireland. In *Ulster Local Studies*, xvi, no. 2, pp 45-58 (1994).

2879 PARKINSON (Danny). Arthur Morrisson, 1765-1837, Lord Mayor of Dublin, 1835. In *Dublin Hist. Rec.*, xlvii, 183-6 (1994).

2880 PARKINSON (Danny). John Gately from Roscommon. In *Gateway to the Past*, i, no. 3, pp 164-5 (1994).
Prominent citizen of East London, South Africa, b. 1829, d. 1902.

PARKINSON (Danny). See 1905.

2881   Parnells Hurling and Football Club. An Cumann Parnell, 1893-1993.   Pp x, 85. Dublin [Parnells Hurling and Football Club], [1993].

2882   PARRY (Jonathan). The rise and fall of liberal government in Victorian Britain. Pp viii, 383. New Haven; London: Yale University Press, 1993. References to Ireland.

2883   PATERSON (David). How wicked were Irish landlords? In *The Historian*, xiv, 19-22 (1987).

2884   PATTERSON (Iain D.). The activities of Irish republican physical force organisations in Scotland, 1919-21.   In *Scottish Hist. Rev.*, lxxii, 39-59 (1993).

PATRICK (Heather). See PATRICK (Ross).

2885   PATRICK (Ross) and PATRICK (Heather). Exiles undaunted: the Irish rebels Kevin and Eva O'Doherty.   Pp xiv, 293.   St Lucia, Queensland: University of Queensland Press, 1989.
        Kevin I. O'Doherty (1823-1905) and Eva O'Doherty (1826-1910).

2886   PATRICK (Ross). Young Irelanders in Australia.   In *Galway Arch. Soc. Jn.*, xxxviii, 73-8 (1981/82).

2887   Patrick W. Nally in Mountjoy prison. In *North Mayo Hist. Jn.*, iii, no. 2, pp 34-43 (1993/94).
        Taken from *The Western People*, 1892.

2888   PEARSON (Peter). Blackrock foreshore: Part two.   In *Blackrock Soc. Proc.*, i, 52-8 (1992/93).

2889   PENNEFATHER (R.S.). The orange and the black: documents in the history of the Orange Order, Ontario and the west, 1890-1940.   Pp 187. Toronto: Orange and Black Publications, 1984.

2890   PERRILL (Martin). Samuel Lewis's descriptions of some east Clare parishes in 1837. In *Sliabh Aughty*, v, 36-8 (1994).

2891   PERRY (Gerald). The last landlord. In *A Window on the Past*, iii, 39-44 (1993).

2892   PEYRONEL (Valérie). Évolution du systéme scolaire nord-irlandais et naissance des écoles intégrées. In *Études Irlandaises*, xviii, no. 1, pp 113-23 (1993).

2893   PHELAN (Jim). The name's Phelan: the first part of the autobiography of Jim Phelan. Pp 298. Belfast: Blackstaff Press, 1993.
        Originally published: London: Sidgwick & Jackson, 1948.   1895-1966, gypsy, actor, writer, blacksmith and convict.

2894   PHELAN (Robert). William Vincent Wallace: a vagabond composer. Pp 125. Waterford: Celtic Publications, 1994.

2895   PHOENIX (Eamonn).   Northern nationalists, Ulster unionists and the development of partition, 1900-21. In *Nationalism and unionism*, pp 107-22 (1994).

2896   PLUNKETT (James).   Jim Larkin and the risen people.   In *Trade union century*, pp 33-41 (1994).

2897   POCHIN MOULD (Daphne).   The barracks of Ballinskelligs Bay.   In *Arch. Ire.*, viii, no. 2, pp 22-4 (1994).
        Early 19th-century coastal fortification.

2898   POLLARD (Kevin J.).   William Thomas Downie.   In *Ir. Family Hist.*, x, 49-52 (1994).

        POLLOCK (Vivienne).   See HILL (Myrtle) .

2899   Poor Clare Monastery, Graiguecullen, Carlow.   A century of prayer 1893-1993: Poor Clare Monastery, Perpetual Adoration, Graiguecullen, Carlow. Pp 40. Carlow: Poor Clare Monastery, 1993.

2900   POTTER (Matthew).   A Catholic unionist: the life and times of William Monsell, first Baron Emly of Tervoe (1812-1894).   Pp 122.   [Limerick?]: [the author], [1994?].

2901   POTTERTON (Homan).   Letters from St Louis. In *Ir. Arts Rev. Yearbk*, pp 245-51 (1994).
        Ireland's exhibit at the St Louis World's Fair in 1904 was 'a brilliant and unqualified success'.   An outline of the contributions of its patrons T.P. Gill and T.W. Rolleston.

2902   POTTERTON (Homan).   Nathaniel Hone and John Quinn: a correspondence. In *Art is my life*, pp 133-53 (1991).

2903   POWELL (Larry).   The discovery of a new master Roderic O'Conor 1860-1940.   In *Etudes Irlandaises*, xviii, no. 2, pp 147-56 (1993).

2904   POWER (Bill).   William O'Brien and the Kingston estate.   In *Mallow Field Club Jn.*, xii, 35-47 (1994).

2905   POWER (Ita).   Love letters to a lady.   In *Mallow Field Club Jn.*, xi, 50-55 (1993).
        Correspondence to Lady Castletown from Oliver Wendall Holmes.

2906   POWER (James).   From Charleville to Kilfane, by the Ballyhoura range of mountains: stories of 100 years ago.   In *The history and legends of Ballyhoura mountains*, pp 41-56 (1993).
        Originally published in *The Kerryman*, 1930s.

2907   POWER (Patrick C.).   Charles J. Kickham (1828-1882).   In *Tipperary County*, pp 63-7 (1993).

2908   POWER (Patrick C.).   County Tipperary & its railways.   In *Tipperary County*, pp 45-7 (1993).

        POWER (Patrick C.).   See 1909.

2909   PRENDERGAST (Ellen). William Prendergast - patriot and historian. In *Carloviana*, xl, 9, 11 (1992/93).

2910   PRESTON (Margaret H.). Lay women and philanthropy in Dublin, 1860-1880. In *Eire-Ireland*, xxviii, no. 4, pp 74-85 (1993).

2911   PRICE (Leslie). The women of 1916. In *An Pobal Éirithe*, v, 3-6 (1991).

        PROBERT (Alan). See 1856.

2912   The Proclamation - the compositors and printers experience investigated. In *An Cosantóir*, li, no. 4, pp 7-8 (1991).
        Investigation of the printing history of the 1916 Proclamation. Courtesy of the *Cork Examiner*.

        PROUDFOOT (L.J.). See 1912, 1913.

        PURCELL (Mary). See HAMILTON (John).

2913   PURDIE (Bob). An Ulster labourist in Liberal Scotland: William Walker and the Leith Burghs election of 1910. In *Scotland and Ulster*, pp 116-33 (1994).

2914   PYLE (Hilary). The different worlds of Jack B. Yeats: his cartoons and illustrations. Pp 343. Blackrock, Co. Dublin: Irish Academic Press, 1994. 1871-1957.

2915   PYLE (Hilary). Jack B. Yeats: his watercolours, drawings and pastels. Pp 214. Blackrock, Co. Dublin: Irish Academic Press, 1994.

2916   PYBURN (Jennifer). A history of the Stoney Memorial Hall, Ballyrisode, Co. Cork. In *Mizen Jn.*, ii, 48-53 (1994).

2917   QUIGLEY (Christy). Presentation School: girls roll book, 1822-1839. In *Old Drogheda Soc. Jn.*, ix, 64-105 (1994).

2918   QUIGLEY (Patrick). Old days in Ardcroney. In *Cloughjordan Heritage*, i, 22-4 (1985).
        Reminiscence recorded in 1939 by Patrick Quigley (1861-194?).

2919   QUINLAN (Tom). The registered papers of the Chief Secretary's Office. In *Ir. Archives*, pp 5-21 (autumn 1994).

2920   QUINLIVAN (Patrick J.). Hunting the Fenians: problems in the historiography of a secret organisation. In *The creative migrant*, pp 133-53 (1994).

2921   QUINN (Hugh, jr). The journal of Hugh Quinn Junr, edited by James McMullan. In *Upper Ards Hist. Soc. Jn.*, i, 7-12 (1977).

2922   Racing 100 years ago. Reminiscences of the Galway Plate. In *Galway Roots,* [i], 18-20 (1993).
        Extract from the *Connacht Tribune*, July 1921.

2923   RADIGAN (Thomas B.). Born in Ireland, buried in Canada. In *Ir. Family Hist.*, x, 61-5 (1994).

2924   RAFFERTY (Oliver P.). Cardinal Cullen, early Fenianism, and the MacManus funeral affair. In *Recusant History*, xxii, 549-63 (1994/95).

2925   RAFTERY (Joseph). A backward look. In *Arch. Ire.*, ii, 22-4 (1988).
A look back at the Irish Antiquities section of the National Museum of Ireland.

2926   RAMSEY (Trevor). A light still burning. The last hundred years of Limerick Baptist Church. In *Ir. Baptist Hist. Soc. Jn.*, n.s., ii, 39-53 (1994/95).

2927   RANKIN (Fred). The east window of Down Cathedral. In *Lecale Miscellany*, viii, 45-50 (1990).

2928   RASHID (Salim). Richard Whately and Christian political economy at Oxford and Dublin. In *Jn. Hist. Ideas*, xxxviii, 147-55 (1977).
Archbishop of Dublin, 1831-63. Established first professorship of political economy in Ireland.

Rathfeigh since the penal days. See 1917.

2929   RAY (Ivor). William 'Bulldog' Young, coastguard and harbour master at Ardglass, Co. Down. In *Lecale Miscellany*, ix, 54-7 (1991).
William Young, 1870-1958.

2930   RAY (John). Edward Hincks and the progress of Egyptology. In *The Edward Hincks bicentenary lectures*, pp 58-74 (1994).

RAYMOND (Raymond James). See 1918.

2931   REAL (Charles E.). A great Irish oak transplanted. My Real ancestors. In *Gateway to the Past*, i, no. 3, pp 114-19 (1994).
Real family.

2932   REAUME (Helen). From Kent Co. (Ontario) marriage records, 1857-1869 [*also* burials *c*.1820-1924; marriage records of Essex County, 1858-1864 (Ontario, Canada)]. In *Ir. Family Hist.*, x, 32-43 (1994).

REDDEN (Jennifer). See 1920.

2933   REDDIOUGH (James). Aspects of Bonniconlon history 1880 to 1910. In *North Mayo Hist. Jn.*, iii, no. 2, pp 31-3 (1993/94).

2934   REECE (Bob). The wild colonial Kellys. In *U.C.D. Hist. Rev.*, iii, 21-30 (1989).

2935   REES (Jim). A farewell to famine. Pp 174. Arklow: Arklow Enterprise Centre, 1994
A party of over 1000 people from Counties Wicklow and Wexford emigrated to the American mid-west led by Fr Thomas Hore.

REID (Richard). See 1922.

2936   REILLY (Catherine). 'Morra Coosy'. In *Swords Voices*, i, no. 2, pp 18-23 (1994).
Memories of Swords.

2937   RICHARDS (Eric). How did poor people emigrate from the British Isles to Australia in the nineteenth century? In *Jn. British Studies*, xxxii, no. 3, pp 250-79 (1993).

2938   RIDLEY (Jane). The Unionist opposition and the House of Lords, 1906-1910. In *Parliamentary History*, xi, 238-53 (1992).

2939   RIGGS (Pádraigín). Pádraic Ó Conaire, deoraí. Pp 258. Baile Átha Cliath: An Clóchomhar, 1994. (Leabhair thaighde, 77)
        Pádraic Ó Conaire, 1882-1928.

2940   RIORDAN (Anthony). Joseph O'Mara operatic tenor. In *Old Limerick Jn.*, xxix, 31-2 (1992).
        Joseph O'Mara, 1866-1927.

2941   RITCHIE (John). 'Taking the pledge' in Strangford. In *Lecale Miscellany*, viii, 10-11 (1990).

2942   ROBERTS (Alan). Rev. Richard Dell, M.A., (*c*.1804-1858) and Magee College. In *Donegal Annual*, xlv, 21-3 (1993).

2943   ROBINSON (David B.). The Fuller family of Dunmore, Co. Galway and Dunmore, N.S.W. Australia. In *Galway Roots*, ii, 98-104 (1994).

2944   ROBINSON (Theo). The pure stream: the story of St Canice's parish church, Finglas. Pp 63. Dublin: Theo Robinson, 1993.
        Church opened in 1843.

2945   ROCHE (Nuala). William Kenealy. In *The book of Cloyne*, pp 197-200 (1994).
        1828-76, journalist, song writer

2946   ROCHE (Richard). Double celebration for Irish Texans. In *Ir. Roots* 1994, no. 3, p. 29 (1994).

2947   ROCHE (Richard). The famine years in Forth and Bargy. In *Wexford Hist. Soc. Jn.*, xv, 1-14 (1994/95).

2948   RODGERS (R.J.). Vision unrealized: the Presbyterian mission to Irish Roman Catholics in the nineteenth century. In *Presb. Hist. Soc. Bull. of Ire.*, xx, 12-31 (1991).

2949   ROGAN (Eddie). James Naughton, Bishop of Killala, 1911-1950: the man, his life, in particular his laws. In *North Mayo Hist. Jn.*, iii, no. 1, pp 39-51 (1992/93).

2950   ROSS (Alexander). Statistical account of the parish of Dungiven by Rev. Alexander Ross (1814) - (from Shaw-Mason's Statistical Survey of Ireland) Extracts. In *Benbradagh*, xxiii, 7-8 (1993); xxiv, 22 (1994).
        Continued from xxii (1992).

        ROSS (Bianca). See 1924.

2951   ROSS (Noel). A survey of the estate of Lord Louth in 1832-33. In *Louth Arch. Soc. Jn.*, xxiii, 231-9 (1994).

2952   Rothe House *c*.1808. In *Old Kilkenny Rev.*, xlvi, 54-6 (1994).
        Excerpt from *The O'Hara family* by John Banim.

2953   Rothe House in 1884. In *Old Kilkenny Rev.*, xlvi, 95 (1994).
        Report to Kilkenny Sanitary Authority, *Kilkenny Journal*, 8.11.1884.
        Submitted by Michael O'Dwyer.

2954   ROUSE (Paul). The politics of culture and sport in Ireland: a history of the
        GAA ban on foreign games 1884-1971.   Part One: 1884-1921.   In
        International Jn. of the History of Sport, x, 333-60 (1993).

2955   ROWAN (Alistair).   Irish Victorian churches: denominational distinctions.
        In *Ireland*, pp 207-30 (1994).

2956   ROYLE (Stephen A.).   Industrialization, urbanization and urban society in
        post-famine Ireland, *c*.1850-1921. In *An historical geography of Ireland*, pp
        258-92 (1993).

        ROYLE (Stephen A.). See JUPP (Peter J.).

2957   RUANE (Kevin M.).   Brother Paul James O'Connor (1796-1878).   In
        Carloviana, xl, 20-22 (1922/93).
        Established Patrician Bros community in Galway in 1826.

2958   RUDDOCK (Thomas).   Watsons' Nurseries: a talk ... Pp 9.   [Foxrock,
        Dublin]: Foxrock Local History Club, [1993]. (Publication, no. 35).
        1880-1967.

2959   RUSSELL (Alys).   Adam's gold.   In *Lecale Miscellany*, viii, 8-9 (1990).
        Refers to article in *Lecale Miscellany*, iii (1985), p.17.

2960   RYAN (Brigid).   My Fenian ancestor.   In *Gateway to the Past*, i, no. 2, pp
        61-4 (1994).
        Stephen O'Donoghue shot in Tallaght in 1867.

2961   RYAN (Christopher).   A visit to Waverley cemetery, New South Wales.   In
        Irish Family History, i, no. 1, pp 3-14 (1993).

2962   RYAN (Des).   Women's suffrage associations in Limerick, 1912-1914.   In
        Old Limerick Jn., xxx, 41-6 (1993).

2963   RYAN (Joseph J.).   Assertions of distinction: the modal debate in Irish
        music.   In *Music and the church*, pp 63-77 (1993).
        19th century.

2964   RYAN (Louise).   Women without votes: the political strategies of the Irish
        suffrage movement.   In *Irish Political Studies*, ix, 119-39 (1994).

2965   RYAN (Martin).   A great Clare man - honest Tom Steele.   In *The Other Clare*,
        ii, 27-9 (1978).
        Tom Steele (1788-1848) an idealist disappointed.

2966   RYAN (Paddy).   Music recordings - a brief history.   In *Treoir*, xxvi, no. 3,
        pp 5-8 (1994).

2967   RYAN (Theresa).   The creamery.   In *Oola Past & Present*, i, 16-18 (1992).

2968   RYAN (Theresa) and BOURKE (Tommy). Farming in Oola long ago. In *Oola Past & Present*, ii, 12-17 (1993).

RYGH (S.). See 1926.

RYNNE (Etienne). See LYSAGHT (P.B.).

2969   Sacred Heart Church, Borrisoleigh, 1893-1993. Pp 36. [S.l.]: [s.n.], [1993?].

2970   SAMUELS (Arthur Warren). The Samuels Collection: a general descriptive listing. Pp [34]. [Dublin]: [Trinity College Library], 1993.

2971   SANDERSON (Agnes). Holiday at Burrishoole. In *Cathair na Mart*, xiii, 117-24 (1993).
        Agnes Sanderson of London, b. 1874 - extract from a journal written when she was 14.

2972   SCALLY (Keith). A tragedy of public voting - Sixmilebridge, 1852. In *The Other Clare*, i, 33 (1977).

2973   SCANLAN (Bill). Lighthouses - a different perspective. In *Galway Roots*, ii, 61-4 (1994).

2974   SCANNELL (James). The funeral of William Dargan. In *Dublin Hist. Rec.*, xlvi, 53-4 (1993).
        William Dargan, engineer, contractor and entrepreneur (1799-1867).

2975   SCANNELL (James). Last train from Harcourt Street (and a short history of the line): a talk ... Pp 17 [Foxrock, Dublin]: Foxrock Local History Club, [1993]. (Publication no. 34)
        1854-1958.

2976   SCANNELL (James). Paying the penalty. In *Dun Laoghaire Jn.*, iii, 41-2 (1993).
        The case of George Lambert Orr, Jan.-Feb. 1914.

2977   SCANNELL (James). Red-faced & empty handed: the adventures of the 'Bonahaven'. In *Wicklow Hist. Soc. Jn.*, i, no. 6, pp 3-8 (1993).

2978   SCANNELL (James). St James's Church, Crinken, Co. Dublin. In *Dublin Hist. Rec.*, xlvii, 100-02 (1994).

SCHELLEKENS (Jona). See 1928.

2979   SCHMIDGALL (Gary). The stranger Wilde: interpreting Oscar. Pp xviii, 494. London: Abacus, 1994.
        1854-1900.

SCHUCHARD (Ronald). See YEATS (W.B.).

2980   SCOTT (Alfred Russell). The Ulster revival of 1859. *Ed.* Eull Dunlop. Pp 220. Ballymena, Co. Antrim: Mid-Antrim Historical Group, 1994. (Mid-Antrim Historical Group, 22)
        Ph.D. thesis, Trinity College Dublin, 1962.

2981   SCOTT (George). 1816 - a terrible year in Dungiven. In *Benbradagh*, xii, 9 (1982).
Excerpt from Rev. George Scott's diary, Minister in Dungiven area, 1814-78.

2982   SCOTT (Peter T.). 'Dishonoured': the 'Colonels' surrender' at St Quentin, the retreat from Mons, August 1914.   Pp [6], 90.   London: Tom Donovan, 1994.
Arthur Edward Mainwaring, 1864-1930, Royal Dublin Fusiliers.

2983   SEERY (James).   Dr Neilson's Irish grammar.   In *Presb. Hist. Soc. of Ire. Bull.*, xx, 5-11 (1991).
Rev. Moses Neilson (1739-1823), book published in 1808.

2984   SEMPLE (Don). Courthouse and shambles. In *Benbradagh*, xii, 1-2 (1982).

2985   SHANNON (Catherine B.).   The legacy of Arthur Balfour to twentieth-century Ireland.   In *Nationalism and unionism*, pp 17-33 (1994).

2986   SHARKEY (Neil). The Third Tipperary Brigade - a photographic record.   In *Tipp. Hist. Jn.*, pp 9-25 (1994).

2987   Shaw, Lady Gregory and the Abbey: a correspondence and a record.   *Ed.* Dan H. Laurence and Nicholas Grene.   Pp xliii, 211.   Gerrards Cross (Bucks.): Colin Smythe, 1993.

2988   SHEEDY (Kieran). 'Soft dull day - trade blue'. The diary of P.J. Dillon, Ennis draper 1861-1869. In *The Other Clare*, xviii, 57-62 (1994).

2989   SHEEHY (James). The Irish at Antwerp. In *Ir. Arts Rev. Yearbk*, pp 163-6 (1994).
Irish artists at the Royal Academy of Fine Arts at Antwerp between 1849 and 1891.

2990   SHEEHY SKEFFINGTON (Andrée).   A coterie of lively suffragists.   In *Writers, raconteurs and notable feminists*, pp 34-52 (1993).
Hanna Sheehy Skeffington her family and friends.

2991   SHEPHERD (Ernie).   The Midland Great Western Railway of Ireland: an illustrated history. Pp 144. East Shilton (Leics): Midland Publishing, 1994.
1840s-1975.

2992   SHERIDAN (David H.V.).   1841 Census - Killeshandra parish.   In *Ir. Family Hist.*, ix, 62-86 (1993).

2993   SILINONTE (Joseph M.).   Cemetery of the Holy Cross, Flatbush, Brooklyn, New York. In *Galway Roots*, pp 35-6 (1993).
Report of a listing of names with Irish birth places from the tombstones.

2994   SILVERMAN (Marilyn).   A tragedy from 1871: a study of stigma, poverty and alienation. In *In the Shadow of the Steeple*, iv, 25-38 (1994).
The case of Anne Aylward who killed her illegitimate daughter of 19 months.

SILVERMAN (Marilyn). See GULLIVER (P.H.).

2995   SIMPSON (Hilary).   'Shawls off for the Lancers'.   In *Ulster Folklife*, xl, 49-55 (1994).

2996   SIMPSON (Lesley).   Balloo House: a house and its people. In *Lecale Miscellany*, ix, 26-31 (1991).

2997   SKY (Patrick).   The forgotten tune collectors. In *Treoir*, xxvi, no. 2, pp 37-40 (1994).

2998   SLATER (Eamonn).   Contested terrain: differing interpretations of Co. Wicklow's landscape. In *Ir. Jn. of Sociology*, iii, 23-55 (1993).

2999   SMARGIE (Aisling).   European sisterhood: feminism as a political force from 1900-1930. In *U.C.D. Hist. Rev.*, vi, 1-11 (1992).

3000   SMITH (Cornelius F.).   The history of Royal Irish Automobile Club, 1901-91. Pp vii, 215. Dublin: Royal Irish Automobile Club, 1994.

3001   SMITH (Des).   Sir Luke O'Connor. In *Roscommon Hist. Soc. Jn.*, iii, 37-9 (1990).
          1831-1915.

3002   SMITH (Des).   Surgeon Major T.H. Parke: a short history of his life. Pp 8, ill. Carrick-on-Shannon: Carrick-on-Shannon & District Historical Society, 1994.

3003   SMITH (Des).   'The world's rarest doctor': Surgeon Major T.H. Parke. In *Roscommon Hist. Soc. Jn.*, iv, 5-9 (1992).

3004   SMITH (Gus).   Irish stars of the opera. Pp xxvi, 339. Dublin: Madison Publishers, 1994.

3005   SMITH (Jeremy).   Bluff, bluster and brinksmanship: Andrew Bonar Law and the third Home Rule Bill. In *Hist. Jn.*, xxxvi, 161-78 (1993).

3006   SMYTH (Bernard T.).   The Chinese batch: the Maynooth mission to China: origins, 1911-1920. Pp 128. Dublin: Four Courts Press, 1994.

        SMYTH (Denis). See 1932.

        SMYTH (William J.). See 1935.

        SMYTH (William J.). See HOUSTON (C.J.).

        SNELL (D.K.M.). See SOMERVILLE (Alexander).

        SNODGRASS (Lee). See 1936.

3007   SOMERVILLE (Alexander).   Letters from Ireland during the famine of 1847. *Ed.* D.K.M. Snell. Pp 219. Blackrock, Co. Dublin: Irish Academic Press, 1994.
          Alexander Somerville, 1811-85. This account originally published as part of 3-vol. work titled *The whistler at the plough*, 1852.

3008   SOMERVILLE (Damien).   Drogheda - the racehorse. In *Old Drogheda Soc. Jn.*, ix, 61-3 (1994).

3009 St Mary's Church Cross. In *Carloviana*, xli, 26 (1993/94).

3010 STACPOOLE-RYDING (Richard J.). Henry de Vere Stacpoole: 1863-1951. In *Dun Laoghaire Jn.*, ii, 18-23 (1991/92).

3011 STAUNTON (Martin). The experience of an Irish town in the First World War. Kilrush and the Munster Fusiliers. In *Old Limerick Jn.*, xxx, 35-8 (1993).

3012 STEMPEL (P. de Bernardo). Rudolf Thurneysen (1857-1940) und sein sprachwissenschaftliches Werk. In *Z.C.P.*, xlvi, 216-48 (1994).

3013 STEWART (Kenneth). Banbridge: the earliest existing Baptist church in Co. Down. In *Ir. Baptist Hist. Soc. Jn.*, n.s., ii, 55-87 (1994/95).

3014 STOKES (John). Who owns the land? In *Oola Past & Present*, ii, 4-5 (1993).

3015 STRAUSS (Valda). Irish famine orphans in Australia. In *Mallow Field Club Jn.*, xi, 132-57 (1993).

3016 STUBBS (Roy St George). Paddy Nolan, K.C. In *Old Limerick Jn.*, xxxi, 31-6 (1994).

3017 SUTTON (Denys). George Moore and Degas. In *Art if my life*, pp 185-95 (1991).

SUTTON (George). See 1941.

3018 SWANTON (Daisy Lawrenson). Emerging from the shadow: the lives of Sarah Anne Lawrenson and Lucy Olive Kingston: based on personal diaries, 1883-1969. Pp 169. Dublin: Attic Press, 1994.
Women activists.

3019 SWIFT (Roger). Anti-catholicism and Irish disturbances: public order in mid-Victorian Northampton. In *Midland History*, ix, 87-108 (1984).

3020 SWIFT (Roger). The historiography of the Irish in nineteenth-century Britain: some perspectives. In *The Irish in British labour history*, pp 11-18 (1993).

3021 SWINFEN (Averil). Turnspit dog-wheels and their dogs. In *The Other Clare*, xviii, 42 (1994).

3022 SYMONDSON (Anthony). Art needlework in Ireland. In *Ir. Arts Rev. Yearbk*, pp 126-35 (1994).

3023 TAHENY (Donal). St Dominic's High School, Esker, Co. Galway, 1847-1857. In *Galway Roots*, ii, 73-5 (1994).

3024 TAKAGAMI (Shin-ichi). The Dublin Fenians after the rising, 1867-79. In *Comparative aspects of Irish and Japanese economic and social history*, pp 182-237 (1993).

3025 TAKEI (Akihiro). The first Irish linen mills, 1800-1824. In *Ir. Econ. & Soc. Hist.*, xxi, 28-38 (1994).

3026   TAYLOR (Lawrence J.). Peter's pence: official Catholic discourse and Irish nationalism in the nineteenth century. In *History of European Ideas*, xvi, 103-7 (1993).

3027   TAYLOR (Patrick). The West Clare Railway. [*Ed.* Allan C. Baker]. Pp 224. Brighton: Plateway Press, 1994.
    1885-1961.

    THOMPSON (Dorothy). See 1945.

    THOMPSON (F. Glenn). See 1946.

    THOMPSON (Valerie). See O'MAHONY (Christopher).

3028   THORNHILL (Aine), compiler. A list of merchants, 1811-12. In *Old Limerick Jn.*, xxx, 21-2 (1993).

3029   THORNTON (Martin). Criminal offences, compensation and breaches of the truce in Drogheda in 1920-21. In *Old Drogheda Soc. Jn.*, ix, 38-41 (1994).

3030   TIERNEY (Mark). A short-title calendar of the papers of Archbishop Michael Slattery in Archbishop's House, Thurles: Part IV, 1847. In *Collect. Hib.*, xxxiv/xxxv, 143-59 (1992/93).

    TILLYARD (Stella). See 1948.

3031   TIMMONS (Martin). The Vartry reservoir, Roundwood. In *Blackrock Soc. Proc.*, ii, 48-55 (1993/94).

3032   TIVNAN (Frank). An t-Athair Tomás Ó Ceallaigh: priest, scholar and patriot. In *Roscommon Hist. Soc. Jn.*, v, 5 (1994).
    1879-1924.

3033   Tomás an Bhlascaoid. *Ed.* Breandán Ó Conaire. Pp 382. Indreabhán, Conamara: Cló Iar-Chonnachta, 1992.
    Tomás Ó Criomhtain, 1856-1937 and the Blasket Islands.

3034   TOWNSHEND (Charles). Making the peace: public order and public security in modern Britain. Pp [9], 264. Oxford: Oxford University Press, 1993.
    References to Ireland.

3035   TOWNSHEND (Charles). The suppression of the Easter Rising. In *Bullán*, i, no. 1, pp 27-47 (1994).

3036   TRAVERS (Pauric). Eamon de Valera. Pp 56. Dundalk: Dundalgan Press for the Historical Association of Ireland, 1994. (Life and times series, no. 3).
    1882-1975.

3037   TROY (B.). Directory of the catholic clergy of the diocese of Cloyne & Ross, 1836-1893: including available obituary lists. 1 vol. (unpaged). [Midleton, Co. Cork]: [the author], [1994?].

3038   TUNNEY (John J.). The famine and the Irish mind. In *Ir.Family Hist.*, x, 120-24 (1994).

3039   TURNER (Larry).   Andrew Byrne: 'intelligent, honest, sober, and industrious'.   In *Irish convict lives*, pp 80-108 (1993).
        1780-1863; 1798 rebel.

3040   TURNER (Michael).   Rural economies in post-famine Ireland, *c*.1850-1914. In *An historical geography of Ireland*, pp 293-337 (1993).

3041   TURTLE (David).   Stewartstown Methodist Church.   In *The Bell*, v, 28-31 (1994).

3042   TWOHIG (Patrick J.).   Green tears for Hecuba: Ireland's fight for freedom. Pp viii, 420.   Ballincollig: Tower Books, 1994.
        Cork, 1916-21.

3043   TYERS (Pádraig).   Ceamara Chorca Dhuibhne = West Kerry camera: English translation of captions in Ceamara Chorca Dhuibhne: a photographic account of life in the Dingle Peninsula 1888-1960 ... [1992].   Pp 32.   Dún Chaoin Inné 1993.

3044   Ua CEARNAIGH (Seán).   Turbulent days beneath Galteemore.   In *Tipp. Hist. Jn.*, pp 88-94 (1993).

3045   Uí MHORÓNAIGH (Eibhlín).   Ár scéal féin.   In *Ó ghlúin go glúin*, pp 1-29 (1993).

3046   URQUHART (Diane).   'The female of the species is more deadlier than the male'?:   the Ulster Women's Unionist Council, 1911-40.   In *Coming into the light*, pp 93-123 (1994).

3047   VALIULIS (Maryann Gialanella).   'Free women in a free nation'.   In *The creation of the Dáil*, pp 75-90 (1994).

3048   VAN DUIN (Pieter).   Ethnicity, race and labour, 1830s-1930s: some Irish and international perspectives.   In *Saothar*, xix, 86-103 (1994).

3049   VAN ESBECK (Edmund).   100 years of Cork Constitution Football Club. Pp 344.   Cork: Cork Constitution Football Club, 1993.
        Rugby football.

3050   VARGA (Nicholas).   Fr John Early: American Jesuit educator.   In *Brieifne*, vi, no. 24, pp 375-89 (1986).

3051   VAUGHAN (Mairéad).   The life and death of a volunteer Captain John Vaughan 1893-1921.   In *Roscommon Hist. Soc. Jn.*, 40 (1990).

3052   VAUGHAN (W.E.).   Landlords and tenants in mid-Victorian Ireland.   Pp xxiii, 339.   Oxford: Clarendon Press, 1994.

3053   VERDON (Michael).   Shawlies, Echo boys, the marsh & the lanes: old Cork remembered.   Pp 219.   Dublin: O'Brien Press, 1993.

3054   Victoria, *Regina*.   Visit to Ireland 1849, extract from the journal of Queen Victoria.   In *Dun Laoghaire Jn.*, ii, 54-60 (1991/92).

3055   VILLIERS-TUTHILL (Kathleen).   Ditched in Derrygimla: the first transatlantic flight of Alcock and Brown.   In *Hist. Ire.*, ii, no. 4, pp 42-7 (1994).

3056   VINCENT (John). A new era for the Irish in South Africa. In *Ir. Roots* 1993, no. 4, p. 13 (1993).

3057   VINCENT (John). San Patricios. The Irishmen who died for Mexico. In *Ir. Roots*, 1993, no. 1, pp 6-7 (1993).

3058   WALKER (Brian) and McCREARY (Alf). Degrees of excellence: the story of Queen's, Belfast, 1845-1995. Pp viii, 234. Belfast: Institute of Irish Studies, Queen's University of Belfast, 1994.

3059   WALKER (Brian). The 1885 and 1886 general elections: a milestone in Irish history. In *Nationalism and unionism*, pp 1-15 (1994).

3060   WALKER (Brian Mercer). Shadows on glass: a portfolio of early Ulster photography. Pp 140. Belfast: Appletree Press, 1994.
        Originally published, 1976.

3061   WALKER (Graham). Empire, religion and nationality in Scotland and Ulster before the first world war. In *Scotland and Ulster*, pp 97-115 (1994).

        WALLACE (Robert H.). See BLACKER (William).

3062   WALLIS (Frank). The revival of the anti-Maynooth campaign in Britain, 1850-52. In *Albion*, xix, 527-47 (1987).

3063   WALLIS (Frank H.). Popular anti-Catholicism in mid-Victorian Britain. Pp viii, 280. Lewiston (N.Y.); Lampeter (Wales): E. Mellen Press, 1993. (Texts and studies in religion, vol. 60)
        References to Maynooth and Irish immigrants.

3064   WALLS (John P.). Hugh Deery. In *Donegal Annual*, xlv, 52-4 (1993).
        Hugh Deery, 1884-1978, stonemason and writer.

3065   WALPOLE (Peggy). Bennettsbridge in the old days. In *In the Shadow of the Steeple*, iv, 58-69 (1994).

3066   WALSH (Christy). The new Church of St Patrick - laying the foundation stone, 1856. In *Bandon Hist. Jn.*, x, 52 (1994).

3067   WALSH (Larry). A German tourist's impressions of Limerick, 1865. In *Old Limerick Jn.*, xxix, 20-21 (1992).

3068   WALSH (Michael) and CUMMINS (Denis). 'The Nightingale'. In *The Past*, xviii, 75-7 (1992).
        Late 19th-century and early 20th-century news sheet from Adamstown, Co. Wexford.

        WALSH (T.J.). See 1951.

3069   WALSH (Walter). Hurling in Mong (1909-1915). In *In the Shadow of the Steeple*, iv, 92-105 (1994).

3070   WATSON (G.J.). Irish identity and the literary revival: Synge, Yeats, Joyce and O'Casey. 2nd ed. Pp x, 326. Washington, D.C.: Catholic University of America Press, 1994. (Critical studies in Irish literature, vol. 4)
        Originally published, London: Croom Helm, 1979.

WEATHERUP (Roger). See FITZGERALD (Desmond).

3071   WEAVER (Paul). The voyage of the Robert Small and the Phoebe Dunbar in 1853. In *Irish convict lives*, pp 231-55 (1993).

WEBB (Marcus). See *Hockey in Trinity*.

3072   WEST (Máire). Kings, heroes and warriors: aspects of children's literature in the era of emergent nationalism. In *John Rylands Library Bulletin*, lxxvi, 165-84 (1994).

3073   WEST (Trevor). Charles Burton Barrington and Trinity Football Club. In *Old Limerick Jn.*, xxx, 32-4 (1993).

3074   WEST (Trevor). Moyne Reid - Western literary pioneer. In *Linen Hall Review*, x, no. 1, pp 9-10 (1993).

3075   WHITAKER (Anne-Maree). Armagh convicts in Australia, 1800-1806. In *Seanchas Ardmhacha*, xvi, no. 1, pp 100-02 (1994).

3076   WHITAKER (Anne-Maree). Unfinished revolution: United Irishmen in New South Wales, 1800-1810. Pp ix, 275. Sydney: Crossing Press, 1994. ('Ireland 1798 Australia' series, no. 1)

WHITE (Anna MacBride). See MacBRIDE (Maud Gonne).

3077   WHITE (Harry) and LAWRENCE (Nicholas). Towards a history of the Cecilian movement in Ireland: an assessment of the writings of Heinrich Bewerange (1862-1923), with a catalogue of his publications and manuscripts. In *Music and the church*, pp 78-107 (1993).

3078   WHYTE (Robert). Robert Whyte's 1847 famine ship diary: the journey of an Irish coffin ship. *Ed*. James T. Mangan. Pp 124. Cork; Dublin: Mercier Press, 1994.

3079   WIEMERS (Amy T.). Rural Irishwomen: their changing role, status and condition. In *Eire-Ireland*, xxix, no. 1, pp 76-91 (1994)

3080   WILLIAMS (Jeremy). A companion guide to architecture in Ireland, 1837-1921. With a foreword by Mark Girouard. Pp xix, 424. Blackrock, Co. Dublin: Irish Academic Press, 1994.

3081   WILLIAMS (John). Ordered to the Island: Irish convicts and Van Diemen's Land. *Ed*. Richard Davis. Pp ix, 226. Sydney: Crossing Press, 1994. Tasmania, 1803-53.

3082   WILLIAMS (Roche). The MacDonaghs. In *Cloughjordan Heritage*, i, 26-30 (1985).

3083   WILLIAMSON (Arthur P.). Enterprise, industrial development and social planning: Quakers and the emergence of the textile industry in Ireland. In *Familia*, ii, no. 9, pp 97-122 (1993).

3084   WILLIAMSON (Jeffrey G.). Economic convergence: placing post-famine Ireland in comparative perspective. In *Ir. Econ. & Soc. Hist.*, xxi, 1-27 (1994).

WILLIAMSON (Jeffrey G.).   See HATTON (Timothy J.).

3085   WILLOUGHBY (Charlie).   Blackrock baths.   In *Dun Laoghaire Jn.*, ii, 34-6 (1990).

3086   WILLS (Clair).   Rocking the cradle?:   women's studies and the family in twentieth-century Ireland.   (Review essay).   In *Bullán*, i, no. 2, pp 97-106 (1994).

3087   WILSON (Anthony M.).   The Downpatrick war memorial;   some further notes.   In *Lecale Miscellany*, xii, 32-7 (1994).
        Comment on article in *Lecale Miscellany*, xi (1993).

3088   WILSON (Joe).   Cobh: now and then: a photographic journey.   Pp 106. Blarney: On Stream Publications, 1993.

3089   WOODCOCK (Caroline).   An officer's wife in Ireland.   Introduction by Tim Pat Coogan.   Pp 95.   Dublin: Parkgate Publications, 1994.
        Originally published as *Experiences of an officer's wife in Ireland.* London: Blackwood, 1921. 'Bloody Sunday' 1920.

3090   WYSE JACKSON (Patrick), ed.   In marble halls: geology in Trinity College Dublin.   Pp 135.   Dublin: Department of Geology, Trinity College Dublin, 1994.

3091   WYSE JACKSON (Patrick) and FALKINER (Ninian).   A portrait of St Columba's College, 1843-1993.   Pp 126.   Dublin: Old Columban Society, 1993.

3092   YEATS (W.B.).   The collected letters of W.B. Yeats.   General *Ed.* John Kelly. Vol. 3, 1901-1904:   *Ed.* John Kelly and Ronald Schuchard.   Pp liv, 777.   Oxford: Clarendon Press, 1994.

3093   YOUNG (James D.).   A very English socialism and the Celtic fringe 1880-1991.   In *History Workshop*, xxxv, 136-52 (1993).

3094   YOUNG (Peter).   Defence and the new Irish state, 1919-39.   In *Ir. Sword*, xix , 1-10 (1993/95).

3095   Ack Ack - sixty years dedicated to service. In *An Cosantóir*, li, no. 9, pp 10-11 (1991).
Summary of articles which were published in 1 Air Defence Regiment Commemorative Magazine, 1989.

AGNEW (Art). See *Naomh Malachi and the Shelagh story.*

3096   AGNEW (Úna). Patrick Kavanagh: early religious work and devotional influences on his work. In *Clogher Rec.*, xv, no. 1, pp 51-73 (1994).

3097   AKENSON (Donald Harman). Conor: a biography of Conor Cruise O'Brien. 2 vols. Pp 573, 356. Kingston, Ontario: McGill-Queen's University Press, 1994.
Vol. 1: Narrative; vol. 2: Anthology.

3098   AKENSON (Donald Harman). Conor: a biography of Conor Cruise O'Brien. Pp xvi, 573. Ithaca, N.Y.: Cornell University Press, 1994.

ALLEN (Donna). See 1962.

ALLEN (Myrtle). See 1964.

ANDREWS (J.H.). See 1968.

3099   ANNETT (Anthony M.). Elections and macroeonomic outcomes in Ireland, 1948-91. In *Econ. & Soc. Rev.*, xxv, 21-47 (1994).

3100   Archaeology in Ireland. Organisations, consultancies and courses. In *Arch. Ire.*, viii, no. 1, pp 29-39 (1994).

3101   ARDAGH (John). Ireland and the Irish: portrait of a changing society. Pp xiii, 466. London: Hamish Hamilton, 1994.

3102   ARNOLD (Bruce). Haughey: his life and unlucky deeds. Pp xii, 308. London: Harper Collins, 1993.
Charles Haughey.

3103   ARNOLD (Bruce). The turning point for Irish modernism. In *Art is my life*, pp 3-13 (1991).
Mainie Jellett and the Society of Dublin Painters.

3104   ARTHURS (Miriam). Down on the farm. In *Swords Voices*, i, 17-22 (1992/93).
Farming in the 1930s.

A.S. See 1974.

3105   AUSTIN (Valerie A.). The Céilí and the Public Dance Halls Act, 1935. In *Eire-Ireland*, xxviii, no. 3, pp 7-16 (1993).

BAKER (Allan C.). See 3027.

3106   BAKER (Susan). Environment. In *Political issues in Ireland today*, pp 186-214 (1994).

Ballypatrick Co-operative Dairy Society Ltd. See 1978.

3107   BANCE (Michael). Smokey Joe: the life and times of a provincial newspaper editor. Pp 168. Dublin: MO Books, 1994.
James Joseph Walsh, 1905-92, of the *Munster Express*.

3108   BARLOW (Dorothy). Aiken's mission to the United States in 1941: a reinterpretation. In *Études Irlandaises*, xix, no. 1, pp 121-37 (1994).

3109   BARNWALL (Richard). 'The Norman invasion'. In *Swords Voices*, i, no. 2, pp 2-5 (1994).
Memories of north County Dublin.

3110   BARRY (Michael). Great aviation stories. Vol. I. Pp 160. Fermoy: Saturn Books, 1993.

3111   BAUMGARTEN (Rolf). Myles Dillon (1900-1972): a bibliography. In *Celtica*, xi, 1-14 (1976).

BEAN (Philip A.). See 1983.

3112   BELL (J. Bowyer). Ireland and the Spanish Civil War, 1936 to 1939. In *Strong words, brave deeds*, pp 240-66 (1994).

BERGER (Pamela). See 1995.

BHREATHNACH-LYNCH (Síghle). See 1998, 1999.

3113   Binneas thar meon: a collection of songs and airs made by Liam de Noraidh in east Munster. Vol. 1. Ed. Dáithí Ó hÓgáin, in collaboration with Marion Deasy. Pp 296. Baile Átha Cliath: An Coláiste Ollscoile, Comhairle Bhéaloideas Éireann, 1994.
Collected between 1940-47. Text in Irish and English.

3114   The Birmingham Six: an appalling vista. Ed. Oscar Gilligan. Pp 239. Dublin: Literéire, 1990.

BOLGER (Pat). See 2003.

BOOTH (John). See 2005.

BOOTH (Lionel). See 2006.

3115   BOURKE (Marcus). Murder at Marlhill: was Harry Gleeson innocent? Pp vii, 123. Dublin: Geography Publications, c.1993.
Harry Gleeson, d. 1941.

BOURKE (Tommy). See 2968.

3116   BOWE (Nicola Gordon). The Friends of the National Collections of Ireland. In *Art is my life*, pp 15-30 (1991).
Founded 1924 by Sarah Purser.

BOWE (Nicola Gordon). See 2015.

3117   BOWMAN (John). 'The wolf in sheep's clothing': Richard Hayes's proposal for a new National Library of Ireland, 1959-60. In *Modern Irish democracy*, pp 44-61 (1993).

3118   BOYCE (Frank). Irish catholicism in Liverpool: the 1920s and 1930s. In *The Irish in British labour history*, pp 86-101 (1993).

        BRADSHAW (Brendan). See GRAHAM (Tommy).

3119   BRADY (Ciaran). 'Constructive and instrumental': the dilemma of Ireland's first 'new historians'. In *Interpreting Irish history*, pp 3-31 (1994).

        BRANDT (Ruth). See McCORMICK (Liam).

3120   BRANNIGAN (Niall R.). Changing of the guard. Curragh evacuation 70 years on. In *An Cosantóir*, lii, no. 12, pp 29-30 (1992).

3121   BREATHNACH (Proinnsias). Bunús sóisialta na polaitíochta in Éirinn: léirmheas stáiriúil. In *Oghma*, i, 8-16 (1989).

3122   BREATHNACH (Proinnsias). An phleanáil réigiúnach in Éirinn. Nár mhaith an rud í? In *Oghma*, iii, 24-33 (1991).

        BRENNAN (Helen). See 2027.

3123   BRENNAN (Robert). That building at the West Pier. In *Dun Laoghaire Jn.*, iii, 32-4 (1993).

        BRENNAN-HOLOHAN (Mary P.). See 2028.

        BRESNIHAN (Brian). See 2029.

        BRIGGS (George). See 2837.

3124   BRODERICK (Eugene). The Blueshirts in Waterford, 1932-1934. Part One. In *Decies*, xlviii, 54-63 (1993). Part 2. In *Decies*, xlix, 55-61 (1994).

3125   BRODERICK (Eugene). The corporate labour policy of Fine Gael, 1934. In *I.H.S.*, xxix, 88-99 (1994).

3126   BRODERICK (Joe). De Valera and Archbishop Daniel Mannix. In *Hist. Ire.*, ii, no. 3, pp 37-42 (1994).

3127   BROPHY (Kevin T.). Walking the line: scenes from an army childhood. Pp 189. Edinburgh: Mainstream Publishing, 1994.
        Galway, *c*.1950s.

3128   BROPHY (P.J.). Circles of friends: a personal memoir. Pp viii, 100. Carlow: Carlovian Press, [1993].
        R.C. priest born Castlemor, Co. Carlow, 1919.

3129   BROSNAN (Declan T.). The Irish Augustinians in Kenya, 1991-1992. In *The Irish Augustinians in Rome, 1656-1994*, pp 211-21 (1994).

3130   BROWN (Alice) and GALLIGAN (Yvonne). Views from the periphery: changing the political agenda for women in the Republic of Ireland and in Scotland. In *West European Politics*, xvi, 165-89 (1993).

3131   BRUNICARDI (Daire). The Mercantile Marine in the second world war. In *An Cosantóir*, lii, no. 4, pp 34-6 (1992.).

3132   BURKE (Jim). Craggaunowen project, Quin, Co. Clare. In *The Other Clare*, i, 13-15 (1977).

3133   BURKE (Pat). The ring of the anvil. Pp 96. Dublin: [s.n.], [1994?]. Dublin 1930s-1950s.

BUTLER (Elizabeth). See 2044.

BUTLER (Katherine). See 2045.

3134   BYRNE (Anne). Revealing figures?: official statistics and rural Irish women. In *Irish women's studies reader*, pp 140-61 (1993). 1961-91.

3135   BYRNE (Damien). Camelot comes to Ireland: the visit of John F. Kennedy in 1963. In *U.C.D. Hist. Rev.*, viii, 1-6 (1994).

BYRNE (Liam). See 2049.

3136   C (WJP). Appreciation. M.J. O'Malley Blackwell (1913-1993). In *Cathair na Mart*, xiii, 160 (1993).

CAHILL (Marie). See 2054.

CAMPBELL (Fergus). See 2059.

CARGEEG (George). See 2064.

3137   CARON (David). An Túr Gloine stained glass in Arizona. In *Ir. Arts Rev. Yearbk*, pp 174-80 (1994).
The stained glass windows in Brophy College, Arizona, were commissioned by Irish-American Mrs Amelia Brophy from 5 Irish stained glass artists in the 1920s and 1930s.

CARROLL (Denis). See 2066.

3138   CARROLL (Joseph). U.S.-Irish relations, 1939-45. In *Ir. Sword*, xix, 99-105 (1993/95).

3139   CARSWELL (Leslie). Health policy. In *Political issues in Ireland today*, pp 143-60 (1994).

3140   CARTY (R.K.). From tradition to modernity, and back again: party building in Ireland. In *Modern Irish democracy*, pp 24-43 (1993).

CASSIN (Maeve). See 2073.

3141   CLAFFEY (Úna). The women who won: women of the 27th Dáil. Pp 158. Dublin: Attic Press, 1993.
20 women T.D.s.

3142   CLARK (Denis). Portraying Irish America: trans-Atlantic revisions. In *Hist. Ire.*, ii, no. 4, pp 48-52 (1994).

3143   COAKLEY (John). Minor parties in Irish political life, 1922-1989. In *Econ. & Soc. Rev.*, xxi, 269-97 (1990).

3144   COHAN (A.S.), et. al. The used vote and electoral outcomes: the Irish general election of 1973. In *British Jn. of Political Science*, v, 363-83 (1975).

COHAN (A.S.). See LIJPHART (Arend).

3145   Coill Dubh, 1952-1992. Pp [10], 210. [Coill Dubh, Co. Kildare]: Coill Dubh Book Committee, [1993].
Village established by Bord na Móna to house workers and their families employed at Allenwood peat-fired generating station.

COLDREY (Barry M.). See 2091.

3146   COLEMAN (Marie). Historians and the Irish Civil War. In *U.C.D. Hist. Rev.*, viii, 37-40 (1994).

3147   COLLEY (Michael). The communicators: the history of the Public Relations Institute of Ireland, 1953-1993. Pp xiii, 113. Dublin: Public Relations Institute of Ireland, 1993.

COLLINS (M.E.). See 2094.

COLLINS (Michael). See 2095.

3148   COLLINS (Neil). Parties and elections: recent developments. In *Political issues in Ireland today*, pp 5-25 (1994).

3149   COLLINS (Peter). Atlantic bridge builder. In *Hist. Ire.*, ii, no. 3, pp 54-6 (1994).
Interview with Catherine Shannon, professor of history at Westfield State College in Massachusetts.

3150   COLLINS (Stephen). Spring and the labour story. Pp 223. Dublin: O'Brien Press, 1993.
Dick Spring and the Irish labour party.

The communists and the Irish revolution (1993). See 2104.

3151   COMYN (James). Leave to appeal: further legal memoirs. Pp 168. Dublin: Round Hall Press, 1994.

3152   COMYN (James). Watching brief: further memoirs of an Irishman at law in England. Pp 170. Dublin: Round Hall Press, 1993.
Born 1921, Q.C. and High Court Judge.

CONNOLLY (Paddy). See 2111

CONNOLLY (Ross M.). See 2113.

3153   CONWAY (Sheelagh). The faraway hills are green: voices of Irish women in Canada. Pp 338. Toronto: Women's Press, 1992.

3154   COOGAN (Tim Pat). De Valera: Long fellow, long shadow. Pp xii, 772. London: Hutchinson, 1993.
Eamon de Valera, 1882-1975.

COOGAN (Tim Pat). See 2117.

COOKE (Jim). See 2119, 2120.

COOLAHAN (John). See NORTH (Reg).

COONEY (Gabriel). See MITCHELL (Frank).

COONEY (D.A. Levistone). See 2122.

3155   CORCORAN (Mary P.). Irish illegals: transients between two societies. Pp xvii, 205. Westport, Conn.: Greenwood Press, 1993. (Contributions in ethnic studies, no. 32)

Cork Archives Institute. See 2124.

3156   CORKERY (John M.A.). Suggestions for a programme. In *Teathba*, i, no. 1, pp 5-9 (1969).
Outline programme for the Longford Historical Society.

3157   COUGHLAN (Anthony). C. Desmond Greaves - politician and historian. In *Reconsiderations of Irish history and culture*, pp 157-77 (1994).

3158   COUGHLAN (Anthony). Ireland's marxist historians. In *Interpreting Irish history*, pp 288-305 (1994).

3159   COUGHLAN (Pat). Too young to vote: 1972 and twenty one years of Brideview United in Tallow. Pp 71. Tallow, Co. Waterford: Brideview United A.F.C., 1993.

3160   COULTER (Carol). Protestants in the South. Beyond the stereotyped views. In *Ir. Reporter*, xvi, 14-16 (1994).

COULTER (Carol). See 2129.

COUSINS (Mel). See 2130.

3161   COYLE (James P.). Transition to peace. In *Ir. Sword*, xix, 72-6 (1993/95).

COX (Ronald C.). See 2132.

CREMIN (Vicky). See 2140.

3162   CRONIN (Mike). Blueshirts, sports and socials. In *Hist. Ire.*, ii, no. 3, pp 43-7 (1994).

3163   CRONIN (Mike). The socio-economic background and membership of the Blueshirt movement, 1932-5. In *I.H.S.*, xxix, 234-49 (1994).

CROOKES (Gearóid). See 2143.

3164   CROWE (Fiona). Towards a history of home economics: a chronology of Irish home economics textbooks. In *Ir. Home Economics Jn.*, ii, no. 2, pp 34-44 (1992).

3165   CROWLEY (Niall). Irish travellers: a contribution denied. In *Eire-Ireland*, xxix, no. 3, pp 147-55 (1994).

3166   CULLEN (Donal). Ireland on the ball: a complete record of the international matches of the Republic of Ireland soccer team, March 1926 to June 1993. Pp 336. Dublin: Elo Publications, 1993.

      CULLEN (Elsie). See 2147.

      CULLEN (L.M.). See WHELAN (Kevin).

      CULLINGFORD (Elizabeth Butler). See 2148.

      An Cumann Parnell [1993]. See 2149.

      CURTIN (Chris). See 2154.

3167   CURTIS (L.P. jr). The greening of Irish history. In *Eire-Ireland*, xxix, no. 2, pp 7-28 (1994).

      CUSACK (Gerard). See 2155.

3168   DALTON (Greg). My own backyard: [Dublin in the fifties]. Pp 112. Dublin: Wolfhound Press, 1994.

3169   DALY (Cahal B.). The ministry of music - remembering Palestrina. In *The Furrow*, xlv, 203-11 (1994).

      DALY (Mairie). See *Eadrainn*(1994).

      DALY (Mary E.). See 2159, 2160, 2162..

3170   DANIELS (Mary). Exile or opportunity? Irish nurses and Wirral midwives. In *Ir. Studies Rev.*, v, 4-8 (1993).

3171   An daonlathas agus an córas rialtais. Basil Chubb ag caint le hOghma. In *Oghma*, i, 43-8 (1989).

      D'ARCY (Fergus). See 2166.

      DAVIES (Mary). See 2169.

3172   DAVIS (Troy). The Irish civil war and the 'international preposition' of 1922-23. In *Eire-Ireland*, xxix, no. 2, pp 92-112 (1994).

3173   DEALE (Julian). Dance macabre: the Ball murder. Attorney General - v - Edward Ball 1936. In *Blackrock Soc. Proc*, ii, 36-9. (1993/94).

      DEASY (Marion). See *Binneas thar meon*.

      De BHALDRAITHE (Pádraig). See 2176.

3174   De BHALDRAITHE (Tomás).   Dáithí - scoláire daonna.   In *Dáithí Ó hUaithne*, pp 73-84 (1994).

3175   De BÚRCA (Séamus).   Brendan Behan: a memoir. 3rd ed.   Pp 72.   Dublin: P.J. Bourke, 1993.
    Previous ed., 1985.

De COGAN (Donard).   See 2177.

3176   DELANY (Hilary).   The Courts acts 1924-1991.   Pp xliv, 339.   Dublin: Round Hall Press, 1994.   (Irish statutes annotated, 3)

3177   DELAP (Breandán).   Úrscéalta stairiúla na Gaeilge.   Pp 181.   Baile Átha Cliath: An Clóchomhar, 1993.   (Leabhair thaighde, 75)
    Irish fiction, 20th century.

De NORAIDH (Liam).   See *Binneas thar meon.*

3178   De PAOR (Liam).   Dáithí an tinteáin.   In *Dáithí Ó hUaithne*, pp 85-98 (1994).
    'Le tacaíocht chuimhne ó Mháire de Paor'.

3179   De PAOR (Tomás).   Eogadh an dá Dháil.   In *Irisleabhar Mha Nuad*, pp 77-81 (1993).

3180   De ROSSA (Proinsias).   Beyond flags and emblems.   In *Times Change*, iii (autumn/winter), 4-5 (1994).

DESMOND (Derry).   See KEATING (Paul).

DEVALLY (Liam).   See 2182.

3181   DICKSON (David).   McDowell at eighty.   In *Hist. Ire.*, i, no. 4, pp 9-12 (1993).
    Interview with R.B. McDowell, who has been associated with the School of History in Trinity College for over sixty years.

3182   DILLON (Martin).   The enemy within.   Pp xxii, 297.   London: Doubleday, 1994.
    The I.R.A. bombing campaign in Britain, 1938- .

DOCKRELL (John H.).   See 2186.

DODD (Joe).   See 2837.

DODD (Luke).   See 2187.

3183   DOHERTY (Richard).   Clear the way! a history of the 38th (Irish) Brigade, 1941-1947.   Pp xvii, 336.   Dublin: Irish Academic Press, 1993.

3184   DOHERTY (Richard).   Irish generals: Irish generals in the British army in the second world war.   Pp 201.   Belfast: Appletree Press, 1993.

3185   DONLEAVY (J.P.).   The history of the Ginger Man.   Pp 517.   London: Viking, 1994.

3186   DONNELLY (Brian).   The National Army enters Cork August 1922.   A diary account by Mr Frank Brewitt.   In *Ir. Archives*, pp 53-8 (autumn, 1994).

DONNELLY (James S. jr).   See 2188.

3187   DONNELLY (Seán) and HOLOHAN (Renagh).   Partnership: the story of the 1992 general election.   Pp 403.   Rathcoole, Co. Dublin: Sean Donnelly, 1993.
Includes data on general elections and by-elections from 1923 to 1992.

DOOLEY (Terence A.M.).   See 2191, 2193.

3188   DOORLY (Mary Rose).   Hidden memories: the personal recollections of survivors and witnesses to the Holocaust living in Ireland.   Pp 112.   Dublin: Blackwater Press, 1994.

3189   DOUGLAS (Francis).   The history of the Irish Pre-School Playgroups Association.   Pp viii, 100.   Dublin: Irish Pre-School Playgroups Association, 1994.

3190   DOYLE (Oliver).   GAA football finals, 1953-4.   In *Irish Railway Rec. Soc. Jn.*, xviii, no. 123, pp 322-30. (1994).
Reduction in travel time with introduction of diesel engines.

DOYLE (Oliver).   See 2201.

DOYLE (Tom).   See 2203.

3191   DRENNAN (Mary Phil).   You may talk now!   Pp 96.   Blarney, Co. Cork: On Stream Publications, 1994.
Memoirs of a Cobh orphanage, 1954- .

3192   DRUDY (Sheelagh) and LYNCH (Kathleen).   Schools and society in Ireland. Pp xi, 289.   Dublin: Gill & Macmillan, 1993.

3193   DRURY (Ronan).   Canon J.G. McGarry, editor [of *The Furrow*] 1950-1977. In *The Furrow*, xxviii, 535 (1977).

3194   DUFF (Frank).   A Free State soldier's memories of the Civil War.   In *Tipp. Hist. Jn.*, pp 57-8 (1993).

DUFFY (Francis).   See 2205.

3195   DUGGAN (J.P.).   Germany and Ireland in World War II.   In *Ir. Sword*, xix, 93-8 (1993/95).

3196   DUKES (Alan).   Éire san Aontas Eorpach.   In *Oghma*, no. 6, pp 57-62 (1994).

3197   DUKES (Jim).   The emergency services.   In *Ir. Sword*, xix, 66-71 (1993/95).

DUNCAN (Mary Frances).   See 2210.

3198   DUNNE (Eamonn).   Action and reaction: Catholic lay organisations in Dublin in the 1920s and 1930s.   In *Archiv. Hib.*, xlviii, 107-18 (1994).

3199   DUNPHY (Richard).   'National self-determination' once again.   In *Times Change*, ii, (summer), 4-5 (1994).

3200   DWYER (T. Ryle). Guests of the state: the story of the Allied and Axis servicemen interned in Ireland during World War II. Pp 252. Dingle: Brandon Press, 1994.

3201   E (P.K.). Martin Joyce 1910-1991. In *Galway Arch. Soc. Jn.*, xlv, 165-6 (1993).

3202   Eadrainn: history of Cork federation, Irish Countrywomen's Association 1936-1994. Compiled by Mairie Daly, Kathleen Gleeson. Pp 134. [Cork]: Cork Federation, Irish Countrywomen's Association, 1994.

        The economic development of Ireland since 1870. See 2217.

3203   EGAN (Desmond). Peter Connolly (1927-1987). In *The Furrow*, xxxviii, 428-35 (1987).
        Priest of the diocese of Meath and professor of English at St Patrick's College, Maynooth.

        ELEBERT (Michael). See 2218.

        EMMONS (David M.). See 2225.

3204   ENGLISH (Richard). Ireland, 1982-94. In *The course of Irish history,* rev. ed., pp 362-81 (1994).

3205   ENGLISH (Richard). 'Paying no heed to public clamor': Irish republican solipsism in the 1930s. In *I.H.S.*, xxviii, 426-39 (1993).

3206   ENGLISH (Richard). Radicals and the republic: socialist republicanism in the Irish Free State, 1925-1937. Pp viii, 309. Oxford: Clarendon Press, 1994.

3207   FAHERTY (Padhraic). Pitch my tent in the Lord: memories of Fr Michael Morahan, S.J. Pp 122. Barna, Co. Galway: P. Faherty, 1993.
        1914-92, missionary priest.

        FAIRHALL (James). See 2232.

        FALKINER (Ninian). See 3091.

3208   FALLON (Ivan). The player: the life of Tony O'Reilly. Pp 364. London: Hodder & Stoughton, 1994.

        Families of Inishbofin Island. See 2233.

        FARMAR (Tony). See 2234.

3209   FARRELL (Brian). 'Cagey and secretive': responsibility, executive confidentiality and the public interest. In *Modern Irish democracy*, pp 82-103 (1993).

3210   FARRELL (Brian). Labour and the political revolution. In *Trade union century*, pp 42-53 (1994).

3211   FARRELL (Brian). The political role of cabinet ministers in Ireland. In *Cabinet ministers and parliamentary government*, pp 73-87 (1994).

FARRELL (Brian). See 2235.

3212   FARRELL (David M.) and WORTMANN (Martin). Party strategies in the electoral market: political marketing in West Germany, Britain and Ireland. In *European Jn. of Political Res.*, xv, 293-318 (1987).

3213   FARRELL (Mark). Sale of de Valera letter. In *Ir. Archives*, pp 2-4 (autumn 1994).
Includes copy of letter to Robert Brennan, ambassador in Washington and his reply, May 1945.

3214   FARSON (Negley). An instinct much stronger than reason. In *Connemara*, i, no. 1, pp 65-9 (1993).
An insight into the mind of Pádraic Ó Conaire by the American writer.

3215   FAY (Patrick). The Amendments to the Constitution Committee 1926. In *Administration*, xxvi, 331-51 (1978).

3216   FENNELL (Desmond). Against revisionism. In *Interpreting Irish history*, pp 183-90 (1994).
Reprinted from *The revision of Irish nationalism* (Dublin, 1989), pp 62-70.

FENNELLY (Teddy). See *Glimpses of Portlaoise*.

3217   FERRIS (Paul). Caitlin: the life of Caitlin Thomas. Pp ix, 278. London: Hutchinson, 1993.
Caitlin Macnamara, wife of Dylan Thomas, 1913-

FERRIS (Tom). See 2241.

FIELDING (Steve). See 2246.

3218   FINN (T. Vincent). Thirty years a'growing: the past, the present and the future of Irish broadcasting. In *Ir. Communications Rev.*, iii, 73-8 (1993).

3219   FITZGERALD (Danny). 20 years of amateur dramatics 1937-1957. In *Oola Past & Present*, i, 31-3 (1992).

3220   FITZGERALD (Danny). Amateur dramatics - Part two 1957-1970. In *Oola Past & Present*, ii, 18-21 (1993).

3221   FITZGERALD (Doireann). How Leon Trotsky was refused admission to the Irish Free State. In *U.C.D. Hist. Rev.*, vii, 10-14 (1993).

3222   FITZGERALD (J.D.). County Donegal railways 1921-23. In *Irish Railway Rec. Soc. Jn.*, xviii, no. 121, pp 210-26 (1993).

3223   FITZGERALD (Seamus). The Arklow war graves. In *Arklow Hist. Soc. Jn.*, pp 22-3 (1992/93).

3224   FITZMAURICE (J.). The military police through the years. In *An Cosantóir*, li, no. 8, pp 4-7 (1991).

FITZMAURICE (James). See 2256.

FITZPATRICK (David). See 2257.

FITZPATRICK (Georgina).   See 2259.

FITZPATRICK (Patrick).   See 2397.

3225   FITZ-SIMON (Christopher).   The boys: a double biography.   Pp 320.
London: Nick Hern Books, 1994.
Micheál Mac Liammóir and Hilton Edwards.

FLANNERY (Michael).   See 2261.

FOLEY (Denis).   See 2264.

3226   FORRISTAL (Desmond).   Edel Quinn, 1907-1944.   Pp 232.   Dublin:
Dominican Publications, 1994.

3227   FOSTER (Roy).   History and the Irish question.   In *Interpreting Irish
history*, pp 122-45 (1994).
Reprinted from *Paddy and Mr Punch*, 1993.

FOSTER (Roy).   See GRAY (Peter).

FREITAG (Barbara).   See 2275.

3228   From Clonsast to Ballyburley, Joe O'Reilly and 4th class, Convent school,
Edenderry.   Pp 176. [S.l.]: [Joe O'Reilly], 1994.
Cos Laois and Offaly.

FULHAM (Brendan).   See 2277.

3229   FURLONG (Nicholas).   The greatest hurling decade: Wexford and the epic
teams of the '50s.   Pp 208. Dublin: Wolfhound Press, 1993.

3230   GABLER (Hans Walter).   What 'Ulysses' requires.   In *Bibliog. Soc.
America Papers*, lxxxvii, 187-248 (1993).
Discussion of the publishing history of James Joyce's *Ulysses*.

3231   GALLAGHER (Michael).   Candidate selection in Ireland: the impact of
localism and the electoral system.   In *Brit. Jn. Political Science*, x, 489-503
(1980).

GALLAGHER (Michael).   See *Irish elections 1922-44*.

GALLAGHER (Michael).   See LAVER (Michael).

GALLIGAN (Yvonne).   See BROWN (Alice).

3232   GARDINER (Frances).   Political interest and participation of Irish women
1922-1992: the unfinished revolution.   In *Irish women's studies reader*, pp
45-78 (1993).

3233   GARVEY (Rosemary).   Senior citizens.   Letters from George Augustus
Moore (1852-1933) to John William Frederick Garvey (1856-1940).   In
Cathair na Mart, xiii, 125-34 (1993).

3234   GARVIN (Tom).   Political power and economic development in Ireland: a
comparative perspective. In *People power*, pp 32-6 (1993).
Irish economic growth, 1922-58.

3235   GARVIN (Tom). Unenthusiastic democrats: the emergence of Irish democracy. In *Modern Irish democracy*, pp 9-23 (1993).

GARVIN (Tom). See 2281.

GATENBY (Peter). See 2282.

3236   GAUGHAN (J. Anthony). Alfred O'Rahilly, 3: Controversialist. Part 2: Catholic apologist. Pp 349. Dublin: Kingdom Books, 1993.
Alfred O'Rahilly, 1884-1969.

3237   GAVIN (Nora) and GOSSON (May). Life is memories. In *Swords Voices*, i, no. 2, pp 28-32 (1994).
Memories of Swords.

3238   GEARY (Eithne). Emigrating from Swords... In *Swords Voices*, i, 11-14 (1992/93).
Emigration to England and America, returning to Ireland.

GEOGHEGAN (Vincent). See 2285.

3239   GERAGHTY (Des). Luke Kelly: a memoir. Pp 156. Dublin: Basement Press, 1994.

3240   GILCHRIST (Joe). Memories & musings: boyhood memories of Leitrim. Pp 48. [Manorhamilton]: Joe Gilchrist, [1993?].
Joe Gilchrist, 1916-

3241   GILLESPIE (Raymond). Historical revisits. T.W. Moody, *The Londonderry plantation, 1609-41* (1939). In *I.H.S.*, xxix, 109-13 (1994).

GILLIGAN (Oscar). See *The Birmingham Six*.

3242   GIRVIN (Brian). Trade unions and economic development. In *Trade union century*, pp 117-32 (1994).

GLEESON (Kathleen). See *Eadrainn* (1994).

3243   Glimpses of Portlaoise: a pictorial parade. Part 1. *Ed.* John O'Brien and Teddy Fennelly. Pp 100. Portlaoise: Leinster Express, 1993.

GOGARTY (Oliver St John). See 2298.

3244   GOLDRING (Maurice). Dissolvers of borders. In *Times Change*, i (spring), 20-23 (1994).
The role of *The Bell*.

GOLDRING (Maurice). See 2300, 2301.

3245   GORMAN (Liam). The school. In *Oola Past & Present*, ii, 6-10 (1993).

3246   GORMAN (Liam). Village arts & farces. The digs, pigs & jigs of wartime. In *Oola Past & Present*, iii, 9-14 (1994).
'The Emergency', 1939-45.

GORMAN (Liam). See 2304.

GOSSON (May).　See GAVIN (Nora).

GRACE (Daniel).　See 2305.

GRAHAM (B.J.).　See 2306.

3247　GRAHAM (Colin).　'Liminal spaces': post-colonial theories and Irish culture. In *The Irish Review*, xvi, 29-43 (1994).

3248　GRAHAM (Mary).　The Cradlehouse ...　In *Swords Voices*, i, 7-10 (1992/93).
Memories of Brackenstown and Swords.

3249　GRAHAM (Tommy).　A man with a mission.　In *Hist. Ire.*, i, no. 1, pp 52-5 (1993).
Interview with Dr Brendan Bradshaw of Queen's College, Cambridge.

3250　GRAY (Peter).　Our man at Oxford.　In *Hist. Ire.*, i, no. 3, pp 9-12 (1993).
Interview with Roy Foster, Carroll Professor of Irish History at Oxford University.

GRAY (Peter).　See NUTT (Kathleen).

3251　GREENSLADE (Liam).　An tonn gheal:　historical reflections on Irish migrants in Britain in the 1980s.　In *The Irish in British labour history*, pp 29-46 (1993).

GRENE (Nicholas).　See 2987.

3252　GRIFFEY (Nicholas).　From silence to speech: fifty years with the deaf.　Pp vi, 186. Dublin: Dominican Publications, 1994.
Education of deaf in Ireland.

3253　GRIFFIN (Alice).　Memories of the Liffey Valley.　Pp 92.　Dublin: FÁS, [1994?].

3254　GRIFFIN (Victor).　Mark of protest: an autobiography.　Pp 235.　Dublin: Gill & Macmillan, 1993.
Dean of St Patrick's Cathedral, b. 1924.

3255　GROGAN (William).　The day Dinny Lacey died.　In *Tipp. Hist. Jn.*, p. 56 (1993).

GUERIN (Michael).　See 2321.

GULLIVER (P.H.).　See 2324.

3256　H. (M.).　Henry A. Wheeler (1916-1993), president 1973-1976.　In *R.S.A.I. Jn.*, cxxiv, 219-20 (1994).

3257　HADFIELD (Brigid).　The Anglo-Irish agreement 1985- :　blue print or green print.　In *N. Ireland Legal Quart.*, xxxvii, 1-28 (1986).

HALL (Michael).　See 2328.

3258　HAMILTON (Douglas).　Industrial development.　In *Political issues in Ireland today*, pp 98-117 (1994).

HAMLIN (Ann). See MAXWELL (Nick).

3259   HANNON (Michael). Being Irish in Britain - yesterday and today. In *Irishways*, iii, 15-16 (1992).

3260   HARDIMAN (Niamh). Pay bargaining: confrontation and consensus. In *Trade union century*, pp 147-58 (1994).

3261   HARKNESS (David). Nicholas Mansergh: historian of modern Ireland. In *Études Irlandaises*, xix, no. 2, pp 87-95 (1994).
Nicholas Mansergh (1910-91).

3262   HARKNESS (David). Phillip Nicholas Seton Mansergh, 1910-1991. In *Brit. Acad. Proc.*, lxxxii, 415-30 (1993).

3263   HARMON (Maurice). Seán O'Faolain: a life. Pp 326. London: Constable, 1994.

3264   HARTE (Stephen). The late Father Christy Walsh, 1917-1991, R.I.P. An appreciation. In *Bandon Hist. Jn.*, ix, 53-6 (1993).

3265   HARVEY (Dan). General Michael Collins's notebook August 1922. In *Cork Hist. Soc. Jn.*, xcix, 130-32 (1994).

HASLEM (Richard). See KNOX (Colin).

3266   HASTINGS (Catríona) and Ó CIOSÁIN (Eamon). Loscadh ag an Stáca? In *Oghma*, no. 5, pp 33-9 (1993).

HATTON (Timothy J.). See 2354,.

3267   HAWKINS (Richard). 'Bending the beam': myth and reality in the bombing of Coventry, Belfast and Dublin. In *Ir. Sword*, xix, 131-43 (1993/95).

3268   HAYDEN (Jacqueline). Lady G: a biography of the honourable Lady Goulding LL.D. Pp 206. Dublin: Town House, 1994.

HAYES (Alan). See 2355.

3269   HAYES (Maurice). 'Local differences': Ireland in the European mosaic. In *Eire-Ireland*, xxviii, no. 1, pp 121-31 (1993).

3270   HAYTER-HAMES (Jane). Cynthia Longfield 1896-1991. In *The book of Cloyne*, pp 190-96 (1994).
Natural scientist.

3271   HAZELKORN (Ellen) and PATTERSON (Henry). The new politics of the Irish Republic. In *New Left Review*, no. 207, pp 49-71 (1994).

HAZELKORN (Ellen). See *Let in the light* (1993).

HEALY (James). See 2356.

3272   HEALY (John). Healy, reporter: the early years. Pp 171. Achill, Co. Mayo: House of Healy, 1991.

HEALY (Roisin). See 2357.

HEALY (T.M.). See 2358.

HEARN (Mona). See 2359.

3273   HEARNE (John M.). The phoenix arises: the early years of Waterford Glass. In *Decies*, l, 67-71 (1994).

3274   HEATHER (Alannah). From Errislannan: scenes from a painter's life. Pp 210. Dublin: Lilliput Press, 1993.
Heather family, Clifden, Co. Galway, 1790s-1960s. Alannah Medora Heather Bent, 1901-92.

HEGARTY (Dave). See 2360, 2361.

HERLIHY (Jim). See 2365, 2366.

HERON (Anastatia). See 2367.

3275   HERON (Marianne). Fighting spirit: Sheila Conroy. Pp [5], 154. Dublin: Attic Press, 1993.
Trade unionist, 1918- .

3276   HERZ (Dietmar). Der Nordirland Konflikt in der Politik Dublins. In *Nordirland in Geschichte und Gegenwart*, pp 257-75 (1994).

HICKEY (Donal). See 2370.

3277   HICKEY (Raymond). The Irish Augustinians in Nigeria, 1939-1992. In *The Irish Augustinians in Rome, 1656-1994*, pp 155-85 (1994).

3278   HILL (Ian). Staging the 'Troubles'. In *Theatre Ireland*, xxxi, 42-6 (1993).

HILL (Myrtle). See 2377.

3279   HILL (Ronald J.) and MARSH (Michael). Introduction: Basil Chubb and Irish politics. In *Modern Irish democracy*, pp 1-8 (1993).

3280   HILLYARD (Paddy). Soapbox. The Prevention of Terrorism Act. In *Ir. Studies Rev.*, iii, 43-4 (1993).

3281   HILLYARD (Paddy). Suspect community: people's experience of the Prevention of Terrorism Acts in Britain. Pp xv, 300. London: Pluto Press, in association with Liberty, 1993.

3282   HINCHY (F.S.). A Palatine childhood. In *Old Limerick Jn.*, xxx, 18-20 (1993).

3283   HINDLEY (Reg). Clear Island (Oileán Chléire) in 1958: a study in geolinguistic transition. In *Ir. Geography*, xxvii, 97-106 (1994).

History of Kilbride G.A.A. Club. See 2378.

Hockey in Trinity. See 2379.

HODGINS (Jack). See 2380.

HOGAN (Edmund M.). See 2381.

HOGAN (Oliver). See 2382.

Hollyford National School [1993]. See 2384.

3284 HOLMES (Michael), REES (Nicholas) and WHELAN (Bernadette). The poor relation: Irish foreign policy and the third world. Pp 229. Dublin: Trócaire and Gill and Macmillan, 1993. (Trócaire world topics, 3)

3285 HOLOHAN (Francis T.). History teaching in the Irish Free State 1922-35. In *Hist. Ire.*, ii, no. 4, pp 53-5 (1994).

3286 HOLOHAN (Peter). Dan Keating - an appreciation. In *In the Shadow of the Steeple*, iv, 39-40 (1994).

HOLOHAN (Renagh). See DONNELLY (Seán).

HOOD (Susan). See 2306.

HOWE (Violet). See McCUTCHEON (Catherine).

HOWLIN (Phil). See 2390.

3287 HUME (John). A new Ireland in a new Europe. In *Northern Ireland and the politics of reconciliation*, pp 226-33 (1993).

3288 HUMPHREYS (Madeleine). Issue of confidence: the decline of the Irish whiskey industry in independent Ireland, 1922-1952. In *Jn. European Econ. Hist.*, xxiii, 93-114 (1994).

HUMPHREYS (Madeleine). See 2395.

A hundred years of Carrigallen school [1993]. See 2396.

A hundred years of Killygarry school. See 2397.

HUNT (John). See 2378.

HURLEY (Frank). See 2399.

3289 HURLEY (Michael). Aubrey Gwynn S.J. (1892-1983); illustration [by] Fiona Kelly. In *Ardmore Jn.*, x, 11-12 (1993).

3290 HUSSEY (Gemma). Ireland today: anatomy of a changing state. Pp 536. Dublin: Town House, 1993.

HYNES (Rory). See 2402.

3291 An iascaireacht in Inis Óirr: sraith léachtaí idir stair agus dian cur síos, a thug Gobnait ní Chonghaile agus Sorcha ní Chonghaile; gcomóradh 50 bliain Scoil Chaomháin Inis Óirr 1942-1992. Pp 40. [Inis Óirr]: [Na hÚdair], 1994. Fishing in the Aran Islands, 1942-1992.

INNES (C.L.). See 2405.

3292 I.R.A.'s courteous arsonists. In *A Window on the Past*, [i], 20 (1987). The burning of Lismullen, home of Sir John Fox Dillon in 1923.

3293   Irish anti-apartheid movement: 1964-1994. Pp 12. [Dublin]: [Irish Anti-Apartheid Movement], [1994?].

Irish Congress of Trade Unions. See 2408.

3294   Irish elections 1922-44: results and analysis. *Ed.* Michael Gallagher. Pp x, 318. Limerick: PSAI Press, 1993. (Sources for the study of Irish politics, 1).

IRWIN (Galen A.). See LIJPHART (Arend).

Is cuimhin linn Kruger. See 2411.

3295   JACOBSEN (John Kurt). Chasing progress in the Irish Republic: ideology, democracy and dependent development. Pp xi, 226. Cambridge: Cambridge University Press, 1994.
        Originally presented as the author's Ph.D. thesis, University of Chicago, 1982.

3296   JEFFARES (Edward). And the British navy provided eats. In *Connemara*, i, no. 1, pp 60-64 (1993).
        Edward Jeffares relates to Breandan O'Scanaill how he was evacuated from Clifden by boat during the Civil War 1922.

JENKINS (William). See 2421.

JOCELYN (Robert). See 2423.

3297   JOHNSON (Nuala C.). Building a nation: an examination of the Irish Gaeltacht Commission report of 1926. In *Jn. Hist. Geog.*, xix, 157-68 (1993).

3298   JOHNSTON (Mairead M.). The Rothe House collection: an Aladdin's cave of costume and textiles. In *Old Kilkenny Rev.*, xlvi, 111-19 (1994).

JOHNSTON (Sheila Turner). See 2425.

3299   JONES (Valerie). The preparatory college system of recruitment to primary teaching. In *Ir. Educational Studies*, xii, 166-78 (1993).

3300   JORDAN (Anthony J.). Seán MacBride: a biography. Pp 199. Dublin: Blackwater Press, 1993.

3301   JORDAN (Anthony J.). To laugh or to weep: a biography of Conor Cruise O'Brien. Pp [13], 253. Dublin: Blackwater Press, 1994.

3302   JORDAN (Heather Bryant). 'A particular flair, a hound's nose, a keen scent': Seán O'Faolain's editorship of *The Bell*. In *Eire-Ireland*, xxix, no. 4, pp 149-60 (1994).

JORDAN (Kieran). See 2429.

3303   K. (H.A.). Helen Maybury Roe. In *Arch. Ire.*, ii, 86 (1988).
        Helen Maybury Roe, 1895-1988.

3304   K. (J.L.). An appreciation. Very Rev. Tobias R. Furlong, P.P., R.I.P. In *Old Wexford Soc. Jn.*, vi, 80 (1976/77).

KAVANAGH (Mary). See 2435.

3305   KEARNEY (Hugh).   The Irish and their history.   In *Interpreting Irish history*, pp 246-52 (1994).
First published in *History Workshop*, xxxi, 149-55 (1991).

KEARNS (Kevin C.). See 2439.

KEATING (Joan). See 2440.

3306   KEATING (Paul) and DESMOND (Derry).   Culture and capitalism in contemporary Ireland. Pp ix, 238. Aldershot: Avebury, 1993.

3307   KELLS (Mary). Religion and the Irish migrant. In *Ir. Studies Rev.*, vi, 16-18 (1994).

3308   KELLY (Aidan). Blackrock in the 1930s. In *Blackrock Soc. Proc.*, i, 2-12 (1992/93).

3309   KENNEDY (Brian P.).   The collecting technique of Sir Alfred Chester Beatty. In *Art is my life*, pp 107-19 (1991).

3310   KENNEDY (Brian P.).   'Ireland To-day' a brave new periodical.   In *U.C.D. Hist. Rev.*, iii, 5-6 (1989).

3311   KENNEDY (Brian P.).   The Irish Free State 1922-49: a visual perspective. In *Ireland*, pp 132-52 (1994).

3312   KENNEDY (Brian P.).   James White: a brief biography.   In *Art is my life*, pp ix-xvi (1991).

3313   KENNEDY (Dennis). Constitutional change in the 1990s. In *Political issues in Ireland today*, pp 26-39 (1994).

KENNEDY (Liam). See 2463.

3314   KEOGH (Dermot) and NOLAN (Aengus).   Anglo-Irish diplomatic relations and World War II. In *Ir. Sword*, xix, 106-30 (1993/95).

3315   KEOGH (Dermot). The Catholic church and the Irish Free State 1923-1932. In *Hist. Ire.*, ii, no. 1, pp 47-51 (1994).

3316   KEOGH (Dermot). Church and state in Ireland 1922-1959. In *Renaissance and Modern Studies*, xxxvi, 70-92 (1993).

3317   KEOGH (Dermot). An eye witness to history: Fr Alexander T. McCabe and the Spanish Civil War, 1936-1939. In *Breifne*, viii, 445-88 (1994).

3318   KEOGH (Dermot).   Twentieth-century Ireland: nation and state. Pp xxiii, 504. Dublin: Gill and Macmillan, 1994. (New Gill History of Ireland, 6)

KEOGH (Dermot). See 2449.

3319   KIBERD (Damien). Countering the liberal newspeak.   Confronted by crass comment and baseless abuse. In *Ir. Reporter*, xvi, 22-3 (1994).

3320   KIBERD (Declan).   Idir dhá chultúr.   Pp 287.   Baile Átha   Cliath:
        Coiscéim, 1993.
        Irish literature in Irish and English.

        KIBERD (Declan).   See 2455.

        KIELTY (Frances).   See 2458.

3321   KILBRIDE-JONES (H.E.).   Adolf Mahr.   In Arch. Ire., vii, no. 3, pp 29-30
        (1993).
        Director of the National Museum of Ireland, 1927-39.

3322   KINANE (Vincent).   Trinity Closet Press, 1973-1994: a chronology and a
        bibliography.   In Long Room, xxxix, 60-63 (1994).

        KING (Carla).   See 2463.

3323   KING (Cecil A.).   28 Inf. Bn.   'In a peculiarly regrettable situation'.   In An
        Cosantóir, li, no. 3, pp 32-3 (1991).
        Reminiscences of the early days of the armed forces.

3324   KINSELLA (Thomas).   Dennis Clark: an appreciation.   In Hist. Ire., ii, no.
        1, p. 6 (1994).
        Irish-American historian who died 17 Sept. 1993.

3325   KIRRANE (Bridy).   My memories of the Harrison Hall, Roscommon.   In
        Roscommon Hist. Soc. Jn., iv, 73 (1992).

        KIRWAN (Elizabeth).   See 2469.

3326   KLAUS (H. Gustav).   Introduction: beyond nationalism and complacency:
        the evolution of Thomas O'Brien.   In Strong words, brave deeds, pp 11-43
        (1994).

3327   KLAUS (H. Gustav).   New Theatre Group plays.   In Strong words, brave
        deeds, pp 93-6 (1994).
        1937-42.

        KLINE (Benjamin).   See 2470.

3328   KNOX (Colin) and HASLEM (Richard).   Local government.   In Political
        issues in Ireland today, pp 55-70 (1994).

3329   KORP (Walter).   Welfare state development in Europe since 1930: Ireland in
        comparative perspective.   Pp ii, 35.   Dublin: Economic and Social Research
        Institute, [1993?].
        Geary lecture.

        KOTSONOURIS (Mary).   See 2475, 2476. 2477.

        KRAUSE (David).   See 2478.

        Labour in art.   See 2482.

3330   LAFFAN (Brigid).   Managing Europe.   In Political issues in Ireland today,
        pp 40-54 (1994).

3331   LANGAN (Tom). Ballycastle seventy years ago.   In *North Mayo Hist. Jn.*,
        iii, no. 1, pp 77-87 (1992/93).

3332   LARRAGY (Joe). Views and perceptions of older Irish people. In *Soc. Pol.
        & Admin.*, xxvii, 235-47 (1993).

        LATHAM (Harry). See 2496.

        LAURENCE (Dan H.). See 2987.

3333   LAVER (Michael) and GALLAGHER (Michael), ed.   How Ireland voted
        1992. Pp xi, 211. Dublin: Folens; [Limerick]: PSAI Press, 1993.

        LAW (Edward J.). See 2497.

3334   Le BROCQUY (Anne Madden). Louis le Brocquy: a painter seeing his way.
        Pp xvi, 317. Dublin: Gill and Macmillan, 1994.

3335   LEE (Joseph). Centralisation and community. In *People power*, pp 37-48
        (1993).

3336   LEE (Joseph). Dynamics of social and political change in the Irish Republic.
        In *Northern Ireland and the politics of reconciliation*, pp 117-40 (1993).

        LENEHAN (John F.). See 2501.

3337   LENIHAN (Padraig). Aerial photography: a window on the past.   In *Hist.
        Ire.*, i, no. 2, pp 9-13 (1993).

3338   Let in the light: censorship secrecy and democracy. [*Ed.* Patrick Smyth and
        Ellen Hazelkorn]. Pp 188. Dingle: Brandon Books, 1993.

3339   LEWIS (Gifford). Gifford and Craven: a small press in Dublin and Co. Cork
        founded in 1972. In *Long Room*, xxxix, 54-9 (1994).

        LEWIS (Gifford). See 2508.

3340   LEWIS (Peter).   Gillie Blackmore Dun Laoghaire's troubadour.   In *Dun
        Laoghaire Jn.*, ii, 38-43 (1991/92).
            Gillie Blackmore (1904-197?), barber and leader of the Borough Minstrels
        of Dun Laoghaire.

3341   LIDDLE (L.H.). Passenger steamers on the Irish Sea, 1919-39, I.   In *Irish
        Railway Rec. Soc. Jn.*, xviii, no. 123, pp 314-21 (1994).

3342   LIJPHART (Arend) and IRWIN (Galen A.).   Nomination strategies in the
        Irish STV system: the Dáil elections of 1969, 1973 and 1977. [followed by]
        Cohan (A.S.) rejoinder. In *Brit. Jn. Political Science*, ix, 362-70 (1979).

        LINEHAN (Thomas P.). See 2510.

3343   Lisacul during the Emergency.   In *Roscommon Hist. Soc. Jn.*, iv, 81-3
        (1992).

3344   LITTON (Frank), ed.   The Constitution of Ireland, 1937-1987.   In
        Administration, xxxv, no. 4, pp 1-225 (1988).
            Special commemorative issue.

LLOYD (David). See 2513.

3345   LOGAN (Eugene). The Monkstown milkmen. In *Dun Laoghaire Jn.*, ii, 14-17 (1991/92).

3346   LOGAN (John). Family and fortune in Kate O'Brien's Limerick. In *With warmest love*, pp 105-30 (1994).

LOHAN (Rena). See 2516.

LUCCAN (Nóra). See 2520.

3347   LUNN (Kenneth).   'Good for a few hundreds at least': Irish labour recruitment into Britain during the second world war. In *The Irish in British labour history*, pp 102-14 (1993).

LYNCH (Kathleen). See DRUDY (Sheelagh).

3348   LYNCH (Michael). Muintir na Tíre. In *Tipperary County*, pp 152-6 (1993). 1931-

LYNCH (Michael). See *Marymount* (1994).

3349   LYNCH (Muireann). Some memories of the 1963 floods. In *Gateway to the Past*, i, no. 2, pp 85-8 (1994).

LYNCH (Patrick). See 2525.

LYNCH (Sighle Bhreathnach). See 2526.

3350   LYONS (F.S.L.). The burden of our history. In *Interpreting Irish history*, pp 87-104 (1994).
       The W.B. Rankin Memorial Lecture, 4 Dec. 1978, published by Queen's University of Belfast.

3351   LYONS (Patricia). Cloyne Mineral Company. In *The book of Cloyne*, pp 286-96. (1994).
       1926-62 silica extraction.

LYSAGHT (P.B.). See 2534.

3352   M. (C). Henry A. Wheeler 1916-1993. In *Arch. Ire.*, vii, no. 4, p. 5 (1993).

MAC A'GHOILL (Pádraig). See 2535.

3353   McALISTER (Denise). Public expenditure. In *Political issues in Ireland today*, pp 71-97 (1994).

Mac an BHUA (Gearóid). See Ó CANNÁINN (Tomás).

3354   Mac an GHALLOGLAIGH (Domhnaill). Brian Ó Mórdha (1918-1986). [Obituary]. In *Breifne*, vi, no. 24, pp [vi-vii] (1986).

3355   Mac an GHALLOGLAIGH (Domhnaill). Dr Terence P. Cunningham. [Obituary]. In *Breifne*, vi, no. 24, pp [ii-v] (1986).

3356   Mac AOGÁIN (Eoghan). An Ghaeilge, na nuatheangacha agus 1992. In *Oghma*, i, 74-86 (1989).

3357   Mac AONGHUSA (Proinsias). Gáire mór na féasóige. In *Dáithí Ó hUaithne*, pp 117-33 (1994).

Mac AONGHUSA (Proinsias). See 2539, 2540.

McAULIFFE (Nicholas). See 2550.

3358   McCABE (Ian). JFK in Ireland. In *Hist. Ire.*, i, no. 4, pp 38-42 (1993).

3359   McCABE (Jane) and McCABE (Paddy). A windy place. In *Swords Voices*, i, 26-7 (1992/93).
        Memories of Swords.

McCABE (Paddy). See McCABE (Jane).

3360   McCAGUE (Eugene). Arthur Cox, 1891-1965. Pp x, 155. Dublin: Gill and Macmillan, 1994.
        Lawyer.

3361   Mac CANA (Proinsias). Dáithí Ó hUaithne. In *Dáithí Ó hUaithne*, pp 9-30 (1994).

3362   Mac CÁRTHAIGH (Micheál). Pádraig Ó Meára: aonach urmhumhan. In *Ó ghlúin go glúin*, pp 30-37 (1993).
        P. Ó Meára, 1893- , writer and teacher.

3363   Mac COIL (Liam). Cianfheachaint. Roinnt tuairmimí, paradacsaí, réamhchlaontaí, agus *Obiter dicta* faoi TnG. In *Oghma*, no. 6, pp 28-33 (1994).

McCONKEY (Kenneth). See 2563.

3364   McCONNELL (David). Regions and minorities: the Adelaide Hospital - the last Protestant general teaching hospital in the Republic of Ireland. In *Culture in Ireland - regions*, pp 130-42 (1993).

3365   McCORMICK (Liam). Two Meath churches; ill. by Ruth Brandt. In *The Furrow*, xxxiv, 279-86 (1983).

McCRACKEN (Donal P.). See 2569.

3366   McCULLEN (John). The Irish National War Memorial Gardens. In *Ir. Garden*, ii, no. 3, pp 30-32 (1993).
        Designed and laid out between 1931 and 1939 by Sir Edwin Lutyens.

3367   MacCURTAIN (Margaret). Moving statues and Irish women. In *Irish women's studies reader*, pp 203-11 (1993).

MacCURTAIN (Margaret). See O'LOUGHLIN (Thomas).

3368   McCUTCHEON (Catherine) and HOWE (Violet). Bandon Grammar School garden fete 1948. In *Bandon Hist. Jn.*, x, 58-61 (1994).

3369   McDERMOTT (Eileen).   Memories of a Knockarush childhood.   In
Roscommon Hist. Soc. Jn., iii, 58 (1990).

3370   McDONAGH (Enda).   Canon J.G. McGarry, editor of *The Furrow*, 1950-
1977. The man, the style and the issues.   In *The Furrow*, xxviii, 739-46
(1977).

3371   McDONAGH (Enda).   New forces for positive change in Ireland.   In
Northern Ireland and the politics of reconciliation, pp 141-9 (1993).

3372   MacDONAGH (Oliver).   Ambiguity in nationalism: the case of Ireland.   In
Interpreting Irish history, pp 105-21 (1994).
Originally published in *Historical Studies* (Melbourne), 19 (1981), pp 337-
52.

3373   McDONALD (Henry).   Irish Batt.: the story of Ireland's Blue Berets in the
Lebanon. Pp 182. Dublin, Gill & Macmillan, 1993.

3374   McDONALD (Rosemarie).   Horses and hospitals: the Irish sweepstakes.   In
Eire-Ireland, xxix, no. 1, pp 24-34 (1994).

McDOWELL (R.B.).   See DICKSON (David).

McDOWELL (R.B.).   See 2585.

3375   McELHONE (Patricia).   Lift the latch: memories of old Rosses Point.   Pp
44. [S.l.]: author, [1994?].

McEVOY (Dan).   See 2587.

MacFHEARGUSA (Pádraig).   See 2589.

3376   Mac GABHANN (Fiachra).   Geographical perspectives on the human
landscape in the flooded valleys of Poulaphouca reservoir, 1939.   In *Baile*, pp
21-7 (1992).

3377   Mac GABHANN (Fiachra).   'The water was the sheriff': the land beneath the
Poulaphouca reservoir.   In *Wicklow*, pp 927-51 (1994).

Mac GAIRBHEITH (Pádraig).   See 2591.

3378   McGARRY (J.G.).   Cardinal William Conway, 1913-1977.   In *The Furrow*,
xxviii, 271-3 (1977).

3379   Mac GEARAILT (Breandán).   Forbairt na Gaeltachta mar aonad.   In *Oghma*,
no. 5, pp 66-70 (1993).

3380   McGOVERN (Frieda).   The education of a linguistic and cultural minority:
Vietnamese children in Irish schools, 1979-1989.   In *Ir. Educational Studies*,
xii, 92-105 (1993).

3381   McGOVERN (Gerard).   Maureen O'Sullivan, a Hollywood exile.   In *Dun
Laoghaire Jn.*, iii, 21-2 (1993).

MacGOWAN (Fiona).   See 2595.

McHUGH (Roger J.).   See 2602.

McINTYRE (H.E.).   See 2605.

3382   McIVOR (Aidan).   A history of the Irish naval service: Pp 256.   Blackrock,
Co. Dublin: Irish Academic Press, 1994.

MACKEY (M.).   See O'REGAN (Joseph).

McLOUGHLIN (Ella).   See 2613.

MacMAHON (Bryan).   See 2615.

McMAHON (Kevin).   See Ó FIAICH (Tomás).

3383   Mac MATHÚNA (Liam).   Donn S. Piatt agus Gaeilge Chúige Laighean.   In
Féile Zozimus, vol. 3: Two Dubliners, pp 69-93 (1994).
Text in Irish, quotes in English.

3384   MacMILLAN (Gretchen M.).   State, society and authority in Ireland: the
foundations of the modern state.   Pp x, 278.   Dublin: Gill & Macmillan,
1993.

3385   McMULLAN (Anna).   Irish women playwrights since 1958.   In *British and
Irish dramatists since 1958*, pp 110-23 (1993).

3386   McQUILLAN (Deirdre).   Mary Robinson: a president in progress.   Pp vi,
122.   Dublin: Gill & Macmillan, 1994.

McQUILLAN (Jack).   See 2622.

3387   Mac Un FRAIDH (Gearóid).   Clocha ceadngailte: léargas ar UNFIL so
Liobáin. Pp 240. Baile Átha Cliath: An Clóchomhar, 1994.
Irish UN forces in Lebanon, 1975- .

3388   MADDEN (Anne).   Seeing his way: Louis le Brocquy, a painter. Pp xvi,
317. Dublin: Gill & Macmillan, 1994.
1916-

MAGUIRE (Martin).   See 2629, 2630.

3389   MAHON (Oliver).   A school photograph examined. In *Sliabh Aughty*, v, 24-
6 (1994).

MAHON (Patrick).   See 2634.

MAHONEY (Joseph).   See 2636.

3390   MAHONEY (Rosemary).   Whoredom in Kimmage: Irish women coming of
age. Pp xv, 307. Boston: Houghton Mifflin, 1993.

3391   MAHONY (R.H.).   The Daunt rescue.   In *The book of Cloyne*, pp 219-28
(1994).
Ballycotton lifeboat, 7 Feb. 1936.

3392   MALLON (Declan).   Nano Reid.   Pp 132, [11].   Drogheda: Sunnyside
Publications, 1994.
Painter, 1900-81.

3393   MANGAN (Colm).   Plans and operations.   In *Ir. Sword*, xix, 47-56 (1993/95).

3394   MANNION (Marie).   Top Irish American business people with Galway roots. In *Galway Roots*, ii, 89-93 (1994).

Mantua N.S.   See 2641.

MARNANE (Denis G.).   See 2643.

3395   MARSH (Michael).   [Political data in 1992]:   Ireland.   ın *European Jn. Political Res.*, xxiv, 455-66 (1993).

3396   MARSH (Michael).   [Political data in 1993]:   Ireland.   In *European Jn. Political Res.*, xxvi, 331-7 (1994).

MARSH (Michael).   See HILL (Ronald J.).

3397   Marymount 1974-1994.   [*Ed*. Michael Lynch].   Pp 108.   [Carrick-on-Shannon]: Marymount College, 1994.

MAUME (Patrick).   See 2648, 2649.

3398   MAXWELL (Nick).   'Exercising professional leadership...'.   A conversation with Dr Ann Hamlin.   In *Arch. Ire.*, iv, 63-4 (1990).

3399   MAYE (Brian).   Fine Gael 1923-1987: a general history with biographical sketches of leading members.   Pp vi, 406.   Dublin: Blackwater Press, 1993.

MAYE (Brian).   See 2651.

MEEHAN (Helen).   See 2654.

3400   MEEHAN (Molaise).   J.G. McGarry - a reminisicence.   In *The Furrow*, xxxii, 531-3 (1981).

Mercy in Rosscarbery.   See 2656.

MITCHELL (Arthur).   See 2659.

3401   MITCHELL (Frank).   Frank Mitchell - a man and the landscape [interviewed by Gabriel Cooney].   In *Arch. Ire.*, iii, 91-5 (1989).

MITCHELL (Mary).   See 2662.

MOLONEY (Joe).   See 2667.

MOLONEY (Mick).   See 2668.

3402   MONGEY (Finian).   Laurence Mongey (1895-1972).   In *Ardmore Jn.*, x, 10 (1993).

3403   MOODY (T.W.).   Irish history and Irish mythology.   In *Interpreting Irish history*, pp 71-86 (1994).
        First published in *Hermathena*, 124 (1978), pp 7-24.

3404   MORIARTY (Seamus). A Bree childhood in the 1930s. In *Gateway to the Past*, i, no. 2, pp 80-84 (1994).

3405   MORRIS (Anthony). Clifden man became 'Father' of our navy. In *Connemara*, i, no. 1, pp 21-4. (1993).

3406   MORRISON (John). The Ulster cover-up. Pp xi, 164. Lurgan: Ulster Society, 1993.

MORRISON (Kristin). See 2682.

3407   MOSS (Joan). Agriculture. In *Political issues in Ireland today*, pp 118-42 (1994).

3408   Mountrath Golf Club: 65 years and growing. Pp 144. Mountrath, Co. Laois: The Golf Club, [1994?].

MULHALL (Tom). See 2683.

MULLETT (Killian). See 2684.

3409   MULLINS (Richard J.). A history of Portarlington Generating Station and Clonsast bog development. Pp vi, 77. [S.l.]: [the author], 1993.
        Co. Offaly, 1936-88.

3410   MULRENNAN (Monica E.). Changes since the nineteenth century to the estuary-barrier complexes of north County Dublin. In *Ir. Geography*, xxvi, 1-13 (1993).

3411   MUNCK (Ronnie) and ROLSTON (Bill). Irish republicanism in the 1930s: new uses for oral history. In *International Jn. of Oral Hist.*, vii, 3-18 (1986).

3412   MURPHY (Brian). The canon of Irish cultural history: some questions concerning Roy Foster's *Modern Ireland*. In *Interpreting Irish history*, pp 222-33 (1994).
        First published in *Studies* (autumn 1993), pp 171-84.

MURPHY (Brian). See 2687.

MURPHY (Della). See 2689.

MURPHY (Hilary). See 2691, 2694.

MURPHY (Ina). See 2698.

3413   MURPHY (Kevin H.). Scoil Uí Chonaill: thirty years a growing 1963-1993. Pp 104. Cahersiveen, Co. Kerry: [Scoil Uí Chonaill], 1994.

MURPHY (Sean). See 2700.

MURRAY (D.). See 2704.

MYERS (Sean). See 2710.

3414   MYRES (Kevin). Fr Browne, S.J. photographer. In *Mallow Field Club Jn.*, xii, 29-34 (1994).

3415   Naomh Malachi and the Shelagh story. [*Ed.* Art Agnew].   Pp 327.
        [Dundalk]: [Naomh Malachi Gaelic Football Club], 1994.

3416   NEALON (Ted). Nealon's guide to the 27th Dáil and Seanad election 92. Pp
        208. Dublin: Gill & Macmillan, 1993.

3417   NEENAN (Michael). The death of Dinny Lacey. In *Tipp. Hist. Jn.*, pp 54-
        55 (1993).

        NESBITT (Ronald). See 2721.

3418   NEVIN (Donal). Decades of dissension and divisions 1923-1959.   In *Trade
        union century*, pp 85-95 (1994).

3419   Ní BHRÁDAIGH (Eilís). Smaointe Fáin.   In *Dáithí Ó hUaithne*, pp 134-43
        (1994).

        Ní CHONGAILE (Gobnait). See *An iascaireacht in Inis Óirr*.

        Ní CHONGAILE (Sorcha). See *An iascaireacht in Inis Óirr*.

3420   Ní DHONNCHADHA (Bríd).   Cáit Ní Ghrifín.   In *Lúise Gabhánach Ní
        Dhufaigh agus Scoil Bhríde*, pp 40-41 (1993).
        Principal of Scoil Bhríde 1950-64.

3421   Ní GHECHÁIN (Mairéad).   Donn Sigerson Piatt, 1905-1970. In *Lúise
        Gabhánach Ní Dhufaigh agus Scoil Bhríde*, pp 38-9 (1993).
        Writer.

3422   Ní NUADHÁIN (Nóirín).   'Foilseacháin na scol': saothar Gaeilge Phádraig
        Uí Mheára. In *Ó ghlúin go glúin*, pp 51-67 (1993).

        Nic CHUMHAILL (Sinead). See 2724.

        NOLAN (Aengus). See KEOGH (Dermot).

        NOLAN (J.C.M.). See 2727.

        NOONAN (J.A.). See ROBERTS (M.J.).

3423   NORTH (Reg) and COOLAHAN (John).   Education.   In *Political issues in
        Ireland today*, pp 161-85 (1994).

3424   NUTT (Kathleen). Irish identity and the writing of history.   In *Eire-Ireland*,
        xxix, no. 2, pp 160-72 (1994).

3425   NUTT (Kathleen) and GRAY (Peter).   Rethinking Irish nationalism.   In
        Studies, lxxxiii, 7-19 (1994).

3426   Ó BEACHAIN (Donnacha). Irish republicans and Europe, 1922-1945.   In
        U.C.D. Hist. Rev., vi, 22-35 (1992).

3427   Ó BEACHAIN (Donnacha).   'We asked for guns' - the question of military
        intervention in Northern Ireland 1969-70. In *U.C.D. Hist. Rev.*, vii, 22-37
        (1993).

3428 Ó BEOLÁIN (Art). Dáithí Ó hUaithne - máistir léinn. In *Dáithí Ó hUaithne*, pp 38-50 (1994).

3429 O'BRIEN (Conor Cruise). The great melody - discordant notes. In *Hist. Ire.*, i, no. 2, pp 23-5 (1993).
  Conor Cruise O'Brien replies to negative reviews of his book *The great melody: a thematic biography and commented anthology of Edmund Burke.*

3430 O'BRIEN (Gerard). The record of the first Dáil debates. In *I.H.S.*, xxviii, 306-9 (1993).

  O'BRIEN (Hugh B.). See 2733.

3431 O'BRIEN (Jack). The Unionjacking of Ireland. Pp 192. Cork: Mercier Press, 1993.
  Great Britain and Ireland.

  O'BRIEN (John). See *Glimpses of Portlaoise.*

  O'BRIEN (Nollaig). See 2734.

  O'BRIEN (Pius). See 2737.

3432 O'BRIEN (Thomas). Spanish correspondence. In *Strong words, brave deeds*, pp 153-85 (1994).
  1938.

3433 Ó BUACHALLA (Breandán). Lugh ildánach. In *Dáithí Ó hUaithne*, pp 99-116 (1994).

3434 O'CALLAGHAN (Margaret). British high politics and a nationalist Ireland: criminality, land and law under Forster and Balfour. Pp 223. Cork: Cork University Press, 1994.

3435 Ó CANAINN (Aodh). Cosslett a chruinnigh. In *Donegal Annual*, xlvi, 23-33 (1994).
  Cosslett Ó Cuinn, collector of Irish lore and language from the 1930s to the 1950s.

3436 Ó CANAINN (Tomás) and Mac an BHUA (Gearóid). Seán Ó Riada: a shaol agus a shaothair. Pp 286. Baile Átha Cliath: Gartan, 1993.
  Seán Ó Riada, 1931-71.

3437 O'CARROLL (Donal). The Emergency army. In *Ir. Sword*, xix, 19-46, (1993/95).

  Ó CARTHAIGH (Seán). See 2745.

  Ó CATHAIN (Diarmuid). See 2746.

3438 Ó CEALLAIGH (Daltún). Sovereign people or crown subjects?: the case for Articles 2 and 3 and against sections 1 and 75. Pp 122. Dublin: Léirmheas, 1993.
  Irish constitution.

3439 Ó CIOSÁIN (Éamon). An t-Éireannach 1934-1937: nuachtán sóisialach Gaeltacha. Pp xiv, 285. Baile Átha Cliath: An Clóchomhar, 1993. (Leabhair thaighde, 74)
A weekly socialist newspaper, founded by Seán Beaumont.

Ó CIOSÁIN (Éamon). See HASTINGS (Caitríona).

O'CLEIRIGH (Nellie). See 2751.

3440 Ó CONAILL (Seamus). Leon Ó Broin 1902-1990. In *Administration*, xxxviii, 9-11 (1990).

Ó CONAIRE (Breandán). See 3033.

Ó CONLUAIN (Proinsias). See 2755.

3441 O'CONNOR (Charles). The fight against T.B. in Ireland in the 1940s. Pp 133. [S.l.]: Charles O'Connor, 1994.
Post-Sanatoria League.

O'CONNOR (David). See 2757.

O'CONNOR (Emmet). See 2758.

3442 O'CONNOR (Kevin). Thou shalt not kill: true-life stories of Irish murders. Pp 231. Dublin: Gill & Macmillan, 1994.
Based on television series 'Thou shalt not kill'.

O'CONNOR (Patrick J.). See 2759.

3443 O'CONNOR (Paul G.). The Irish Augustinians in Ecuador, 1977-1992. In *The Irish Augustinians in Rome, 1656-1994*, pp 187-209 (1994).

3444 O'CONNOR (Tom). A civil service career - some reflections. In *Administration*, xxxviii, 365-72 (1990).

O'CONNOR LYSAGHT (D.R.). See 2104.

3445 Ó CRUALAOICH (Gearóid). County Cork folklore and its collection. In *Cork*, pp 919-40 (1993).
1920s -

3446 O'D. (P.). Jimmy O'Connor 1928-1993. In *Galway Arch. Soc. Jn.*, xlvi, 212-13 (1994).

3447 O'D. (P.). John Monahan 1918-1992. In *Galway Arch. Soc. Jn.*, xlv, 166-8 (1993).

Ó DANACHAIR (Caoimhín). See 2761.

O'DAY (Alan). See 2762, 2763.

Ó DEIRG (Íosold). See 2095).

3448 Ó DOCHARTAIGH (Gearalt). Gall mór mo linne - an tAthair Peadar Mac Loinsigh. In *Donegal Annual*, xlvi, 60-63 (1994).

3449   Ó DONNCHADHA (Proinsias). A harvest of memories: reflections of a lifetime. Pp 32. Dublin: Night Owl Early Bird Bureau, 1994.

3450   Ó DONNCHADHA (Proinsias). A stack of stories: reflective memories. Pp 57. Dublin: Night Owl Early Bird Bureau, 1994.

O'DONNELL (Declan). See 2765.

3451   O'DONNELL (E.E.). Father Browne's Dublin photographs, 1925-50. Pp 96. Dublin: Wolfhound Press, 1993.

O'DONNELL (E.E.). See 2766.

3452   O'DONNELL (Jimmy). The Arranmore disaster. Pp [2], iii, 80 [S.l.]: [the author], [1993?].
        Saturday 9 Nov. 1935. Donegal.

3453   O'DONOGHUE (Dan). A history of handball in Bally. Pp 77. [S.l.]: [s.n.], [1994?].

3454   O'DONOGHUE (Martin). Public policy making: the uneasy case of political economy. In *Modern Irish democracy*, pp 123-36 (1993).

3455   O'DONOGHUE (Thomas A.). Sport, recreation and physical education: the evolution of a national policy of regeneration in Eire, 1926-48. In *Brit. Jn. of Sports Hist.*, iii, 216-33 (1986).

O'DRISCOLL (J.). See 2776.

Ó DUBHTHAIGH (Niall). See 2777.

Ó DUIBHÍR (Ciarán). See 2778.

Ó DUINN (Seamus). See 2782.

Ó DÚSHLÁINE (Tadhg). See 2411.

O'FARRELL (Padraic). See 2784.

O'FARRELL (Patrick). See 2785.

3456   Ó FIAICH (Tomás). Tomás Ó Fiaich's letters from Louvain: letters, 1950-1952, from Tomás Ó Fiaich, St Anthony's College, Louvain, to his father, Patrick Fee, Anamar. *Ed.* Kevin McMahon. Pp iv, 68. [Cullyhanna]: Cullyhanna Community Enterprises, [1994?].
        Tomás Ó Fiaich, 1923-90.

3457   Ó FIANNACHTA (Pádraig). Nessa Ní Shéaghdha (1916-1993). In *Éigse*, xxvii, 139-40 (1993).

3458   Ó FLAITHIMHÍN (Séamus). Monsignor Pádraig de Brún (1889-1960): cathaoirleach Chomhairle na hInstitiúide (1940-1960). In *Irisleabhar Mha Nuad*, pp 9-32 (1994).

Ó GLAISNE (Risteard). See 2788, 2789, 2791.

O'GORMAN (Dermot). See 2793.

O'GORMAN (Ronnie). See *Thanks for the memories, 1954-1994.*

3459   Ó GRÁDA (Cormac). Making history in Ireland in the 1940s and 1950s: the saga of *The great famine.* In *Interpreting Irish history*, pp 269-87 (1994). Reprinted from *The Irish Review* (1992), pp 87-107.

3460   Ó GRÁDA (Cormac). Determinants of Irish emigration. In *Int. Migration Rev.*, xx, 650-56 (1986).

Ó GRÁDA (Cormac). See 2217.

Ó GRÁDA (Liam). See 2805.

3461   O'HALPIN (Eunan). Army, politics and society in independent Ireland, 1923-1945. In *Men, women and war*, pp 158-74 (1993).

3462   O'HALPIN (Eunan). Aspects of intelligence. In *Ir. Sword*, xix, 57-65 (1993/95).

3463   O'HANLON (Danny). Out of the ashes: a chronicle of fifty years of the fire service in Cavan. Pp 232. [S.l.]: [s.n.], [1993?].

3464   O'HANLON (Gerard). Culture and the gospel in a changing Republic of Ireland. In *Milltown Studies*, xxxii, 5-23 (1993).

3465   Ó hAODHA (Micheál). Siobhán: a memoir of an actress. Pp 190. Dingle: Brandon, 1994.
    Siobhán McKenna, 1922-86.

3466   O'HARA (Bernard). Regional Technical College, Galway: the first 21 years. Pp 206. Galway: Research and Consultancy Unit, Regional Technical College, Galway, 1993.

O'HARE (Colmán). See 2810.

3467   Ó HÉALAÍ (Pádraig). Fear an leabhair: Pádraig Ó Fiannachta. In *Stáir na Gaeilge*, pp 1-21 (1994).
    1927-

3468   Ó hEIDIRSCEOIL (Seán). A personal memoir of the thirties. In *Strong words, brave deeds*, pp 188-214 (1994).

Ó hÓGÁIN (Dáithí). See *Binneas thar meon.* (1994).

O'KEEFE (Patrick). See 2811.

3469   O'KEEFE (Patrick D.). Clann na Poblachta: its origin and growth. Part 1-2. In *Tipp. Hist. Jn.*, pp 19-30 (1993); pp 1-8 (1994).

3470   O'LEARY (Brendan). Election report: the Irish general election of November 1992. In *West European Politics*, xvi, 401-12 (1993).

O'LEARY (Liam). See 2815.

3471   Ó LOINGSIGH (Pádraig). Dáithí Ó hUaithne: Uachtarán Acadamh Ríoga na hÉireann, 1973-1976. In *Dáithí Ó hUaithne*, pp 59-67, ill. (1994).

3472   O'LOUGHLIN (Thomas). Sister act. In *Hist. Ire.*, ii, no. 1, pp 52-4 (1994).
Interview with Margaret MacCurtain of University College, Dublin.

Ó LUANAIGH (Dónall). See 2818.

3473   Ó LÚING (Pádraig). Memories of St Brendan's seminary, Killarney. Pp 43. [S.I.]: Pádraig Ó Lúing, 1994.

3474   Ó LÚING (Seán). Donn Sigerson Piatt: Laighneach ó Linn life. In *Féile Zozimus, vol 3: Two Dubliners*, pp 46-68 (1994).
Text in Irish, quotes in English.

3475   O'MAHONEY (Anne). Growing up in Limerick's pig market. In *Old Limerick Jn.*, xxxi, 44-7 (1994).

3476   O'MALLEY (Anthony). Reminiscences. In *Cathair na Mart*, xiii, 137-44 (1993).
Anthony O'Malley, b.1899, a farmer with a lifelong interest in folklore and history.

3477   O'MALLEY (Cormac K.H.). Appreciation Helen Hooker O'Malley Roelofs. In *Cathair na Mart*, xiii, 161-2 (1993).
Artist (sculptor). Married Ernie O'Malley 1935 and divorced from him in 1952.

3478   O'MALLEY MADEC (Mary). The Irish travelling woman: mother and mermaid. In *Irish women's studies reader*, pp 214-29 (1993).

3479   Ó MAOILMHICHÍL (Gearóid). Fostaigh an Óige agus oibreoidh sí. In *Oghma*, no. 4, pp 26-31 (1992).

3480   Ó MATHÚNA (Dónal). Pádraig uasal Ó Gallchóir. In *Bandon Hist. Jn.*, x, 49-51 (1994).
Pádraig Ó Gallchóir, 1913-93.

Ó MÓRDHA (Pilib B.). See 2832.

Ó MURCHADHA (Diarmuid). See 2835.

3481   Ó MURCHADHA (Felix). Violence, reconciliation, pluralism: a critique of Irish nationalism. In *Canadian Jn. of Irish Studies*, xix, no. 2, pp 1-12 (1993).

3482   Ó MURCHÚ (Helen). An duine agus an náisiún. In *Náisiún na hÉireann*, pp 58-85 (1993).
Irish language and nationality.

100 years of the L.F.A. See 2837.

O'NEILL (Assumpta). See 2838.

O'NEILL (Jenny). See 2839.

3483   O'NEILL (Kevin). Revisionist milestone. In *Interpreting Irish history*, pp 217-21 (1994).
    Originally published in *Irish Literary Supplement* (fall 1989), pp 1, 39. Roy Foster's *Modern Ireland 1600-1972*.

O'NEILL (Marie). See 2840.

3484   O'NEILL (Thomas P.). Dr J.C. McQuaid and Eamon de Valera: insights on church and state. In *Breifne*, viii, 327-37 (1992/93).

3485   ORAM (Hugh). Paper tigers: stories of Irish newspapers by the people who make them. Pp 143. Belfast: Appletree Press, 1993.

3486   O'REGAN (Joseph). Memories of life on the island of West Skeam; recorded in April 1993, edited for this journal by M. Mackey. In *Mizen Jn.*, ii, 8-19 (1994).

3487   O'REILLY (Barry). North Dublin - a case in point: the Skerries Heritage Project. In *Traditional architecture in Ireland*, pp 21-7 (1994).

O'REILLY (Joe). See *From Clonsast to Ballyburley*.

O'REILLY-HYLAND (Kathleen). See 2847.

Ó RIAIN (Seamus). See 2848.

Ó RIAIN (Seán). See 2849, 2850.

3488   O'RIORDAN (Manus). Communism in Dublin in the 1930s: the struggle against fascism. In *Strong words, brave deeds*, pp 215-39 (1994).

3489   O'RIORDAN (Manus). James Larkin junior and the forging of a thinking intelligent movement. In *Saothar*, xix, 53-68 (1994).

O'ROURKE (Alan). See 2852.

O'ROURKE (Kevin). See 2853, 2854.

O'SCANAILL (Breandan). See JEFFARES (Edward).

3490   Ó SIADHAIL (Micheál). Athair de mo chuid. In *Dáithí Ó hUaithne*, pp 31-7 (1994).

Ó SIADHAIL (Pádraig). See 2859.

3491   Ó SIORADÁIN (Mártín). Ag cuimhneamh ar Dháithí. In *Dáithí Ó hUaithne*, pp 68-72 (1994).

3492   O'SULLIVAN (Michael). Mary Robinson: the life and times of an Irish liberal. Pp iii, 226. Dublin: Blackwater Press, 1993.
    b. 1944; president of Ireland, 1990-97.

O'SULLIVAN (Michael). See 2862.

3493   O'SULLIVAN (Patrick). I heard the wild birds sing: a Kerry childhood. Pp 207. Dublin: Anvil Books (1993).
    First published 1991.

3494   O'SULLIVAN (Tadhg). Hubert Butler memorial lecture, Kilkenny, 12 September 1991. In *Butler Soc. Jn.*, iii, 65-9 (1994).

3495   O'TOOLE (Fintan). Blackhole green card: the disappearance of Ireland. Pp 223. Dublin: New Island Books, 1994.

3496   O'TOOLE (Fintan). Meanwhile back at the ranch: the politics of Irish beef. Pp 292. London: Vintage, 1994.

O'TOOLE (Fintan). See 2482.

Ó TUATHAIGH (Gearóid). See 2865.

3497   Ó TUATHAIGH (M.A.G.). Irish historical 'revisionism': state of the art or ideological project? In *Interpreting Irish history*, pp 306-26 (1994).

3498   OWEN (Arwel Ellis). The Anglo-Irish Agreement: the first three years. Pp x, 263. Cardiff: University of Wales Press, 1994.

PAINE (Derek). See 2870, 2871.

3499   PARLE (Jim). Solving a wartime fuel crisis in Co. Wexford. In *Wexford Hist. Soc. Jn.*, xv, 15-33 (1994/95).

Parnells Hurling and Football Club. See 2881.

3500   PARSONS (Denis). Mobilisation and expansion, 1939-40. In *Ir. Sword*, xix, 11-18 (1993/95).

PATTERSON (Henry). See HAZELKORN (Ellen).

3501   PELLETIER (Martine). Telling stories and making history: Brian Friel and Field Day. In *Ir. University Rev.*, xxiv, 186-97 (1994).

PHELAN (Jim). See 2893.

3502   PHELAN (Margaret M.). Kilkenny Archaeological Society, 1945-1994. In *Old Kilkenny Rev.*, xlvi, 96-104 (1994).

PIHL (Lis). See TOKSVIG (Signe).

3503   Plane crash in the Blue Stacks remembered. In *Donegal Annual*, xlv, 66-8 (1993).
        British Sunderland flying boat which crashed on 31 Jan. 1944.

3504   Political data 1945-1990: Ireland. In *European Jn. Political Res.*, xxiv, 62-4 (1993).

POLLOCK (Vivienne). See 2377.

Poor Clare Monastery, Graiguecullen, Carlow. See 2899.

POWELL (Larry). See 2903.

3505   POWER (David). Long way from Tipperary. Pp 146. Clonmel: Glen Publications, [1993].
        World war 2 - personal narratives Irish.

3506   POWER (Louis). + Kevin: a portrait of Archbishop Kevin McNamara. Pp x, 176. Dublin: Blackwater Press, 1993.

POWER (Patrick C.). See 2908.

3507   POWER (Vincent). Send 'em home sweatin': [the showbands' story]. Pp 400. Dublin, Kildanore Press, 1990.

PRENDERGAST (Ellen). See 2909.

3508   Professor Michael V. Duignan, 1907-1988. In *Arch. Ire.*, ii, 45 (1988).

3509   PRONE (Terry). Irish murders: 2. Pp 204. Dublin: Poolbeg, 1994.

3510   Publications by Basil Chubb. In *Modern Irish democracy*, pp 192-4 (1994).

PYLE (Hilary). See 2914, 2915.

3511   PYPER (George West). The rectory ghost. In *Swords Voices*, i, 23-5 (1992/93).
        The old rectory in Swords.

3512   QUIGLEY (Aidan). Air aspects of the Emergency. In *Ir. Sword*, xix, 86-90 (1993/95).

QUIGLEY (Patrick). See 2918.

QUINLAN (Tom). See 2919.

3513   QUINN (Aren). The coastwatching service. In *Ir. Sword*, xix, 91-2 (1993/95).

3514   QUIRKE (David). Great greyhounds of our parish. In *Oola Past & Present*, i, 23-5 (1992).

3515   R. (E.). Professor Thomas Fanning, 1933-1993. In *Arch. Ire.*, vii, no. 3, p. 7 (1993).

3516   RAFTER (Kevin). Neil Blaney: a soldier of destiny. Pp 151. Dublin: Blackwater Press, 1993.

RAFTERY (Joseph). See 2925.

3517   Raheen pipe band (a little village miracle). In *Roscommon Hist. Soc. Jn.*, iv, 43-4 (1992).

RAMSEY (Trevor). See 2926.

3518   REA (J.). Irish state forestry: government policy 1948-1959. In *Ir. Forestry*, xlii, 7-15 (1985).

3519   REDMOND (Mary). Trade unions and the law. In *Trade union century*, pp 99-105 (1994).

REES (Nicholas). See HOLMES (Michael).

REILLY (Catherine). See 2936.

3520   REYNOLDS (Brian).   Casalattico and the Italian community in Ireland.   Pp
         191. Dublin: U.C.D. Foundation for Italian Studies, 1993. (Publications of
         the Foundation for Italian Studies, University College, Dublin, [8]).

3521   RICHARDSON (Hilary).   The fate of Kingsley Porter.   In *Donegal Annual*,
         xlv, 83-7 (1993).

         RIGGS (Pádraigín).   See 2939.

         RIORDAN (Anthony).   See 2940.

3522   ROBERTS (M.J.) and NOONAN (J.A.).   Bunratty Folk Park and its potential
         as an education centre. In *The Other Clare*, ii, 36-9 (1978).

         ROBINSON (David B.).   See 2943.

         ROBINSON (Theo).   See 2944.

3523   ROCHE (Patrick J.).   Contemporary Irish nationalism.   In *Nordirland in
         Geschichte und Gegenwart*, pp 309-33 (1994).

3524   ROCHE (W.K.).   Industrial relations.   In *Trade union century*, pp 133-46
         (1994).

3525   ROCKETT (Kevin).   Aspects of the Los Angelesation of Ireland.   In *Ir.
         Communications Rev.*, i, 18-23 (1991).

         ROGAN (Eddie).   See 2949.

         ROLSTON (Bill).   See MUNCK (Ronnie).

3526   ROSE (Kieran).   Diverse communities: the evolution of lesbian and gay
         politics in Ireland.   Pp 84.   Cork: Cork University Press, 1994.
         (Undercurrents).

3527   ROWAN (Paul).   The team that Jack built.   Pp 192.   Edinburgh:
         Mainstream, 1994.
         Jack Charleton and Irish soccer.

3528   RUANE (Joseph).   Colonial legacies and cultural reflexivities.   In *Études
         Irlandaises*, xix, no. 2, pp 107-19 (1994).

3529   RUANE (Joseph).   Ireland, European integration, and the dialectic of
         nationalism and postnationalism. In *Études Irlandaises*, xix, no. 1, pp 183-93
         (1994).

3530   RUDD (Niall).   Pale green, light orange: a portrait of bourgeois Ireland,
         1930-1950. Pp [5], 168. Dublin: Lilliput Press, 1994.

         RUDDOCK (Thomas).   See 2958.

3531   RUDDY (Bridie).   Memories of Garden Street and it's (*sic*) lanes.   In *North
         Mayo Hist. Jn.*, iii, no. 2, pp 27-30 (1993/94).
         Ballina.

         RYAN (Christopher).   See 2961.

3532   RYAN (Gerard). Life on North Street. In *Swords Voices*, i, no. 2, pp 10-13 (1994).
        Memories of Swords and of the fire service.

3533   RYAN (Theresa). Dancing at Will Gavin's. In *Oola Past & Present*, iii, 3-6 (1994).

        RYAN (Theresa). See 2967, 2968.

3534   RYAN (Thomas) and STUART (Imogen). Remembering Canon McGarry. In *The Furrow*, xxxi, 518-21 (1980).

3535   RYAN (Tim). Albert Reynolds: the Longford leader: the unauthorised biography. Pp viii, 226. Dublin: Blackwater Press, 1994.

3536   RYAN (Tim). Dick Spring: a safe pair of hands! Pp 224. Dublin: Blackwater Press, 1993.

3537   RYAN-SMOLIN (Wanda). Leo Whelan (1892-1956). In *Ir. Arts Rev. Yearbk*, pp 227-34 (1994).
        Irish portrait painter.

        RYNNE (Etienne). See 2534.

        Sacred Heart Church, Borrisoleigh. See 2969.

3538   SANDS (Christopher). The Gresham for style. Pp 144. Dublin: Eblana Publications, 1994.
        Gresham Hotel, Dublin.

3539   SAVAGE (Joe). 'The good old days ...'. In *Swords Voices*, i, 15-16 (1992/93).

        SCANLAN (Bill). See 2973.

3540   SCANNELL (James). The bomb that never was. In *Arklow Hist. Soc. Jn.*, pp 17-18 (1992/93).
        Epilogue to 'Arklow's 1941 narrow escape' by James Scannell in *Arklow Hist. Soc. Jn.* 1990/91.

3541   SCANNELL (James). Wicklow - prelude to the 'Emergency' June to September 1939. Part 1, June 1939. In *Wicklow Hist. Soc. Jn.*, i, no. 7, pp 5-14 (1994).

        SCANNELL (James). See 2975.

3542   SCUDDS (Colin). O'Connor jewellers, 51 Lr Georges Street, Dun Laoghaire. In *Dun Laoghaire Jn.*, iii, 30-31 (1993).
        Shop built on lane leading to an old slaughter yard.

3543   SHANNON (Catherine B.). The Kennedys, Ireland and Irish America: a healthy intersection. In *The Irish Review*, xiv, 10-14 (1993).

        SHANNON (Catherine). See COLLINS (Peter).

        SHARKEY (Neil). See 2986.

Shaw, Lady Gregory and the Abbey. See 2987.

SHEPHERD (Ernie). See 2991.

SILINONTE (Joseph M.). See 2993.

SILVERMAN (Marilyn). See 2324..

3544   SIMPSON (W.G.). The Fleet Printing Company: recalling a trade printing house in the early 1950s. In *Long Room*, xxxix, 48-53 (1994).

3545   Sligo Regional Technical College. Sligo Regional Technical College, 1970-1990. Pp 352. Sligo: Regional Technical College, 1991.

SMARGIE (Aisling). See 2999.

SMITH (Cornelius F.). See 3000.

3546   SMITH (Desmond). The dissolution of the Irish Republic: a step on the way to peace. In *Studies*, lxxxiii, 55-63 (1994).

SMITH (Gus). See 3004.

3547   SMITHERS (Brigid). Tales from Mountgorry. In *Swords Voices*, i, 28-32 (1992/93).
      Memories of Mountgorry and Swords.

3548   SMYTH (Ailbhe). The women's movement in the Republic of Ireland, 1970-1990. In *Irish women's studies reader*, pp 245-69 (1993).

3549   SMYTH (Jim). Dancing, depravity and all that jazz. The Public Dance Halls Act of 1935. In *Hist. Ire.*, i, no. 2, pp 51-4. (1993).

SMYTH (Patrick). See *Let in the light* (1993).

3550   An spás a réiteach. An t-Aire Mícheál D. Ó hUiginn, T.D. ag caint le Peadar Kirby. In *Oghma*, no. 5, pp 19-28 (1993).
      Higgins, Michael D.

3551   St Mary's Baldoyle: silver jubilee 1967-1992. Pp 44. [Dublin]: [St Mary's Baldoyle], [1993?].

STACPOOLE-RYDING (Richard J.). See 3010.

STEMPEL (P. De Bernardo). See 3012.

3552   STOKES (Dick). Memories of the past. In *Oola Past & Present*, i, 27-30 (1992).

3553   STOKES (Roy). The wreck of the Bolivar. In *Dun Laoghaire Jn.*, i, pp [9-10] (1990).

3554   STOUT (Geraldine). Grant-aided change in the Boyne Valley Archaeological Park: agricultural grants, 1950-1990. In *Ir. Geography*, xxvi, 79-88 (1993).

3555   STRONG (Eithne). Mullaghareink: aspects in perspective. In *Eire-Ireland*, xxviii, no. 4, pp 7-15 (1993).

STUART (Imogen). See RYAN (Thomas).

3556   SUENENS (Léon Joseph). The hidden hand of God: the life of Veronica O'Brien and our common apostolate. Pp 338. Dublin: Veritas, 1994.
Originally published in French, 1993. 1905- Legion of Mary and charismatic renewal.

3557   SUTTON (Ralph). Pictures in a friend's eye. In *O'Mahony Jn.*, xii, 33-7 (1982).
Eoin O'Mahony memorial lecture in Dublin.

SWANTON (Daisy Lawrenson). See 3018.

3558   SWEENEY (George). Irish hunger strikes and the cult or self-sacrifice. In *Jn. Contemporary Hist.*, xxviii, no. 3, pp 421-37 (1993).

3559   SZUCHEWYCZ (B.G.). The rhetoric of religious innovation: perceptions and reactions to the Catholic charismatic renewal in Ireland. In *Canadian Jn. of Irish Studies*, xix, no. 1, pp 37-53 (1993).

TAYLOR (Patrick). See 3027.

3560   Thanks for the memories, 1954-1994: Forty years of the Galway international oyster festival. *Ed.* Ronnie O'Gorman. Pp [6], 106. Galway: Galway International Oyster Festival, 1994.

3561   TIERNEY (Erin). Ideology of women in Irish education - a historical perspective. In *Alumnus*, pp 15-19 (1993).
Outline of the author's thesis-in-progress.

3562   TIERNEY (Erin). A look behind the bar. In *Alumnus*, pp 87-94 (1994).
The marriage bar for women national teachers, 1933-58.

TIVNAN (Frank). See 3032.

3563   Todhchaí na hEaglaise Caitlicí in Éirinn. Peter McVerry, Brendan Ryan agus Catherine Dunphy ag caint le Peadar Kirby. In *Oghma*, no. 3, pp 97-110 (1991).
McVerry, Peter; Ryan, Brendan; Dunphy, Catherine.

3564   TOKSVIG (Signe). Signe Toksvig's Irish diaries, 1926-1937. *Ed.* Lis Pihl. Pp 450. Dublin: Lilliput Press, 1994.
Danish writer and wife of Irish novelist Francis Hackett.

Tomás an Bhlascaoid (1992). See 3033.

3565   TOUHER (Patrick). Free as a bird: [the shadow of Artane]. Pp 196. Dublin: Gill & Macmillan, 1994.
Born 1942, 8 years in Artane School as orphan, 1950-58.

TOWNSHEND (Charles). See 3034.

TRAVERS (Pauric). See 3036.

3566   TREACY (Steve). Scythe to setaside: 30 years of agricultural photography. Pp v, 97. Dublin: I.A.W.S. Group, 1993.
1960s- .

3567   Tully graveyard, Lehaunstown, Cabinteely, Co. Dublin.   In *Dun Laoghaire Genealogical Soc. Jn.*, ii, 25-7 (1993).

TYERS (Pádraig).   See 3043.

3568   Uí DHOMHNAILL (Máire).   Mar is cuimhin linn Pádraig Ó Meára.   In *Ó ghlúin go glúin*, pp 39-49 (1993).

Uí MHORÓNAIGH (Eibhlín).   See 3045.

VAN ESBECK (Edmund).   See 3049.

3569   VAUGHAN (Paddy).   The last forge in Lismore.   Pp xi, 98.   Dublin: Poddle Press, 1994.
        Lismore, Co. Waterford.

VERDON (Michael).   See 3053.

VINCENT (John).   See 3056.

3570   W. (P.F.).   Thomas Fanning 1933-1993.   In *R.S.A.I. Jn.*, cxxiv, 220-21 (1994).

3571   WALLACE (Joe).   Waterford 1947: the year of the two congresses.   In *Saothar*, xix, 139-44 (1994).

WALLS (John P.).   See 3064.

WALPOLE (Peggy).   See 3065.

3572   WARKE (R.A.).   Ripples in the pool.   Pp 164.   Dublin: Mercier Press, 1993.
        Autobiography of Church of Ireland Bishop of Cork, Cloyne and Ross, b.1930.

WEBB (Marcus).   See *Hockey in Trinity*.

WEST (Máire).   See 3072.

WHELAN (Bernadette).   See HOLMES (Michael).

3573   WHELAN (Kevin).   Watching the detective.   In *Hist. Ire.*, ii, no. 2, pp 10-12 (1994).
        Interview with Professor L.M. Cullen of Trinity College Dublin.

3574   WHITAKER (T.K.).   Éire mo linne.   In *Náisiún na hÉireann*, pp 86-93 (1993).
        Irish society and language in modern Ireland.

WIEMERS (Amy J.).   See 3079.

WILLIAMS (Roche).   See 3082.

WILLIAMSON (Jeffrey G.).   See 3084.

WILLIAMSON (Jeffrey G.).   See 2354.

WILLOUGHBY (Charlie). See 3085.

WILLS (Clair). See 3086.

3575   WILSON (Andrew J.). The conflict between Noraid and the Friends of Irish Freedom. In *The Irish Review*, xv, 40-50 (1994).

WILSON (Joe). See 3088.

3576   Working life in Fingal 1936-1959: recollections from north County Dublin. Pp 79. Dublin: Fingal Heritage Group, 1994.

WORTMANN (Martin). See FARRELL (David M.).

WYSE JACKSON (Patrick). See 3090, 3091.

YOUNG (James D.). See 3093.

YOUNG (Peter). See 3094.

3577   ADAMS (Gerry).   Selected writings.   Pp 316.   Kerry: Brandon, 1994.

3578   ALCOCK (Antony).   Understanding Ulster.   Pp 178.   Lurgan: Ulster
        Society Publications, 1994.
        Rev. and updated version of Northern Ireland: problems and solutions,
        Sindelfingen: Libertas Verlag, 1985.

3579   Amnesty International. International Secretariat. Political killings in Northern
        Ireland. Pp 75. London: Amnesty International British Section, 1994.

3580   ANDERSON (Don).   Fourteen May days: the inside story of the loyalist
        strike of 1974. Pp xiii, 180. Dublin: Gill & Macmillan, 1994.

3581   ANDERSON (James) and SHUTTLEWORTH (Ian).   Sectarian readings of
        sectarianism: interpreting the Northern Ireland census.   In *The Irish Review*,
        xvi, 74-93 (1994).

        ARDAGH (John).   See 3101.

3582   ARMSTRONG (Lord).   Ethnicity, the English, and Northern Ireland:
        comments and reflections.   In *Northern Ireland and the politics of
        reconciliation*, pp 203-07 (1993).
        Secretary to the British cabinet in the 1980s.

3583   ARTHUR (Paul).   The Anglo-Irish Agreement: a device for territorial
        management? In *Northern Ireland and the politics of reconciliation*, pp 208-25
        (1993).

3584   ARTHUR (Paul).   Northern Ireland: religion, national identity and distorted
        history. [Review article]. In *Parliamentary History*, xii, 312-20 (1993).

3585   AUGHEY (Arthur).   Conservative party policy and Northern Ireland.   In *The
        Northern Ireland question*, pp 121-50 (1994).

3586   AUGHEY (Arthur).   Contemporary unionist politics.   In *The Northern
        Ireland question*, pp 53-75 (1994).

3587   AUGHEY (Arthur).   Light at the end of the tunnel?: the conflict today.   In
        Nordirland in Geschichte und Gegenwart, pp 237-56 (1994).

3588   AUGHEY (Arthur).   The Unionists.   In *Nordirland in Geschichte und
        Gegenwart*, pp 363-80 (1994).

3589   BAILLIE (John).   Solution for Northern Ireland: a king's perspective.   Pp
        282. Lewes (Sussex): Book Guild, 1994.
        Scottish example.

        BAIRNER (Alan).   See SUGDEN (John).

        BAKER (Joe).   See 1977.

BAKER (Susan).   See 3106.

3590   BARAKAT (Sultan).   Civil unrest shaping the built environment in Northern Ireland: the case of Belfast.   Pp iv, 66.   York: University of York, Institute of Advanced Architectural Studies, 1993.   (Post-war Reconstruction and Development Unit Working Paper 3)

3591   BARTON (Brian).   Lord Brookeborough and the Andrew's premiership.   In *Nordirland in Geschichte und Gegenwart*, pp 171-83 (1994).

BASSETT (John).   See 1981

3592   BEEMAN (Josiah Horton) and MAHONY (Robert).   The institutional churches and the process of reconciliation in Northern Ireland: recent progress in Presbyterian-Roman Catholic relations.   In *Northern Ireland and the politics of reconciliation*, pp 150-59 (1993).

3593   BELL (Desmond).   Acts of Union: youth sub-culture and ethnic identity amongst Protestants in Northern Ireland. In *Brit. Jn. Sociol.*, xxxviii, 158-83 (1987).

3594   BELL (J. Bowyer).   The Irish troubles: a generation of violence, 1967-1992. Pp xvii, 872.   Dublin: Gill & Macmillan, 1993.

3595   BELL (Robert).   A democracy of print.   The periodical literature of the Northern Ireland troubles.   In *Linen Hall Review*, xi, no. 3, pp 9-11 (1994).

3596   BELL (Robert).   The Northern Ireland political collection at the Linen Hall Library.   In *Hist. Irá.*, i, no. 1, pp 47-51 (1993).

3597   BELL (Robert).   Northern Ireland political periodicals, 1966-1992:   a bibliography of the holdings of the Linen Hall Library.   Pp x, 531.   Belfast: Linen Hall Library, 1994.

3598   Belleek Chamber of Commerce.   Belleek community & visitors' guide.   Pp 128.   Belleek: Belleek Chamber of Commerce, [1994?].

3599   BENNETT (Ronan).   Double jeopardy: the retrial of the Guilford Four.   Pp 71.   London: Penguin, 1993.

3600   BERLINKE (Helge).   Die Unendliche Krise: Ökonomische und socioökononische Entwicklungen in Nordirland.   In *Nordirland in Geschichte und Gegenwart*, pp 354-62 (1994).

3601   BEW (Paul) and DIXON (Paul).   Labour party policy and Northern Ireland. In *The Northern Ireland question*, pp 151-65 (1994).

3602   BEW (Paul) and GILLESPIE (Gordon).   Northern Ireland: a chronology of the troubles, 1968-1993.   Pp xii, 344.   Dublin: Gill & Macmillan, 1993.

BEW (Paul).   See *Passion and prejudice* (1993).

3603   BLOOMFIELD (Ken).   Stormont in crisis: a memoir.   Pp 295.   Belfast: Blackstaff Press, 1994.
        Private secretary to Terence O'Neill and head of Northern Ireland civil service.

3604   BONNER (David).   Combating terrorism: supergrass trials in Northern Ireland. In *Modern Law Review*, li, 23-53 (1988).

BOYCE (Frank). See 3118.

3605   BRADLEY (Anthony). Requiem for a spy: the killing of Robert Nairac. Pp 158. Cork; Dublin: Mercier Press, 1992.

BRADLEY (John). See 2023.

BRADY (Ciaran). See 3119.

3606   BRADY (Ronan). An end to vitriol. Eventually getting the message across. In *Ir. Reporter*, xvi, 3-4 (1994).

BRANAGH (Kenneth). See LAWRENCE (Norman).

3607   BREE (Declan). The road to peace: from Downing Street to Bodenstown. Pp 24. Sligo: Graltan Labour History Committee, 1994.

BREEN (Muriel). See 2026.

3608   BREWER (John D.).   Sectarianism and racism, and their parallels and differences. In *Ethnic and Racial Studies*, xv, 352-64 (1992).

3609   BRIERLEY (G.J.), GAILEY (I.B.) and GILLESPIE (W.F.). The Territorials in Northern Ireland 1947-1992. Pp 119. [s.l.]: Northern Ireland Territorial Auxiliary and Volunteer Reserve Association, 1993.

3610   BROWN (Terence). The cultural issue in Northern Ireland, 1965-1991.   In *Northern Ireland and the politics of reconciliation*, pp 160-70 (1993).

BROWNE (Jeremy). See LAWRENCE (Norman).

3611   BRUCE (Steve). The edge of the union: the Ulster loyalist political vision. Pp viii, 176. Oxford: Oxford University Press, 1994.

3612   BRUCE (Steve). Northern Ireland: reappraising loyalist violence. In *Ethnic and religious conflicts*, pp 113-33 (1994).

3613   BRUCE (Steve). The politics of the loyalist paramilitaries. In *The Northern Ireland question*, pp 103-20 (1994).

3614   BRUCE (Steve). The Red Hand: loyalist paramilitaries in Northern Ireland. In *Nordirland in Geschichte und Gegenwart*, pp 381-95 (1994).

BRYSON (Lucy). See McCARTNEY (Clem).

BUCKLAND (Patrick). See 2038.

3615   BURNETT (Harry).   Childhood memories of regattas at Strangford.   In *Lecale Miscellany*, xi, 61-5 (1993)

3616   BURNETT (Harry).   Hauling up 'Armyne' for the winter.   In *Lecale Miscellany*, v, 22-3 (1987).
        Yachting in Strangford in the 1920s.

3617   BURNETT (Harry). Memories of school days in Strangford. In *Lecale Miscellany*, vii, 60-64 (1989).

3618   BURNETT (Harry). Memories of school days in Strangford. In *Lecale Miscellany*, viii, 16-23 (1990).

3619   BUTLER (David). Documenting the Troubles: a question of perspective. In *Ir. Communications Rev.*, ii, 35-45 (1992).

3620   BUTLER (David E.). British broadcasting in Northern Ireland: a contradiction in terms? In *Nordirland in Geschichte und Gegenwart*, pp 453-68 (1994).

BYRNE (Anne). See 3134.

3621   CALDWELL (John Taylor). Severely dealt with: growing up in Belfast and Glasgow. Pp 163. Bradford: North Herald Books, 1993.

3622   CALLAGHAN (Hugh). Cruel fate: one man's triumph over injustice. Pp [11], i, 207. Swords, Co. Dublin: Poolbeg Press, 1993.

3623   CALLAGHAN (Kevin) and GORRY (Terry). A price on my head. Pp 175. Wigan: Owl Books, 1993.
    British Army bomb disposal in Northern Ireland.

3624   CAMERON (Margaret). The women in green: a history of the Royal Ulster Constabulary's policewomen: golden jubilee, 1943-1993. Pp 120. Belfast: R.U.C. Historical Society, 1993.

3625   CAMPBELL (Annie). Let us be true each to the other. A covenant for a new Ireland. In *Ir. Reporter*, xvi, 12-14 (1994).

CAMPBELL (Brian). See *Nor meekly serve my time.*

3626   CAMPBELL (Colm). Extradition to Northern Ireland: prospects and problems. In *Modern Law Review*, lii, 585-621 (1989).

CANAVAN (Paul). See 2061.

3627   CARROLL (Valerie). From Belfast's Sandy Row to Buckingham Palace: the story of John Gibson. Pp 144. Cork; Dublin: Mercier Press, 1994.
    John Gibson, 1926-

CARSWELL (Leslie). See 3139.

CARVILLE (P.J.). See 2071.

CASSIDY (Dennis). See 2072.

3628   CATHCART (Rex). Ireland and 'King Billy' usage and abusage. In *History Today*, xxxviii, no. 7, pp 40-45 (July 1988).

3629   CHABANAIS (Paula) and GOLDBERG (David). Sidney Smith: painter and moralist (1912-1982). In *Ir. Arts Rev. Yearbk*, pp 235-44 (1994).
    Belfast artist.

CHRISTENSEN (M.). See 2078.

3630   CLARK (Wallace). Mull of Kintyre - the hard way. In *The Glynns*, viii, 11-12 (1980).

3631   CLARKE (Liam). Contemporary republican politics. In *The Northern Ireland qusetion*, pp 76-102 (1994).

3632   CLEMENTS (Roy). Memory of memories of Derry. *Ed*. Martina McLaughlin. Pp 108. Derry: Guildhall Press, 1994.

        CLIFFORD (Gerard). See DUNLOP (John).

3633   COCHRANE (Elizabeth). Downpatrick characters of bygone days. In *Lecale Miscellany*, viii, 42-3 (1990).

3634   COCHRANE (Feargal). Any takers? The isolation of Northern Ireland. In *Political Studies*, xlii, 378-95 (1994).

3635   COCHRANE (Feargal). Progressive or regressive?: the Anglo-Irish Agreement as a dynamic in the Northern Ireland polity. In *Irish Political Studies*, viii, 1-20 (1993).

3636   COCHRANE (Gerry). The return of the County Down. In *Lecale Miscellany*, v, 17-19 (1987).
        Reconstructing the Downpatrick-Ardglass branch line.

        COLLINS (Neill). See 3148.

3637   COLMER (Albert W.K.). D.J. McNeill - a tribute. In *Lecale Miscellany*, vi, 2 (1988).

3638   COLMER (Albert W.K.). 'The Hilda Parnell' or 'The Hilda' over 30 years ago. In *Lecale Miscallany*, vi, 45 (1988).
        The remains of a small wooden schooner now lying near Quoile Quay.

3639   COLMER (Albert W.K.). P.J. Lennon - a tribute. In *Lecale Miscellany*, v, 2 (1987).

        COLMER (Albert). See 2102.

        CONNOLLY (Al). See 2109.

        COOLAHAN (John). See 3423.

        COUGHLAN (Anthony). See 3158.

3640   COULTER (Colin). The character of Unionism. In *Irish Political Studies*, ix, 1-24 (1994).

3641   COULTER (Colin). Class, ethnicity and political identity in Northern Ireland. In *Ir. Jn. of Sociology*, iv, 1-26 (1994).

3642   CRADDEN (Terry). Trade unionism, socialism and partition: the labour movement in Northern Ireland, 1939-1953. Pp xi, 244. Belfast: December Publications, 1993.

        CRADDEN (Terry). See 2135.

3643   CRAWFORD (Steve).   The SAS at close quarters. Pp 192.   London: Sidgwick & Jackson, 1993.
Pp 112-47 Northern Ireland, including Loughall and Gibralter.

3644   CROSKERY (Mary E.).   The Gibraltarians in County Down.   In *Lecale Miscellany*, xii, 39 (1994).
Note to article in *Lecale Miscellany*, iii (1985) on Gibraltarian World War II evacuees.

CURTIS (L.P. jr).   See 3167.

3645   DALLAS (George).   Prophet for Protestants.   In *The Furrow*, xxxiv, 89-94 (1983).
W.S. Armour, author of *Facing the Irish question.* .

3646   DALY (Cahal B.).   Peace - now is the time: Northern Ireland.   Pp 31. Dublin: Veritas, 1993.

DARWIN (Kenneth).   See *Passion and prejudice* (1993).

DAVEY (Peter).   See 2168.

3647   DAVEY (Ray).   A channel of peace: the story of the Corrymeela Community. Pp 170. London: Marshall Pickering, 1993.
Ecumenical centre, Co. Antrim.

3648   DAVIS (Richard).   Mirror hate: the convergent ideology of Northern Ireland paramilitaries, 1966-1992. Pp vi, 345. Aldershot: Dartmouth, 1994.

De ROSSA (Proinsias).   See 3180.

3649   DEVLIN (Paddy).   Straight left: an autobiography. Pp vii, 303.   Belfast: Blackstaff Press, 1993.
Co-founder of SDLP in 1970.

DICKSON (David).   See 3181.

DILLON (Martin).   See 3182.

3650   DINWOODIE (Robbie).   A fireman writes ... a reporter's view of Scotland's press and the Irish question. In *Scotland and Ulster*, pp 134-49 (1994).
Ulster 1981-

3651   DITCH (J.S.) and MORRISSEY (M.J.).   Northern Ireland: review and prospects for social policy. In *Soc. Pol. & Admin.*, xxvi, 18-39 (1992).

3652   DIXON (Paul).   European integration modernisation and Northern Ireland, 1961-75. In *Études Irlandaises*, xix, no. 1, pp 167-82 (1994).

3653   DIXON (Paul).   'The usual English doubletalk': the British political parties and the Ulster unionists 1974-94. In *Irish Political Studies*, ix, 25-40 (1994).

DIXON (Paul).   See BEW (Paul).

3654   DOHERTY (Paul).   Agape to Zoroastrian: religious denomination in Northern Ireland, 1961-1991. In *Ir. Geography*, xxvi, 14-21 (1993).

3655 DOHERTY (Richard). Escort base. In *Ulster Local Studies*, xvi, no. 1, pp 31-42 (1994).

DOUGLAS (Wm). See 2196.

3656 DOYLE (John). Workers and outlaws: unionism and fair employment in Northern Ireland. In *Irish Political Studies*, ix, 41-60 (1994).

3657 DRAPER (Vivienne). The children of Dunseverick. Pp 160. Dingle: Brandon, 1994.
Ardglass.

3658 DUFFY (Joseph). Northern Ireland. The way forward as I see it (1). In *The Furrow*, xxxiii, 399-406 (1982).

3659 DUGGAN (Dave). Todhchaí iarchogaidh Deachrachtaí agus rianta dóchais. In *Oghma*, vi, 6-10 (1994).

3660 DUNLOP (Eull). Jack McCann, a Ballymena man. In *The Glynns*, xxii, 8-9 (1994).

3661 DUNLOP (John), CLIFFORD (Gerard) and ELLIOTT (Eric). Pastoral dimensions of the Northern Ireland conflict. The Presbyterian Church; the Catholic Church; the Church of Ireland. In *The Furrow*, xxxiii, 36-50 (1982).

DUNPHY (Richard). See 3199.

3662 EDWARDS (Owen Dudley). Rodney Green: an appreciation. In *Lurgan*, p 185 (1993).
Historian E.R.R. Green, 1920-81.

ELLIOTT (Eric). See DUNLOP (John).

ELLIOTT (Sydney). See FLACKES (W.D.).

ENGLISH (Richard). See 3204.

3663 FARREN (Aidan). Harvest-men. In *Benbradagh*, xii, 15 (1982).

FARREN (Seán). See MACAULAY (Ambrose).

FAUSKE (Christopher). See 2237.

3664 FENTON (James). The homely tongue: the story so far. In *Ulster Local Studies*, xvi, no. 2, pp 22-8 (1994).

FERRIS (Tom). See 2242.

FINLAY (Andrew). See 2248.

3665 FINN (Gerry B.). Sporting symbols, sporting identities: soccer and intergroup conflict in Scotland and Northern Ireland. In *Scotland and Ulster*, pp 33-55 (1994).

FITZGERALD (Desmond). See 2251.

3666 FITZGERALD (Garret). The origins and rationale of the Anglo-Irish Agreement of 1985. In *Northern Ireland and the politics of reconciliation*, pp 189-202 (1993).

3667 FITZGERALD (J.D.). Forbes on the L & LSR, 1928. In *Irish Railway Rec. Soc. Jn.*, xviii, no. 120, pp 184-97 (1993).

3668 FLACKES (W.D.) and ELLIOTT (Sydney). Northern Ireland: a political directory, 1968-93. Revised ed. Pp xiv, 513. Belfast: Blackstaff Press, 1994.
Previous ed., 1989.

3669 FOSTER (Roy). Anglo-Irish relations and Northern Ireland: historical perspectives. In *Northern Ireland and the politics of reconciliation*, pp 13-32 (1993).

FOSTER (Roy). See 3227.

3670 FRIEL (Charles P.). Witham Street to Cultra. In *Irish Railway Rec. Soc. Jn.*, xviii, no. 122, pp 278-81 (1993).
Transfer of locomotives to Ulster Folk & Transport Museum, 1993.

3671 FRIERS (Rowel). Drawn from life: an autobiography. Pp 216. Belfast: Blackstaff Press, 1994.

FULTON (Eileen). See 2278.

GAILEY (I.B.). See BRIERLEY (G.J.).

GALLAGHER (Jim). See MAGUIRE (Anne).

3672 GALLAGHER (Lyn) and ROGERS (Dick). Castle, coast and cottage: the National Trust in Northern Ireland. Pp 208. Belfast: Blackstaff Press, 1992. 2nd ed.
Gazetteer plus history of National Trust since 1935.

3673 GALLAGHER (R.D. Eric). Northern Ireland. The way forward as I see it (2). In *The Furrow*, xxxiii, 406-12 (1982).

GARDINER (Frances). See 3232.

3674 GARLAND (Roy). The Ulster Volunteer Force negotiating history. Pp 174. [Belfast]: [the author], 1991.

3675 GIFFORD (Dick). The Hilda Parnell. In *Lecale Miscellany*, v, 28-30 (1987).
The remains of a small schooner now lying near Quoile Quay.

GILLESPIE (Gordon). See BEW (Paul).

GILLESPIE (Gordon). See *Passion and prejudice* (1993).

GILLESPIE (W.F.). See BRIERLEY (G.J.).

3676 GIRVIN (Brian). Constitutional nationalism in Northern Ireland. In *The Northern Ireland question*, pp 5-52 (1994).

GLENDINNING (James). See 2295.

3677   GLENDINNING (Miles) and MUTHESIUS (Stefan). Tower block: modern public housing in England, Scotland and Northern Ireland. Pp viii, 420. New Haven: Yale University Press, 1994.

GOLDBERG (David). See CHABANAIS (Paula).

GORRY (Terry). See CALLAGHAN (Kevin).

3678   GRAHAM (Brian J.). The search for the common ground: Estyn Evans's Ireland. In *Inst. Br. Geog. Trans.*, n.s., xix, 183-201 (1994).

GRANT (J.R.). See 2307.

3679   GRAY (John). Flan Campbell (1919-1994). In *Hist. Ire.*, ii, no. 2, p. 7 (1994).

3680   GREER (Alan). Policy networks and state-farmer relations in Northern Ireland, 1921-72. In *Political Studies*, xlii, 396-412 (1994).

3681   GROSSHEIM (Bernd). Speaking Gaelic in the Troubles: Irischer nationalismus und seine sprache. In *Nordirland in Geschichte und Gegenwart*, pp 487-94 (1994).

3682   GUELKE (Adrian). The peace process in South Africa, Israel and Northern Ireland: a farewell to arms? In *Ir. Stud. in Int. Affairs*, v, 93-106 (1994).

3683   GUELKE (Adrian). The United States and the Northern Ireland question. In *The Northern Ireland question*, pp 189-212 (1994).

3684   HADDEN (Peter). Beyond the troubles?: Northern Ireland's past and future: a socialist analysis. Pp 103. Belfast: Herald Books, 1994.

HADFIELD (Brigid). See 3257.

HAINES (Keith). See 2325.

3685   HALLIDAY (Colin). Downpatrick & Ardglass railway. In *Irish Railway Rec. Soc. Jn.*, xviii, no. 121, pp 227-30 (1993).

HALTZEL (Michael H.). See KEOGH (Dermot).

HAMILTON (Douglas). See 3258.

HAMILTON (S.N.). See 2335.

3686   HAMLIN (Ann). Emyr Estyn Evans, 1905-1989. In *Arch. Ire.*, iii, 115 (1989).

3687   HAMMILL (Brendan). Emigrant brother. The politics of emigration. In *Irishways*, i, 10-11 (1991).

3688   HANNA (Cona). Downpatrick World War II airmen honoured. In *Lecale Miscellany*, vi, 33-6 (1988).

HANNA (Conac). See 2336.

3689   HARKNESS (David W.).   From Sunningdale to Hillsborough.   In *Nordirland in Geschichte und Gegenwart*, pp 223-36 (1994).

3690   HARRIS (Mary).   The Catholic Church, minority rights, and the founding of the Northern Irish state.   In *Northern Ireland and the politics of reconciliation*, pp 62-83 (1993).

HARRIS (Mary). See 2344.

3691   HARTMANN (Klaas) and SCHUMACHER (Christopher).   Chronologie des Nordirlankonflikt.   In *Nordirland in Gescheschte und Gegenwart*, pp 554-64 (1994).

HASLEM (Richard). See 3328.

3692   HAYES (Maurice).   Sweet Killough, let go your anchor.   Pp 219.   Belfast: Blackstaff Press, 1994.
        Memoir of growing up in Co. Down village, 1927-

HAYES (Maurice). See 3269.

HAZELKORN (Ellen). See 3271.

HEGARTY (Lawrence). See 2362.

3693   HELLE (Andreas).   Nordirland als Problem der britischen Politik.   In *Nordirland in Geschichte und Gegenwart*, pp 276-98 (1994).

3694   HELLE (Andreas).   ' Die widersprüchliche Autonomie Nordirlands.   In *Nordirland in Geschichte und Gegenwart*, pp 151-70 (1994).
        Semi-independence of Northern Ireland.

3695   HENRY (Brian).   Portstewart Football Club: the first 25 years.   Pp 84. [Portstewart, Co. Antrim]: Portstewart Football Club, [1993?].

3696   HERZ (Dietmar).   Nordirland und die Europäische Gemeinschaft.   In *Nordirland in Geschichte und Gegenwart*, pp 299-308 (1994).

3697   HEWITT (Christopher).   Catholic grievances and violence in Northern Ireland.   In *Brit. Jn. Sociol.*, xxxvi, 102-05 (1985).

3698   HEWITT (Christopher).   Discrimination in Northern Ireland: a rejoinder.   In *Brit. Jn. Sociol.*, xxxiv, 446-51 (1983).

3699   HEWITT (Christopher).   Explaining violence in Northern Ireland.   In *Brit. Jn. Sociol.*, xxxviii, 88-93 (1987).

3700   HEWITT (Christopher).   Catholic grievances, Catholic nationalism and violence in Northern Ireland during the Civil Rights period: a reconsideration.   In *Brit. Jn. Sociol.*, xxxii, 362-80 (1981).

HILLYARD (Paddy). See 3280, 3281.

3701   HOGAN (Edmund).   The church and Northern Ireland.   In *The Furrow*, xxxi, 232-9 (1980).

3702   HOROWITZ (Donald L.).   Conflict and the incentives to political accommodation.   In *Northern Ireland and the politics of reconciliation*, pp 173-88 (1993).
        Comparisons with African and Asian countries.

3703   HUGHES (A.J.).   Manx speaker Ned Maddrell and Irish Gaelic author Liam Mac Neachtain.   In *Seanchas Ardmhacha*, xv, no. 2, pp 125-9 (1993).

        HUME (John).   See 3287.

3704   IGNATIEFF (Michael).   Blood and belonging: journeys into the new nationalism.   Pp 201.   London: BBC Books/Chatto & Windus, 1993.
            Chapter on N. Ireland.

3705   Institute for European Defence and Strategic Studies.   Ulster after the ceasefire: the report of an independent study.   Pp 36.   London: Alliance for the Institute for European Defence and Strategic Studies, 1994.   (European security study, no. 21)

3706   JACKSON (Alvin).   Unionist history.   In *Interpreting Irish history*, pp 253-68 (1994).
            First published in *The Irish Review* (autumn 1989), pp 58-65 and (spring 1990), pp 62-9.

        JACKSON (Alvin).   See 2414.

3707   JACKSON (J.D.).   The Northern Ireland (Emergency Provisions) Act 1987.   In *Northern Ireland Legal Quart.*, xxxix, 235-57 (1988).

        KEARNEY (Hugh).   See 3305.

3708   KEARNEY (Richard) and WILSON (Robin).   Northern Ireland's future as a European region.   Submission to the Opsahl Commission.   In *The Irish Review*, xv, 51-69 (1994).

        KELLS (Mary).   See 3307.

3709   KELLY (Mary Pat).   Home away from home: the Yanks in Ireland.   Pp 164.   Belfast: Appletree Press, 1994.
            1942-5 Northern Ireland.

3710   KENNEDY (Dennis).   The European Union and the Northern Ireland question.   In *The Northern Ireland question*, pp 166-88 (1994).

        KENNEDY (Dennis).   See 3313.

        KENNEDY (S.B.).   See 2443.

3711   KEOGH (Dermot) and HALTZEL (Michael H.).   Introduction.   In *Northern Ireland the the politics of reconciliation*, pp 1-10 (1993).

3712   KILLEN (Pat).   Dying trades.   In *Lecale Miscellany*, vi, 41 (1987).

3713   KIRKPATRICK (Noel).   Take a second look: [around County Down].   Pp [8], 231.   Newtownards: Alkon Press, 1993.
            County Down in 20th century.

KNOX (Colin). See 3328.

3714 KOCKEL (Ulrich). Mythos und Identität: der Konflikt in Spiegel Volkskultur. In *Nordirland in Geschichte und Gegenwart*, pp 495-517 (1994).
Popular culture.

3715 KOVALCHEK (Kassian A.). Catholic grievances in Northern Ireland: appraisal and judgement. In *Brit. Jn. Sociol.*, xxxviii, 77-87 (1987).

LAFFAN (Brigid). See 3330.

3716 LAWRENCE (Norman). Parallel realities of Northern Ireland. Foreword by Kenneth Branagh; the photographers Jeremy Browne [et al]. Pp xi, 140. Belfast: Blackstaff Press, 1994.

LEDWIDGE (John). See 2499.

3717 LENNON (Brian). Catholic praxis and the Northern Ireland conflict. In *Nordirland in Geschichte und Gegenwart*, pp 442-52 (1994).

3718 LENNON (P.J.). Earning a living in Strangford over 60 years ago. As I remembered it. In *Lecale Miscellany*, ix, 38-9 (1991).

3719 LENNON (P.J.). Earning a living in Strangford in the 1930s as I remembered it. In *Lecale Miscellany*, xii, 16-18 (1994).

3720 LENNON (P.J.). Hiking the roads to make a living. In *Lecale Miscellany*, v, 24-7 (1987).

3721 LEONARD (Jane). Archives relating to Northern Ireland. In *The Longman guide to sources in contemporary British history 1: organisations and societies*, pp 342-51 (1994).

LIDDLE (L.H.). See 3341.

3722 LIJPHART (Arend). Review article: the Northern Ireland problem: cases, theories and solutions. In *Brit. Jn. Political Science*, v, 83-106 (1975).

3723 LISTER (Ruth). Social policy in a divided community: reflections on the Opsahl Report on the future of Northern Ireland. In *Ir. Jn. of Sociology*, iv, 27-50 (1994).

3724 LIVINGSTONE (Stephen). The House of Lords and the Northern Ireland conflict. In *Modern Law Rev.*, lvii, 333-60 (1994).

3725 LOFTUS (Belinda). Mirrors: orange & green. Pp 112. Dundrum (Co. Down): Picture Press, 1994.
Politics and art, Northern Ireland.

3726 LONGLEY (Edna). A Northern 'Turn'? In *The Irish Review*, xv, 1-13 (1994).

3727 LONGLEY (Michael). Obituary - Jack McCann. In *The Glynns*, xxii, 6-7 (1994).

3728   LONGLEY (Michael). Tuppenny stung: autobiographical chapters. Pp 82. Belfast: Lagan Press, 1994.

LOUGHRAN (Gráinne). See *The radio catalogue* (1993).

3729   LOUGHRAN (Louise). Cluntoe aerodrome. In *The Bell*, v, 73-84 (1994).

3730   LUCY (Gordon). Northern Ireland: local government election results, 1993. Pp vi, 195. Belfast: Ulster Society (Publications), 1994.
        1981-

LUNN (Kenneth). See 3347.

3731   LYNCH (John). 'Ceasefire in the Academy'? In *Hist. Ire.*, ii, no. 4, pp 11-14 (1994).
        Interview with Paul Bew, professor of politics at Queen's University of Belfast.

LYONS (F.S.L.). See 3350.

3732   MACAFEE (Caroline).   Why are we waiting?:   a report on the Ulster dictionary project. In *Ulster Local Studies*, xvi, no. 2, pp 7-17 (1994).

McALLISTER (Denise). See 3353.

3733   McALLISTER (Ian). Political parties and social change in Ulster: the case of the SDLP. In *Social Studies*, v, 75-89 (1976/77).

3734   MACAULAY (Ambrose), WORRALL (Stanley) and FARREN (Seán). Church and school in Northern Ireland: a Catholic view; a Protestant view; a politician's view. In *The Furrow*, xxxi, 623-40 (1980).

MacCABA (Anton). See 2553.

3735   McCARTNEY (Clem) and BRYSON (Lucy). Clashing symbols?: a report on the use of flags, anthems and other national symbols in Northern Ireland. Pp vii, 196. Belfast: Institute of Irish Studies, Queen's University of Belfast for the Community Relations Council, 1994.

McCARTNEY (David James). See 2560.

McCAULEY (Iain). See McKEOWN (Cahir).

McCAVANA (Marian). See *The radio catalogue* (1993).

3736   McCOLGAN (John). 'Ulster's midwife': Sir Ernest Clark and the birth of the Northern Ireland administration.   In *Administration*, xxxviii, 41-69 (1990).

McCONVILLE (Michael). See 2565.

McCORD (M.E.). See 2567.

3737   McCOURT (Harry). 'Oh how we danced'. Pp 56. Derry: Guildhall Press, 1992.
        History of Derry showbands.

McCREARY (Alf). See 3058.

3738   McCUSKER (Breege). Castle Archdale and Fermanagh in World War II. Pp [x], 174. Irvinestown: Necarne Press, 1993.

McDONAGH (Enda). See 3371.

MacDONAGH (Oliver). See 3372.

McDONALD (B.). See 2578.

McDOWELL (R.B.). See 3181.

McGARRY (John). See O'LEARY (Brendan).

McGARRY (J.G.). See 3378.

3739   McKEOWN (Cahir). Enniskillen reminiscences. *Ed.* Iain McCauley. Pp 80. Enniskillen: Cahir McKeown, 1993.

McKEOWN (Laurence). See *Nor meekly serve my time* (1994).

3740   McKERNAN (James). Value systems and race relations in Northern Ireland and America. In *Ethnic and Racial Studies*, v, 156-74 (1982).

3741   McKITTRICK (David). Endgame: the search for peace in Northern Ireland. Pp x, 341. Belfast: Blackstaff Press, 1994.

3742   McLAUGHLIN (Eithne). Women and the family in Northern Ireland. A review. In *Women's Studies International Forum*, xvi, 553-68 (1993).

McLAUGHLIN (Martina). See CLEMENTS (Roy).

3743   McLAUGHLIN (Mitchel). Escaping from divisions and dependency. A new beginning for the next generation. In *Ir. Reporter*, xvi, 7-8 (1994).

McMEEKIN (Donald). See 2618.

McMULLAN (Anna). See 3385.

McNEILL (Ian). See 2620.

McNEILL (Linda). See 2621.

3744   MacPÓILIN (Aodán). The work of the ULTACH Trust in promoting the Irish language. In *Ulster Local Studies*, xvi, no. 2, pp 29-37 (1994).

3745   McVEIGH (Ann). Australia for ten pounds. In *Hist. Ire.*, i, no. 3, pp 44-6 (1993).

3746   McVICKER (John). Hugh and Sadie Mitchell. In *Ir. Baptist Hist. Soc. Jn.*, n.s., i, 21-48 (1993/94).

3747   McWILLIAMS (Monica). The church, the state and the women's movement in Northern Ireland. In *Irish women's studies reader*, pp 79-99 (1993). 1960-93.

3748   MAGUIRE (Anne) and GALLAGHER (Jim). Why me? One woman's fight for justice and dignity. Pp vi, 137. London: Harper Collins, 1994.

MAHONY (Robert). See BEEMAN (Josiah Horton).

3749   MAPSTONE (Richard). The military in a divided society: the occupational outline of soldiers in Northern Ireland. In *International Jn. of Sociol. and Soc. Pol.*, xiii, nos 1-2, pp 3-17 (1993).

3750   MASON (David). Nationalism and the process of group mobilisation: the case of 'loyalism' in Northern Ireland reconsidered. In *Ethnic and Racial Studies*, viii, 409-25 (1985).

MAXWELL (Frank). See 2650.

3751   MAYBIN (Mike). A nostalgic look at Belfast trams since 1945. Pp 99. Peterborough: Silver Link Publishing, 1994.

3752   MERRIGAN (Matt). Strike across the empire. In *Labour History News*, ix, 20-21 (1993).
        Seamen's strike 1925 in Britain, Australia, New Zealand, South Africa and Northern Ireland.

3753   MILLER (David). Don't mention the war: Northern Ireland, propaganda and the media. Pp xii, 368. London: Pluto Press, 1994.

3754   MILLER (Kerby A.). Revising revisionism: comments and reflections. In *Northern Ireland and the politics of reconciliation*, pp 52-61 (1993).

3755   MITCHELL (Paul). Conflict, regulation and party competition in Northern Ireland. In *European Jn. Political Res.*, xx, 67-92 (1991).

MITCHELL (Walter F.). See 2663.

3756   MOLLAN (Kenneth). Cultivating the supergrass - recent developments in law and order in Northern Ireland. In *Social Studies*, viii, 109-21 (1984/85).

MOODY (T.W.). See 3403.

3757   MORGAN (Hiram). A scholar and a gentleman. In *Hist. Ire.*, i, no. 2, pp 55-8 (1993).
        Interview with A.T.Q. Stewart of Queen's University.

MORRISON (John). See 3406.

MORRISSEY (M.J.). See DITCH (J.S.).

3758   MORROW (Duncan). Faith and fervour: religion and nationality in Ulster. In *Nordirland in Geschichte und Gegenwart*, pp 422-41 (1994).

3759   MORROW (Duncan). Games between frontiers: Northern Ireland as ethnic frontier. In *Nordirland in Geschichte und Gegenwart*, pp 334-53 (1994).

MOSS (Joan). See 3407.

MUNCK (Ronnie). See 3411.

MUTHESIUS (Stefan). See GLENDINNING (Miles).

NELSON (Charles). See 2717.

3760 NELSON (E. Charles). 'Glory of Donard': a history of the Slieve Donard Nursery, County Down, with a catalogue of cultivators. Pp 128. Belfast: Northern Ireland Heritage Gardens Committee, 1993.

3761 NELSON (Havelock). A bank of violets: the musical memoirs of Havelock Nelson. Pp vii, 62. Belfast: Greystone Books, 1993.
Doctor and musician, 1917-

3762 NELSON (Sarah). Belfast: walking the Shankill. In *Scotland and Ulster*, pp 22-32 (1994).
Personal account of social worker in Belfast 1972 to 1978.

3763 NELSON (Sarah). Developments in Protestant working-class politics. In *Social Studies*, v, 202-24 (1976/77).

3764 NEWSINGER (John). Thatcher, Northern Ireland and 'The Downing Street years'. In *Ir. Studies Rev.*, vii, 2-6 (1994).

3765 Nor meekly serve my time: the H Block struggle, 1976-1981. Compiled by Brian Campbell. *Ed.* Brian Campbell, Laurence McKeown, Felim O'Hagan. Pp xvi, 267. Belfast: Beyond the Pale Publications, 1994.

NORTH (Reg). See 3423.

NUTT (Kathleen). See 3424.

3766 Ó BEACHÁIN (Donnacha). Minority versus minority: constitutional nationalism and republicanism in Northern Ireland 1981-1988. In *U.C.D. Hist. Rev.*, v, 11-15 (1991).

Ó BEACHÁIN (Donnacha). See 3427.

3767 Obituary - George Robert Chapman. In *Review*, v, no. 3, p. 2 (1986/87).

3768 Ó BRÁDAIGH (Ruairí Óg). Submitting to the loyalist veto. A new Ireland cannot be the old Ireland in disguise. In *Ir. Reporter*, xvi, 9-11 (1994).

3769 O'BRIEN (Brendan). The long war: the IRA and Sinn Féin, 1985 to today. Pp 319. Dublin: O'Brien Press, 1993.

3770 O'CONNELL (Michael). Truth: the first casualty. Pp 254. [S.l.]: Riverside Ltd, 1993.
Miscarriages of justice.

3771 O'CONNOR (Fionnuala). In search of a state: Catholics in Northern Ireland. Pp 393. Belfast: Blackstaff Press, 1993.
Northern Ireland since 1969.

3772 O'DOHERTY (Shane). The volunteer: a former IRA man's true story. Pp 243. London: Fount, 1993.

Ó DIOBHLIN (Diarmaid). See 2764.

O'HAGAN (Felim).   See *Nor meekly serve my time.*

O'HAGAN (Kevin J.).   See 2806.

3773   O'HEARN (Denis).   Catholic grievances, Catholic nationalism: a comment.
In *Brit. Jn. Sociol.*, xxxiv, 438-45 (1983).

3774   O'HEARN (Denis).   Again on discrimination in the North of Ireland: a reply
to the rejoinder. In *Brit. Jn. Sociol.*, xxxvi, 94-101 (1985).

3775   O'HEARN (Denis).   Catholic grievances: comments.   In *Brit. Jn. Sociol.*,
xxxviii, 94-100 (1987).

3776   O'LEARY (Brendan) and McGARRY (John).   The politics of antagonism:
understanding Northern Ireland.   Pp 358.   London: Athlone Press, 1993.
(Conflict and change in Britain series - a new audit, 3)

3777   O'LEARY (Cornelius).   Northern Ireland, 1921-72: misshapen constitutional
development and scholarly silence.   In *Modern Irish democracy*, pp 137-56
(1993).

3778   O.MALLEY (Padraig).   Northern Ireland: a manageable conflict?   In *The
Irish Review*, xv, 14-39 (1994).

Ó MAOLÁIN (Ciarán).   See *Register of research on Northern Ireland.*

3779   O'MEARA (J.).   The GNR(I) crisis 1938.   In *Irish Railway Rec. Soc. Jn.*,
xviii, no. 123, pp 342-52 (1994).

Ó MURCHADHA (Felix).   See 3481.

O'NEILL (Kevin).   See 3483.

3780   O'NEILL (Shane).   Pluralist justice and its limits: the case of Northern
Ireland.   In *Political Studies*, xlii, 363-77 (1994).

3781   ORAM (Dick).   Losing a heritage.   In *Lecale Miscellany*, xii, 10-15 (1994).
Preservation of architectural heritage.

OSBORNE HARPER (W.).   See 2857.

Ó TUATHAIGH (M.A.G.).   See 3497.

OWEN (Arwel Ellis).   See 3498.

3782   PARKER (Tony).   May the Lord in his mercy be kind to Belfast.   Pp [9],
358.   London: Cape, 1993, 1994.
Interviews.

3783   PARKINSON (David L.).   Lead Hill primary school 1968-1993.   Pp 27.
Belfast: Practice Books, 1993.

PARKHILL (Trevor).   See 2878.

3784   Passion and prejudice: nationalist/unionist conflict in Ulster in the 1930s and the origins of the Irish Association. *Ed.* Paul Bew, Kenneth Darwin, Gordon Gillespie. Pp xvii, 128. Belfast: Institute of Irish Studies, Queen's University of Belfast, 1993.
        Collection of letters between politicians .... about government policies and north-south relations.

3785   PATTERSON (Henry).   The republican tradition.   In *Nordirland in Geschichte und Gegenwart*, pp 396-421 (1994).

        PATTERSON (Henry). See 3271.

        PENNEFEATHER (R.S.).   See 2889.

3786   PETERS (Derek).   Memories of a sea gipsy.   Pp 156.   Belfast: Arc Publications, 1994.

        PEYRONEL (Valerie). See 2892.

3787   PHOENIX (Eamon). Northern nationalism: nationalist politics, partition and the Catholic minority in Northern Ireland, 1890-1940. Pp xix, 485. Belfast: Ulster Historical Foundation, 1994.

        POWER (Vincent). See 3507.

3788   PRIOR (Pauline). Mental health policy in Northern Ireland. In *Soc. Pol. & Admin.*, xxvii, 323-34 (1993).

3789   Public Record Office of Northern Ireland. A guide to cabinet conclusions, 1921-1943. Pp 333. Belfast: Public Record Office of Northern Ireland, 1993.

3790   PURDIE (Bob).   Oppressive solidarity. The Northern Ireland civil rights movement and Irish America. In *Irish Studies Rev.*, ii, 6-8 (1992).

        QUAYLE (Ethel). See TAYLOR (Maxwell).

3791   QUINN (Dermot).   Understanding Northern Ireland.   Pp ix, 114. Manchester: Baseline, 1993.

3792   The radio catalogue: BBC Northern Ireland archives at the Ulster Folk and Transport Museum. Compiled and edited by Gráinne Loughran and Marian McCavana. Pp 342. Belfast: Ulster Folk and Transport Museum, 1993.

        RAY (Ivor). See 2929.

3793   Register of research on Northern Ireland, 1993 edition.   *Ed.* Ciarán Ó Maoláin. Pp 216. Coleraine: University of Ulster, Centre for the Study of Conflict, 1993.

3794   Research Institute for the Study of Conflict and Terrorism. Northern Ireland: reappraising republican violence: a special report. In *Ethnic and religious conflicts*, pp 83-111 (1994).

3795   RICHTARIK (Marilynn J.).   Acting between the lines: the Field Theatre Company and Irish cultural politics, 1980-1984.   Pp 356.   Oxford: Clarendon Press, 1994. (Oxford English Monographs)

3796 ROCHE (Patrick J.). Northern Ireland and Irish nationalism - a unionist perspective. In *The Irish Review*, xv, 40-78 (1994).

ROCHE (Patrick J.). See 3523.

ROGERS (Dick). See GALLAGHER (Lyn).

3797 ROLSTON (Bill). Ceasefire! The IRA cashes in its chips. In *Ir. Reporter*, xvi, 5-6 (1994).

3798 ROLSTON (Bill). Index to *Fortnight Magazine*, nos 1-300, 1970-1992. Pp 106. Belfast: Fortnight Publications, 1992.

ROLSTON (Bill). See 3411.

3799 RUANE (Joseph). Conflict management vs conflict resolution: an emancipatory approach to the Northern Ireland conflict. In *Ir. Jn. of Sociology*, iv, 51-66 (1994).

3800 RYAN (Mark). War and peace in Ireland: Britain and the IRA in the new world order. Pp xi, 173. London: Pluto Press, 1994.

3801 SCHRÖDER (Gottfried). Nordirland im Film. In *Nordirland in Geschichte und Gegenwart*, pp 469-86 (1994).

SCHUMACHER (Christopher). See HARTMANN (Klaas).

SEMPLE (Don). See 2984.

SHUTTLEWORTH (Ian). See ANDERSON (James).

3802 SIDWELL (Robert). Ulster: the cost of being British. Pp 145. [Enniskillen]: Dreamland Publications, 1993.

SIMPSON (Hilary). See 2995.

SIMPSON (Lesley). See 2996.

SMITH (Desmond). See 3546.

3803 SPRJUT (R.J.). Internment and detention without trial in Northern Ireland 1971-1975: ministerial policy and practice. In *Modern Law Review*, xlix, 712-40 (1986).

STEWART (A.T.Q.). See MORGAN (Hiram).

STEWART (Kenneth). See 3013.

3804 STOCKDALE (Aileen). Rural service provisions and the impact of population revival: a study of public opinion in Northern Ireland. In *Area*, xxv, 365-78 (1993).

3805 STOCKMAN (Gerard). The sounds of Ulster Irish: a guide for non-Irish-speakers. In *Ulster Folklife*, xl, 39-48 (1994).

3806 STURM (Roland). Der Nordirlandkonflikt: Lösungsmodelle in Geschichte und Gegenwart. In *Nordirland in Geschichte und Gegenwart*, pp 518-53 (1994).
Proposals for solving Northern Ireland conflict.

3807 SUGDEN (John) and BAIRNER (Alan). Sport, sectarianism and society in a divided Ireland. Pp vii, 151. Leicester: Leicester University Press, 1993. (Sport, politics and culture).

3808 SUTTON (Malcolm). Bear in mind these dead: an index of deaths from the conflict in Ireland, 1969-1993. Pp 226. Belfast: Beyond the Pale Publications, 1994.

3809 TANNAHILL (Anne). Ingredients of regional identities (Northern Ireland). In *Cultures in Ireland - regions*, pp 116-22 (1993).

3810 TAYLOR (Maxwell) and QUAYLE (Ethel). Terrorist lives. Pp vi, 223. London: Brassey's, 1994.
Two chapters deal with Northern Ireland.

3811 TAYLOR (Peter). States of terror: democracy and political violence. Pp xiii, 375. London: Penguin, 1994.
Updated reprint; originally published, 1993.

3812 TEAGUE (Paul). Governance structures and economic performance: the case of Northern Ireland. In *International Jn. Urban and Regional Res.*, xviii, 275-92 (1994).

3813 TODD (Jennifer). History and structure in loyalist ideology: the possibilities of ideological change. In *Ir. Jn. Sociol.*, iv, 67-79 (1994).

3814 TODD (Jennifer). Unionist political thought, 1920-72. In *Political thought in Ireland since the seventeenth century*, pp 190-211 (1993).

3815 TOMLINSON (Mike). What price Northern Ireland. The costs of the conflict and the dividends of peace. In *Ir. Reporter*, xvi, 20-21 (1994).

3816 TOWNSHEND (Charles). The supreme law: public safety and state security in Northern Ireland. In *Northern Ireland and the politics of reconciliation*, pp 84-99 (1993).

TURTLE (David). See 3041.

3817 Ulster: the internal colony. Pp 22. Belfast: Queen's University of Belfast, Ulster Unionist Association, [1993?].

URQUHART (Diane). See 3046.

WALKER (Brian). See 3058.

3818 WARD (Alan J.). A constitutional background to the Northern Ireland crisis. In *Northern Ireland and the politics of reconciliation*, pp 33-51 (1993).

3819 WEATHERUP (D.R.M.). 'Ireland's eye: the photographs of John Welch:' review. In *Ulster Local Studies*, iv, no. 1, pp 21-3 (1978).
Robert John Welch, d. 1936.

WEATHERUP (Roger).   See 2251.

3820   WEITZER (Ronald).   Transforming settler states: communal conflict and internal security in Northern Ireland and Zimbabwe.   Pp xiv, 278.   Berkeley: University of California Press, 1990.

3821   WELLS (Ronald A.).   A fearful people: religion and the Ulster conflict.   In *Eire-Ireland*, xxviii, no. 1, pp 53-68 (1993).

3822   WHYTE (John).   Bibliography.   In *Northern Ireland and the politics of reconciliation*, pp 235-55 (1993).

3823   WHYTE (John).   Dynamics of social and political change in Northern Ireland. In *Northern Ireland and the politics of reconciliation*, pp 103-16 (1993).

3824   WHYTE (John H.).   How is the boundary maintained between the two communities in Northern Ireland.   In *Ethnic and Racial Studies*, ix, 219-34 (1986).

3825   WICHERT (Sabine).   Bloody Sunday and the end of unionist government. In *Nordirland in Geschichte und Gegenwart*, pp 201-22 (1994).

3826   WICHERT (Sabine).   The role of nationalism in the Northern Ireland conflict. In *History of European Ideas*, xvi, 109-14 (1993).

3827   WICHERT (Sabine).   Terence O'Neill and his politics.   In *Nordirland in Geschichte und Gegenwart*, pp 184-200 (1994).

3828   WILLIAMSON (Arthur P.).   Policy for higher education in Northern Ireland: the New University of Ulster and the origins of the University of Ulster.   In *Ir. Educational Studies*, xii, 285-301 (1993).

3829   WILSON (Andrew J.).   The American congress for Irish freedom and the Northern Ireland civil rights movement, 1967-70.   In *Eire-Ireland*, xxix, no. 1, pp 61-75 (1994).

WILSON (Andrew J.).   See 3575.

3830   WILSON (Carrie).   The Australian project at Down County Museum.   In *Lecale Miscellany*, xi, 35-7 (1993).

WILSON (Robin).   See KEARNEY (Richard).

3831   WOOD (Ian S.).   Thin red line? - Scottish soldiers in the Troubles.   In *Scotland and Ulster*, pp 150-71 (1994).

WORRALL (Stanley).   See MACAULEY (Ambrose).

INDEX

AALEN (F.H.A.), 0088
ABBOTT (William M.), 1412
ABRAMS (Lesley), 0074
ACK ACK, 3095
ADAMS (Gerry), 3577
ADAMS (Jack), 0089
ADAMS (J.R.R.), 1613
ADAMS (Valerie), 0439
ADAMSON (Ian), 0090
THE AGE OF MIGRATING IDEAS, 0001
AGNEW (Art), 3415
AGNEW (Úna), 3096
AHERN (Mary), 1413
AHERN (Michael), 0091, 1414
AHERN (Richard), 1960
AHLQVIST (Anders), 0092
AIBIDIL GAOIDHEILGE &
 CAITICIOSMA, 1415
AITCHISON (N.B.), 1062-1064
AKENSON (Donald Harmon), 0093, 3097, 3098
ALCOCK (Antony), 3578
ALDERMAN (Geoffrey), 0030
ALLEN (Andrew W.), 0094
ALLEN (Denis), 1961
ALLEN (Donna), 1962
ALLEN (Gregory), 0095, 1963
ALLEN (J. Romilly), 0953
ALLEN (Myrtle), 1964
ALONG THE BLACK PIG'S DYKE, 0096
ALOYSIUS OF MARY (Brother), 1965
AMNESTY INTERNATIONAL, 3579
ANDERSON (Amy), 0097
ANDERSON (Audrey), 1966
ANDERSON (Don), 3580
ANDERSON (Hugh), 1614
ANDERSON (James), 3581
ANDERSON (Robert), 0098
ANDERSON (R.S.W.), 0046
ANDERSON (W.K.), 1967
ANDREWS (J.H.), 0040, 0099, 1968
THE ANNALS OF CLONMACNOISE, 0100
ANNESLEY (Cressida), 1969
ANNESLEY (Patrick G.), 0101
ANNETT (Anthony M.), 3099
ANTON (Brigitte), 1970, 1971
ARCHAEOLOGY IN IRELAND, 3100
ARCHAEOLOGICAL INVENTORY OF
 COUNTY CORK, 0102
ARCHER (Jean), 1972
ARDAGH (John), 3101
ARMSTRONG (Lord), 3582
ARNOLD (Bruce), 3102, 3103
ARNOLD (L.J.), 1416
ARNSTEIN (Walter L.), 1973

ART AND THE NATIONAL DREAM, 0002
ART IS MY LIFE, 0003
ARTHUR (Paul), 3583, 3584
ARTHURS (Miriam), 3104
ARTHURSON (Ian), 1307
A.S., 1974
AS OTHERS SAW US, 1975
ASCH (Ronald G.), 0077, 0103, 1615, 1616
ASPECTS OF IRISH GENEALOGY, 0004
ASSOCIATION OF CRICKET
 STATISTICIANS, 0104
'AS TIME GOES BY', 0105
ATHLONE'S COUNTRY WOMEN'S
 ASSOCIATION, 0106
AUBREY (John), 1617
AUDLEY (Brian), 1618
AUGHEY (Arthur), 3585-3588
AUGNEY (John), 0107
AUSTIN (Valerie A.), 3105
AVERY (Michael), 0108
AYLMER (Richard J.), 0109
B. (P.P.), 1619
THE BACKBONE, 1620
BAGENALSTOWN CYMS, 1976
BAILEY (Bee), 1621
BAILEY (John), 0110
BAILLIE (John), 3589
BAILYN (Bernard), 0111
BAIRNER (Alan), 3807
BAKER (Allan C.), 3027
BAKER (Augustine F.), 0112
BAKER (David J.), 1417
BAKER (Joe), 1977
BAKER (John Austin), 0113
BAKER (Susan), 3106
BALLHATCHET (Kenneth), 1622
BALLARD (Linda), 0114, 0115
BALLARD (Linda M.), 0116
BALLYNOE CEMETERY, 0117
BALLYPATRICK CO-OPERATIVE, 1978
BANCE (Michael), 3107
BANE (Liam), 1979
BARAKAT (Sultan), 3590
BARBOUR (Bill), 1496
BARDON (Jonathan), 1980
BARKLEY (John M.), 0118
BARLOW (Dorothy), 3108
BARNARD (T.C.), 1418-1422, 1623
BARNARD (Toby), 0119, 1423
BARNWALL (Richard), 3109
BARRETT (Evelyn), 0120
BARRON (Thomas J.), 0014
BARRY (Ann), 0121
BARRY (Deirdre), 0122

INDEX

INDEX

INDEX

INDEX

INDEX

INDEX